OUR LADY of CONTROVERSY

Chicana Matters Series

DEENA J. GONZÁLEZ AND ANTONIA CASTAÑEDA, EDITORS

Chicana Matters Series focuses on one of the largest population groups in the United States today, documenting the lives, values, philosophies, and artistry of contemporary Chicanas. Books in this series may be richly diverse, reflecting the experiences of Chicanas themselves, and incorporating a broad spectrum of topics and fields of inquiry. Cumulatively, the books represent the leading knowledge and scholarship in a significant and growing field of research and, along with the literary works, art, and activism of Chicanas, underscore their significance in the history and culture of the United States.

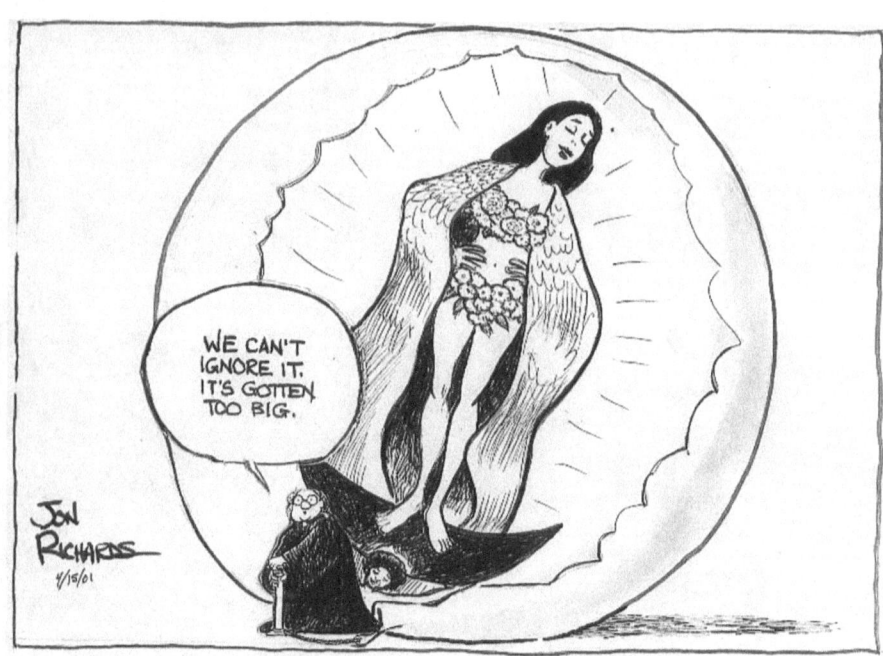

OUR LADY OF CONTROVERSY

ALMA LÓPEZ'S "IRREVERENT APPARITION"

EDITED BY
Alicia Gaspar de Alba and Alma López

University of Texas Press ⦦ AUSTIN

Second paperback printing, 2012

Requests for permission to reproduce material
from this work should be sent to:
    Permissions
    University of Texas Press
    P.O. Box 7819
    Austin, TX 78713-7819
    http://utpress.utexas.edu/about/book-permissions

"The Artist of *Our Lady* (April 2, 2001)," by Alma López;
www.lasculturas.com.

"Art Comes for the Archbishop: The Semiotics of Contemporary
Chicana Feminism and the Work of Alma López," by Luz Calvo, is
reprinted by permission of Indiana University Press from *Meridians:
Feminism, Race, Transnationalism* 5.1 (2004).

Library of Congress Cataloging-in-Publication Data

Our Lady Of Controversy : Alma López's "Irreverent Apparition" /
Edited by Alicia Gaspar de Alba and Alma López. — First edition.
        pages cm. — (Chicana matters series)
    Includes index.
    ISBN 978-0-292-71992-7 (cloth : alk. paper) — ISBN 978-0-292-
72642-0 (pbk. : alk. paper)
    1. López, Alma (Alma Lorena), 1966– Our Lady. 2. López, Alma
(Alma Lorena), 1966– —Criticism and interpretation. 3. Guadal-
upe, Our Lady of—Art. 4. Mexican American art—Public opinion.
I. Gaspar de Alba, Alicia, 1958– —editor of compilation. II. López,
Alma (Alma Lorena), 1966– —editor of compilation.
    N6537.L655A72 2011
    709.2—dc22   2010047372

doi:10.7560/719927

CONTENTS

LIST OF IMAGES

COLOR PLATES

ACKNOWLEDGMENTS

ALMA'S ACKNOWLEDGMENTS

My darling Alicia is an awesome writer, professor, and editor. On April 6, 2001, Chicana Matters Series co-editor Antonia Castañeda approached me about a publication focusing on the controversy, but it was not until after Alicia and I married that this book was born. We are grateful for our mothers and families. I am especially grateful to my favorite sister, Leti, for her concern and encouragement. The models: Raquel Salinas and Raquel Gutiérrez.

Tey Marianna Nunn for living in the fire during this most unexpected controversy. Her family, especially her mother, Tey Diana Rebolledo, who publicly denounced the principal controversy organizers and the archbishop.

The Cyber *artistas*: Elena Baca, Marion Martínez, and Teresa Archuleta-Sagel, who stood in solidarity, and whose work was amazing but who, unfortunately, did not receive all of the attention they deserved because of the controversy.

The museum staff and others who took the difficult high road, including the New Mexico Museum director, Thomas Wilson; MOIFA director, Joyce Ice; the chief museum security officer, John McCarthy; the museum staff; and the exhibition docents, who spoke bravely in counterprotests.

Good friends who were always around to talk, particularly at the most difficult moments, when I was threatened and when I received hate mail from children: Lizette Sánchez and her family, especially her mom, Dorcas; Rigo Maldonado; Tongues members Aurora García, Raquel Gutiérrez, Stacy Macías, Claudia Rodríguez, Cristina Serna; Lindsey Haley and Ayde González for dressing as "Our Ladies" at one of our slumber parties to make me laugh.

The folks at 18th Street Arts Complex, where I was living and working as an artist in residence, who were concerned enough to keep a watchful eye after we received threats to burn down my studio. Professor Chon Noriega, director of the UCLA Chicano Studies Research Center, who encouraged me to write an essay on the controversy for *Aztlán*. Self Help Graphics and Tomás Benítez, who invited me to create the silkscreen *Our Lady of Controversy* and who exhibited the print while the zealous America Needs Fatima members protested their annual print exhibition.

There were countless people, artists, activists, and community organizations that spoke, wrote, and gathered in support of freedom of expression, in particular, journalist Hollis Walker, and the NCAC (National Coalition Against Censorship) programs director, Svetlana Mintcheva. I am so deeply grateful to the hundreds who took the time to write letters and e-mails of support.

And of course the contributors to this publication, who represent the most genius of Chicana feminist activists.

ALICIA'S ACKNOWLEDGMENTS

First, I want to express my deepest respect and admiration for my beloved wife, Alma López. If it weren't for her courage, vision, integrity, and dedication to the spirit of love and the power of transformation, *Our Lady* would not have come into being, and the controversy would not have spawned this volume.

My heartfelt gratitude to all the contributors for their fabulous work; to the reviewers for their glowing remarks; to my eagle-eyed and energetic research assistant and index maker extraordinaire, Allison Wyper; to series editors, Antonia Castañeda and Deena González, for their remarkable Chicana Matters series of which Alma and I are proud to be a part; and, of course, to our *querida* editor, *la* twinkle-toed Theresa May, and the rest of the production staff at U.T. Press. Special thanks to Georgina Guzmán for stepping in to help put this book to bed. As Violeta Parra once said: "Gracias a la vida que me ha dado tanto." Y gracias a las Madres, who make everything possible.

OUR LADY of CONTROVERSY

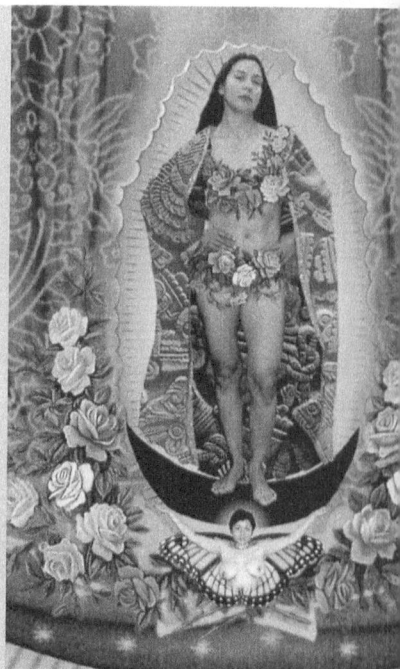

Cyber Arte

Computer-inspired art combines elements
traditionally defined as "folk" with state of
the art computer technology to create a
new aesthetic for the 21st Century.

OPENING RECEPTION

Sunday, February 25, 2001
2:00 - 4:00 pm
hosted by the Women's Board of the
Museum of New Mexico

Panel Discussion

2:00 - 3:00 pm
"Tradition Meets Technology"
with Curator Dr. Tey Marianna Nunn
and special guests in Museum Auditorium
By museum admission

EXHIBITION DATES

February 25, 2001 - October 28, 2001

ALMA LÓPEZ "OUR LADY" LUPE & SIRENA S
IRIS/GLICEE ON CANVAS 14" x 17.5" 1999

I.1.　MOIFA *Cyber Arte* exhibition flyer. September 2000. Alma López personal papers.
Courtesy of Alma López.

Our Lady of Controversy

A SUBJECT THAT NEEDS NO INTRODUCTION

Alicia Gaspar de Alba

IN THE BEGINNING of a new millennium, Our Lady appeared in Santa Fe during Holy Week. Her appearance caused passionate discussions throughout the Americas. Hundreds met in a geographic space called Holy Faith to discuss and debate her contemporary apparition to a Chicana artist named Alma, a resident in the City of Angels."[1]

So begins Alma López's *"respuesta"* to her twenty-first-century inquisitors in Santa Fe, New Mexico, who racked and pinioned her constitutional rights as an artist, her identity as a Mexico-born Chicana, and her integrity as a woman. Like Sor Juana Inés de la Cruz three centuries earlier, who in her own "Respuesta a Sor Filotea" had to defend her rights as a writer and a woman to a persecuting archbishop, bishop, and father confessor, Alma López had to take a stand against another trinity of church fathers—an archbishop, a deacon, and a chaplain—who were all beset with the notion that a 14" × 17.5" digital collage in a museum had magically transformed itself into an irreverent apparition of La Virgen de Guadalupe.

On February 25, 2001, the *Cyber Arte: Tradition Meets Technology* exhibition opened at the Museum of International Folk Art (MOIFA) in Santa Fe, New Mexico. One of the pieces in the show was Alma López's *Our Lady*, a digital collage representing the artist's interpretation of the Virgin of Guadalupe wreathed in roses, held on high by a bare-breasted butterfly angel, and draped with a cloak engraved with symbols of the Aztec moon goddess, Coyolxauhqui. The exhibition showcased the work of four Chicana/Hispana/Latina artists who combine folk iconography with computer technology in the creation of their digital-media artworks.

In September of 2000, in response to a brochure sent out by MOIFA to announce the exhibition several months before the show opened, the museum started receiving calls from community activists and representatives of the Catholic Church protesting the image and demanding that it be removed from the exhibition. For months after the opening, protest rallies and prayer vigils were organized outside the museum, spearheaded by a community activist cum volunteer chaplain for the city's police department, a deacon of Guadalupe Parish, and the archbishop of the Santa Fe Archdiocese. The three men agitated and inflamed the protestors, who grew more and more belligerent at what they saw as the museum's patent disregard of New Mexico's religious beliefs and, in particular, as Alma López's "blasphemy" of their holy symbol, which the newspapers had labeled the "Bikini Virgin."

Not only did the protestors demand the removal of *Our Lady* from the *Cyber Arte* exhibition but they also demanded a public apology from the Museum of New Mexico and the immediate resignations of the exhibition curator, Tey Marianna Nunn; MOIFA director, Joyce Ice; and the director of the Museum of New Mexico, Tom Wilson. And they called for the return of all "sacred" Catholic art to the custody of the church.

In a blatant display of the alignment between church and state, even lawmakers were on the side of the protestors. Calling the work an "outrageous desecration," all but two members of the New Mexico legislature (all Democrats, by the way) demanded that the piece be immediately removed from the exhibition or the museum would risk losing funding.[2] This position drew the scorn of then-governor Gary Johnson, a Republican, who said he did not believe *Our Lady* violated community standards and that legislators should not be in the business of telling art museums what to show and what not to show. The governor asked an important question: "If you take it down, then where do you draw the line on the next piece of art?"[3] The museum's Committee on Sensitive Materials was summoned to evaluate the sensitivity quotient of the work,[4] and after weeks of deliberation, community forums, and a media blitz that had the unintended effect of making Alma López world famous, the committee determined that *Our Lady* was not a religious object and that there was nothing culturally denigrating in the image, and concurred that all of the artwork of the *Cyber Arte* exhibit should remain on display. Nor did the curator and museum director lose their jobs.[5]

Apart from the protests, "[m]useum staff logged an enormous volume of comments, letters, emails, and phone calls from all over the state, and nearly 24,000 preprinted postcards from across the United States, demanding that the work be removed."[6] One particular phone call inventoried in the museum's phone log on the morning of July 6, 2001, was especially chilling. Identifying himself as a friend of Timothy McVeigh's, who had been executed a few weeks earlier for bombing a building in Oklahoma City and killing 168 people—considered to be "the deadliest act of terrorism in the United States prior to 9/11"[7]—the caller made his position on *Our Lady* known loud and clear: "Did you know who Timothy McVeigh was? . . . Did you know he was Catholic and had a special relationship with the Virgin? . . . Just listen to me a minute, I knew him see, and the last thing he said to me was for me to see if the painting/collage of the Blessed Virgin was still up, and if it was for me to flatten the building. I knew him and I helped him blow up that building. I'm gonna call next week and if that thing is still there, I will blow up your building. You got that!!! Dial tone."[8]

Alma López and Tey Marianna Nunn also received e-mail and phone threats. Cathryn Keller, writing in *Museum News*, called the artist and the curator "trauma survivors" and detailed their shock and confusion at being accosted by men both before and after the April 4 meeting. Tey Marianna Nunn described the experience: "We were suddenly surrounded by eight or ten men saying 'crucify her' and calling us 'fea' [ugly] as we left . . . I was very shocked and upset that what I consider my culture would do this to me."[9]

For Joyce Ice the controversy became "a metaphor for issues of difference and diversity; the economic divide in Santa Fe, the sense of art being for the elite and not the common people."[10]

The *Santa Fe Reporter* dubbed the controversy "the best local scandal,"[11] but it was not limited to a local audience. News of the scandal spread nationally and was covered in dailies across the country: South Florida's *Sun Sentinel*, the *Milwaukee Journal Sentinel*, the *Los Angeles Times*, the *New York Times*, the *Reno Gazette Journal*, and even *Reforma*, one of the main newspapers of Mexico City, among many others. Online coverage multiplied exponentially, and national arts journals like *Museum News* and *Art in America* also weighed in.

Regardless of the Committee on Sensitive Materials' eventual decision not to censor *Our Lady*, the very fact that the controversy went on as long and as far as it did attests to the power that was wielded by the alignment of church, state, and community against a twenty-first-century Malinche, or "traitor" to her race, culture, and gender. To the Guadalupanos, Alma López was a traitor to their faith. To Chicano and Mexican nationalists, she was a traitor to their race and culture. To Hispanos she was a Californicated outsider in New Mexico.

This book is about the controversy over *Our Lady*, or as she was called in the newspapers, "Our Lady of Preposterous Assumptions," "Our Lady of I Should Look So Good," "Our Lady of All This Fuss,"[12] and "Our Lady of Eternal Conflict."[13] The ten scholars who have trained their attention on a subject that needs no introduction all approach *Our Lady* from a feminist standpoint, critical of the persecution that Alma López and Tey Marianna Nunn received from the media, the fundamentalist Catholic community of Santa Fe, New Mexico's legislators, the museum's Board of Regents, and the nameless, countless others who added their match to this modern-day witch burning.

Located in the fields of art history, Chicana history, Chicana/o cultural studies, literary studies, queer studies, religious studies, and women's studies, the essays gathered in this collection offer us different ways to approach the subject of the controversy and the controversy of the subject that is *Our Lady*. The controversy took place in 2001, but the issues that it raised have been part of a much larger national struggle in the art world since the 1980s, and they are still current—censorship in the arts, accountability, the role of the artist, community representation and the public museum, First Amendment rights of artists, and the right-wing reactionary appropriation of the discourse of social justice and civic action. By focusing on one controversial piece of art in one small exhibition in Santa Fe, the chapters show the complex intersectionality of cultural politics, historical memory, and gender dynamics that informs exhibition practices and public reception, whether in New York or New Mexico. They also use *Our Lady* as a case study for examining the different *chiasmi*—or opposing ideas—that took center stage in the controversy.

A *chiasmus*, explains Richard Nordquist, is "a verbal pattern (often a type of antithesis) in which the second half of an expression is balanced against the first but with the parts reversed ... From the Greek, 'to invert' or 'to mark with the letter X.'"[14] An antithesis is "a juxtaposition of opposing ideas in balanced phrases."[15] By inverting a phrase, that is, by applying a crisscrossed structure to the phrase in which the first part is reversed in the second, we get

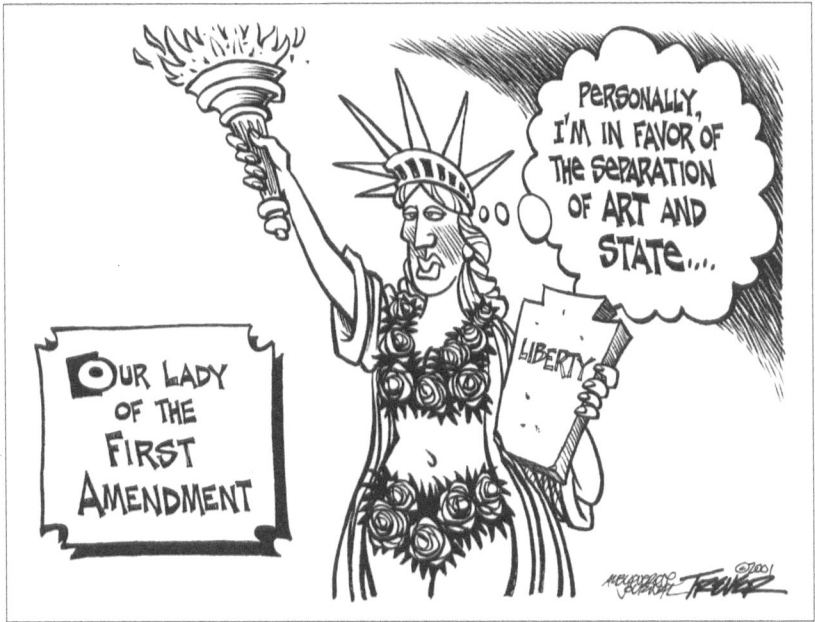

I.2.   Our Lady of Liberty. Cartoon, *Albuquerque Journal* (April 17, 2001),
by John Trever, © 2001. Courtesy of John Trever.

a new reading of the same idea. Mae West's famous line—"It's not about the
men in my life, but about the life in my men"—demonstrates how using the
chiastic structure can dramatically alter an interpretation. The first phrase is
meant as a judgment of a woman who is accused of having too many men in
her life. By inverting the phrase, the speaker turns the judgment on its head;
rather than defend herself against the accusation, the speaker acknowledges
the presence of all those men in her life but makes the point be about the
quality of those men not the quantity. In the same way, the chapters in this
book reverse the readings and interpretations of Alma López's *Our Lady* that
were given by the religious "right." Feeling wronged by the artist, the protestors proceeded to wrong the artist's constitutional rights.

In this collection, the opposing ideas that are turned inside/out and up-
side/down are many; they include private/public, insider/outsider, body/
faith, church/state, colonial/decolonial, secular/sacred, identity/representa-
tion, community/museum, freedom of speech/freedom of religion, Anglo/
Hispanic, virgin/whore, masculine/feminine, and male/female. Thus, some
of the titles in the collection employ a ludic or playful tone to underscore the

antithetical ideas under scrutiny, such as Tey Marianna Nunn's "It's Not about
the Art in the Folk, It's about the Folks in the Art: A Curator's Tale," which
shows that the controversy was unleashed not because of the art on display in
the *Cyber Arte* exhibition at the Museum of International Folk Art but because
some community members, aided and abetted by the media, misperceived
and misrepresented the work in the show and the curator's intentions for the
exhibit. Deena González's "Making Privates Public: It's Not about La Virgen
of the Conquest, but about the Conquest of La Virgen" sees the controversy
as a consequence of New Mexico's long struggle for economic survival in
the face of continued colonization and looks at the history of Virgen worship in Santa Fe and the competition that exists between the older Virgin
of the Conquest, La Conquistadora, and the younger Virgin of Guadalupe.
Emma Pérez's "The Decolonial Virgin in a Colonial Site: It's Not about the
Gender in My Nation, It's about the Nation in My Gender" extends the analysis of colonialism and concerns over the nation in Santa Fe by analyzing the
gendered discourse created by the e-mail correspondence that Alma López
received and collected on her website, taking to task the Chicano nationalist
attacks against *Our Lady* and their critiques of what they saw as Alma López's
betrayal of Aztlán as yet one more manifestation of the male colonized mind.
Cristina Serna pays homage to Mae West with her title, "It's Not about the
Virgins in My Life, It's about the Life in My Virgins," as she discusses the
different representations of the Virgin of Guadalupe in Alma López's work
and the work of other Chicana artists, as well as in the work of a Mexican
artist, Rolando de la Rosa, who was similarly ostracized in Mexico City for
his depictions of the Virgin of Guadalupe with the face of Marilyn Monroe.
Alma López herself participates in the chiastic language game with her closing piece, "It's Not about the Santa in My *Fe*, But about the Santa Fe in My
Santa," which, in the tradition of the *Nican Mopohua*, tells her own version of
the Virgin of Guadalupe apparition and deconstructs the "codex" represented
by the different symbols that appear on the original image of La Virgen. It is
also the story of the evolution of her work as a digital artist and of how *Our
Lady* came into being. In reading the story of *Our Lady* from the artist's perspective, and learning about the personal meaning and history of each detail
in the piece, we understand how mistaken were the interpretations of the
protestors, and how hypocritical was their righteous trampling of an artist's
First Amendment rights in the name of the "true" and all-embracing Mother
of God.

The other five pieces, though they do not employ the chiastic structure in their titles, nonetheless examine, juxtapose, and invert other conflicting and paradoxical issues that emerged in the controversy. Kathleen FitzCallaghan Jones's "The War of the Roses: Alma López, Guadalupe, and Santa Fe," based on her 2002 art history Master's thesis, was written in the immediate aftermath of the conflict. Drawing on personal interviews with the major players in the drama—Alma López, José Villegas, Tey Marianna Nunn, and Frank Ortiz—Jones's chapter sheds light on the more emotional aspects of the controversy that created a civil war of power and allegiance in Santa Fe. Luz Calvo's "Art Comes for the Archbishiop: The Semiotics of Contemporary Chicana Feminism and the Work of Alma López," originally published in *Meridians* in 2004, playfully alludes to Willa Cather's *Death Comes for the Archbishop*, about the pervasive power of the Catholic religion in New Mexico. In Calvo's work, *Our Lady* is the pervasive force that visits the archbishop. Calvo argues that the controversy brought to light the multitude of desires embedded in the Virgin of Guadalupe, from the nationalist desire to return to the motherland to the queer desire to love your own kind. In a new Afterword to her piece, Calvo discusses how Alma López tropes or twists the icon of La Virgen to signify new directions for radical cultural workers.

Puerto Rican scholar Clara Román-Odio's piece, "Queering the Sacred: Love as Oppositional Consciousness in Alma López's Visual Art," argues that *Our Lady*, as one of a series of works that pay homage to and yet deconstruct the mythological trappings of the Virgin of Guadalupe narrative, is an example of both Chicana spirituality and the oppositional consciousness of "love," which for Chela Sandoval constitutes part of the "methodology of the oppressed." Catrióna Rueda Esquibel's "Do U Think I'm a Nasty Girl?" is written from the femme lesbian spectator's position to show the author's identification with *Our Lady*. What is reflected back for the critic is not only the beauty of the brown women's bodies that are the central focus of the image but the contours of the author's own desire. My "Devil in a Rose Bikini: The Second Coming of Our Lady in Santa Fe" offers an in-depth analysis of the protest by comparing the different audience responses to the work as seen in the comment book of the museum, the media coverage, and especially the performance art of the protest, the staged processions and pilgrimages that simultaneously decried and created an irreverent apparition.

The idea of using chiasmus as an organizing principle for the book originated in a colorful kitchen in Oakland, California, in October 2007. Alma and

I had come to the Bay Area to see an excerpt of the opera that Carla Lucero had written based on my novel, *Sor Juana's Second Dream* (another story altogether), and Catrióna and Luz had invited us to stay at their home. We were sipping juice from fresh coconuts hewn in the backyard by a machete-wielding Luz and nibbling on Catrióna's freshly baked blueberry scones as we worked at conceptualizing the roundtable that we wanted to propose at the 2008 meeting of the National Association for Chicana and Chicano Studies, which was to take place the following March in Austin, Texas. For this roundtable, we wanted to gather some of the scholars who had written on or had something to say about *Our Lady*, as a kind of retrospective look at the controversy from a vantage point seven years later. Luz, Alma, Cristina Serna (also in this volume), and I ended up presenting on the panel, which was moderated by Antonia Castañeda, a longtime advocate of *Our Lady*, who for years had actually been encouraging Alma and Tey Marianna Nunn to put together a book about the controversy. The roundtable, "Irreverent Apparitions: Chiasmatic Interpretations of Alma López's *Our Lady*," filled the venue, and we saw how contemporary and captivating the topic of *Our Lady* continued to be for that group of Chicana and Chicano studies scholars. Luz broke it down for us in her presentation: "Chiasmus, by reversing the original, allows us to see reality in a new light—we create a new way of seeing and hopefully a new way of being in the world. This particular trope provides the rhetorical ground for us to make new political claims on the social world. Perhaps, chiasmus is the perfect trope for radical activists, artists, and critics—for it reverses the order of things."[16]

It is our hope that this collection helps us "make new political claims" about the contradictory issues that were at the heart of the controversy and that it "allows us to see [*Our Lady*] in a new light," as indeed Alma López has already done in her painting on the cover, where Our Lady's acrylic metarepresentation stands taller and meaner than the original, which caused "all this fuss." Like Ester Hernández's karate-kicking La *Virgen de Guadalupe Defendiendo los Derechos de los Xicanos*, like the women warriors of the boxing ring that Delilah Montoya has captured in her book on women boxers, *Our Lady of Controversy II* is more *"malcriada"* than ever. Says Delilah Montoya: "A *malcriada* is a woman who will not behave and is determined to do what she wants, regardless of what society rules or even good sense dictates. When a family is confronted with this sort of unseemly member, they struggle to

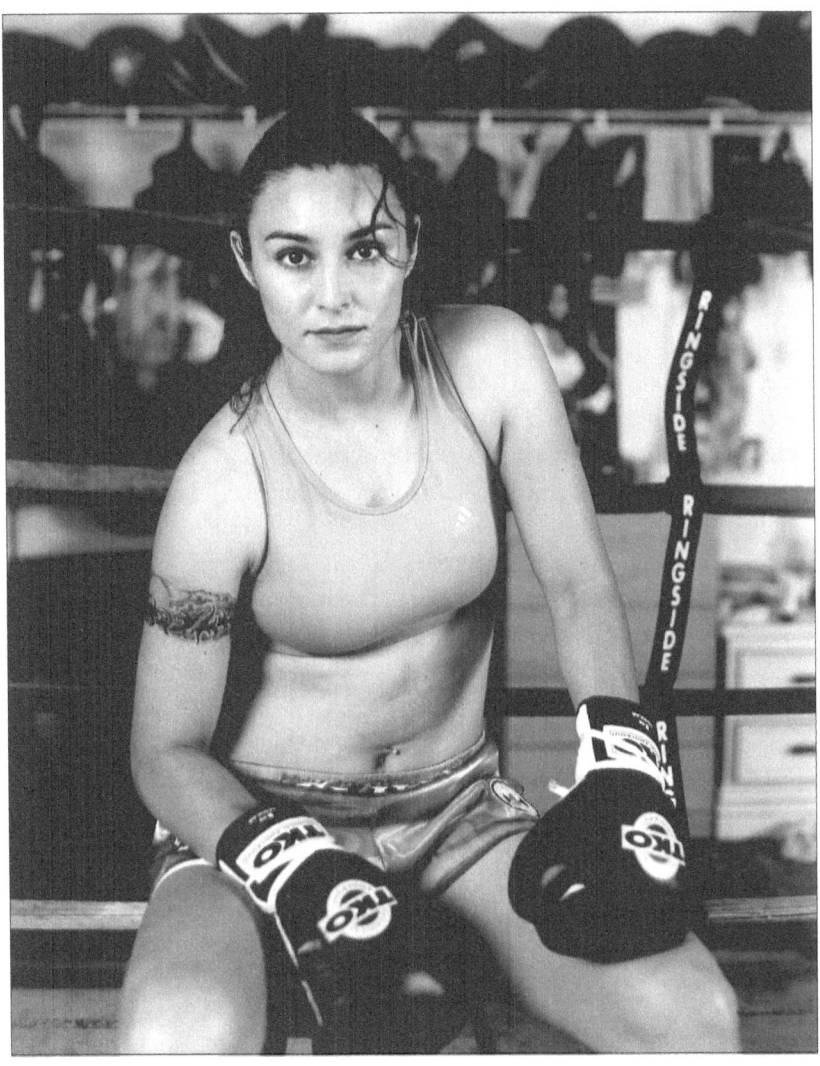

1.3. *Jackie Chávez*. Black-and-white Photograph by Delilah Montoya, © 2005. Courtesy of Delilah Montoya.

change her. Welcoming the uphill battle, the *malcriada* remains unchanged; in the end, the family learns to accept her and even become proud of her accomplishments."[17]

What also remains unchanged is the zealous homophobia of the Chicano nationalist hate group La Voz de Aztlán. In August 2004, Ernesto Cienfuegos, La Voz de Aztlán's head honcho, "attacked Fullerton Museum Center Director Joe Felz for including 'decadent lesbian artist' Alma López in an exhibition titled 'The Virgin of Guadalupe: Interpreting Devotion,'" whose *Our Lady*, he went on to say in his e-mail (which he copied to the Fullerton mayor and other city officials) "denigrate[s] the values of [Mexicans] in collusion with those in the homosexual and lesbian lifestyles and of those others who have a deep hate against us."[18] Although the piece Alma had agreed to display in the Fullerton exhibition was not *Our Lady*, just the mention of her name paired with a Virgen de Guadalupe exhibition was enough to rekindle the group's hateful torch.

Then, in April 2010, nine years after the *Our Lady* controversy in Santa Fe, La Voz de Aztlán again went after Alma López as well as Cherríe Moraga this time, who were guest speakers at a Chicana feminist conference organized by the student group Conciencia Femenil at California State University, Long Beach. According to La Voz de Aztlán, or "La Voz de Pendejos," as Gustavo Arellano calls the organization in his *OC Weekly* blog, "feminism is a Jewish conspiracy to 'emasculate' Mexican men, and . . . Jews also promote homosexuality 'in order to destroy our culture.'"[19]

But La Voz de Aztlán is not alone. Even among college students in the twenty-first century, these same reactionary attitudes persist, as we can see by reading the cyber comments in response to an article in the Cal State, Long Beach *Daily 49er* announcing the Chicana feminist conference organized by Conciencia Femenil:

> ¡QUE ASCO!
> The name Conciencia Femenil should be changed to Conciencia Maricona because the organizers and participants of this conference are a bunch of lesbians hiding under the guise of feminism. Worst, Alma López is a decadent artist who has painted sacrilegious images of Mexico's most revered religious icons, the Virgen de Guadalupe. She has depicted La Virgen in a bikini and with obvious erotic sapphic symbolisms. This "mariflora" is a sick pervert.[20]

The comments that follow this one get progressively more intolerant and hateful, culminating in "La Ley Azteca," some mythical Aztec law which supposedly calls for hanging sodomites, impaling the active party in a homosexual relationship and disemboweling the passive party, and the use of a big stick to kill lesbians.[21] It is because this vicious ignorance persists in our community that a book such as *Our Lady of Controversy* hits home. TKO.

NOTES

1. Alma López, "Silencing Our Lady: La Respuesta de Alma," *Aztlán: A Journal of Chicano Studies* 26.2 (Fall 2001): 249.

2. Mark Hummels, "Lawmakers Denounce Artwork," *Santa Fe New Mexican* (April 4, 2001). *Cyber Arte* Collection, Museum of International Folk Art Archives.

3. Deborah Baker, "Governor: 'Our Lady' Doesn't Violate 'Community Standard,'" *Albuquerque Tribune* (April 7, 2001). *Cyber Arte* Collection, Museum of International Folk Art Archives.

4. This committee was formed in 1986 "to deal with repatriation issues arising from the Native American Graves and Repatriation Act of 1990." See Anne Constable, "Museum Director Rejects Appeal," *Santa Fe New Mexican* (July 14, 2001). *Cyber Arte* Collection, Museum of International Folk Art Archives.

5. Tom Wilson's days as director of the Museum of New Mexico were numbered, however. In 2002, he was fired from his position by the incoming governor, Bill Richardson (both a Democrat and a Chicano). As Hollis Walker tells it: "Though no specific reference to the art controversy was made, many people assumed it was the impetus for, or at least a major factor in, Wilson's firing." See Hollis Walker, "Whose Lady? Laying Claim to the Virgin Mary," in *The New Gatekeepers: Emerging Challenges to Free Expression in the Arts* (New York: Columbia University/ National Arts Journalism Program, 2003), 44 (42–44).

6. Cathryn Keller, "Faith and the First Amendment Santa Fe Style," *Museum News* (July/August 2001): 31 (30–35). *Cyber Arte* Collection, Museum of International Folk Art Archives.

7. Wikipedia entry on Timothy McVeigh.

8. Incident report, Museum of New Mexico phone log, July 6, 2001. *Cyber Arte* Collection, Museum of International Folk Art Archives..

9. Quoted in Keller, "Faith and the First Amendment," 33.

10. Ibid., 35.

11. *Santa Fe Reporter* (July 25–31, 2001). *Cyber Arte* Collection, Museum of International Folk Art Archives.

12. Kate Nelson, "Our Lady of All This Fuss Can't Rock a Faith Built on More Than Scorn," *Albuquerque Tribune* (April 5, 2001). *Cyber Arte* Collection, Museum of International Folk Art Archives.

13. Steven Robert Allen, "Our Lady of Eternal Conflict," *Weekly Alibi* 10.16 (2001): 14. *Cyber Arte* Collection, Museum of International Folk Art Archives.

14. Quoted online in About.com: Grammar & Composition, www.grammar.about .com.

15. Ibid.

16. Luz Calvo, "It's Not about the Gender in My Nation, but the Nation in My Gender," paper presented at the "Irreverent Apparitions: Chiasmatic Interpretations of Alma López's 'Our Lady,'" NACCS Roundtable, March 20, 2008.

17. Delilah Montoya, artist's essay in *Women Boxers: The New Warriors* (Houston, Tex.: Arte Público Press, 2006), 19.

18. See Gustavo Arellano, "Nuestra Señora de Censorship: Who Says the Virgin of Guadalupe Can't Be Sexy?" *OC Weekly* 9.50 (August 20–26, 2004).

19. See Gustavo Arellano, "The Hilarious Haters: Jew-Bashing, Gay-Trashing La Voz de Aztlán Harasses Long Beach State Chicanas," http://blogs.ocweekly.com/navelgazing/the-hilarious-haters/jew-bashing-gay-trashing-la-vo/. The blog can also be accessed on http://www.almalopez.com/ORnews3/20104130Cweekly.html.

20. See http://www.daily49er.com/opinion/chicana-feminists-must-be-heard-1.221 0967. The full text can also be accessed on http://www.almalopez.com/ORnew s3/2010404CSULB.html.

21. Ibid.

1

The Artist of *Our Lady* (April 2, 2001)

Alma López

P LEASE THINK OF ME and send me really good and supportive energy at 12 noon Los Angeles time or 10 am New Mexico time this Wednesday, April 4. Thank you.

On Wednesday, April 4, at 10 am at the Museum of International Folk Art, the governing board of New Mexico's state museum system will consider removing an artwork that has offended some Roman Catholics in New Mexico. *Cyber Arte* is scheduled through October 28, 2001, and features four contemporary Chicana/Latina/Hispana artists who combine traditional "folk" elements with current computer technology.

The "offending" work, *Our Lady*, is a photo-based digital print on exhibition in a museum, and not an object of devotion in a church. It is an image that could possibly arouse conversations on topics such as use of cultural images in art, gender issues, or the use of technology as a tool for creative expression.

This work features performance artist Raquel Salinas as an assertive and strong Virgen dressed in roses and cultural activist Raquel Gutiérrez as a nude butterfly angel and was inspired by Sandra Cisneros's essay, "Guadalupe the Sex Goddess." Like many other Chicanas throughout the United States, Raquel Salinas, Raquel Gutiérrez, and I grew up in Los Angeles with the image of La Virgen in our homes and community. La Virgen is every-where. She's on tattoos, stickers, posters, air freshener cans, shirts, and corner store murals, as well as church walls. Many, including myself, feel that there is nothing anyone can do to change how the original image of La Virgen de Guadalupe is generally perceived.

Catholic or not, Chicana/Latina/Hispana visual, literary, or performance artists grew up with the image of La Virgen de Guadalupe, therefore enti-tling us to express our relationship to her in any which way relevant to our own experiences. Many artists, such as Yolanda M. López, Ester Hernández, Santa Barraza, Delilah Montoya, Yreina D. Cervantez, and Raquel Salinas, have shared their own personal experiences using La Virgen de Guadalupe.

More than twenty years ago, artists Yolanda M. López and Ester Hernán-dez were threatened and attacked for portraying La Virgen in a feminist and liberating perspective. Yolanda M. López received bomb threats for her por-trayal of La Virgen wearing low-heeled shoes. In this image La Virgen walks with her head bowed, hands clasped, wearing a dress below the knee. I think that people were upset because La Virgen was able to walk.

The protest against *Our Lady* is organized and led by community activ-ist José Villegas. New Mexico's archbishop, Michael J. Sheehan, has joined him, calling the artwork "sacrilegious." Mr. Villegas's first and only attempt to communicate with me was through a threatening e-mail. One week later, on television I saw the rally he organized against the museum.

Mr. Villegas and the archbishop see the *Our Lady* digital print with exposed legs and belly and a female angel's breasts as "offensive." Yet I know that many churches, in Mexico and Europe and the United States, house images of nude male angels and most prominently, a Crucifixion practically naked except for a skimpy loincloth.

When I see *Our Lady* as well as the works portraying La Virgen by many Chicana artists, I see an alternative voice expressing the multiplicities of our lived realities. I see myself living a tradition of Chicanas who, because of cul-tural and gender oppression, have asserted our voice. I see Chicanas creating a deep and meaningful connection to this revolutionary cultural female image. I see Chicanas who understand faith.

Even if I look really hard at my work and the works of many Chicana art-ists, I don't see what is so offensive. I see beautiful bodies that are gifts from our creator. I see nurturing breasts. I see the strong nurturing mothers of all of us. I am forced to wonder how men like Mr. Villegas and the Archbishop are looking at my work that they feel it is "blasphemy" and "the Devil." I wonder how they see bodies of women. I wonder why they think that our bodies are so ugly and perverted that they cannot be seen in an art piece in a museum?

For me, this experience at times has been confusing and upsetting, primarily because men like Mr. Villegas and Archbishop Sheehan self-righteously believe that they have the authority to dictate how a particular image should be interpreted. They believe they can tell me as well as other Chicanas how to think. I am a woman who has grown up with La Virgen. Who are these men to tell me what to think and how to relate to her?

It scares me to see so many people organized to attack me. It makes me sad that this has been a divisive issue especially along gender lines, to see brothers and sisters fighting, and to see politicians trying to use this as an excuse to cut funds for art and education.

Although there are people like Mr. Villegas and Archbishop Sheehan who are offended by the *Our Lady* digital print, not everyone agrees that it should be removed. E-mails, calls, and letters of support have included Catholics, Latinas/os, artists, educators, and various communities throughout the United States. This experience has also evoked an outpouring of positive feedback and support, which has affirmed my belief that there really isn't anything wrong with this image. So many people have e-mailed me and contacted the museum expressing their concern over these attacks. I want to thank everyone who has been wonderfully supportive.

Perhaps time and place play prominent roles in this controversy. This is Lent, a time of devotion between Ash Wednesday and Easter. Santa Fe is a place with deep spiritual and traditional roots, and the Museum of International Folk Art is the place where many images of saints reside.

I hope that my digital print *Our Lady* is not removed from the exhibition. I know that not everyone likes my work, but no one person has the right to remove it and therefore prevent others from seeing it. This museum, like other museums, is a site of learning. Museums are not churches or sites of spiritual devotion.

I don't think there should be any threats to funding or to museum directors because I have exhibited my work here. As artists, museums, and allies, we need everyone to know that we are also taxpayers. We need to tell our political representatives that we also decide what to do with our vote and our money. We need to tell everyone that we oppose censorship and funding cuts to art and education.

If my work is removed, that means that I have no right to express myself as an artist and a woman. It means that there must be something wrong and sexually perverted with my female body. It means that it's okay for men to look at our bodies as ugly. It means that as Chicanas we can only be sexualized or only be virgins. It means that only men can tell us how to look at La Virgen. It means that we cannot look upon La Virgen as an image of a strong woman like us.

Special thanks to every person who wrote beautiful and affirming e-mails and letters of support. My heart is full with love because of you.

—Alma López, Los Angeles[1]

NOTES

1. I wrote this statement in preparation for meeting with the protestors at the Museum of International Folk Art. The meeting was to take place on April 4, 2001, but had to be cancelled because there were hundreds of protestors who were not allowed into the meeting for safety concerns. An impromptu press conference was convened after the April 4 gathering at which I read this statement. I had the piece published online to generate a wide audience of cyber support for *Our Lady*. I later expanded the piece, which was then published as "Silencing Our Lady: La Respuesta de Alma," in *Aztlán: A Journal of Chicano Studies* 26.2 (Fall 2001): 249–267. This version includes some letters sent to the curator as well as the museum director, the model, and me expressing support for the work and outrage at the attacks on our First Amendment rights.

2

It's Not about the Art in the Folk, It's about the Folks in the Art

A CURATOR'S TALE

Tey Marianna Nunn

FOR ALMA, ELENA, MARION, AND TERESA

THE FOLK ART MUSEUM

THIS CHAPTER IS PART *testimonio* and part scholarly research. As such I will start by sharing a few anecdotes about my experience at the University of New Mexico (UNM) and how it led me to where I am today. As a UNM graduate student in the interdisciplinary Latin American Studies Program, I was taught to think critically about Spanish colonial art and history, as well as contemporary Hispanic, Chicano, and Latino art and culture. I reveled in the classes that actually reflected components of me—my interests, my experiences, my culture, and my identity.

I remember the first day a Chicano art history course was officially taught at UNM. At the beginning of her lecture on that day, my professor shed tears because of the sheer magnitude of the message being conveyed.

In the summer of 1994, I was selected to be one of the first group of fifteen Latina and Latino graduate students to participate in a two-week seminar in Washington, DC, sponsored by the Intra-University Program for Latino Research and the Smithsonian Institution's Center for Museum Studies. This intensive program was a direct result of a critical study issued about this American cultural institution in our nation's capital. The report, titled *Willful*

Neglect: The Smithsonian and U.S. Latinos (Smithsonian Institution Task Force, 1994), cited an alarming lack of Latino representation among staff who held decision-making positions as well as the lack of Latino representation in Smithsonian exhibitions and programming.

My experience at the Smithsonian impacted me greatly and made me realize that I could work in a museum and make a difference. I believed that in doing so, I could find my Nuevomexicana and Latina experience reflected in a museum exhibition and, more important, I could serve as a "gatekeeper" to assist others previously not represented in museums into the *templos* as well.

In my position as curator of contemporary Hispano and Latino collections at the Museum of International Folk Art (MOIFA) in Santa Fe, I confronted aspects of cultural conflict every day. I held this position for more than nine and a half years. For years local Hispano/a and Chicano/a artists (yes, there are Chicanas and Chicanos in New Mexico) have criticized our sister museum, the Museum of Fine Arts in Santa Fe (now named the New Mexico Museum of Art) for its failure to represent local Hispanic artists within their exhibition galleries.[1] Similar battles took place in other New Mexican venues, such as the State Fair complex, where, finally, in the early 1990s, a building devoted to showcasing Hispanic art was formally named. While New Mexico's Department of Cultural Affairs (formerly the Office of Cultural Affairs) has now established the National Hispanic Cultural Center in Albuquerque, Santa Fe's state-run arts-related institutions continue largely to ignore the incredible talent of Hispana/o, Nuevomexicana/o, Latina/o, and Chicana/o artists who make their home in New Mexico. Furthermore, Santa Fe, Albuquerque, and Las Cruces have only a handful of private art galleries that show Hispanic art—contemporary or traditional. Even fewer galleries are owned by Hispanics. As far as mainstream institutions go, the Museum of International Folk Art is the only Santa Fe state-affiliated institution in which Hispanic and Latin American art is shown on a regular basis. Of course, the fact that a "folk" art museum is one of the few museums that exhibit traditional and contemporary art can be viewed as extremely problematic, since the institution provides the context through which the art is interpreted.

Despite such critical observations, MOIFA has been a national leader in representing Hispanic art since the 1950s. Early on, the curator of Spanish colonial collections recognized the value of the traditional art of New Mexico and acquired stellar examples for the permanent collection. In the late 1980s, the museum opened the Hispanic Heritage Wing (HHW) with the first large-scale permanent exhibition in the country dedicated to Hispanic art. The exhibition, titled *Familia y Fé* (family and faith), is devoted to the traditional core values of Hispanic New Mexico. It features hundred of examples of Hispanic New Mexican religious and vernacular art, including *bultos* (three-dimensional religious sculptures), *retablos* (two-dimensional paintings or panels), hide paintings, other religious objects, furniture, weaving, tinwork, straw appliqué, and jewelry from the colonial period through the Mexican, territorial, and early revival periods. *Familia y Fé* ends with a section about art produced in the 1930s and 1940s. This exhibit also highlights extraordinary nineteenth- and twentieth-century examples of traditional Mexican and New Mexican images of La Virgen de Guadalupe by Rafael Aragón, Pedro Antonio Fresquís, A. J. Santero, as well as unidentified artists.

Adjacent to the large permanent exhibit space that houses *Familia y Fé* is a small gallery (approximately 600 square feet) tucked in the far corner of the museum. Named the Contemporary Changing Gallery, this space was mandated by the original HHW community advisory board to showcase contemporary Hispanic art. The board, consisting of Nuevomexicanos/as, wanted to ensure that the museum continued to present Hispanic art and culture not solely in the context of a colonial past but also in a dynamic and changing present with an eye toward the future. It is important to note that the Contemporary Changing Gallery is the only space in the entire Museum of New Mexico system that is dedicated to contemporary Hispanic art.

THE ART

On February 25, 2001, an exhibition titled *Cyber Arte: Tradition Meets Technology* opened in the Contemporary Changing Gallery in MOIFA's HHW. *Cyber Arte* was one of the first exhibitions nationwide to highlight digital art. Prior to opening day, a tremendous amount of advance press about *Cyber Arte* had run in such publications as *American Art*, *Art and Antiques*, *Hispanic Magazine*, and the *Santa Fe New Mexican*. The reviews, prior to February 25, praised this small exhibition for the cutting-edge show that it was meant to be—and that it was.

Three weeks after opening day, two male members of the local Hispanic religious community, one a police chaplain and self-proclaimed community activist, and the other a deacon at Our Lady of Guadalupe Church in Santa Fe, visited MOIFA. They brought with them one of approximately six thousand brochures mailed by the museum during the previous September (2000). The brochure featured all of the ongoing exhibits and announced upcoming projects for early 2001. The color image accompanying the description of Cyber Arte was that of Our Lady, by Los Angeles–based artist Alma López. This work is a computer-generated print on canvas depicting a strong Latina with attitude.[2] Her head is raised and her confident gaze meets directly with that of the viewer. With her hands on her hips, she assumes the "Latina Power pose." Her robe, decorated in pre-Columbian symbols, is draped over her shoulders. She also wears a modest 1930s bathing suit (or a 2004 Olympic women's running suit, depending on how you look at it) made of pink, white, and yellow roses. Her face, neck, torso, and legs are exposed. There is no cleavage. She stands on a black crescent moon held by a female angel with bare breasts and butterfly wings.[3] Larger roses and decorative elements from the traditional iconography of La Virgen de Guadalupe frame these central images.

With the pamphlet image in hand, the two men met with MOIFA director, Dr. Joyce Ice, and demanded that the "offensive," "blasphemous," and "sacrilegious" piece be removed immediately from Cyber Arte.[4] In discussion with the museum director, the chaplain and the deacon agreed to "open a dialogue" to discuss the piece. However, rather than entering what could have been a very important, respectful, and illuminating cultural dialogue for all involved, the two men went directly to the local press after the meeting. The next day, an article outlining their concerns and demands appeared in the local paper.

On March 17, 2001, the headline that ran across the Albuquerque Journal's northern New Mexico edition read: "Skimpily Attired 'Our Lady' Protested," and the subheading read, "Critics Say Nudity, Virgin Do Not Mix." Personally, I'm not sure how one can be skimpily attired and nude at the same time, but that discussion would take a whole other chapter.[5] Nevertheless, in that article, the term "Bikini Virgin" was coined by a non-Hispanic male newspaper reporter to describe this image of a strong, garland-draped Latina. In the article, the deacon was quoted as saying: "What bothers me about it is that it was termed devotion to Our Lady of Guadalupe . . . and if that qualifies as devotion, it's very distorted."[6] The police chaplain stated: "To see Our Lady displaced with a woman in a bikini and a woman with her bosoms sticking out . . . that's totally disrespectful. It violated the sacred boundaries of our culture."[7] In many subsequent articles, the police chaplain mentioned that both his mother and grandmother were named Guadalupe. In one article, he elaborated, saying that López's *Our Lady* was "disrespectful to Santa Fe residents with strong personal connections to the Virgin of Guadalupe."[8]

From that point on, the image of López's *Our Lady* was splashed, in its entirety, all over the local television news and newspapers—above the fold, in color, and rarely with permission. The use of the sensational "Bikini Virgin"— rather than "the Virgin" adorned in "rose-encrusted garments," the description utilized by a female reporter during the same time period—recalled other recent controversial catch phrases in art such as "Piss Christ" (a color photograph by Andrés Serrano) and "Dung Virgin" (regarding a painting titled *The Holy Virgin Mary* by Chris Ofili shown in the *Sensation* exhibition at the Brooklyn Museum in 1999).[9]

In the wake of these high-profile events, the idea of a Bikini Virgin, used completely out of the context of the exhibition, the museum, the artist, and the curator, spread like wildfire across New Mexico and beyond. The tone of the initial wave of print and television reporting was sensationalist and inflammatory. It is no wonder people reacted emotionally and vehemently. Although fallout continues to this day, to a great extent, the *Our Lady* controversy lasted from March 2001 to late February 2002, despite the fact that the piece, along with the entire *Cyber Arte* exhibition, closed on its original date of October 28, 2001.

On the surface, this incident may appear to be simple in nature. A nontraditional Virgin version gets shown in a state-funded museum and the local Hispano Catholic community gets upset. However, this was an extremely complicated, intricate, intense, and in some ways unique episode, so much so that I am convinced that the Virgin was on both sides.

CURATORIAL INTENT

Addressing and collapsing stereotypes regarding Latinos and Latino art is not only a scholarly interest for me but also an ongoing necessity in the art and museum world. Imagine being one of only a handful of Hispanic/Latina curators in the entire country. Although the situation has certainly improved since the Smithsonian's "willful neglect" report was published in 1994, the fact remains that the ongoing representation of Latino culture and art is still minimal in museums, galleries, university classes, and related books and articles, when compared to representatives of the population as a whole. In the wake of the North American and Central American Free Trade Agreements and increased globalization, the focus has been on art and artists from Latin America, not necessarily on the "Minority Majority"—Latino and Hispanic art and artists in the United States. This is especially true for Nuevomexicano artists, whose work is often stereotyped (and more often dismissed) as "folk" because of an economically and artistically successful "Spanish-colonial" style.

With few exceptions, the art by Nuevomexicano/a artists does not get included in the national discourse on Latino/a, Chicano/a, and Hispanic arts and culture. This is a frustrating yet intriguing dynamic, as the "traditional" and "contemporary" work is well executed, carefully composed, and powerfully provocative. Often the Nuevomexicana/o artists who achieve artistic recognition and success have done so as a result of acknowledgment from outside the Land of Enchantment rather than from their exposure within the state's boundaries. In the art world, success is commonly based on recognition by collectors, galleries, museums, and curators. In New Mexico, all of these issues have to do with identity, awareness, perceptions, and stereotypes, as well as representation of these artists within the Museum of New Mexico System. And all of these issues played integral roles in the *Our Lady* controversy.

My original curatorial intent in putting together the *Cyber Arte* exhibition was to highlight the Hispanic and Latina/o arts and cultural presence on the Internet, a trail-blazing curatorial notion at the time. The secondary purpose of the exhibition as it was originally conceived was to address stereotypes of Latinos, technology, and art, especially because Latinos are one of the "minority" groups greatly affected by the digital divide. I had noticed for a number of years that many traditional and contemporary artists were looking toward the computer either to set up their own websites or to create art. I was especially intrigued by the fact that many of these artists experimenting with technology were women. I wondered how these women negotiated the borders of identity as they pertained to combining tradition and technology. Thus, *Cyber Arte: Tradition Meets Technology* was born. Little did I know it would become a metaphor for tradition meeting modernity, as well as many other issues, in Santa Fe, New Mexico, and beyond.

THE EXHIBITION

For the exhibition, I chose the work of four Hispana/Latina/Chicana artists: Teresa Archuleta-Sagel, Elena Baca, and Marion C. Martínez, all from New Mexico, and Alma López from California.[10] These strong, talented, and intelligent women explore traditional elements in their work by using technology. Whether digitally rendering family photos to convey family history or constructing saints out of computer parts, each artist grapples with how to be modern and traditional simultaneously.

I realized as the show went up that all four *artistas* were responding to modern high-tech times and at the same time honoring tradition. Supplementary and educational materials for the exhibit included two gallery handouts: a guide to Latino resources and arts-related websites, with a list of Spanglish terms for the Internet (reprinted from the *New York Times*); and a separate handout containing artist's statements by the featured artists along with their web addresses (see the statements at the end of this chapter).

The computer-rendered works by award-winning master weaver Teresa Archuleta-Sagel were among the first pieces selected for the *Cyber Arte* exhibition. Archuleta-Sagel is from Española, New Mexico. In the early 1970s

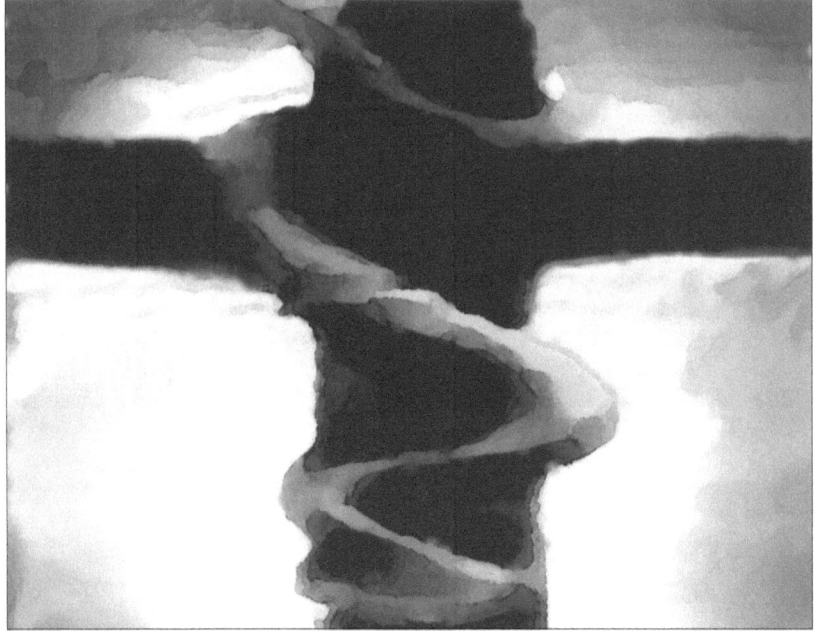

2.1.   *Crossroads*. Digital print by Teresa Archuleta-Sagel, © 1999. Courtesy of the International Folk Art Foundation, Santa Fe, New Mexico.

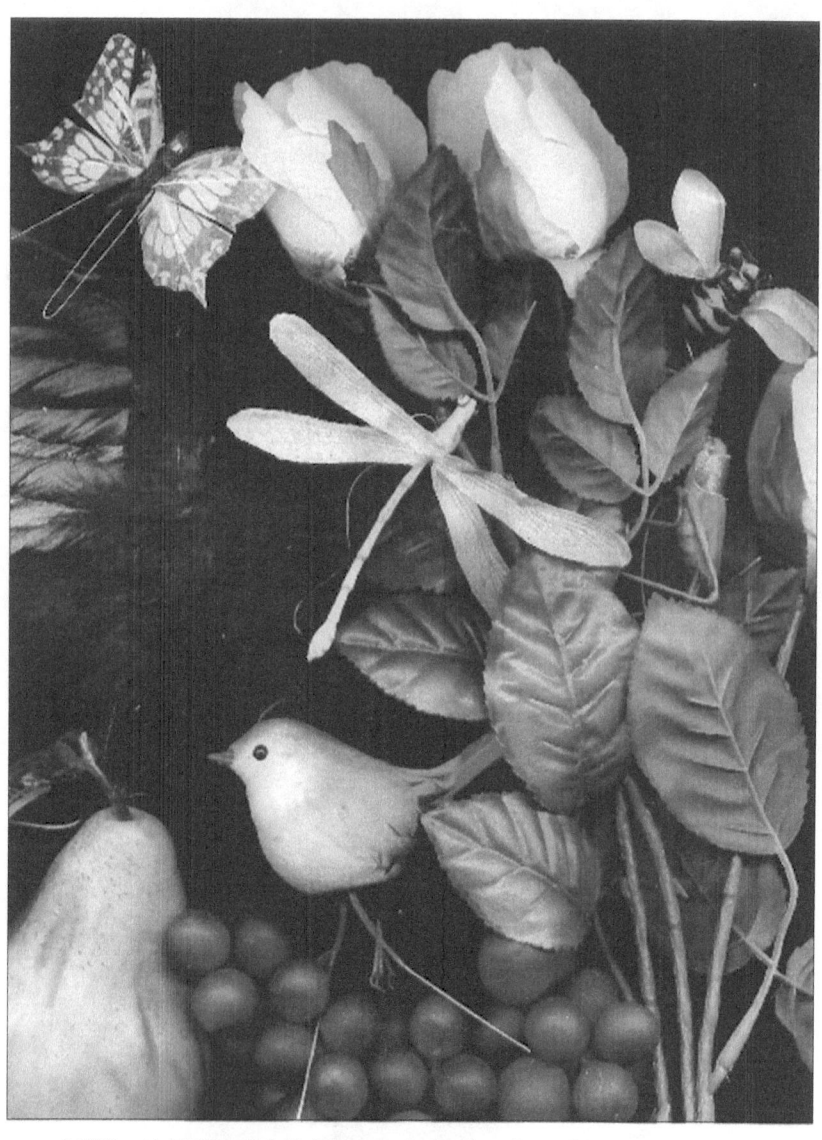

2.2. *Still Life with Walking Pink Bird*. Digital print by Elena Baca, © 2001.
Courtesy of Elena Baca.

she studied weaving with renowned Doña Águeda Martínez and researched the history and techniques that contribute to this art form in New Mexico. Examples of her "traditional" work are represented in MOIFA's permanent textile collection. A few years before *Cyber Arte*, Archuleta-Sagel became ill from the environmental effects of the weaving process and as a result had to set her weaving aside. Yearning for a creative outlet, she turned to the computer. Her fiber-inspired digital tapestries as well as her use of family photos and religious icons provided for cathartic healing and expression and helped her produce, as she says, "emotions and dreams that reflect my life."

Elena Baca from Albuquerque also uses family stories, photos, and religious components in her unique photo print process and combines them with modern digital technology. She creates riveting and evocative images inspired by her Nuevomexicana roots.

Along with these "traditional" cultural elements, Baca began a series of "FakeLifes" playing on the still life tradition found in both folk and fine art. In these works, composed of fake flora and fauna purchased in craft stores, she comments on tradition and modernity—natural and artificial.

"Techna" artist Marion C. Martínez was born in Española and raised in the community of Los Luceros. She creates religious images and traditional *matachines* masks from old circuit boards, mother boards, and other technological components she finds in the Black Hole, a used-computer outlet in Los Alamos. For Martínez the process in which she creates is deeply spiritual and devotional in the same way the traditional *santeros* and *santeras* of northern New Mexico sculpt and paint their images in wood.

Finally, Chicana artist Alma López often recounts growing up in El Sereno, California, during the Chicano Mural Renaissance of the 1970s and 1980s amid murals mostly depicting Emiliano Zapata, Francisco Villa, and Aztec warriors. Among the works by López chosen to support the exhibition's vision were images of women and the border and symbols of women negotiating tradition with technology.

I was drawn to the work of Archuleta-Sagel, Baca, Martínez, and López specifically because they combine traditional folk and cultural iconography and recast them to reflect the twentieth and now twenty-first centuries. Although such sources of inspiration have informed Chicano and Latino art for decades, Hispano, and especially Hispana, works utilizing a contemporary approach in New Mexico have had to struggle to position themselves alongside (and oftentimes against) the embedded Spanish colonial historical and stylistic works while defying stereotypes in the process.

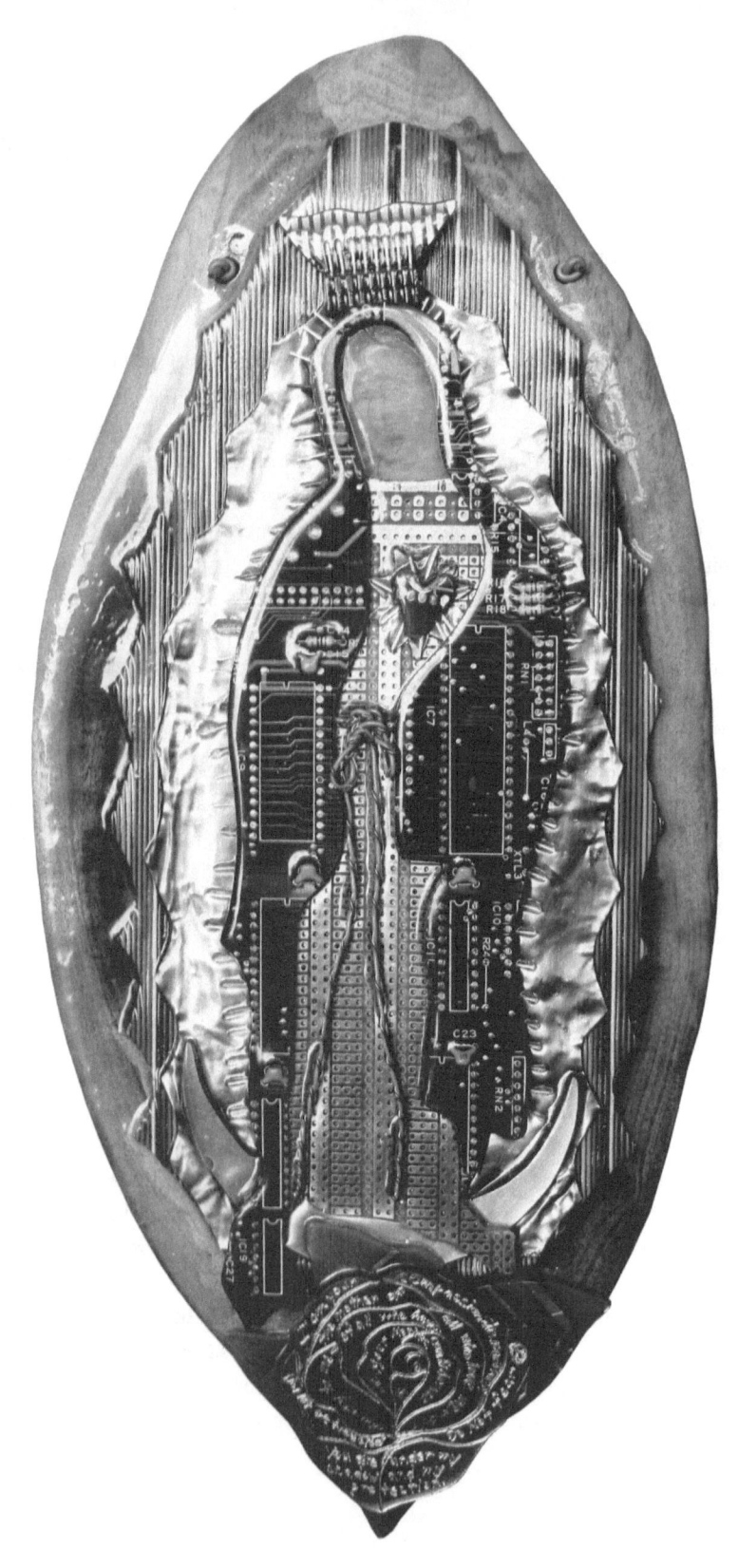

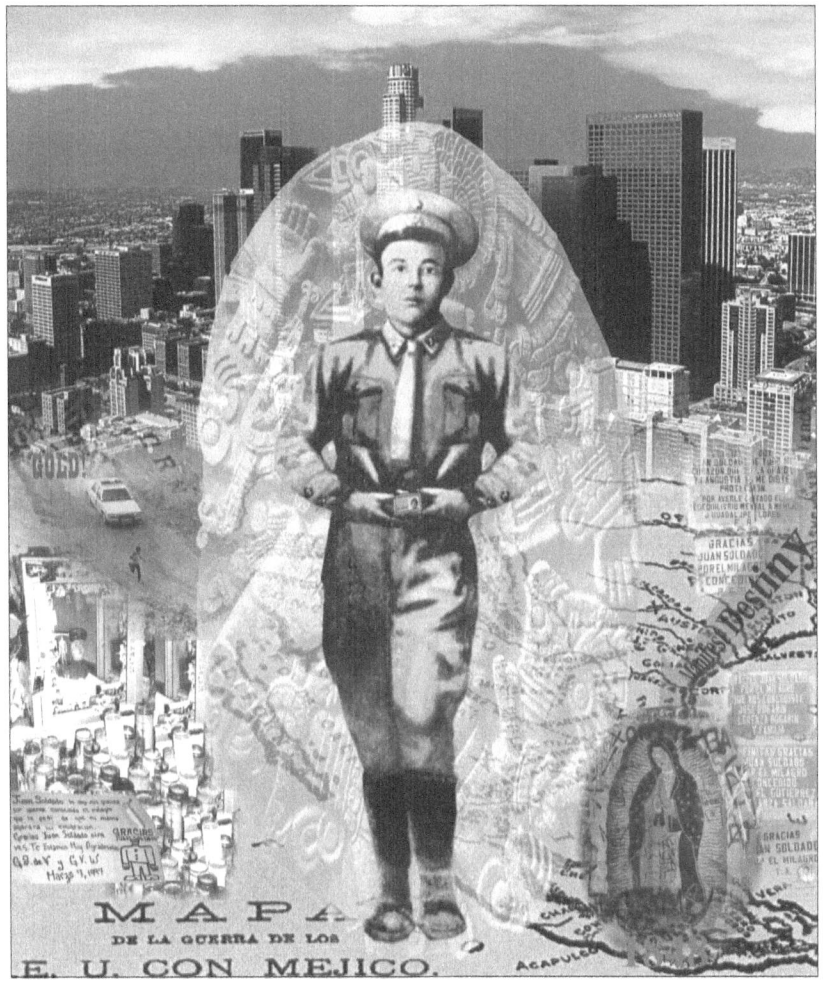

2.3.   FACING *Mi Madre Santa*. Mixed media sculpture by Marion C. Martínez, © 1998.
       Courtesy of Marion C. Martínez. From the collection of Alma López.

2.4.   ABOVE *Juan Soldado*. Digital print by Alma López, © 1997.
       Courtesy of Alma López.

HISTORICAL IMAGES OF GUADALUPE

According to legend, the Mexican image of La Virgen de Guadalupe appeared in 1531. At that time, it was already dramatically changed from the image of the same name in Spain. She had indigenous features and elements when she appeared to Juan Diego on the hill of Tepeyac. In the early nineteenth century and during the Mexican War for Independence, her image was utilized to help Father Miguel Hidalgo and those who fought for freedom from Spain. Around this time, the colors of her dress and cloak, as well as the wings of the angel that appeared below her feet, changed to reflect *mexicanidad,* or Mexican identity, with the *colores nacionales* (national colors) of red, white, and green. In the twentieth-century United States, César Chávez and Dolores Huerta used La Virgen's image in the United Farm Workers' struggle for farmworkers' rights. Clearly, even before the recasting by contemporary artists and writers, the image of La Virgen de Guadalupe was used for political and personal statements and reflected the changing times.

Beginning in the 1970s, Chicana artists such as Ester Hernández, with her karate-kicking Virgin, and Yolanda M. López, with her triptych of her grandmother, her mother, and herself each rendered as Guadalupe, interpreted the icon, portrayed in the traditional image with downcast gaze, as a less-passive model for female behavior.[11] Their Virgen is strong, active, and mobile. She looks and acts like a contemporary woman. You would not want to mess with her, because she is in control.

Examples of these personal and artistic interpretations often reflect another connection to Mexico and an acknowledgment of indigenous identity with references to pre-Columbian Mother Goddess images including Tonantzin, Coatlicue, and Coyolxauhqui. Men got into the revisioning act too, with Alfredo de Batuc's *Seven Views of City Hall* (1987) and César Martínez's *Mona Lupe: The Epitome of Chicano Art* (1992). Sometimes male images are depicted dressed as Guadalupe. Examples of this phenomenon can be seen on Mexican soap packages featuring the folk saint El Niño Fidencio and Mita Cuarón's *Guadalupe Baby* (1992), depicting the artist's son surrounded by symbols of La Virgen de Guadalupe.

Many other examples of this revisionist tradition can be found in literature and art, including stories by Sandra Cisneros and Ana Castillo, as well as a performance called "Heat Your Own," in which Raquel Salinas, the model for López's *Our Lady*, portrays La Virgen de Guadalupe.[12] And months before the *Cyber Arte* exhibition opened, an edited version of Alma López's *Our*

Lady appeared on the cover of an award-winning book, *Puro Teatro: A Latina Anthology.*[13]

Armed with all of this information and more, I selected López's *Our Lady* for the exhibition. My selection was based on historical knowledge of and current discourse about Hispana/o, Chicana/o, and Latina/o artists and writers who have strongly felt the need to reshape and recast the image of La Virgen de Guadalupe into something they can personally identify with. López was not the first artist to render La Virgen de Guadalupe in a different and personal manner. Her work is in no way an aberration. It is simply one of the more recent examples in a long-running and legitimate conversation that artists have been having since the 1970s. In fact, reimaging La Virgen is now so common in the community that it has become an established tradition in the Chicano and Latino art historical canon. Revisioning the Virgin of Guadalupe's image and inscribing her into American art history was an ongoing cultural war fought by artists, activists, and community members who intentionally positioned themselves in the museum and art worlds with passion and an agenda. Nevertheless, it seems unlikely that awareness of this history would have changed the protestors' justification in Santa Fe, even though the struggles were similar.

THE FOLKS IN THE ART

When the protest against *Our Lady* started in March 2001, the protestors' objective was to have the piece removed from the exhibition and the museum. In addition, the protestors asked for a formal apology and the resignations of the state's Office of Cultural Affairs administrators, MOIFA'S director, and its curator. Later, protestors asked the museum to return all Catholic sacred images and icons to the church and that the museum give all receipts from admission to the *Cyber Arte* exhibit to the Catholic ministry.[14] In regard to the artwork, one of the main protestors stated: "I see the devil" and declared a "holy war" (his words) on the state museum. "They started the fire, and we're going to put it out. No one has a right to attack our religion."[15]

As the first wave of this very emotional protest gained energy, arguments of insider-outsider, taxpayer-funded institutions, church versus state, First Amendment rights, censorship and self-censorship, gender, sexuality, education and class, as well as who had the right to use the Guadalupe image rose quickly to the forefront. The archbishop of Santa Fe, Michael Sheehan, voiced his opinion in the press, saying that "such a picture has no place in a tax-supported museum." His official statement continued: "I wish that those who want to paint controversial art would find their own symbols to trash and leave the Catholic ones alone."[16] He later labeled Raquel Salinas, a rape survivor and the model for *Our Lady*, a "tart" and a "prostitute."[17] Next he questioned Alma López's religious affiliation, remarking: "I don't know if she is Catholic or not. I'd like to see a letter of support from her pastor."[18]

The events of these first weeks began an extremely difficult and painful year and a half for me, for the artists, for my colleagues, and for the community. Those of us directly involved were the recipients of many threatening phone calls, menacing letters, and personal attacks. The artwork was called blasphemous and sacrilegious. I was called insensitive and malicious. I was accused of trafficking in cyber porn and of Catholic bashing. I was told God would strike me down, and I was even accused of not being Hispanic. It was declared that I was starting a new religion and promoting Satanism. Members of our own Board of Regents called me to demand that I go immediately into the gallery and remove the piece. One regent stated: "It is very difficult for me to comprehend that a curator in one of our four museums would come up with something so vile and so offensive to the community that it should be removed."[19] Another regent told me that my decision to include the piece was one of the "greatest misjudgments since that of Helen of Troy."[20]

Although supporters, both local and national, always outnumbered those calling the "Bikini Virgin" blasphemous, one would have never known it from the unbalanced and polarizing media coverage (I state this now as many members of the press have since personally apologized to me).[21] A newspaper editorial came out saying that "Guadalupe is held in high esteem by many New Mexicans as a symbol of purity" and that the curator of the exhibition should have been more sensitive to this and not displayed "a modern, sexy interpretation of a popular religious icon."[22]

Hundreds of articles and political cartoons followed. During the first few months, the mainstream press failed to give coverage to the artist's or curator's perspective. The major newspapers in Albuquerque and Santa Fe, which have historically supported the Catholic Church, had been receiving phone calls from the archbishop as well as one of the deeply religious museum regents.

For me personally, the things most difficult to swallow in interviews, articles, and editorials were words to the effect that because I was educated I had lost touch with my community and that I was a thinker and not a believer. My integrity, scholarship, and identity were all challenged, and for most of that year, I was vilified in the local press. Because of my unusual first name and slanderous misconceptions by some protestors, a rumor spread that I was the head of a secret Vietnamese lesbian sisterhood. This, by the way, was news to my husband at the time, who in turn was told he was "sleeping with the devil."

On April 4, 2001, during the first of two museum-sponsored public hearings on the issue, both Alma López and I were scheduled to give prepared statements at the beginning of the meeting but were silenced by the protestors and prevented from presenting our points of view to the large audience and assembled press corps. Law enforcement authorities, because of the extremely intimidating, emotionally charged, and violent atmosphere, canceled the meeting. Upon news of the cancellation, López and I were immediately surrounded by male audience members, most shouting: "Burn her, burn them!" We were escorted away by security staff and U.S. marshals who helped us get back to the museum in a getaway car and motorcade.

Despite the fact that Gary Johnson, the Republican governor at the time, came out in support of keeping the piece on display, stating that it did not violate community standards, things got worse before they got better over the course of the next six months. Death and bomb threats continued, so much so that the FBI was brought in to bug and monitor the museum's phone system. Museum administrators wrote a letter of apology to the archbishop. Under the direction of the state attorney general's office, the museum's Committee on Sensitive Materials, which previously had dealt only with NAGPRA (Native American Graves Repatriation Act) issues, met and considered whether *Our Lady* was a "ritual" object. The archbishop and many priests preached from the pulpit against the museum and the artists. The American Civil Liberties Union threatened to bring a lawsuit against the museum, stating that López's First Amendment rights would be violated if the exhibit closed early. A Pennsylvania-based organization, the American Society for the Defense of Tradition, Family and Property/America Needs Fatima, which is struggling to rid Brazil of the samba, held a national rosary rally and prayer vigil on museum grounds. A key group of protestors and parishioners obtained all the exhibit-related records, including curatorial correspondence, through the Freedom of Information Act. Throughout the entire span of the controversy, the exhibition artists and my museum colleagues, from security staff to upper administration, experienced extreme stress and criticism as well.

Although the brochure lists the closing date of the exhibition as October 28, 2001, the museum intended to extend the run of the show by four months, for a new closing date in February 2002. As a result of the controversy, the exhibition did not stay open those extra months, against my own and the four artists' wishes. Museum officials made this decision in "the spirit of reconciliation" toward the community component that claimed spiritual degradation and felt that the image "violated the sacred boundaries" of "their" culture.[23]

Ignoring this good-faith effort to reconcile differences, some protestors continued their crusade. Public hearings continued and lawsuits were filed. Members of the New Mexico State Legislature continued to threaten the funding of the museum, claiming no separation of church and state in New Mexico, and repeatedly stated that they wanted the "outrageous desecration" of the Virgin removed immediately.

In November 2001, after the exhibit had been removed, I was called to testify before the Legislative Finance Committee. During the budget hearing that addressed the museum's role in the controversy, those who spoke before me and against *Our Lady*—a general, a PhD, and an ambassador (all male)—were addressed by their proper titles; I, the only native Nuevomexicana curator in the state's museum system, with a PhD from the state's flagship university, was addressed as "Miss Nunn." A few months later, when the legislative session began, a couple of state senators and representatives sponsored a Memorial to investigate my qualifications and to censure "the curator's behavior."

Things did not begin to quiet down until almost a year to the day after the exhibition opening, when a state district court judge issued a final ruling in a lawsuit. He stated that the curator was not liable for not holding a public hearing about including *Our Lady* before the exhibition went up.

Whenever I speak or write about this controversy, a question is always at the forefront of the minds of most people. How did this situation reach the emotional pitch that it did? Why weren't the voices of all sides reflected in the media coverage? What was the protest really all about? As can be imagined, I have asked myself these very questions on more than one occasion. In my opinion, there were a number of extenuating factors.

First, one of our museum regents was a multigenerational Hispanic New Mexican, a devout Catholic, a Knight of Malta, and a former U.S. ambassador to several Latin American countries. He actively voiced his opinion against the work, the exhibition, museum administrators, and the curator. This was exactly the opposite of the situation experienced by the Brooklyn Museum and that institution's showing of Chris Ofili's so-called Dung Virgin. In Brooklyn, the entire Board of Regents stood by the decisions of the director and the curator of the *Sensation* exhibit. In contrast, our regent actively helped incite the protesting faithful rather than explain the museum's point of view, thus positioning himself as a champion of the people and at the same time disparaging the museum that he was charged to advise.

Second, on a near-daily basis, the media called for the removal of the work from the museum while at the same time repeatedly featuring the entire image unedited on the front page (often above the fold) of their respective papers. The coverage on the local nightly news was similar. When the affiliates were not showing the image on screen behind the anchorperson, they were including a slow camera pan of the image, highlighting the figure's torso and legs. In general, the media bombarded the public with the image completely out of the context of the exhibition while never once asking for permission to use the image and rarely crediting the artist. The media coverage was so intense that over the course of assembling the archives dealing with this period in MOIFA's institutional history, we documented well over 450 local, national, and international newspaper articles and thousands of pieces of written documentation in the form of letters and e-mails.

Third, the identity politics of "place and space" factored heavily into this experience, as did intense issues of cultural loss. For years, Santa Fe and northern New Mexico have in various ways tried to maintain a "traditional culture" while dealing with issues of cultural loss. *Our Lady* became a critical flashpoint for the convergence of these issues. Nuevomexicanos often intentionally position themselves based on longevity of familial ties as well as geographic place in order to retain identity. Long-term residence is used as an integral marker of authenticity and a symbol of pride. This idea of cultural authenticity to prove legitimacy was utilized as a major argument in the *Our Lady* controversy, so much so that just before the second public forum was held, one reporter wrote an article with the headline "N.M. Heritage Stirred into Debate over 'Our Lady.'" The article, subtitled "Cultural Issues Drive Discussion," detailed how the issue of long-term cultural ties in New Mexico played a role and complicated the controversy.[24]

Additional statements found in the newspaper archives support the importance and emotionality of the idea of territory and place. A vocal protestor stated: "You may do whatever you want to in Los Angeles, but traditionally here in New Mexico, this is old school . . . If she [López] can't get that message, that's her problem."[25] Interestingly, this same protestor, who relied on the use of the geographic "place" card in his arguments, was not originally from New Mexico. In addition, although Alma López, from California, was shunned, the faith-based organization Tradition, Family and Property, from Pennsylvania, was heartily welcomed with open arms by the Santa Fe protestors.

Fourth, aspects of identity politics mentioned earlier manifested themselves in an argument over ownership of the image of the Virgin of Guadalupe and, by extension, over who owned its history. Despite the fact that the image appears and is marketed on everything from nail clippers to puzzles and is emblazoned on low riders and in tattoo form on the bodies of many Latinos and Latinas, Alma López was repeatedly admonished for using and changing the image. One letter to the editor even declared that the basilica in Mexico City held the copyright and that no one was allowed to use it without the basilica's permission.

In response, López often stated in articles that the claim that the Virgin of Guadalupe did not "belong" to her and that she thus did not have a "right" to reimage her in her art was the most upsetting aspect of the controversy for her personally. As one journalist recorded in the *Wall Street Journal*: "In fact the artist, born in Mexico and, by her own account a devout Roman Catholic and devotee of Our Lady of Guadalupe, could make a better case for 'ownership' of the Mexican apparition of the Virgin Mary Icon than could most of the protestors."[26] But some protestors did not agree and felt that neither López nor the museum had a right to the image. One stated: "The sacred image was a miracle given by God. And that image belongs to God. It doesn't belong to her [López] or anyone for interpretation."[27]

Finally, protestors perceived MOIFA and the Museum of New Mexico System, despite a long legacy of representing and supporting Hispano art and culture, and despite the fact that three of the artists and the curator were native born, to be insensitive Anglo-oriented institutions bent on assaulting the local Hispanic culture. Protestors were often quoted as saying: "It isn't about censorship, it's about respect." I maintain that at the beginning of the controversy, the non-Hispanic museum administrators perceived a need to be politically sensitive to the "Hispanic community." But because museum administrators, for the most part, were unfamiliar with the multiplicity of communities and identities within the so-called community, coupled with the fact that no one had ever dealt with such an impassioned protest, they felt a need to apologize and acquiesce. In doing so, however, they empowered one segment of the community and ignored the others.

Not all Hispanics, Catholics, men, women, and New Mexican taxpayers were offended by the piece. In short, the Catholic Church, key legislators, and vocal protestors were heard and allowed to speak freely, but Hispanic and Latino supporters, the female museum director, the exhibit designer, the graphic designer, the Nuevomexicana/Latina curator, and the artists—one of whom is a Chicana and three of whom are Nuevomexicanas—were not.

The protestors tried to put *Our Lady* and La Virgen de Guadalupe back in her place, but in many ways *Cyber Arte* lives on. In the years since the controversy, many New Mexican Hispanic artists who work in traditional styles have experimented with different versions of La Virgen. In some representations she is holding out her arms, in others, her foot peeks out from under her robes; still other traditional *retablos* (done with tongue in cheek) depict her wearing a rose-covered 1930s bathing outfit.

Fulfilling my original curatorial intent regarding an Internet presence, Alma López, the artist under fire, started a website devoted to the controversy (www.almalopez.com). There she has posted articles as well as e-mails both for and against the piece. In a 2004 interview she stated that she was glad she did it because at least the Internet was a "safe place for people to have a voice."[28]

IDENTITY AND ITS DISCONTENTS

There can be no doubt that significant cultural issues played out in the *Our Lady* controversy. Issues of identity, both the perceived loss of identity and its political positioning, were hidden behind the cloak of *Our Lady*. While La Virgen was able to shield some, she was not able to protect others. The now-historic controversy has had its repercussions. State-run institutions have shied away from doing exhibitions featuring anything that might be construed as "controversial." This has included many aspects of Nuevomexicano and Latino art, because museum officials and state administrators misperceive such visual production to be political and problematic. When possibly controversial work is exhibited, large disclaimer signs are exhibited as well. It is almost as if the protestors not only silenced the museum but silenced themselves and those who have fought alongside them in similar cultural battles.

I have come to the conclusion that culture wars are inevitable. Representing Latino art and culture is problematic and will continue to be so as demographics shift and the Hispanic communities jostle for position. Our culture is complex and contradictory, not homogeneous by any means. To be Hispanic or Latino in the twenty-first century is to be many different things, both traditional and contemporary, simultaneously. To date, these varied voices have not necessarily been welcomed into museums with open arms. My job as curator is to interpret, preserve, and present the multiple artistic manifestations of our dynamic communities and experiences. As I do so, someone is probably going to be offended.

EPILOGUE

On the afternoon of September 10, 2004, I presented a preliminary version of this chapter in the Student Union Building on the University of New Mexico campus in Albuquerque. My paper was one of the invited contributions to a National Endowment for the Humanities (NEH)–supported conference titled "Expressive Culture in the Hispanic Southwest: A Colloquium on Curriculum, Research, and Retention at an Hispanic Serving Institution of Higher Education." I was four minutes into my presentation when two men arrived in the conference room. Both individuals had been active in the protest against the *Cyber Arte* exhibit and MOIFA. One of the men made his way to the front row and turned on a tape recorder.[29] Three and a half years later the controversy was still emotional.

EPILOGUE TO THE EPILOGUE

I wish I could say the persecution around the controversy ended in 2004, but that is not the case. It was still going strong in January 2007. At that time I was asked by Off-Center Community Arts Project, an Albuquerque nonprofit, to participate on a panel for their Guadalupe Exhibit and Conference. The conference included the exhibit opening, the discussion panel, and a shrine-making workshop as well as a tour of local shrines dedicated to the Virgin. The events were funded by an NEA Challenge America: Reaching Every Community Fast-Track Review Grant. This national funding helped pay for local public radio announcements. These ads listed the names of the panelists, including me, acclaimed artist Yolanda (not Alma) López, and Dr. Jennifer Colby, a professor and Guadalupe expert at California State University, Monterey Bay. Upon hearing these announcements, and hearing my surname paired with a "López," some of the protestors who had been key in the 2001 events at MOIFA began calling around and protesting my participation on the panel. At the time I had just taken a new position as director and chief curator of the National Hispanic Cultural Center Art Museum in Albuquerque. A few days before the scheduled panel, I received phone calls from the chair of the NHCC Board (National Hispanic Cultural Center, appointed by the governor) as well as the secretary of the Department of Cultural Affairs for the State of New Mexico. Both had received phone calls from protestors including the archbishop of Santa Fe. The people who contacted me were concerned about what I was going to be talking about and how I was professionally representing the center as a state employee. I assured them that it was to be a general slide lecture on images of Guadalupe focused on New Mexico. I was asked if I was planning to discuss Alma López's image of Our Lady. I replied that I had not planned on it but maybe now I was going to have to address it, given the circumstances. They insisted that I was to do this on my own time and not in my capacity as director and chief curator of the state's premier Latino art museum.

I attended and presented at the panel, and there were protestors. I never mentioned Alma López's work, which disappointed the agitators in attendance. However, my fellow panelists did, and they experienced firsthand the passion of the protestors. That Saturday in January, six years after the opening of the *Cyber Arte* exhibition, I learned that keeping quiet and intentionally not mentioning *Our Lady* was as powerful as bringing *Our Lady* into the room.

CYBER ARTE ARTIST'S STATEMENTS

Teresa Archuleta-Sagel

As a young girl growing up in Española, New Mexico, I did not know how to articulate my dreams.[30] Never having been exposed to "art," I lived a life of unknown and untapped possibilities. There was always a restless spirit within me that needed expression, but I had no mentors.

When I was eighteen, I saw my future in the clear blue eyes of a poet and two weeks later eloped with Jim Sagel, who supported my excessive spirit. He was my husband, my friend, my mentor, and a gentle genius who encouraged me to become, complicated as it might be, the woman I am today.

When we returned to the Española Valley in the early 1970s, I began studying weaving under the tutelage of renowned master weaver doña Águeda Martínez. I researched all aspects of Rio Grande weaving and its history, including the Mexican and Spanish techniques that contributed to my art.

In the early 1990s, I became environmentally ill and had to curtail my weaving in order to focus on my health. It was during this time that I began seriously to delve into the fascinating world of multimedia and computer graphics. My first attempts were amateurish collage pieces, but with time came the techniques and ability to produce, on paper, the emotions and dreams that reflect my life. As Frida Kahlo once said, "I paint my own reality."

In 1995, I was well enough to return to my loom and began to weave again with renewed enthusiasm and conviction. I decided that I would endeavor to try gently to change the course of Rio Grande weaving by using finer yarns and a closer warp count. Somehow, now that we have left the twentieth century behind, I find myself working in two different mediums: fiber and paper. My loom, which in reality is a medieval computer and requires a much slower, methodical approach, is well suited to the enduring values of my heritage. And the "box"—my computer—allows me the nontoxic exploration of digital art creation, as it hurls me into the twenty-first century.

Elena Baca

The ideas for my images derive from dreams, traditional ideas of storytelling, oral history, and personal occurrences. I am captivated by the moment between reality and memory that generates a powerful narrative.

The computer became a good tool for me as a lazy photographer or a hyper artist. Impatience led me to use the computer to cut, paste, and manipulate quickly, to scan objects and capture images. My technical process developed after trying a variety of photographic printing processes that suited my perceptions of magical realism and narrative. The printing process I use is labor intensive and in some cases toxic. Using the computer has allowed me to wean myself from the darkroom.

Sometimes I look at *Atocha Dream*, and call it my "Gee, I was learning PhotoShop image, and look, I can use a rubber stamp too!" The hardest thing about using a computer and having all those tools is knowing when to stop. I think of the computer and scanner as tools that are a step to achieve the final images.

The FakeLife series is another exploration, influenced by the idea of digital and traditional themes in art. I had been laying out objects on the scanner for a while and making "scan-o-grams." I started purchasing objects found in (seventeenth-century) still-life paintings at craft stores with UPC codes still on them and creating my own contemporary still-lifes. My images are kind of a mush of plastic, inorganic, faux fruit, bugs, and flowers.

Alma López

I grew up in northeast Los Angeles in a community named El Sereno during the Chicano Mural Renaissance of the 1970s and early 1980s. My visual world included wall-sized meticulously spray-painted black, Old English, graffiti lettering, bakery and market calendars of sexy Ixtacihuatl draped over the lap of Popocateptl; tattoos of voluptuous bare-breasted women with long-feathered hair; burgundy lips and raccoon eyes—painted cholas; and murals mostly depicting Emiliano Zapata, Francisco Villa, and Aztec Warriors.

I did not realize the impact of this aesthetic until I graduated from the University of California at Santa Barbara, where I could catch glimpses of students (and me) standing in a studio in front of an easel holding a brush and a palette posed like French painters wearing berets in art history books. When I returned to El Sereno, I knew I would paint murals. To this visual world, my contribution would go beyond the sexualized images of Ixtacihuatl and the tattooed women; to create images of women parallel in presence to Zapata, Villa and Aztec warriors.

So I began to paint and create digital murals. The work I do comes from my heart and is not meant to disrespect or offend. I was born in Mexico, baptized Catholic, and grew up in East L.A. with the Virgen in my home and community.

Marion C. Martínez

Marion C. Martínez was born in Española, New Mexico, and raised in the community of Los Luceros, just north of Española. Throughout her life, she has created art, including pottery and woodcarving. Martínez has always had a fascination with technology. In 1984, she became interested in and began working with computer-generated images. During the time Martínez was experimenting with video camera work and computer images on video, she discovered the computer circuit board. After several years of working with boards, she began creating jewelry, sculpture, and wall hangings utilizing circuit boards and other electronic components.

Since September 1992, Martínez's circuit board art, which she refers to as "mixed tech media" art, has shown in museums, galleries, and invitational shows throughout the United States, Canada, and Mexico. Her work is in many permanent collections including those of San Juan Community College, Northern New Mexico Community College, Fidelity Investments, and the Nokia Corporation. During the 1999 Christmas season, her work hung on the New Mexico tree at the White House.

About her work, Martínez says: "My artwork represents the coming together of the dichotomy of my rural life experiences. I was born into the Hispanic tradition and influenced by the Native American surroundings of my childhood. I was born to a family and community of farmers and ranchers, and yet I was raised in the shadows of one of our nation's foremost high technology research facilities (the Los Alamos National Laboratory). My artwork combines the images and symbols of my culture and of my environment with the components derived from the technology developed in my backyard."

NOTES

An earlier version of this essay was published under a different title in Phillip B. Gonzales, ed., *Expressing New Mexico: Nuevomexicano Creativity and Ritual* (Tucson: University of Arizona Press, 2007), 162–183.

1. The Museum of International Folk Art, the Museum of Fine Art, the Palace of the Governors, and the Museum of Indian Art and Culture, along with state monuments, make up the Museum of New Mexico System, part of the state's Department of Cultural Affairs.
2. Raquel Salinas, a performance artist based in Los Angeles, was the model for *Our Lady*.
3. Raquel Gutiérrez, a cultural activist based in Los Angeles, was the model for the angel.
4. "Parishioners Request Removal of Collage," *Santa Fe New Mexican* (March 17, 2001).
5. Morgan Lee, "Skimpily Attired 'Our Lady' Protested," *Albuquerque Journal North* (March 17, 2001).
6. Deacon Anthony Trujillo quoted in ibid.
7. José L. Villegas Sr., quoted in ibid.
8. Morgan Lee, "Museum Keeps Controversial Work," *Albuquerque Journal North* (March 20, 2001).

9. Ellen Berkovitch, "Recasting Roots," *Pasatiempo* (February 23–March 1, 2001): 16–18.

10. The *Cyber Arte* exhibition featured the following works: *Sor Juana, Frida, y Yo* (1998), *This Woman Is My Mother* (1998), *Apparitions* (1999), *Digital Milagros* (1999), *Birds Take Flight* (1999), *Grace* (1998), and *Crossroads* (2000), by Teresa Archuleta-Sagel; *Atocha Dream* (1996), *Baptism* (2000), *Nature's Bounty* (2001), *Still Life with Walking Pink Bird* (2001), *Country Market—Genetically Modified* (2001), *Spring Bushes* (2001), and *Still Life with Sunflowers and Parrot Head* (2001), by Elena Baca; *Juan Soldado* (1997), *California Fashion Slaves* (1997), *María de los Ángeles* (1997), *La Línea* (1998), *Our Lady* (1999), *Heaven* (1999), *Santa Niña de Mochis* (1999), and *Selena in the Sky with Roses* (2000), by Alma López; *Oratorio a La Virgencita* (2000), *Santo Niño de Atocha* (2001), *Sacred Heart, Sacred Hands* (2000), *Jesús con la Cruz* (2000), *Compassionate Mother* (1999), *Danza de la Matachine III* (1999), *Danza de la Matachine IV* (2000), *Danza de la Matachine V* (2000), and *Danza de la Matachine VI* (2000), by Marion C. Martínez.

11. See Ester Hernández's *La Virgen de Guadalupe Defendiendo los Derechos de los Xicanos* (1976) and her *Paseo Cósmica* or *Cosmic Cruise* (1990); and Yolanda M. López's *Victoria F. Franco: "Our Lady" of Guadalupe* (1978), *Margaret F. Stewart: "Our Lady" of Guadalupe* (1978), *Portrait of the Artist as the Virgin of Guadalupe* (1978), and *Tableau Vivant (Photograph of the Artist as La Virgen de Guadalupe* (1978).

12. See Cisneros's "Guadalupe the Sex Goddess" and other essays by leading authors in *Goddess of the Americas / La Diosa de las Américas: Writings on the Virgin of Guadalupe*, edited by Ana Castillo (New York: Riverhead, 1996).

13. *Puro Teatro: A Latina Anthology*, edited by Alberto Sandoval-Sánchez and Nancy Saporta Sternbach (Tucson: University of Arizona Press, 2000).

14. Along with thousands of examples of Catholic religious art and material culture, the Museum of International Folk Art houses and cares for the Archdiocese of Santa Fe collection. In fact, MOIFA, a state-funded museum, maintained this agreement, free of charge, for a number of years.

15. Full text: "Yes, it is a holy war on our state institution," Villegas said. "They started the fire and we're going to put it out. No one has a right to attack our religion." Cited in Jennifer M. Barol, "'Our Lady' Art Unrobes Icon and Unleashes Parish Protest," *Albuquerque Tribune* (March 22, 2001).

16. Archdiocese of Santa Fe press release, 26 March 2001.

17. Morgan Lee, "Archbishop Says Art Trashes Virgin, Insults Catholics," *Albuquerque Journal* (March 27, 2001).

18. Archbishop Michael Sheehan quoted in Morgan Lee, "'Our Lady' Debate Heats Up Wednesday," *Albuquerque Journal* (April 2, 2001).

19. Anne Constable, "Attorney: Board Can Remove Offensive Artwork," *Santa Fe New Mexican* (April 14, 2001).

20. Conversation with Regent Frank V. Ortiz, March 2001. A similar statement was made by Ortiz in a letter dated March 31, 2001, to Georgia Simms Carson, a MOIFA docent. Cyber Arte Collection, MOIFA.

21. For two informative essays written by journalists covering the controversy, see Kevin Dolan, "Blinded by 'Objectivity': How News Conventions Caused Journalists to Miss the Real Story in the 'Our Lady' Controversy in Santa Fe," *Journalism* 6.3 (2005): 379–396; and Hollis Walker's "Whose Lady? Laying Claim to the Virgin Mary," in *The New Gatekeepers: Emerging Challenges to Free Expression in the Arts* (New York: National Arts Journalism Program/Columbia Graduate School of Journalism, 2004), 42–43.

22. "State Curators Need to Show Sensitivity," editorial, *Albuquerque Journal* (March 21, 2001); www.abqjournal.com.

23. José Villegas, a member of Our Lady of Guadalupe Parish in Santa Fe and one of the main protestors, is quoted as saying this. See Morgan Lee, "Our Lady in Bikini Protested," *Albuquerque Journal* (March 17, 2001).

24. See Morgan Lee, "N.M. Heritage Stirred into 'Lady' Debate," *Albuquerque Journal* (April 16, 2001).

25. Tom Sharpe, "Virgin Controversy Comes to Boil at Rally," *Santa Fe New Mexican* (April 1, 2001).

26. Hollis Walker, "Another Day, Another Inquisition?" *Wall Street Journal* (March 21, 2001).

27. Jennifer M. Barol, "'Our Lady' Protest Has Raised Exhibit's Profile, Officials Say," *Albuquerque Tribune* (March 28, 2001).

28. Personal communication with the artist, August 2004.

29. Personal observation by the author, conference participants, and attendees. University of New Mexico Student Union Building Lobo Rooms A&B, September 10, 2004.

30. "Cyber Arte: Tradition Meets Technology Artist Statements." This was an exhibition handout available for the taking during the duration of the *Cyber Arte* exhibition in the Contemporary Hispanic Changing Gallery. Designed by Anita Quintana (another Nuevomexicana) and published by the Museum of International Folk Art, 2001.

3

The War of the Roses

GUADALUPE, ALMA LÓPEZ, AND SANTA FE

Kathleen Fitzcallaghan Jones

THE CONTROVERSY

ANTA FE IS A PLACE inherently riddled with paradox and op-position: tradition versus the avant-garde in the arts to centuries-old Spanish Catholicism versus the infringement of outsiders and secularism. These forces came to a head in 2001 with Alma Ló-pez's *Our Lady*. In September 2000, the Museum of International Folk Art (MOIFA) in Santa Fe printed 11,000 brochures for upcoming shows and immediately released 750 to the public. The announcement for *Cyber Arte: Tradition Meets Technology* was found in the center with a reproduction of *Our Lady*.

In retrospect, since the explosion of emotion and turmoil in Santa Fe in 2001, it is interesting to recall the initial lack of response to the show on February 25, 2001. In fact, the museum received only six complaints from the public. However, a brochure found its way into the hands of José Villegas, a conservative Catholic and self-proclaimed community activist. On Friday, March 16, 2001, Villegas, with brochure in hand, and Deacon Anthony Trujillo from Our Lady of Guadalupe Church visited the museum with the stated intention of opening a dialogue. The curator of the show, Tey Marianna Nunn, was out of town, so the director of the museum, Joyce Ice, invited and welcomed the men to return the following week. The next day, Saturday, March 17, 2001, the *Albuquerque Journal* published a front-page article about the exhibit and the image of *Our Lady*. The article announced: "Skimpily Attired 'Our Lady' Protested" and proceeded in the first line to describe the "Virgin of Guadalupe in a floral bikini" and "scantily clad Virgin Mary."[1] José Villegas and Deacon Trujillo never returned to the museum to start the dialogue, but maybe they never really needed to, for the forces of indignation had already taken hold in the community, spurred on by the inflammatory words of journalist Morgan Lee. Dr. Nunn explained to me during an interview that as much as she had tried to understand both sides of the conflict, she believed that the leaders of the protest never truly gave the dialogue a chance for they (the opponents of the show) never wanted to listen to the museum's position.[2]

In the days, weeks, and months to come, the protests, conflict, and attempts at reconciliation grew, consuming virtually everyone in the community. But where did it really start? What was the actual moment of conception? Was it the brochure? Could this all have been avoided if the brochure had had another image from the show and not *Our Lady*? Is the media to blame for inciting reaction and a "movement"? The answers to these questions will never be clear, but one thing is certain: the tremendous reaction to such a small, rather innocuous image in the back room of the Museum of International Folk Art (in fact, the only room in the museum to be dedicated to the work of contemporary Hispanic artists) truly indicated that political, racial, and gender tensions in Santa Fe were running high, and something kindled those tensions.

The controversy ultimately was not about *Our Lady*, and community conflict would in time have erupted with or without it. This work, printed in this brochure and falling into the hands of José Villegas and Deacon Trujillo, was the incendiary moment that catalyzed the controversy that divides many segments of an otherwise united Santa Fe and northern New Mexico society.

After looking at the chronology of events, from prayer vigils and protests, to meetings and committee hearings, it is obvious that *Our Lady* became secondary, and primary issues began to emerge. Interestingly, many in the community, whether in town meetings, letters to the editor, or newspaper articles, recognized that the controversy was really about "something else," but it was difficult for people to say exactly what it *was* about. In hindsight, several community conflicts began to unravel, all of which centered on binary control struggles, threats, and fears. The *Our Lady* controversy, like many before it, truly centered on the power struggle between secular and sacred (thinkers and believers), between "insiders" and "outsiders" such as New Mexican Hispanics, Anglo-Americans, and California Chicanas, and between men and women.

Almost immediately after initial reports in local and national newspapers, conflict between church and museum began. After members from the parish of Our Lady of Guadalupe asked for the removal of *Our Lady*, museum director Joyce Ice announced on March 21, 2001 that it would not be taken down. On March 23, delegates from the church officially asked museum officials and Edson Way, the state's cultural affairs officer, to have the piece removed. Archbishop Michael Sheehan then joined the struggle as he asked the museum to remove "the tart," *Our Lady*, on March 26.[3] On March 30, the Association of Art Museum Directors officially supported the museum in its decision to display *Our Lady* in the *Cyber Arte* show.

Further division was demonstrated in a prayer vigil and rally of one hundred *Guadalupanos* (those devoted to Guadalupe) in the museum parking lot on March 31, 2001, and also in the flood of letters to the editor. The oppositional force at the rally was an emotional group, with some members crying, others emotionally hurt, and a few angry. Few had actually been into the museum to see the work but protested *Our Lady* and the museum's decision to include it nonetheless.

On Sunday, April 1, 2001, a letter from the docents of the Museum of International Folk Art supported the museum's decision to exhibit *Our Lady* and other work by Alma López. This position was countered by a letter from many members of the Deanery (of the Catholic Church) of Santa Fe in which they voiced their concerns and worries about the image and their displeasure with the museum. This developed into a problematic struggle for control as the church cultivated its role as art and cultural authority in its demands on the museum: "Art museums are at the service of the community. New Mexico's citizen community has one-third of its members calling themselves Roman Catholic. To have our taxes support what is in effect an attack on our religion is distasteful, to say the least. We are consequently respectfully asking that the Board of Regents seriously consider the removal of said artwork and in the future enter into dialogue with various faith leaders before such examples of religious art be admitted to display for our citizens."[4] The letter went on to explain: "It is culturally insensitive," and "to say that the artist is one of 'their' own is no excuse for this attack on Hispanic identity. Some Hispanics are not in touch with their cultural history and its religious underpinnings."[5] Though this point was coming from a group that might base its arguments on the grounds of blasphemy, it was clear that questions of cultural and ethnic identity were intimately involved. The accusation that Alma López was not in touch with her "'cultural history and its religious underpinnings'" was not evident. The authors, both Hispanic and Anglo, did not recognize that Alma López *was* in touch with her Mexican and Chicana heritage.

However, the insinuations go much deeper, as the letter referenced a profound division between the people of northern New Mexico and "others." Though López would not deny she was Hispanic, she called herself Chicana or Mexican American. The letter does not use these terms.

As quickly as the church became involved in the controversy, local lawmakers jumped in with attacks and demands on the museum. This no doubt was only another element of the power struggle in the city of Santa Fe but a very important one in that it reflected Hispanic authority. Exhibit curator Tey Marianna Nunn explained: "The legislature is one of the last strongholds of Hispanic power. It historically has been from the 1800s through the territorial period and statehood."[6]

The obvious struggle was between the power and role of the legislature and that of the museum, its curatorial staff, boards, and committees. The ramifications of the entrance of the legislators into the conflict would have long-lasting effects on the autonomy of the museum system of New Mexico, which will be explored later.

On March 27, 2001, nine Santa Fe–area legislators, all Hispanic and Democrats, wrote a reprimanding and demanding letter to Wood "Mike" Arnold II, the president of the Board of Regents of the Museum of New Mexico System. After pointing out the "outrageous desecration" and "flagrant disrespect" of the museum, the authors of the letter reminded the museum that they (the legislators) were "trying to fund" the programs of the museums but this was difficult when the museum did not act responsibly toward its public.[7] Mark Hummels, in the *Santa Fe New Mexican*, pointed out that this resembled a slight threat to the museum's economic future.[8] It also brought into question who or what entity was in control of the museum's curatorial decisions.

In its best efforts to invite dialogue in the community, the Museum of New Mexico Board of Regents opened its meeting to the public on Wednesday, April 4, 2001. In the end, however, the whole venture was a disaster because of a lack of space, a large turnout, and high emotion. The Museum of Indian Arts and Culture (MIAC) holds 350 people and was presumably a large enough space. However, the venue reached its capacity and people were turned away. Rumors spread in the crowd outside that many Anglos were admitted and Hispanics were kept out.[9] The *Albuquerque Journal* and the *Santa Fe New Mexican* reported that at least 600 people showed up to voice their opinions on the hottest topic in town. The available space thus left 300 people out of the discussion. John McCarthy, then head of security for the Museum of New Mexico, adamantly denied these figures and blamed the press for gross exaggeration. He explained that the media ignored the 350 attendees inside and focused its attention on the protestors who were not allowed to enter for security and safety reasons, numbering 20 in all.[10] Apparently, those outside, whether 20 or 300, certainly made a lot of noise, praying, chanting, and demanding entrance. Finally, as tensions mounted, the meeting was postponed until April 16 and moved to the Sweeney Convention Center, a larger facility.

Alma López described the audience at that first meeting to be about half supporters and half protestors. The supporters were mostly Latinas, artists, writers, professors, and young women. In contrast, the protestors were primarily men, priests, and middle-aged women who were brought to the meeting on buses from local churches. José Villegas, a priest, and three other men dominated the conversation. She explained that the meeting was interrupted just as Tey Marianna Nunn was about to speak. Alma López and Tey Marianna Nunn had to be escorted from the meeting by police to protect their safety.

Interestingly, Alma López and José Villegas had had a meeting earlier in the day. She explained that it was cordial. Villegas told her that he just wanted to be heard, and she pointed out that they had that in common.[11]

José Villegas's interpretation of the meeting between the two is curious, as is much of what he says. He explained that he accepted her as a "sister" and the meeting "was an embracement." Villegas welcomed her to his "neighborhood," a sign of acceptance, but said that they needed to sit down to talk. He said Alma agreed and overall felt the whole experience was positive and spiritual. But then museum officials took her away and the conversation was over.[12]

Throughout the entire controversy, however, José Villegas expressed hostility toward the museum, with its "PhDers," and Alma López, who came into his "neighborhood" without asking permission. When you do that, he explained, "you get the wrath of the community." He admitted that this attitude was territorial, but "the Catholic faith has been here before the sixteenth century [*sic*] and people ought to just leave it alone."[13] Over the months, Villegas sounded very much like this, hostile and emotional in his actions, words, and writings. He was at the center of every protest, legal action, and meeting, all the while decrying the pain and suffering placed on his people, his neighborhood, and even his mother by the desecration of La Virgen de Guadalupe in the *Our Lady* interpretation.

While his position generally lacked credibility because of its often-contradictory nature, Villegas accurately addressed the issues that underlay the controversy. He was giving voice to real concerns and worries in the community. Specifically, Villegas was referencing the conflict of power between the "Anglo" museum and the "'Hispanic" community, between government and church, between insiders and outsiders, despite his obsession with the image of bare legs and exposed stomach.

The next major interaction between the museum and the church before the large town hall meeting on April 16 was a letter written by Thomas H. Wilson, the director of the Museum of New Mexico, to His Excellency Michael J. Sheehan dated April 11, 2001. In the communication, Dr. Wilson extended his apologies for the pain caused in the Catholic community and extended an offer for dialogue on cross-cultural issues. Later, the two did meet to talk, and Archbishop Sheehan reiterated his position that such an offensive work had no place in a state-funded museum.[14] Tey Marianna Nunn felt that this letter was a mistake for it undermined her position and authority as a curator with decision-making abilities. It made her look as if she had done something wrong, which she maintained she had not.[15]

The postponed town hall meeting/debate was finally called to order on Monday, April 16. The media had been preparing for weeks, and the city was bracing itself for a large turnout with extra police on site, child care, sack lunches, and free parking. The meeting at the downtown Sweeney Convention Center was set up so that people could address the audience in three-minute time slots, write comments on a board, or participate in roundtable discussions. The majority of the 600–1,000 people came to protest the work rather than support it. Comments covered an emotional spectrum ranging from exclamations of mothers waking crying at night to pleas for Hispanic and Catholic cultural respect. Many encouraged Alma to learn her faith and to recognize what a "real" woman looked like.[16] Overall, the meeting was successful as a democratic event. The community was allowed to voice its opinions, but nothing was truly solved. *Our Lady* stayed put on the wall in the Museum of International Folk Art, and the protestors continued to protest it. The debate was an attempt at democratic process, but ultimately the final decision was made by higher powers and not by "the people."

POLITICS AND POLICY

Politics and policy concerns emerged within the museum system. The question of authority and jurisdiction over the controversial work came to the forefront of the discussion. Who could make the ultimate decision on whether or not to keep *Our Lady*? Would it be the Board of Regents, state government, the Office of Cultural Affairs, the director of the museum, or possibly the already existing Committee on Sensitive Materials? John Grubesic, an attorney with the State Attorney General's Office, was of the opinion that the Board of Regents had the authority to order the museum to remove the work based on the museum's collections policy.[17] Regent's president Arnold agreed with this position, despite disagreement by cultural affairs officer Edson Way, who explained that the regents had no authority over museum exhibits.[18]

At this point, discussion about using the Committee on Sensitive Materials began. It was decided that this committee would listen, gather information, and make a recommendation on the status of *Our Lady* in the museum. With this information in hand, director Tom Wilson would extend his recommendation to the Board of Regents. Lastly, the Board of Regents would make a decision on whether to remove the image. These activities became an impetus for further controversy surrounding the political authority and power of various factions and people in the museum system.

There was division on whether or not it was the role of the Committee on Sensitive Materials to make a decision about *Our Lady* at all. There was conflict within the Board of Regents. For example, Ambassador Frank Ortiz strongly pushed for the committee's involvement, and Paul Rainbird asserted that the committee had no jurisdiction over works like Alma López's *Our Lady*, for the committee had been created to deal with repatriation of Native American objects.

Ambassador Ortiz was in favor of removing the image due to the great conflict it had created in the community and the harm being done to the reputation of the museum system. He in fact contended that he had warned the Board of Regents and the museum when the brochures were released, in

September of 2000, that the image would be offensive to the community of Santa Fe.[19] Paul Rainbird, on the other hand, strongly supported Alma López and *Our Lady*. Even members of the committee, such as Robin Gavin of the Museum of International Folk Art, believed that they should not be involved in the decision.

The Alma López controversy was so complicated, as seen in the mediation of these positions, because the power struggle and "sides" were not clear-cut or consistent. In this complex situation, power became a responsibility that many wanted but also one that many others would rather not have had. In fact, it became even more complicated as the controversy grew, for there were no two clear sides to the debate. José Villegas and his contingency were clearly on one far-reaching end of the spectrum, and Alma López and her supporters, like Paul Rainbird and Tey Marianna Nunn, were on the other. However, there was a faction of diplomats like Ambassador Ortiz in the middle.

Ortiz's interests, at first glance, lay in pacifying the community's conflict and saving the reputation and funding capacity of the museum system by removing the image. He was the spokesman for the *people* of Santa Fe in the political and decision-making arena. (However, there was no collaboration between the two.) The ambassador explained that even though the image did not upset him, it upset so many in the community that it was the responsibility of the Board of Regents and the Committee on Sensitive Materials to review and ultimately remove *Our Lady*. Further, in his opinion, Tey Marianna Nunn had made serious curatorial misjudgments in choosing the piece and misreading the community. However, he too may have been misreading the community, which over the last hundred years had ethnically and religiously changed considerably with the migration of eastern and western Americans and Mexicans. Ambassador Ortiz explained that the jurisdiction of the board over the museum's exhibit was very clearly laid out in the Museum of New Mexico's collections policy, which was approved by the Board of Regents on May 20, 1999.[20] Therefore, the board could override curatorial decisions or, as he posited, curatorial mistakes.

The root of the disagreement surrounding the committee was found in the question of its role. The committee was originally created to deal with issues of repatriation of ceremonial and burial objects to Native American tribes. When tribes approached the museum with requests to return such objects, the committee convened to decide whether or not the "sensitive material" should be returned. However, throughout the *Our Lady* controversy, the term *sensitive* in the committee name was misinterpreted to apply to works that upset the *sensitivities* of a group of people versus the bona fide right to repatriation due to native religious or cultural mandates.

The collections policy is very clear in its explanation of the committee's role in responding "to the ethical concerns surrounding culturally sensitive materials" in the Museum of New Mexico's collections, displays, and exhibits and the appropriate action of repatriation of the said materials.[21] The policy defines the following objects but does not limit itself to these as "culturally-sensitive materials": "objects whose treatment or use is a matter of profound concern to living peoples." Culturally sensitive materials include human remains from a death rite or ceremony, associated funerary objects, unassociated funerary objects, sacred objects, objects of cultural patrimony, and culturally sensitive documents. An authorized representative of an Indian tribe or another community that has cultural, familial, or geographic ties may request the repatriation of culturally sensitive materials.[22] Frank Ortiz felt that the committee was perfect for resolving the *Our Lady* conflict despite how the committee's duties and sensitive materials had been defined:

> When the museum finally looked at the policy it was supposed to be following, which was very late in the game—too late—they said: "Oh, this only refers to Indian graves." So that is, in my judgment, a total cover-up, because if you read the collections policy it says of "a living community." Sensitive material is not limited to Indian graves. The original instructions had to do with Indian graves, but this was modified very substantially. And as I say, it is statutorily mandated so you have to follow the letter of the law.[23]

Ambassador Ortiz, in an attempt to defend his position, likened the display of *Our Lady* to dressing a Zuni kachina doll in a flowered bathing suit.[24] While he was correct in asserting that this would be problematic, it still was not an accurate correlation with the sensitive ceremonial and sacred objects with which the committee was concerned. In a memorandum to the Committee on Sensitive Materials dated April 19, 2001, Ambassador Ortiz more aggressively likened the offenses of the exhibited piece to the impact of the words "savages," "niggers," and "faggots," and the like in the greater community.[25] This information was not made public until later.

On April 20, 2001, the Committee on Sensitive Materials started a long series of meetings (that would take a month to complete) to decide the fate of *Our Lady*. The meetings were closed to the public, which upset many in the community, but this was legal according to Director Tom Wilson and the Attorney General's Office.[26] On May 22, the committee announced its recommendation to not remove *Our Lady* but to take it down on October 28, 2001—"four months early."[27]

This compromise, of course, pleased few. For critics of *Our Lady*, such as José Villegas and other Catholics, this was not soon enough, and for López and museum supporters, it was an affront to the right of freedom of speech. The dramatic rhetoric of José Villegas came as no surprise when he learned of the committee's decision. They were "biased and disrespectful to the cultures of Northern New Mexico. They violated the principles of respect in my *barrio*." He promised to "hit them where it will hurt" by filing an appeal with Tom Wilson and the state district court to remove *Our Lady* in the name of public safety. Villegas explained that he was getting death threats from "their freedom-of-speech people, whoever they are. I think this is going to promote more hate crime in our community."[28]

Naturally, Ambassador Frank Ortiz was not pleased with the findings of the committee, nor was the committee pleased with Frank Ortiz's earlier comments. On May 15, 2001, the committee wrote a letter to the ambassador outlining its decision-making process. Committee members, based on the collections policy (the policy that Ortiz and all members of the Board of Regents had approved exactly two years earlier), denied, point by point, their jurisdiction over the decision. Their authority in the matter of *Our Lady* was most obviously explained by clarifying that they, as the Committee on Sensitive Materials, did not find *Our Lady* to be a sensitive material as defined by the policy. They explained that the committee distinguished "devotional art and material culture from art and material culture that is non-devotional or secular in nature." For example, Juan Diego's *tilma* (long apron) would be a devotional object and it must remain in its religious context in the Basílica de Guadalupe in Mexico City, but Alma López's *Our Lady* would be a secular object, a work of art inspired by the *tilma*. It was not, and never was intended to be, used in a devotional ceremony or religious context.[29]

The letter continued by expressing the committee's understanding of the rights of the community to object to the *Cyber Arte* exhibit, and it defended the role of the museum to "explore the rich art and culture of the greater Hispanic Community." In the letter, Ambassador Ortiz's metaphor of racial epithets to describe the museum's decision to exhibit the work was denounced as "inappropriate, inaccurate and dangerous hyperbole."[30] These exchanges, however confrontational and surprising, crystallized the great division in the community between Hispanics as traditional insiders and Anglos as invasive outsiders.

INSIDER/OUTSIDER

Amidst the hurrah and fighting at the political and decision-making levels, the tensions at the community level remained. Though these tensions were fought out in the legislature and between the museum and the church, it must be recognized that these conflicts were also taking place in the streets. If nothing else, this controversy was instrumental in opening the channels of communication in the community. Controversies such as these are what art historian Erika Doss explores as essential to democratic debate and "how democratic expression is shaped in contemporary America."[31]

Ironically, much of the democratic dialogue took place through the modems and digital highways of the Internet. The number of letters, reactions, responses, supportive messages, and protests found on websites and in online journals is virtually uncountable. The irony lies in the fact that one of Tey Marianna Nunn's intentions for *Cyber Arte* was to demonstrate the wealth of the Latino presence on the Internet.[32] As Hispanics in northern New Mexico and Latinos around the country protested *Cyber Arte* on the Internet, they were simply validating Nunn's exhibit.

Civic involvement was also obvious in the tremendous amount of letter writing and number of protests and voices in the real-world community of Santa Fe. On the side of the opposition, a common complaint was the lack of understanding, appreciation, and recognition by the predominantly Anglo museum. Naturally, the museum countered this position by citing its exhibition history and staff. The very show that caused the uproar was in fact created by a Hispanic curator of contemporary Hispano and Latino collections with a PhD in art history, had three other Hispanic artists from New Mexico, and was intended to celebrate contemporary Hispanic arts within the history of Hispanic tradition and culture.

The feelings of resentment and views of ethnic inequality were no doubt just below the surface throughout the spring of 2001, where they had been festering since the Anglo-Americans' entrance into the territory of New Mexico in the 1800s and the conception of the museum system in the early 1900s.

As controversy developed a hundred years after the creation of the museum system, public voices began to emerge that echoed those of the "pure blood" Spaniards a century before. One voice was once again that of Ambassador Frank Ortiz in letters and announcements claiming that MOIFA's staff and docents dramatically underrepresented the Hispanic community. He feared that this fostered a lack of understanding of the particular culture of Santa Fe on the part of the museum.[33] He questioned the docents' names, race, religion, and connection to New Mexico. Ortiz explained that of the letters he received from docents in support of the museum, the majority of the writers were newcomers to New Mexico, knew little about New Mexico history, were not Hispanic, and did not have religious human images in their places of worship. From this evidence he then questioned: "If this interpretation of the majority of the Folk Art docent corps is half accurate, is there any wonder that they cannot fully understand our community?"[34] Once again, Ortiz was ignoring the complexity and ethnic richness of the community of Santa Fe. Santa Fe is not, and never has been, only "our community" of Spanish Americans.

Though his observation concerning the lack of Hispanic docents may have been true, there were, from the point of view of the museum, several reasons for this. First, there are people in New Mexico without Hispanic names who are in fact Hispanic. For example, Joan Fleetwood, the volunteer coordinator for the Museum of New Mexico System, explained in a letter to Ambassador Ortiz dated April 12, 2001: "I personally was born in Santa Fe, my grandfather is Roybal and my grandmother is Gonzales, yet my married name gives no indication of my heritage."[35] Second, Fleetwood noted that despite her greatest efforts to recruit bilingual and Hispanic volunteers, cultural forces generally did not allow for much response from the Hispanic community. It appears that she had a greater understanding of the community than did Ambassador Ortiz. She explained that, generally speaking, Hispanic candidates were more reticent about public speaking and were more involved with their families as primary caretakers for children and grandchildren, and hence had less time for volunteering.[36]

Docents were infuriated by the accusations that they were inadequate at their jobs in the museum system. Many of the docents were highly educated in the region, history, art, and culture of New Mexico and the Southwest. Before working at MOIFA, volunteers must take a six-month intensive training course, which focuses on history and art of the state of New Mexico. Dr.

Dorothy Parker, the chair of the Docent Council at the time of the contro-versy, had a doctorate in the history of New Mexico and was a professor at Eastern New Mexico University. Georgia Carson, who could have been seen as a newcomer with her arrival in Santa Fe nine years earlier, had familial ties to New Mexico, as her husband's great-grandfather was territorial governor of the state.[37]

The credentials of the docents were simply not enough to pacify the al-ready agitated Hispanic community in Santa Fe. This was obvious through-out the summer as conflict continued in an "us" versus "them" battle within and between the city and the museum. One complaint came from an angry Gloria Mendoza, who expressed her frustration with the perceived inequality of Hispanic representation in the museum system. In an outspoken letter in July she reiterated Ambassador Ortiz's position that the Museum of Inter-national Folk Art had double standards and was insensitive to the Spanish culture. Mendoza felt that the city must demand that the legislators "cre-ate drastically more sensitive and inclusive policies and have definitely more Spanish representation in our museums."[38]

Mendoza conveyed the position that for centuries the Spanish people had been very tolerant of their mistreatment, misrepresentation, and disrespect and that they would no longer be silent. The museum and *Cyber Arte* threat-ened "the very foundation of our dignified and impenetrable culture."[39] She pointed out that the Spanish, despite their long history in New Mexico, were still struggling for respect, and exhibits such as this did little to help.

Paul Rainbird, a Tewa Indian and member of the Board of Regents, had pointed out months before, at the April 4 meeting at the museum, that time in a certain place did not grant authority. "You can't claim the subject matter and the sensitivity *just because you were here longer* (original emphasis). That doesn't make it right or wrong, it's not based on that." He pointed this out to the inflamed "Spanish" representatives at the meeting and explained that their claims of hundreds of years of presence in New Mexico were inconse-quential to the thousands of years [sic] his people had been in the region.[40]

Mendoza questioned how people who had never lived in a culture could make decisions and policies about that culture. She was not very specific about what people and what culture she was addressing, but presumably she was referencing the Anglo community and the Spanish culture.

Though many in the community shared Mendoza's position and opinions, it appears that they were often ill informed. This is made evident by looking at the museum, its curators, shows, and the artists themselves. First, Mendoza's accusation that the museum was insensitive to the Spanish culture was simply incorrect. This is made clear when one enters the Museum of International Folk Art and the Hispanic Heritage Wing or reads the newspaper. For example, an article in the *Santa Fe New Mexican* on May 23, 2001 had a list of folk art exhibits over the years. The list of exhibits of Spanish colonial and contemporary Hispanic art began in 1959 with *Guatemalan Textiles* and *Popular Art of Colonial New Mexico*. The list continued with sixty-three shows, which included such subjects as *Comparative Santos* (1962), *Días de Más, Días de Menos* (1976–1978), *Hispanic Art in the United States* (1988), *New Mexican Madonnas* (1999), and *Cyber Arte: Where Tradition Meets Technology* (2001).[41]

Many point out that those central to the *Cyber Arte* exhibit—the artists and the curator—were Hispanic. How could two Hispanic women who were deeply rooted in their cultural and ethnic histories misrepresent themselves? If the history of La Virgen de Guadalupe has demonstrated anything, it is that self-representation is a deeply personal and subjective exercise. That history also indicates that *anyone* may appropriate this image for self-representation, and it is, in fact, part of an evolving tradition. This is precisely what Tey Marianna Nunn was conveying in her exhibit: the perpetuation, evolution, and transcendence of Hispanic/Latina tradition and culture.

GENDER

The show *Cyber Arte*, as Dr. Nunn explained it, was meant to portray the balance between or negotiation of traditional and contemporary identities of Hispana women.[42] It was a display of how these artists "translate and recast their deeply-rooted cultural beliefs, images and history by utilizing computers to create a new type of visual art."[43] The show was set deep within a traditional context yet expanded out into the contemporary world. Unfortunately, people became caught up in one particular image in the show and ignored both the intention of the show and the other artists.

Indirectly, however, there was reaction to the overall intentions of *Cyber Arte* as seen in the specific reaction to *Our Lady*. Though the controversy, as already explored, greatly focused on racial tensions and dichotomies like newcomers versus century-old families in New Mexico, gender tensions also emerged. The show was about Hispanic art, but it was more specifically about *women* and what they were doing within the traditional culture of northern

New Mexico. Hispanic/Chicana artists pushing the limits of "tradition" no doubt were a catalyst for controversy in a traditionally patriarchal culture.

All four of the women in the show appropriated the image of La Virgen de Guadalupe and other Mexican icons such as Frida Kahlo and Sor Juana Inés de la Cruz in their exploration of art and identity. However, Alma López was the only one to disrobe La Virgen, and hence was the target of the wrath of the community. Marion C. Martínez of Glorieta, New Mexico (just northeast of Santa Fe), is famous for her Virgenes made of computer wiring and hard drives. Martínez describes one work, *Guadalupana Aztechna*, as "a total mother board," humorously personifying a distinct computer part. She explains that her technological-compilation works are in fact very similar to traditional folk art in that she works with found objects.[44] Elena Baca, of Santa Fe, creates still-life collage images on her computer and scanner. Teresa Archuleta-Sagel, formerly a traditional master weaver, now uses the computer to make digital tapestries. Three of the four artists were native New Mexicans, and whether they called themselves Hispanic or Chicana or Spanish, their ultimate connection was their gender, their adherence to tradition, and their reimaging of appropriated icons like Guadalupe.

Another group to appropriate La Virgen de Guadalupe was the national group America Needs Fatima, which led a rally on June 30, 2001 in the parking lot of the museum. As appeals and protests continued to be battled in the courts and before the public of Santa Fe, the male-dominated Christian front asserted itself against the image of a female body exhibited in the museum. The campaign, part of the American Society for the Defense of Tradition, Family and Property—based in Hanover, Pennsylvania—had hundreds of people attend the rally from all over the country. As this had now become a national movement against *Our Lady*, Alma López, and the museum, the organization bused in protestors and prayers from Albuquerque and other parts of the state. The overarching organization was founded in Brazil in the 1960s to warn the public of the consequences of society's sins and the need for penance and conversion.[45]

The great sin found in Santa Fe was the "blasphemous" visual representation of La Virgen de Guadalupe by Alma López. Though this group was not from Santa Fe, or even New Mexico, or Mexico, or the Southwest, members were confident they had authority over the body of a female icon as being significant to a person's cultural, spiritual, and self-identity—as it was for Alma López. Try as they might, they had no authority over Alma López.

Despite the inherent ironies of the organization's presence in Santa Fe, it did however mirror deeply held sentiments and customs found in the patriarchal Catholic and cultural traditions of northern New Mexico. This group, like many locals, felt threatened by the assertion of power by a female artist using the female form and by the fact that a public institution supported this assertion of power. The Catholic Church, a pillar of authority in New Mexico, is historically patriarchal in its power structure, tenets, and belief system, and therefore in its visual representations and iconography. These deep-seated traditions translate into contemporary fears of female assertion as manifested in the visual arts and the appropriation of Catholic icons for feminine affirmation and validation.

This is particularly true in this time of difficulties facing the Catholic Church. The controversy surrounding Alma López's *Our Lady* came at a time when the church was attempting to retain power. Pedophilia scandals from Boston to Santa Fe had created for the Catholic Church not only great financial difficulties but also tremendous blows to its authority and respectability. Concurrently, the Catholic stronghold of power was weakened by the decreasing number of priests, from 1,000 yearly vocations in the 1960s to 600 in the 1990s. In the 1990s, 300 women became nuns while 2,000 retired, resigned, or died.[46]

Similarly, there had been a great division between the *people* and the church since Vatican II in the early 1960s, despite the Council's attempts to create a stronger connection between the church and its public. Church attendance had dropped, and there had been public demand for a lay voice in running parishes and greater dialogue about issues of clergy conduct and responsibility.[47] Also, there had been questions about the role of women in the Catholic Church and its culture. There was interest in a more prominent place for women in the church, and even more interest in questioning the church's power over women since Pope Paul VI's 1968 ban on artificial birth control. In a sense, the church's unbudging position in these situations has contributed to its dwindling power.

Despite the church's problems regarding sex scandals, the greatest attacks made by Catholics against *Our Lady* concerned the female body. The so-called blasphemy was blamed on La Virgen's exposed body, but this claim suggested a thinly veiled fear of the reality of feminine corporeality, power, and voice. In cries to remove *Our Lady* from the museum, men were denying a woman's fundamental right to assert her voice. By doing this, they were not only attacking the image of *Our Lady* but that of every woman in their community. Archbishop Sheehan's description of *Our Lady* as "a tart" and the now-ubiquitous Catholic claims that *Our Lady* and the bare-breasted angel were "offensive" beg the question, "Why or how are they offensive?" There was apparently something offensive about the female body, a most regrettable perception, especially as male bodies, *in churches*, are not perceived as such. Alma López is quite clear when she says: "Their faith and masculinity is threatened by my portrayal of the Virgen as a contemporary Latina."[48]

López explains her opinion of the female body, one, unfortunately, which the Catholic men (and women!) in northern New Mexico do not share:

> Even if I look really hard at "Our Lady" and the works of many Chicana artists, I don't see what is so offensive. I see beautiful bodies: gifts from our creator. Maybe because my mother breastfed me as a baby, I see breasts as nurturing. Maybe because I love women, I see beauty and strength. I also see the true representation of Mary. Mary was an awesome woman and mother with a difficult task. She had a child that was not her husband's, she kept her son safe from a murderous king, she suffered her son's struggles and death, and most of all she raised her son to have love and compassion for everyone, including female prostitutes. I think Mary was a lot like some of our mothers.[49]

Paul Rainbird, a retired member of the Board of Regents, was one of Alma López's and Tey Marianna Nunn's staunchest supporters. He saw the controversy as nothing other than a gender issue, founded in a religious structure's inherently sexist position. Paul Rainbird is a Tewa Indian from San Ildefonso Pueblo and grew up within the dualism of the Tewa belief system and Catholicism. At the age of sixteen or seventeen, Rainbird broke from his Catholic upbringing despite his grandmother's complete acceptance of both the Tewa worldview and Catholicism. He saw this double acceptance as a direct contradiction in beliefs and a ploy of the Catholic Church to manipulate and control his people.

Despite his opposition to the belief system of Catholicism, Rainbird recognized the cultural and historical significance of Catholicism to his pueblo. Today, community activity, council positions, and pride focus on the church that the pueblo built after killing the priests and destroying the church during the Pueblo Revolt in 1680. Many community members who are involved in the caretaking and upkeep of the San Ildefonso church are equally and intimately involved with the kiva society of the pueblo.

All of the interconnectedness in the pueblo and his education informed Paul Rainbird's sympathy with and understanding of Alma López's attempts to express the syncretism of her Aztec and Catholic roots. He also personally understood the church's history of oppression and therefore appreciated López's struggle and artistic critique of these forces.[50] The fundamental issue, as Paul Rainbird saw it, was that all religions are constructs that have been created by men in order to control women, power, and society. In Catholicism's defense, all religious structures are guilty of this, even in the Tewa world, Rainbird explained. When religions have this power, it is inculcated in the traditions of the greater community. This is even seen in the Tewa pueblos. For example, in familial disputes, men are generally favored in the council's decisions concerning property and ownership.[51]

Rainbird's views are validated by the Alma López controversy. The movement against López was fundamentally a male-dominated one, orchestrated by priests, senators, fathers, and grandfathers. Even when women were against the image or Alma López, it was because they were part of, or accepted, the male-constructed hierarchy or they served as a mouthpiece for their male counterparts. Rainbird felt that it was these men who were scripting the letters written and the speeches made by women, for it was the men who were truly outraged.[52]

According to Rainbird (and Alma López and her other supporters), the issue was simple. She was an artist, expressing herself in her art. It was not complicated, but obviously threatening, that she was a woman doing this within a community that had a certain vision of women and their expected role in that community.

The community's characteristic male dominance is apparent in civic and religious rituals such as Las Fiestas de Santa Fe. The core reality of Las Fiestas is symbolic of a patriarchal societal structure that is threatened by women and any authoritative images of women. The celebrations and rituals of Las Fiestas truly represent the sentiments and positions that have been mandated in the city by centuries of proud tradition. It is worth reiterating that Las Fiestas are deeply rooted in a strong Spanish cultural identity from the days of *los conquistadores* and the reconquest of the region of New Mexico in the 1600s. The prevailing female images and icons to emerge in this time were the

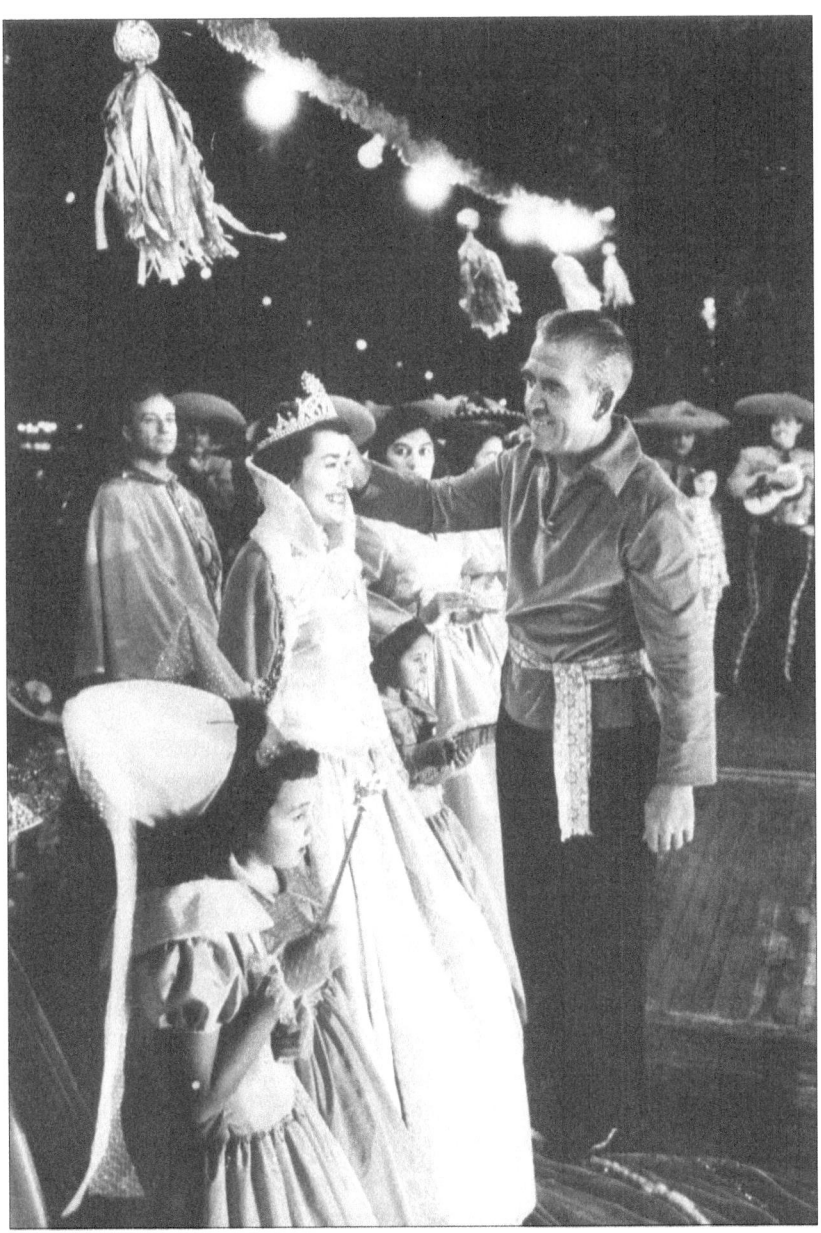

3.1.   *The Queen Being Crowned at the Santa Fe Fiesta.* Photograph by A. Y. Owen. Time Life Pictures/Getty Images, © 1957. Courtesy of Time Life Pictures/Getty Images.

unflattering La Malinche and the pure and heavenly La Virgen as represented in the cults of La Virgen de Guadalupe and La Conquistadora. Santa Fe's Fiestas, to this day, perpetuate the feminine ideals of virginity, beauty, and submissiveness.

Las Fiestas is a popular celebration deeply rooted in the blended Catholic faith and Spanish cultural heritage. A reenactment of the historical events of Don Diego de Vargas's "peaceful" entrance into the region is made up of locals playing the roles of Don Diego, his captains and lieutenants, Franciscans, Indian governors, musicians (including a black drummer), and soldiers. In the reenactment, the characters are symbolic of an ethno-civic, religious organization.[53] To portray Don Diego a man must be of Spanish descent, at least twenty-one years old, a resident of Santa Fe County for at least a year, and bilingual. Also important are appearance, poise, and personality. The general trend in Don Diego portrayers as represented in Las Fiestas is that he is married, a member of the city's civic and business community, and therefore perceived not as an adolescent but as a man.[54]

The distinctions and qualifications for the Fiesta queen, on the other hand, are in turn demanding and specific. She must be "of good character," have a Spanish surname, be between the ages of nineteen and twenty-four, unmarried before and during Las Fiestas, born in Santa Fe County, a resident of the country for the last five years, bilingual, and able to present birth or baptismal certificates. She must also be capable of meeting the public with "responsibility, dignity, and poise." There are additional social responsibilities and restrictions placed on the queen and her court that are not found in the men's contracts. She has to attend all functions and rehearsals and cannot consume alcoholic beverages in either public or private during her reign.[55] The double standard is obvious.

It is unclear whom the queen is literally representing in the history of the conquest. It appears that she symbolically represents La Conquistadora, a virgin, and is simultaneously a construct of the ideal woman in the eyes of the male public, a construct that Chicana feminists have been resisting for decades. The Fiesta queen is young and innocent like an unmarried virgin. Although ostensibly a virgin, the Fiesta queen is regally heterosexualized with ornately made up hair, face, clothes, and accessories. She stands to the side of the older, authoritative, and paternal Don Diego.

The Fiesta queen, with her court of princesses, is a far cry from López's *Our Lady*. If the queen is somehow symbolic of the idealized woman, it is no wonder *Our Lady* and Alma López were a threat to the greater male population of the city and its traditional Catholic fundamentalism. *Our Lady* is not a depiction of a sweet, submissive mother or a virginal princess. She is an assertive force in the face of a threatened population that is slowly losing civic and religious power.

CONCLUSION

Legal attempts were made to preserve the intangible male stronghold on tradition and culture in the New Mexico State Legislature. This not only greatly impinges on the fundamentals of free speech and freedom of expression by female artists like Alma López but also on the future sovereignty of the museum system. During the winter 2002 legislative session, over a dozen legislators, including Rep. Luciano "Lucky" Verela (Democrat-Santa Fe), presented a House Joint Memorial. The Memorial opened with a request that the New Mexico Legislative Council designate an interim committee to study the Office of Cultural Affairs and entities under its jurisdiction (i.e., the Museum of New Mexico.) The Memorial was in response to complaints about MOIFA's handling of opposition to the *Cyber Arte* exhibit.[56] The Memorial called for clarifying the roles of the Board of Regents and hired museum curators. The council was also to reevaluate "the role and composition of the sensitivities committee . . . to reflect societal sensitivities in this technological era."[57]

In the eyes of the museum, artists, and curators, the Memorial was dangerously overbearing. Although a Memorial is only an expression of an opinion and not binding, this one reflected the position of the mostly male, Hispanic legislators of northern New Mexico, who were perpetually antagonistic toward the museum, *Cyber Arte*, its curator, Tey Marianna Nunn, and Alma López. It was a similar, though not as violent, reaction to López's *Las Four* by an equally antagonistic group of male "judges" a few years earlier. First installed in the Community Center of the Estrada Courts housing project in Boyle Heights in Los Angeles in 1997, *Las Four* focused on the young women of the neighborhood, sitting on their front steps, lost in their dreams. Floating above them were powerful images of Dolores Huerta, cofounder of the United Farm Workers; Sor Juana Inés de la Cruz, seventeenth-century Mexican poet; Adelita, the female soldier symbolic of the many unrecognized women who fought with Zapata and Villa in the Mexican Revolution of the early 1900s; and Rigoberta Menchú, the Guatemalan civil rights fighter who won the Nobel Peace Prize in 1992. The Aztec moon goddess Coyolxauhqui and the four female leaders have protected the young women throughout their difficult and violent lives.

The image was attacked by young men from the projects, who pulled down the vinyl mural and slashed it because they did not like the choice of girls in the image. They felt López and her collaborators should have chosen "better girls."[58]

In both cases, *Our Lady* and *Las Four*, men were threatened by what they perceived the works to be saying about their (the men's) position in the communities. In both the Estrada Courts and the New Mexico State Legislature there was a negative reaction, for the men did not have control over the artist, the works, the women depicted in the work, or the decision making surrounding the works.

In reflecting on this debate and controversy in the city of Santa Fe, it is apparent that this was not the first time that such conflict had arisen, nor will it be the last. These conflicts are everywhere, from the Brooklyn Museum of Art to the Jewish Museum's controversial show in March 2002, *Mirroring Evil: Nazi Imagery/Recent Art* in New York. The most similar case to precede *Our Lady* is Renée Cox's *Yo Mama's Last Supper* (2001) in the Brooklyn Museum of Art's exhibit *Committed to the Image: Contemporary Black Photographers*. *Yo Mama* is a photograph of a naked Cox as Jesus Christ at the Last Supper. Her symbolic representation of the female body is similar in style to that of Alma López's. Reaction by "important" men in the community was also painfully similar to that in Santa Fe. Cox and López found the female body a powerful creation of God while the opposition found it offensive.

Mayor Rudy Giuliani attacked the Brooklyn Museum of Art, the artist, and the artwork. In response to the "outrageous, disgusting, and anti-Catholic" work (created by a woman raised and educated as a Catholic), Mayor Giuliani threatened to take his case for removal to the Supreme Court, create a "decency" commission to stop the display of art that "decent" people would find offensive, and to withhold funding to art institutions that displayed such works.[59] He had done this before. In 1999, he pulled the museum's city funding when his sensitivities were offended by Chris Ofili's elephant dung and female genitalia–covered *Holy Virgin Mary*.

There is something reassuring in the thought that Alma López is not alone in her struggle. She has a history of Guadalupe appropriation to support her, and a community of Chicanas, artists, women, and men to defend her, from

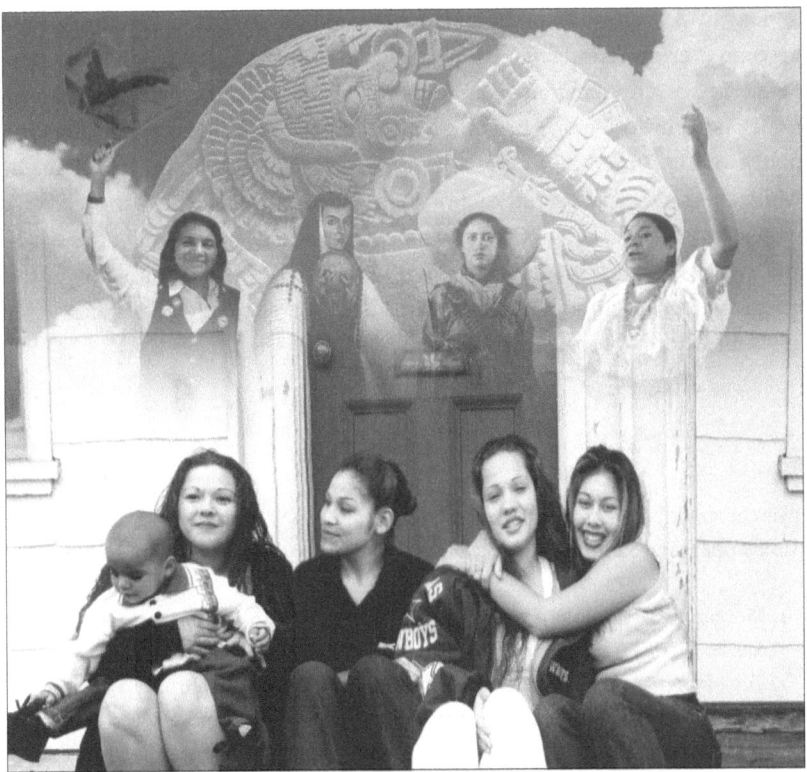

3.2. *Las Four.* Digital print by Alma López, with the SPARC/César Chávez Digital
Mural Lab, © 1997. Courtesy of Alma López and the SPARC Archives.

Tey Marianna Nunn to Paul Rainbird, and a contemporary culture of controversial images, such as Cox's *Yo Mama*, to sustain her.

Within the larger context of the changing world exists the perpetual merging of the past and the present, creating new traditions for the future. The appropriation of the icon of La Virgen de Guadalupe exemplifies this through
her image's history in Mexico, California, and New Mexico. Tey Marianna
Nunn and MOIFA exemplify this in their exhibition *Cyber Arte: Tradition Meets
Technology.* Alma López manifests this new tradition in her revolutionary, yet
profoundly traditional, work, *Our Lady.* As much as people fear the emer-
gence of suppressed voices and try to censor the right to create art, hope
remains that no one will ever hinder the expanding and merging realms of
modern art, technology, and spirituality.

Day by day, as art and religion have entered the twenty-first century, they become ever more intertwined in the world of technology. Just as the Internet served as an incredible palette for the discussion surrounding the Alma López controversy, it has become a new and powerful source for spreading myths of La Virgen de Guadalupe. In December 2001, Pope John Paul II, while announcing the sainthood of Juan Diego, unveiled the website www. virgendeguadalupe.org.mx, which accepts petitions, offers real-time Mass, and even has a gift shop. It is just another example of the dissemination of the image of La Virgen de Guadalupe into the universe, ready and available for any soul who wishes to claim her for herself.

NOTES

This chapter is based on Kathleen FitzCallaghan, "The War of the Roses: Guadalupe, Alma López, and Santa Fe," Master's thesis, University of Colorado, 2002, 47–82.

1. Morgan Lee, "Apology for 'Our Lady' Distress Sent to Archbishop," *Albuquerque Journal North* (April 13, 2001).
2. Tey Marianna Nunn, interview with the author, Santa Fe, February 13, 2002.
3. Nancy Warren, "Some Like a Virgin, Some Don't: Alma López Generates Controversy in New Mexico," *San Francisco Chronicle* (April 27, 2001), www.sfgate.com.
4. The Very Rev. Fr. Jerome Martinez y Alire et al., "It's Open Season on Catholic Symbols," letter, *Albuquerque Journal North* (April 1, 2001).
5. Ibid.
6. Tey Marianna Nunn, interview with the author, Santa Fe, February 13, 2002.
7. Speaker Ben Lujan et al., Santa Fe, to Mr. Wood "Mike" Arnold II, Board of Regents President, Museum of New Mexico, Santa Fe, March 27, 2001. *Cyber Arte* Collection, Museum of International Folk Art Archives, complete Record of correspondence received by the Museum of New Mexico regarding the *Cyber Arte* exhibition, April 11, 2001.
8. Mark Hummels, "Lawmakers Denounce Artwork," *Santa Fe New Mexican* (April 4, 2001).
9. Jennifer McKee, "Shouts, Shoves, Prayers Filled Foyer Outside," *Albuquerque Journal North* (April 5, 2001): 3.
10. John McCarthy, personal interview, Santa Fe, February 15, 2002.
11. Alma López, "What's Going On? As of August 28, 2001," *Los Angeles Chicana Artist Alma López*, August 28, December 12, 2001, www.almalopez.com.
12. José Villegas, personal interview, Santa Fe, February 15, 2002.

13. Ibid.
14. Morgan Lee, "Apology for 'Our Lady' Distress Sent to Archbishop," *Albuquerque Journal North* (April 13, 2001).
15. Tey Marianna Nunn, interview with the author, Santa Fe, February 13, 2002.
16. Anne Constable, "The Debate Rages On," *Santa Fe New Mexican* (April 17, 2001).
17. Anne Constable, "Attorney: Board Can Remove Offensive Work," *Santa Fe New Mexican* (April 14, 2001).
18. Morgan Lee, "From Lady to Lightning Rod," *Albuquerque Journal North* (April 5, 2001).
19. Ambassador Frank Ortiz, interview with the author, Santa Fe, February 14, 2002.
20. Ibid.
21. Museum of New Mexico Collections Policy, approved by Museum of New Mexico Board of Regents, May 5, 1999, 28.
22. Ibid., 29.
23. Ambassador Frank Ortiz, interview with the author, Santa Fe, February 14, 2002
24. Anne Constable, "Regents Says Museum's Policy Wasn't Followed," *Santa Fe New Mexican* (May 23, 2001).
25. Ibid.
26. Morgan Lee, "Museum Asks Patience of 'Our Lady' Critics," *Albuquerque Journal North* (May 18, 2001).
27. The committee said "four months early" because members wanted it to seem like a concession they were making to the community's demands. In actuality, October 28, 2001 was the original closing date of the show, as per the brochure.
28. Anne Constable, "Controversial Exhibit Will Come Down in October," *Santa Fe New Mexican* (May 23, 2001).
29. Anita K. McNeece et al., Committee on Sensitive Materials, letter to Ambassador Frank Ortiz, May 15, 2001.
30. Ibid., 4.
31. Erika Doss, *Spirit Poles and Flying Pigs: Public Art and Cultural Democracy in American Communities* (Washington, DC: Smithsonian Institution Press, 1995), 14.
32. Tey Marianna Nunn, interview with the author, Santa Fe, February 13, 2002.
33. Morgan Lee, "Regent under Fire for Attack on Exhibit, Volunteers," *Albuquerque Journal North* (May 23, 2001).
34. Anne Constable, "'Our Lady' Correspondence Reveals Rift," *Santa Fe New Mexican* (May 25, 2001).
35. Joan Fleetwood, letter to Frank Ortiz, Santa Fe, April 12, 2001.
36. Constable, "'Our Lady' Correspondence Reveals Rift."
37. Ibid.
38. Gloria Mendoza, "Museum Should Embrace Community," opinion, *Albuquerque Journal North* (July 8, 2001).

39. Ibid.

40. Paul Rainbird, interview with the author, Santa Fe, February 14, 2002.

41. "Folk-Art Exhibits through the Years," *Santa Fe New Mexican* (May 23, 2001).

42. Tey Marianna Nunn, interview with the author, Santa Fe, February 13, 2002.

43. Emily Van Cleve, "Modern Art," *Albuquerque Journal* (February 18, 2001).

44. Ibid.

45. Anne Constable, "More Than 500 Expected at 'Our Lady' Protest Today," *Santa Fe New Mexican* (June 30, 2001).

46. Terry Golway, "The Faithful and Their Faith," *New York Times* (March 17 and 18, 2002), www.nytimes.com.

47. Ibid.

48. Alma López, "Silencing Our Lady: La Respuesta de Alma," *Aztlán* 26.2 (2001): 254–255.

49. Ibid.

50. Paul Rainbird, interview with the author, Santa Fe, February 14, 2002.

51. Ibid.

52. Ibid.

53. Ronald L. Grimes, *Symbol and Conquest: Public Ritual and Drama in Santa Fe* (Albuquerque: University of New Mexico Press, 1992), 116.

54. Ibid., 117.

55. Ibid., 247.

56. Morgan Lee, "'Our Lady' Cyber Art Prompts House Measure," *Albuquerque Journal North* (February 8, 2002).

57. Luciano "Lucky" Verela, House Joint Memorial 88, 45th Legislature, State of New Mexico, second session, 2002.

58. To read more about the *Las Four* controversy, see http://www.members.labridge.com.

59. Amy Reiter, "New York's Bully in Chief Meets His Match: 'Yo Mama' artist Renée Cox Won't Let Adulterer Rudy Giuliani Use Catholicism to Beat Her Up," February 16, 2001, www.salon.com.

Making Privates Public

IT'S NOT ABOUT LA VIRGEN OF THE CONQUEST,
BUT ABOUT THE CONQUEST OF LA VIRGEN

Deena J. González

W HAT HAPPENS when controversy over an art piece in a museum develops in an environment redolent of religious tradition, cultural lifeways and manners, and extreme wealth or poverty? These are the historical contexts in which the controversy that developed over Alma López's *Our Lady* must be read. The manner in which López's interpretation of the mestiza Virgen de Guadalupe would affront a small but exceedingly vocal, media-savvy group of New Mexican protestors has historical origins in devotional practices that date back to the sixteenth century as much as in the economic and cultural colonization that has taken place in the region since the nineteenth century. As *I Am Joaquín*, a film and manifesto in Chicano history from the 1960s recognized, Mexicans in the conquered territory of the north "had won the battle for cultural survival, but lost the one for resources."[1]

With the arrival of *Our Lady* in Santa Fe, New Mexicans recognized both a connective historical resonance (a new Virgen de Guadalupe had made her way to Santa Fe) and an old condition: their colonized status. The traditional Catholic Church in this instance was evoked as a place of support for the community, although in New Mexico, the church and its priests and officers have not always supported the poor and the disenfranchised, including farmworkers and union movements.[2] When we are asked to view New Mexicans as colonized people, the example of *Our Lady* must be included but understood against the longer historical backdrop of Virgen worship, Catholic politics, and economic survival.

To unravel the layers of complexity embedded in the fierce public denunciations of *Our Lady*, we also need to understand the migratory patterns of successive generations of the colonizers of New Mexico, beginning from the southern Mexican point of origin in 1598, when the Spanish pushed northward from Zacatecas; to the journeys that followed of successive generations (1600–1821) of Spanish Mexicans, who brought the legend, stories, and images of La Virgen de Guadalupe from the Mexican interior to the frontier; to the eastern-based, westward-moving, primarily Protestant and anti-Catholic Euro-Americans much later in the 1820s, '30s, and '40s; and, finally, the arrival contemporarily in Santa Fe of the wealthy and ensconced East Coast art establishment and the kitsch-driven merchants who pander to a certain tourist market. The blueprint for easy targeting, cultural confusion, and misunderstanding makes sense if seen within this wave of migrations, or within the migration patterns long a part of a region's economic, political, and artistic landscape.

The noncolonialist interventions of Chicana art require exploration of these other historical precedents first, to clarify why the reaction by a select group of New Mexicans received so much attention. Without a grasp of the political, religious, and economic precedents, Alma López's representation of La Virgen de Guadalupe seems to be simply provocative, that is, artistic and meritorious on that ground alone, in a postmodern era, "the thing artists do," but without context about *why* it emboldened groups of New Mexicans and some religious leaders to demand its removal.

VIRGEN WORSHIP THEN AND NOW

The various Spanish expeditions against the indigenous peoples of the far northern frontier, today's Southwest or Mexico's northern territories, were armed with symbols designed to present and implant a venerable Catholic tradition in regions that were yet to be captured or settled by Spanish-speaking Catholics. In other words, they played important roles in the conversion of natives but also in retaining the faith practices of the loyal, if frightened, frontierspeople who were banished to the hinterlands or were escapees seeking a better life, and increasing the royal treasury in need of financial gain by conquest. Two such symbols were La Conquistadora and La Virgen de Guadalupe.

While it is difficult to compare a frontier icon or image with a national one, particularly because one is more obscure and belongs to a particular time while the other is also of its time and place but achieves national significance and transcends it contemporarily across the Americas, the former is critical to understanding how the early Spanish Mexican colonists and their descendants choose today to link their military and religious pasts. Symbolically, La Conquistadora is emblematic of a return, or a win, while La Virgen de Guadalupe is emblematic of loss but through indigenous survival.

La Conquistadora, or the Virgin of the Conquest, arrived in Santa Fe under a different name, and her image was constructed varyingly as Our Lady of the Assumption, Our Lady of the Conception, Our Lady of the Rosary, Our Lady of the Ransom, and, most recently, Our Lady of Peace, all one and the same Virgin or image wrapped in festive veneration as La Conquistadora. She had traveled northward with the confraternities, or *hermandades*, with the friars and priests.

Las Fiestas de Santa Fe, one of the largest annual public gatherings or festivals in Santa Fe, is the reenactment of Don Diego de Vargas's 1692 *entrada*, or "reconquest," of New Mexico, marking the return of the Spanish after the 1680 Pueblo Revolt when the Pueblo Indians successfully repelled the colonizers southward toward what is now the El Paso–Juárez border. The festival is also a commemoration of La Conquistadora, who is reputed to have been saved from a burning church, returned to her niche by the victorious soldier-settlers, or colonizers, to become the city of Santa Fe's patron saint.[3] The official website of the annual commemorative pageant emphasizes as well her beauty and fashionable appearance: "La Conquistadora is among the most venerated Marian figures in the world. She was crowned in 1954 by Cardinal Francis Spellman and again in 1960 by an apostolic representative of Pope John XXIII. Her golden crown is studded with precious stones, including a three-carat diamond. Her extensive wardrobe includes an exquisite lace mantilla from Seville, Spain, and an elaborate costume fashioned from ancient French vestments found in the old cathedral museum."[4]

Until the current century, La Conquistadora was rarely described as the patron saint honoring Spanish over native. Cognitive dissonance reigned between the celebrated colonialism of Santa Fe, or the official story, and an

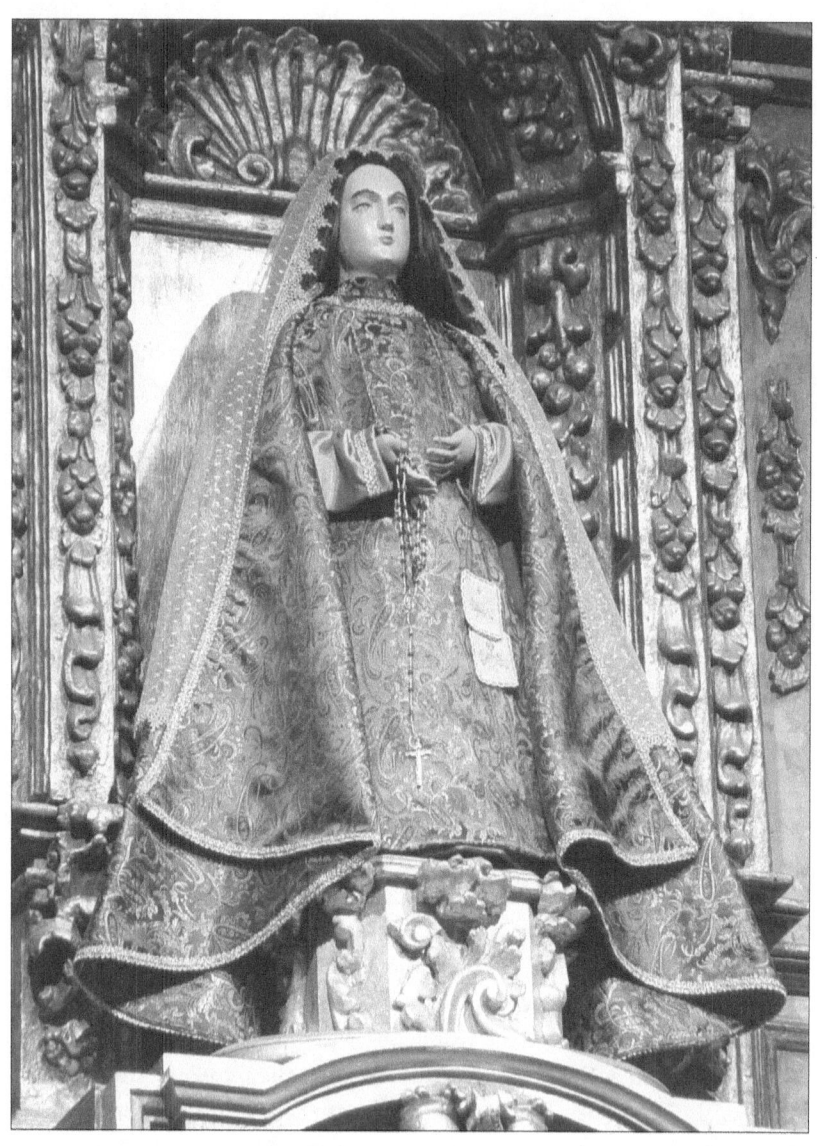

4.1.   La Conquistadora. Digital Photograph by Delilah Montoya, © 2009.
Courtesy of Delilah Montoya.

eventual "remedy" about some aspects of the city's historical amnesia. The recognition that conquest affected negatively a population of native, displaced, or enslaved people meant that La Conquistadora and the Santa Fe Fiestas relabeled her role as a reminder or symbol of a "peaceful reoccupation," or so states the website of the Fiestas' organizing committee, in other words, a "bloodless" takeover.[5] The initial meeting between native occupants of the Spanish buildings remaining when the Spanish retreated was indeed a negotiation and without warfare. One Tewa leader met the Spanish conqueror wearing a cross and also carrying an image of La Virgen de Guadalupe. La Conquistadora was with the returning Spaniards on a makeshift wagon, and a chapel in her honor would not be constructed until later, by other Indians after the native leaders of the occupied city were ousted and summarily executed.[6]

The worship of La Conquistadora, paraded from the cathedral and about town as she is during the heavily tourist-driven annual Fiestas, layers complexity on the matter of the official regard normally reserved for another "Lady," or "Virgin," the nationalistic Mexican icon, La Virgen de Guadalupe, said to have appeared in 1531 to a "poor" Mexican Indian whose name is Hispanicized as Juan Diego. La Virgen de Guadalupe, thought to have been the goddess Tonantzin in Aztec tradition, would some two hundred years later become the patron saint of the wounded but resistant Spanish-colony-turned-nation, Mexico (1821), and be heralded as the "mother" of the Mexican republic of which New Mexico was a part during the transition from Spanish colony to the Mexican nation (1820s–1840s).

One might even argue that in Santa Fe a certain competition developed between the Spanish Virgin of the Conquest and the mestiza Virgin of Guadalupe, which already had a following deep in Mexico by the late seventeenth century. From the beginning of Catholic and Spanish colonization in 1598, with the criollo (of Spanish blood but born in the Americas) Juan de Oñate's expedition and settlement, to the later centuries of symbolic renewal and rejuvenation in religious worship and practices, many studies document La Virgen de Guadalupe's artistic and religious significance in New Mexico. Although many believe that she was one among several religious figures worshipped on the northern frontier, the truth is that her significance continued to rise as it did throughout the Mexican republic from independence forward. Waves of Mexican migrants to New Mexico (pre-1848) and immigrants (post-1848) ensured that her traditional image adorned church walls and home altars. In other words, the renewal of her image, and thus her status and ven-eration, traverses the centuries as it has the geographic landscape of Old and New Mexico.

Another example of the longer-lived status La Virgen de Guadalupe oc-cupies in the lives of New Mexican villagers can be found in her presence among such local and colorful performances as the dances of the *matachines*, costumed characters drawn from historical events. The ritualized dances link Old and New Mexico because, as some scholars say, the *matachines* originated in Central Mexico. Scholars believe the word to have derived "from 16th cen-tury French and Spanish, and Italian *mattacino* is thought to have come from the Arabic word *muttawajjihin* . . . which means to assume a mask . . . from wajh, face."[7] The reenactments of conquest and of religious veneration of La Virgen de Guadalupe, including her appearance to the native, Hispanicized, and beatified Juan Diego, remain part of New Mexican folklore.

A few blocks from the Guadalupe *santuario*, said to be the oldest Marian parish in the United States, La Conquistadora is ensconced in the far larger ca-thedral, with its French limestone and nonadobe walls and designated in 2005 by Pope Benedict XVI as a basilica. The title confers landmark status on the cathedral and acknowledges it as the seat of the Spanish/Catholic incursion many centuries previously, but more important, as the seat of a new incur-sion: the French transplant, in this case, Archbishop Jean Baptiste Lamy, who commissioned it due to his disdain for the native materials and architecture of the older cathedral. On the ruins of the adobe church arose a monument or testament to Euro-American intrusion and success. It took many decades to build, as masons who could work the imported stone also had to be import-ed. The tenacious archbishop nevertheless succeeded, although the cathedral was completed only after his death.

The juxtaposition, therefore, of a Spanish colonialist symbol, La Con-quistadora, with that of an emerging mestiza figure of national identity, La Virgen de Guadalupe, would not be lost in the farthest corners of the Span-ish empire. Twin traditions—colonialist, on the one hand, celebrant of the racial and cultural mixing of Europeans and natives, on the other—would be conjoined, partnered, if unwittingly or against church doctrine. The par-adox of this partnership is illustrated in the controversies that attend each Virgin. Beginning with doubts about her appearance to an Indian man, Juan Diego Cuauhtlatloatzin, Nuestra Señora Virgen de Guadalupe's legitimacy has been questioned across the ages. In other words, long before she was declared patron of the Americas by Pope Benedict the XIV in 1754, her story, legend, and history circulated throughout Mexico, but some church officials and others still disputed her apparition, her portrayals, and her origins among the Aztecs. Her image and history, thus, are not fixed but have evolved across time and adapted to the exigent religious, ethnic, and racial consciousness particular to their eras.

La Conquistadora, literally, the female conqueror, while acknowledged as a historical icon and an important figure uniting Spanish Santa Fe with Spain, the country of origin that so many New Mexicans claim as the homeland (versus Mexico), presents her own difficulties. Because she is Spanish (*criolla*) and embodies the conquest of native people, or the wresting of land from the natives by Spanish speakers, she is emblematic of the once-honorable warrior tradition within which Spanish Mexicans prevailed in language and religion. As they moved generationally out of that tradition, they necessarily reached uneasy truces to survive in the distant lands of the Spanish empire. It became increasingly irrelevant that many were in fact of mixed race and had indigenous ancestors in their recent family histories, because they chose to call themselves "Hispanos," or not truly native to the land, until perhaps many centuries later. The curious case of claiming "colonialist" heritage but being of mixed racial and ethnic makeup, is something still debated among all "native" New Mexicans. Technically, a native would not be a New Mexican, an Anglicized term, or even a Spanish-speaking Catholic. To parse the technicalities along racial and ethnic lines, a native would be indigenous, a descendant of many of the thousands who survived the original Spanish conquest as well as subsequent migrations of Spanish-speaking, Catholic-worshipping "settlers." Yet the current predicaments of mixed-race "Hispanos" who claim a degree of "Mexicanness" in worshipping La Virgen de Guadalupe reside precisely in reformatted displacement, this one engineered or occurring contemporarily through the Mexican workers migrating to Santa Fe and by the Euro-American transplants who employ them.

It is relevant and interesting that in a class- and color-based society, moved northward to the farthest reaches of the empire, La Conquistadora marries history, purpose, and religion. She smoothed out the wrinkles until the 1960s, when her display became less popular in the face of indigenous survival, and tales of mistreatment and of horrors too numerous to detail were published and read. Still, Spanish Mexicans have been determined to reserve La Conquistadora for public presentation just one day a year, during the annual Santa

Fe Fiestas, when she is paraded through the street, in *sevillano* style and fashion.[8] Otherwise, she remains safely sequestered in the chapel in the Basílica of Saint Francis, which dedicated to her a place of reverence and safety—not surprising, given her rescue, re-placement, and the revision of Santa Fe's history that accounts for the Spanish conquest of native peoples as a commemorative event for the winners, who now face their own "loss" or defeat at the hands of the westering Euro-Americans. Interestingly, within the Catholic frontier tradition in New Mexico, her chapel is all that remains of the original Santa Fe cathedral, removed in the 1870s when Archbishop Lamy began construction of the current one in a European vernacular.

Unlike her sequestered sister of the conquest, the other Virgin, La Virgen de Guadalupe, is a very public figure and is on display outside the Guadalupe Church, easily accessed by her followers and near the central plaza, where several museums and galleries or shops also house and sell her likenesses. Her history sustains a different political message of nationalistic fervor. The Guadalupe Church, or chapel behind the large statue, was under museum control, but the parishioners lobbied for its return to the community and finally achieved it in 2001. It was constructed in 1781 and a few years later housed an early painting of La Virgen de Guadalupe by José de Alzibar. The *santuario* and its artwork attested to the importance of La Virgen de Guadalupe across these centuries for people in northern New Mexico.

In 2001, a twelve-foot bronze statue of La Virgen de Guadalupe was commissioned from a Mexican sculptor, purchased by the Guadalupe Historic Foundation of the Santuario, and, seven years later, carried along the Spanish migratory and conquest route known as El Camino Real, the Royal Road, from the center of Mexico northward to Santa Fe.[9] Fresh from a tumultuous journey beginning in Mexico City, including being held at the border to ensure that drugs were not being transported inside her cavities, or, metaphorically, as in the case with many drug runners, inside her body, she is visible to all passersby, tourists, and worshippers.[10] The Virgen statue, momentarily lost by the U.S. Immigration and Customs Services, indeed met with a chilly reception at the harshly demarcated border but now is "home" in Santa Fe.

Interestingly, the statue's journey from south to north mimics the colonial journey of La Conquistadora. Thus, Santa Fe's and the nation of Mexico's patron saint, in effect, unite symbolically (dare we say marry?) in the "City Different," as Santa Fe is continually referenced in its tourist literature.[11]

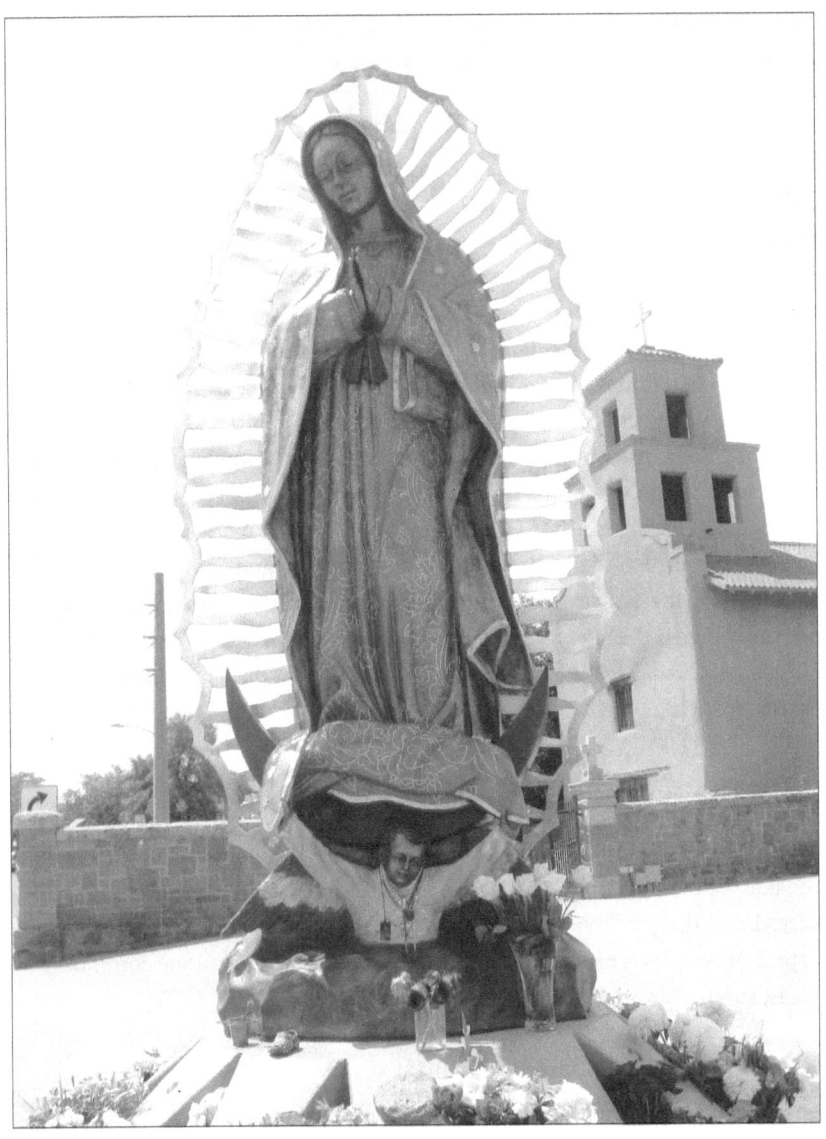

4.2. Our Lady of Guadalupe Statue. Digital Photograph by Alicia Gaspar de Alba, © 2008.
Courtesy of Alicia Gaspar de Alba.

Whether historically or contemporarily controversial, each female icon or saint occupies an established location in regional and national history, a history that is often disjointed.

A traditional symbol of resistance and affirmation, but in a modern context, today's Virgen de Guadalupe of Santa Fe inhabits an outdoor space more akin to the Mexican one, where La Virgen de Guadalupe is also placed outdoors in statue form while the original artistic rendition (*tilma*) in Mexico City is safely indoors but recognized as belonging to the ages and to nature, or to the land.

The placement of the new statue of La Virgen de Guadalupe is said to have been generated by the controversy produced in 2001 by Alma López's *Our Lady*. With yet another traditional image in the form of a large statue in a parking area, available for the tourist passersby, the implication or message is rife with "Behold, all, this is our true Virgen."

Specific characteristics of the statue send several messages. She is either twelve or fourteen feet tall, weighs 4,000 pounds, and is visible from a distance. Also, she is brown-skinned. Her figure, in this context, is large and assertive but also enlisted to convey what New Mexicans "really think" La Virgen de Guadalupe deserves: public display and a proper, that is, subdued, demeanor.

CHURCH AND STATE

The role of the Alma López art piece bears directly on questions of insider/outsider status, on public/private venerations, and on concerns about the sacred and the profane. The bitter judgment of the archbishop of Santa Fe captured well the ensuing local angst and public confusion, or conflation of ideas, surrounding the image:

ALBUQUERQUE—(March 26, 2001)
Statement of Archbishop Michael J. Sheehan on the offensive depiction of Our Lady of Guadalupe:

Upon my return on Friday evening, March 23, from leading a pilgrimage to Fatima and Lourdes I found out about the controversy regarding yet another trashing of the image of Our Lady of Guadalupe. To depict the Virgin Mary in a floral bikini held aloft by a bare breasted angel is to be insulting, even sacrilegious, to the many thousands of New Mexicans who have deep religious devotion to Guadalupe.

To place such a repulsive picture in the Museum of International Folk Art shows insensitivity to a large segment of Santa Feans and imprudence in the administration of a State-funded institution. Such a picture has no place in a tax supported public museum.

As the Archbishop of Santa Fe, I find it offensive that the Catholic symbol of Guadalupe has been so disrespectfully treated. In the recent past the Virgin Mary has been shown in contemporary art smeared with elephant dung and she has been depicted as a golden haired Barbie doll. Now this! I doubt that the Jewish community would be patient with such a mistreatment of symbols sacred to their faith.

I wish those who want to paint controversial art would find their own symbols to trash and leave the Catholic ones alone. I urge the Board of Regents of the Museum to see that the offensive image is removed and that those responsible for the unfortunate decision to display it, apologize.[12]

With this statement, the archbishop was asking museum attendees to view the artwork as religious in character while, contradictorily, his message was laced with popular cultural rhetoric, including "trashing," "to trash," and "golden haired Barbie doll." The archbishop, while chiding the museum for what he considered a misapplication of state funds, seemed blissfully unaware of his own precarious position in that regard; that is, the separation of church and state also demands that any tax-exempt religious institution not "endorse particular political positions" at the pulpit or from the office.

The controversy over López's *Our Lady* could also be contextualized within the role art has played in New Mexico. Across the decades, many outsiders in the art world and art patron community have made their way to New Mexico. They seek to exploit the religious heritage and mythic beliefs of people or communities long considered enclaves of "indigeneity" and folkloric in composition. In the Smithsonian style and application of such concepts, whether as stylized presentations of art or as "field-workers," to name just two formats for "Americanizing," the practice of Euro-American conversion (or colonization) reaches across two centuries. The attempt is to convert New Mexicans into proper Americans and it had its origins in the 1820s, when Euro-Americans developed the St. Joseph–Santa Fe–Chihuahua routes for carrying manufactured items, including alcohol, cloth, and tools or implements, from the United States into northern Mexico.[13]

Labeled "Spanish Americans," sometimes by themselves as well as by outsiders, Spanish-speaking, predominantly Catholic New Mexicans, or Hispanos, have mostly tolerated the waves of strangers or conquerors in their midst, beginning in the early nineteenth century (1810–1821) and followed by the U.S. war with Mexico (1846–1848) and the former's subsequent claim to New Mexico. Over one hundred years later, the descendant artists' "colonies," whether in Taos or Santa Fe, in Ruidoso or Abiquiu, circulated artwork in East Coast galleries and artistic circles. Many came west in the pre– and post–World War II period to cure their ailments or just to escape the stifling cities. They were enormously successful in selling images of landscapes or their own rather simplified, anthropological versions of "lost cultures." Although New Mexican Hispano culture was not in need of discovery and had not been lost, it was cast as if on the precipice of extinction, holding on tenaciously to its eras, especially after the 1930s New Deal unleashed "modernization" programs aimed at rural electrification, home economics, and general cultural repair by focusing on recovering "lost" cultural techniques.[14]

The presentation in a new millennium of a more current and particularly Chicana-from-California artistic "intrusion" into the New Mexico landscape, if viewed from the perspective of outsider/insider, can also be assessed along similar lines, pertaining to origins, migrants or homesteaders, and image repair. López's *Our Lady* trekked west to southwest, from urban California to New Mexico, and not east to west, as has generally been the case for large artistic trends or movements. López reversed the role of the artist or migrant against the wave or current of westward expansion and colonization. She is a fellow Chicana ("Hispana" in the New Mexican lexicon), and her photo-based digital collage but a single submission by invitation in a small show with three other artists. Others from the East have imported entire schools or methods without controversy. Examples include the Nathaniel Wyeth landscape school, led by Peter Hurd, San Patricio, New Mexico and the most famous and considered by far the most original, the Georgia O'Keeffe school.[15]

It is difficult to imagine that a 14" × 17.5" piece could upset any of these trends or tendencies or upend the overabundant and popular landscape stylizations found in hundreds of Santa Fe galleries, shops, and museums. In the ensuing debate and outcry, however, it almost appeared to be the case that the entire art world was at issue. Similarly, it seemed that this one small piece would undermine the other popular theme in the established and wealthy museum culture of Santa Fe—depicting religious, devoted peasant-worshippers—which are as ubiquitous as the fetishized, howling coyote. Working against the established and popular artistic themes or schools, we can understand the unpredictability of the outcry for the artist and the art-

going public, as we might begin to review the unmanageability of the growing scrutiny given to a revisionary rendition of a saintly icon.

TOURIST ECONOMY AND CONTROL OF OUTSIDERS

Because the allegations of "anti-Catholicism" suited the public arena and reinforced the popular economic, tourist notion of "pious, mantilla-clad" New
Mexican villagers pained by an outsider's depiction of "their" venerable symbol of virginity, that is, a woman without sexuality, the organized marches
and spiteful and threatening messages sent to the museum's trustees, the
show's curator, and the artist herself, were strategic. The letter writers and
commentators in the media, as well as the protestors, were dedicated to the
idea of their own traditional "cultural and religious authenticity" or interpretation of "proper" iconography as well as sexuality. Their message carried a
distinctly NIMBY flavor ("not in my backyard"), or a clear invective that any
reconfiguration or nontraditional depiction of La Virgen de Guadalupe was
incompatible with "traditional" northern New Mexican values.

I am not suggesting that the organized protests, joined in chorus by select
Catholic bishops and priests, were pandering to the tourist economy, but in
the background we must consider the following details crucial to an evalua-
tion of *Our Lady* in Santa Fe: the city is now almost entirely under the control
of "outsiders," with its working-class residents having sold their historic family properties for upwards of $300,000 each, or more money than any retire-
ment account. The workers who service the wealthy in Santa Fe tend now
to live on the outskirts of the city in mobile homes and are also being sup-
planted by Mexican undocumented workers. The homes in the older sections
of the city are ever more valuable in the context of Euro-American median
family incomes because the incomes of Hispano residents of New Mexico
hover precariously close to national poverty lines.[16] As entire sections of the
now tourist Mecca of Santa Fe began to be sold to outsider and wealthy migrants from the 1970s onward, the locals' influence in cultural production
and religious festivals waned. Is it any wonder, then, that such an easy target
as something that could be made out to be as central to, or confrontational
toward, a person's religious beliefs would merit the attention of the displaced
people of northern New Mexico? Literally squeezed between the transnational economies binding the United States and Mexico, holding on to the
dearest of symbols, emblematic of *mestizaje* and of conquest, lends a different
angle to or perspective on the protestors.

Moreover, many of the artistic traditions have been supported by outsiders who arrive in New Mexico and become converts to historical preservation, forgetting that the traditions themselves have changed across time and are laid claim to for practical or economic reasons as much as for historical custom. The annual "Spanish," or "Hispanic," market, selling millions of dollars of religious crafts and artwork in Santa Fe each year, with its band of experts, juried shows, and publicity junkets, underscores how truly important is each artist's product to village economies, family household income, and the regional tourist draw. Without outside organizers and patrons, many aspects of this artistic trade fair would suffer.

Other New Mexicans, activists especially, continue to fret about the ways collectors descended on their villages and communities, supposedly eager to buy or sell cultural icons and antiques; New Mexicans into the 1920s had little concept of what made something an antique or lent it capitalistic value, as they used to say that an article was simply great-grandmother's old chest, or a saint (*bulto*) that belonged to relatives living several hundred years ago. These familial and familiar items composed the average New Mexican household until the mid-twentieth century, and many New Mexican families continue to practice the tradition of preservation, lineage, and longevity in location.

Today, markets and economies have shifted, and it is not uncommon to see family homes sold in Santa Fe and Taos at prices equal to those in the housing markets of the West and East coasts. One result is the difference between rural, small-village mindfulness and the necessity of cultural preservation in the face of overdeveloped national economies. Physical survival mirrors cultural preservation to the extent that the manufactured houses (mobile homes, trailers) to which Spanish Mexicans move as they sell their centrally located family homes today reflect the continuing pattern of historical displacement and of "frontier" exploitation. Living outside the center or core of the ancient city, now so dolled up as to have become consumed in its own clichéd Disneyland caricature, the Santa Fe locals are more and more distant from their early settlement.[17]

Spanish Market, the annual venerable explosion of juried art and rented booths and attendant fees on the Santa Fe Plaza dating back to the 1920s, indicates the extent of the selling and manufacturing of art, whether religious, village-based, organic or natural, or postmodern. The contest and the presentation to the public, from art dealers to small collectors, dictates intricate linkages between art patrons, wealthy decorators in need of items, and the much poorer local artists or artisans themselves, many of whom have resurrected lost techniques or recuperated crafts in an effort to keep their familial and cultural traditions alive.

ICONOGRAPHY

Virgin of Guadalupe images have circulated among New Mexicans for many hundreds of years. In the case of Santa Fe, Virgin saints or icons are to be venerated, if at different times on the calendar, and all require vigilance and preservation to be saved from either burning churches or rapacious outsider Chicana feminist artistic depiction. If properly housed, that is, near the *santuario* or inside a cathedral or chapel, outfitted to suit the Catholic and traditional tastes of worshippers, little controversy exists. But if they are taken away from their "restricted" homes or sites and put in museums, for example, the recipe for controversy is ripe for historical amnesia, misinterpretation, and an effort to make up for the lack of formal education about cultural adaptation, theological constructs, and artistic license and freedom. In this case, the lowest common denominator, folkloric in nature and advanced by church and conservative religious groups, propelled the negative publicity and public outcry about the artistic image of a "new" Guadalupe across the New Mexican landscape. One of the protest's leaders, José L. Villegas Sr., wrote threateningly in an e-mail to Alma López: "Let me reassure you one thing about your New Mexico supporters, we will find out who they are and when we do, we will do whatever it takes to admonish them in the public form [*sic*] and hold thier [*sic*] actions accountable. We will take them to a higher level. They have no clue on what a controversy is in New Mexico, especially when you mess with a sacred image that does not belong to you."[18] Through it all, the hatred or fear of women was palpable.

Another element within the controversy or debate, this one based on the economy, and about the role of museums within it, requires explanation. While many churches in New Mexico are now virtually museums, or owned by the large museum culture that frequents and promotes views of "quaint" New Mexican history for non–New Mexicans, New Mexicans are likely to resist efforts to privatize church buildings.

The celebration during the new statue's unveiling revealed the layers of issues and was reported in the *Albuquerque Journal*:

There was a moment just after the unveiling of the bronze Our Lady of Guadalupe statue Friday evening when Santa Fe's old and new were facing each other.

La Peregrina, the three-foot-high traveling replica of La Conquistadora, was just off to the side looking toward the new 14-foot statue that arrived earlier last month from Mexico to be placed outside Our Lady of Guadalupe Church. La Conquistadora was made in Spain and brought to New Mexico on the Camino Real in about December 1625.

"It is the old and the new," Cliff Russell, a parish member and a lector, said during the outdoor Mass with more than 500 people attending to dedicate the statue. "This really started seven years ago, when we fought to get the santuario back." Given the Catholic Church's need to sell church property, especially in the wake of expensive settlements in the cases against it and its pedophile priests, and the lack of local fundraising to retain active parishes, the museums as well as local businesses have in fact played a significant role in the historic preservation of buildings and sites.[19]

Northern New Mexicans have consistently held at bay certain contradictions about public displays of folk culture, including the religious, and about exposure, which brings tourist dollars as well as needed funds for religious and artistic preservation. For this reason, the debate about insiders and outsiders, in this invocation of Alma López's artistic and spiritual license, presented a necessary corrective to the dilemma of welcoming strangers for the goal of relieving them of their money and rejecting their outsider views or offerings at the same time.[20] The controversy, although painful for its participants, the museum directors, curators, and the artist herself, as well as an inducement for the newspaper reporters and media on the scene, nevertheless generated money for an area marked by enormous gaps between the wealthy transplants to Santa Fe and the New Mexicans who serve them. Deeper or more focused journalism might have used that contemporary economic gulf, and some regard for historical accuracy, to achieve a nuanced understanding of the various sides involved: what was the stake or claim of each group within the ensuing firestorm, and why would this have been important to the museum-going public?

The hostility toward the museum or museum culture itself was omnipresent. Outsiders thought they had brought fame and glory to New Mexico, and many residents acted as if they were either grateful or uninterested entirely, much as they greet the Hollywood crews busily filming subsidized movies in the State of New Mexico today.[21]

Added to this fear or concern about outsiders, especially on the part of villagers whose communities date back several centuries, is the recognition that others do not understand fully the role of Catholicism or of the church in New Mexicans' daily existence. The sentiment predates the arrival of Euro-Americans in the 1840s; many Euro-American traders and merchants commented in the 1820s about what they perceived as a "priest-ridden culture," as they sold their manufactured goods to the same "backward" population. Their earliest prejudicial reflections enticed subsequent generations to view New Mexicans as more than religious devotees governed by their Catholicism; rather, it made New Mexicans appear to be meek and humble, when not macho or patriarchical.

For New Mexicans, another dilemma ensued. The critics provided needed items manufactured more efficiently than the Mexican republic was able to do to send to the frontier. The ambivalence about strangers peddling new items, artistic or religious in scope, or the right to display them is thus historical and predates the Euro-American concepts of freedom of expression or freedom of speech. Instead, within a culture where church and state were intricately intertwined (Roman law, ecclesiastical law and practices, and the heritage of the Inquisition), northern New Mexicans used art and folk traditions to support their political and worldviews, as well as their religious devotions. In other words, New Mexicans have a heritage of subtle commentary against established governing authority in the case of a frontier against its republican center, or Santa Fe versus Mexico City, and they have supported and continue to support artistic expressiveness. Their support occurs across several arenas—the practical, the political, and the economic—and does not harbor or reserve devotion for just one, the museum or the church.

It is unfortunate that the journalists reporting the outcry about López's *Our Lady* did not focus on these complex purposes. The political and religious climates might shift and be emboldened in dynamic exchange, but sometimes the pattern of center (Spain or Mexico City; La Conquistadora, La Virgen de Guadalupe), versus the periphery or margin (Santa Fe or East L.A.) remains in play long after the colonial and neocolonial relationship is severed. Thus, the newer and larger, more "genuine" twelve-foot Virgen de Guadalupe makes her way northward once again, to refresh the old, to symbolize a wealthier or funded Catholic community, or to evoke the center and make a statement on the margins against "inappropriate" intrusions of the Los Angeles variety.

THE POLITICAL ECONOMY OF FOLKLORE

The economic context of the art produced and its longevity is nearly as important in the controversy that ensued in 2001 right at the turn of the new millennium. As the religious, the homophobic, the antifeminist, or the secular-versus-sacred debate mushroomed, what the mainstream media seemed incapable of contextualizing was that New Mexico remained one of the poorest states in the nation, although its artists and artisans produced prized products; the wealth of northern New Mexico's second- or vacation-home owners (the outsiders) does not translate into a larger tax base or improved health care and educational systems for those whose spiritual and religious fervor continues to grow even in the face of economic downturns.[22] Instead, the newspapers and television news reports created a scenario for representing "tradition-bound" residents, led in protest by some Catholic authorities, to maintain an image that sells or that helps retain local citizens in poses that pander to the image of subservient, devout Catholics. The ultraconservative American Society for the Defense of Tradition, Family and Property (TFP), a national organization with local chapters, rallied supporters, including Catholic priests, in a postcard-writing campaign and public gatherings.[23] While the TFP website and articles suggest how it mustered support, the organization also advanced a traditional scare tactic grounded in anti-Catholicism and reminiscent of nineteenth-century Euro-American strategies.

Indisputably, La Virgen de Guadalupe's traditional image helps Catholics retain control of their parishes, or resist church authorities when defending local practices in the face of change, but, contrarily, it also locks them into a particular pose; they become part of the artistic canvas that such public protests involving art also encourage. Videotaping these nontraditional art patrons simply enhances their folkloric, naïve-about-the-meaning-of-"real"-art ways. For museum directors and artists, the groundswell of devout religious folk also makes responding to the protestors far more difficult, because few artists, patrons, or museum officials wish to be seen as resistant to local customs or practices. In fact, at the exact moment when such museums as the renowned Museum of International Folk Art were seeking ways to encourage more public participation, the protest grew and brought bad or poor publicity along with a heightened, if overly sensitive, awareness to this particular, rather nonmainstream, museum. In fact, the point of the exhibition had the opposite purpose: to bring New Mexicans into the sacred or refined (confined) spaces of the museum.

That the Museum of International Folk Art and its employees, including the curator of the show within which Alma López's digital photo collage was included, are considered, contradictorily, both a part of New Mexico and apart from New Mexico is as important as economy, history, and artistic or religious heritage. The museum's mission statement reads: "The mission of the Museum of International Folk Art is to enrich the human spirit by connecting people with the arts, traditions, and cultures of the world."[24] The museum houses the splendid Alexander Girard collections, gathered by an avid collector fascinated throughout his lifetime with Mexican and Latin American crafts and folk art. A newer Neutrogena wing was established just before the controversial show and debate ensued and pays tribute to the corporate sponsorship now so necessary to museum sustenance. Another wing on New Mexico traditions and history is a permanent feature of the museum.

Part of the museum's stated mission is the understanding that cultures do change. However, the exhibitions reinforce traditional or staged notions of the "folkloric" because of the artifacts that are captured in time and rendered in smaller spaces for the viewing public. That is, try as museum staff might to re-create a Spanish village, as the Smithsonian attempted in one of its museums, the point is that the dioramas, images, collections, and objects are all removed and homeless; the museum is not a home, just as it is not a chapel. The educational value encouraged by preservation and reflection make up for the artificiality of the museum environment, some would argue, particularly when a stream of school buses dislodge their cargo at the museum doors.

The question to be asked is: "How many native New Mexicans visit this museum?" Not as many as might be imagined. A 2006 governor's report on tourism and marketing allowed for public growth in some museums, including Natural History and Science (Albuquerque), the UFO Museum (Roswell), and the New Mexico Farm and Ranch Museum (Las Cruces). The other art museums of New Mexico, located primarily in a cluster in Santa Fe, saw a decline in attendance. Their appeal remains primarily among outsiders. In the same period, park attendance increased at the local lakes, dams, and campgrounds.[25] Locals are voting with their feet, as they say, and supporting the sites where they feel comfortable, or where the large families that compose Mexican America can gather, versus the smaller, confined, and quiet spaces a museum necessarily requires.

COMPUTER TRICKERY AND GENUINE WOMEN

Long before Alma López set foot in the Museum of International Folk Art in Santa Fe, proper religious conduct during both public and private female veneration dominated the New Mexican religious and geographic landscape.[26] Privately, men have worshipped female saints, women have built altars to female virgins and other saints, and publicly, under traditional, frontier Catholicism, holy or saints' days have been preserved.[27] Worshippers and New Mexicans are generally uncomfortable with public depictions of sexuality in many contexts but especially those deemed religious. *Our Lady* introduced the key element of sexuality into the discourse of gender that undergirded much of the protest, although all of Alma López's artwork provides a distinctly lesbian lens or perspective meant to provoke discussions about the sacred in women's bodies. The lesbian subtext of *Our Lady*, particularly in honoring the female body as an embodiment of the spirit of La Virgen de Guadalupe, was also at play, but the homophobia was generally channeled through a religious filter.

Some hoped the dreaded topic of women's sexuality would remain restricted to the private domain. This is evident in the lack of explicit or venomous commentary about "lesbian" representation, lesbian subtext, or the like. "In your computer trickery, you say you want to portray a strong woman," said one man at the second community forum to which the public had been invited to express its views about *Our Lady*. Dressed in cowboy boots and a cowboy hat and addressing the absent artist, the white man pontificated: "Alma López, you don't know what a real woman is. Look around you. New Mexico has genuine women."[28]

A real woman, a genuine woman, or a strong woman—are they mutually exclusive terms? La Conquistadora and La Virgen de Guadalupe both embody "proper" elements of femaleness under Catholicism—motherhood and modesty primary among them—while Alma López's digital *Our Lady* embodies its opposite. La Virgen de Guadalupe appears within the art controversy as the property of men and of the Catholic Church's hierarchy, who deem only certain elements of femaleness acceptable, or as proper female depiction, veneration, and display, whether in museums or churches.[29] It seems a strange supposition, the control of women's worship, given a "new" or changing church hoping to retain Catholics and to humanize the liturgy in nonsexist ways.

The rose-clad, defiant figure of Raquel Salinas staring directly at the viewer was one important revision to more typical images of women and saints. And the expressly sexual defiance in the placement of the figure countered the prevailing idea that a Guadalupe image must remain without sexuality, because in the stereotypical rendition of La Virgen, or Mother of God, a breast's contour is barely visible under the shawl and dress she wears. Curiously, the explicit sexual pose itself was a "silent" or "silenced" element in the ensuing debate while the affront to respectful religious devotion or veneration took center stage among the protestors. The debate also advanced discussions of artistic freedom (and the artistic merit of the work), but these were consistently subsumed in the media by the topic more likely to sell newspapers and increase ratings: angry, pious Catholics. The supposed impropriety in the depiction or adaptation of La Virgen de Guadalupe was thus laced with moralistic judgment and resulted in the call, ultimately, for the removal of the work.

López and the Museum of International Folk Art might have erred in imagining that an audience saturated with television and its countless horrific and violent sexual images would be unwilling to suspend the notion that art in a religious center and religious thematic content in a museum are two entirely different propositions or perspectives,[30] or that some elements of capitalism would have inured the New Mexican protestors. La Virgen de Guadalupe, after all, decorates low rider cars, is found on hippie jewelry and oven mitts, and brings some shops a handsome profit. This is also not the first reconfiguration of La Virgen de Guadalupe by Chicanas, so one is left to wonder where this particular New Mexican audience got left behind, or have they just had enough of these adaptive patterns?[31] López herself and the model for the image were interested less in the public's religious attitudes than in making the point about violence against women, about women interpreting their symbols of veneration for themselves. López saw the work as contributory, not as an affront, and was surprised at how the misogynistic invective of many protestors was cloaked in religious zeal. The zeal, as her website indicates, continued well past 2001:

On December 2002, I was invited to exhibit *Our Lady* by a young artist curator, only to be censored by the director from an annual Virgen de Guadalupe exhibition at the Aztlan Cultural Center in San Antonio, Texas. During the summer of 2003, a conservative religious group from Pennsylvania came to Self Help Graphics in East Los Angeles to protest a silkscreen based on *Our Lady* titled *Our Lady of Controversy* where the standing female figure is wearing boxing gloves ready to defend her constitutional rights. This summer, a curator for the Fullerton Museum declined to exhibit "Our Lady." Although, the curator selected a "safe" Guadalupe image that I produced in 1997, the museum received hate emails from Hector Carreon aka Ernesto Cienfuegos of *La Voz de Aztlán* website.[32]

Once they were intertwined, any effort to disentangle the elements of the controversy became hostage to a quagmire of anti-Catholicism, of perceived affronts to a religious but not terribly "Christian" hateful and spiteful sensibility. Lost were how those in turn were also an affront to the objectives of a talented artist, of believing subjects who posed for the image, and of feminist-derived and -inspired creativity. Indeed, some Chicano male scholars like Octavio Romano labeled López "narcissistic," perhaps thinking she was the one portrayed in the image (it is Raquel Salinas), or "ideological" and insisted that the symbolic content of La Virgen could be transposed by the real body of a Chicana clad in roses.[33] The latter were again subsumed in the quest to provide examples of a "proper" religious sentiment, much like the Spanish conquerors had done four hundred years previously against the native peoples of the northern frontier. The irony was lost on some of these men, who were less able than in any other historical era to control women and their saints.

Multiple political issues also bore down on the surrounding debate and focused on the Museum of International Folk Art. The era of George W. Bush's presidency, with its license to assert "family values" at a moment when households were witnessing the "failure" of one out of every two heterosexual marriages, when composite households of nonconsanguineous kin and female-headed households were more the norm, is particularly interesting. López's rendering engendered all of these issues because it was held up as the provocation or cause of the debate, but perhaps the discussion should have been held all along. Given that Chicano/a studies is practically outlawed in New Mexico's public schools, and its children and citizenry are therefore held back from acquiring the analytical and historical focus needed to unravel this type of discussion, it is small wonder that many artists of necessity instead resort to traditional symbols and depictions to support their families and communities in the face of a public able to consume only one version of authentic art.[34] Art patrons endorse these developments as they snap up the less-risky renditions and use those on napkin rings, dishware, and other consumer items. As a result, conversation, creativity, and community are impoverished victims of "art for hire." Luckily, some sojourners like Alma López will find their way past the sanctified walls or fences, crossing borders to assist the effort for a richer and more expansive female depiction and feminist representation of La Virgen de Guadalupe.

The artist Alma López did not colonize New Mexican Catholics with her depiction of *Our Lady* of Guadalupe as an embodiment of Mexican womanhood, sensuality, and survival. On the contrary, her artwork embraces female empowerment to turn La Virgen's eye back to the viewer, who then must question his or her perspective of the symbol, its spiritual content, and the religious relic all at once. Gazing at art is not the same as religious veneration. New Mexican protestors confused the two, whether intentionally or not. The artist had hoped to encourage greater interest in the symbol of La Virgen de Guadalupe away from its traditional, patriarchal anchor in submissiveness, shame, and sexual ambivalence; she hoped to engage the public in a specifically feminist-constructed interpretation. For feminist patrons and museumgoers, she accomplished this objective.[35] For others, perhaps dislodging them from their comfortable understandings of Mexican and Chicana womanhood is sufficient.

The local, regional, and national Mexican character of both La Conquistadora and the Virgin of Guadalupe, each situated in the colonial era but also transhistorical, is elided under the umbrella presented by attention instead to their legendary status. The legends embody historical moments commemorated in celebrations, but the history of their mythic dimensions is recast in light of each new conquest, whether economic, political, or religious. Alma López's adaptive depiction offered an opportunity for historical correction, and in that task, she succeeded. The media, however, failed to grasp and portray the complexity of the issues, resorting instead to underscoring the sensationalism and fanning the lucrative flames of the controversy.

NOTES

1. The movie is based on a poem by Rodolfo "Corky" Gonzales, *I Am Joaquín: Yo Soy Joaquín, an Epic Poem: With a Chronology of People and Events in Mexican and Mexican American History* (New York: Bantam, 1972).

2. The blog, website, and information center created by Alma López to gather up the discussion also contains helpful articles of the period from the newspapers and speeches by Catholic Church officials on the pedophilia reports and cases and their connection to church policies. See www.almalópez.com. From the e-mail section of the same website: "To me one of the very saddest aspects of the entire episode is the using of your art to drive yet another wedge in this community. As a scapegoat for all the pent up resentment and ill will; you have manifestly been very badly treated.—Nicky Watts, Santa Fe, New Mexico."

3. See Fray Angélico Chávez, *La Conquistadora: The Autobiography of an Ancient Statue* (Paterson, N.J.: St. Anthony Guild Press, 1954); for a novel about another Virgin icon, see idem, *The Lady from Toledo: An Historical Novel in Santa Fe* (Santa Fe: Friends of the Palace Press, 1993, reprint of the 1960 edition). Earlier work on La Conquistadora can be found in J. Manuel Espinosa, "The Virgin of the Reconquest of New Mexico," *Mid-America* 18 (April 1936): 79–87; and in Oakah L. Jones Jr., *Los Paisanos: Spanish Settlers on the Northern Frontier of New Spain* (Norman: University of Oklahoma Press, 1979).

4. See www.santafefiesta.org/history.

5. See Sarah Bronwen Horton, *The Santa Fe Fiesta, Reinvented: Staking Ethno-Nationalist Claims to a Disappearing Homeland* (Santa Fe: SAR Press, 2010), introduction.

6. See Ramón A. Gutiérrez, *When Jesus Came, the Corn Mothers Went Away: Marriage, Sexuality, and Power in New Mexico, 1500–1846* (Stanford, Calif.: Stanford University Press, 1991), 144–145; also see Ana Pacheco, ed., *La Herencia del Norte: Our Past, Our Present, Our Future* (Summer 1994, inaugural issue, Santa Fe: Gran Via, Inc.) for images, and about how the *cofradía's*, or confraternity's, women dress La Virgen, including in the costume stitched by Cochiti Pueblo member Dorothy Trujillo to symbolize Native-Hispano reconciliation around La Conquistadora, p. 33.

7. Douglas Kent Hall, "Matachines: Soldiers of the Virgin," *Borderlands* 11 (Spring, 1993): 13, an El Paso Community College local history project, at www.epcc.edu/nwlibrary/borderlands.

8. See www.santafefiesta.org; comparisons of Spanish origins can be viewed, for Seville, at www.exploreseville.com. See also Camille Flores-Turney, "Dressing La Conquistadora with Care and Devotion," in Pacheco, ed., *La Herencia*, including the discussion of La Conquistadora's 1990s tour of Seville, her reception there, and the gown sewed for her by *sevillanas*, p. 31.

9. Occupying an important position in full view of the tourist nexus, at one of its entry points into the plaza, the statue is said to have been one response to Alma

López's *Our Lady*. See Anne Constable, "Journey of Devotion," *Santa Fe New Mexican* (July 26, 2008), www.santafenewmexican.com.

10. See www.santafe.com for details of the statue's "imprisonment," or lost status at the border; see the blog on its journey at www.guadalupejourney.blogspot.com. The same website contains the video of its unveiling.

11. Gay and lesbian marriages are illegal in New Mexico to date, but the likeness of this new journey or travelogue and of its symmetry with gay and lesbian marriage, should not be lost as we evoke an LGBTQI (Lesbian, Gay, Bisexual, Transgender, Queer, Questioning, and Intersex) perspective, or a feminist one about the meaning of La Conquistadora, La Virgen de Guadalupe, and "Our Lady." In essence, the protestors of the López digital photo collage raised *Our Lady* as well into that pantheon or platform, acknowledging it as a symbol, albeit an improper one.

12. Archbishop Sheehan also said: "Instead of showing her as the innocent Mother of Jesus, she is shown as a tart or a street woman, not the Mother of God!" (May 22, 2001), www.archdiocesesantafe.org.

13. See Pablo Mitchell, *Coyote Nation: Sexuality, Race and Conquest in Modernizing New Mexico, 1880–1920* (Chicago: University of Chicago Press, 2005).

14. On an exhibition and Native American artists in the New Deal, including the implications and impact of recovery, see Jori Finkel, "In Santa Fe, on the Trail of New Deal Artists," March 12, 2008, www.nytimes.com; also see www.tfaoi.org for the Museum of International Folk Art's 1999 exhibit description of the impact of the New Deal on local artists.

15. See Kathleen Pyne, *Modernism and the Feminine Voice: O'Keeffe and the Women of the Stieglitz Circle* (Berkeley: University of California Press; Santa Fe: Georgia O'Keeffe Museum; Atlanta: High Museum of Art, 2007); and Barbara Buhler Lynes, Lesley Poling-Kempes, and Frederick W. Turner, eds., *Georgia O'Keeffe and New Mexico: A Sense of Place* (Princeton, N.J.: Princeton University Press; Santa Fe: Georgia O'Keeffe Museum, 2004).

16. On income distribution by ethnicity and the importance of context in interpreting the data, see Bureau of Business and Economic Research, http://bber.unm.edu/economy.htm; on poverty statistics, see the 2007 report of the Food Research and Action Center, Washington, DC: "State of the States," 83 and 84, on New Mexico's children, www.frac.org.

17. See Jeffrey Mitchell, *The Economic Importance of the Arts and Cultural Industries in Santa Fe County* (Albuquerque: University of New Mexico, 2004), 17.

18. Message dated March 17, 2001, in the e-mail section of www.almalopez.com. An example of the defense of artistic freedom and expression, in the e-mail section of the same website: "Will the Board allow Mr. Villegas, the archbishop, or anyone else for that matter, to come to the museum and summarily order

the removal of any other works, because they are sacrilegious, offensive, in bad taste, historically incorrect, badly composed, oddly dimensioned or too big or too small?"—Armando Durón.

19. Polly Summer, "Parish Completes a Character Transformation," *Albuquerque Journal* (August 16, 2008). The question would be whether the "character" in the title refers to the Alma López *Our Lady* or to the reclamation of the parish itself from the state and museum network. See www.guadalupejourney.blogspot.com.

20. See newer secondary work on the foundations of this discussion in Andrew Leo Lovato, *Santa Fe Hispanic Culture: Preserving Identity in a Tourist Town* (Albuquerque: University of New Mexico Press, 2004); and John M. Nieto-Phillips, *The Language of Blood: The Making of Spanish-American Identity in New Mexico, 1880s–1930s* (Albuquerque: University of New Mexico Press, 2004).

21. For an example of the propaganda and legislative initiatives promoting tourism and tax dollars, see www.nmfilmmuseum.org.

22. See Verónica C. García, "Poverty Isn't an Excuse: It's a Call to School Reform," *Albuquerque Journal* (February 9, 2008), for a discussion of the poverty indexes, adult education, and household incomes.

23. See J. Horvat II at www.tfp.org/current-campaigns/anti-blasphemy/the-Santa-fe-chill.html (November 8, 2007).

24. See MOIFA's mission statement at www.internationalfolkart.org.

25. See New Mexico Tourism Department National State and Regional Trends 2006 Governors Conference on Tourism, Slides 22, 23, at www.newmexico.org (2006_Research_Presentation.pdf).

26. Although not a New Mexico surname, López is popular there. On male forms of worship, see the rich bibliography on the *hermandades*, confraternities, or Penitente Brotherhood, including Michael P. Carroll, *The Penitente Brotherhood: Patriarchy and Hispano-Catholicism in New Mexico* (Baltimore, Md.: Johns Hopkins University Press, 2002). On female spiritual practices, see Jeanette Rodríguez, *Our Lady of Guadalupe: Faith and Empowerment among Mexican-American Women* (Austin: University of Texas Press, 1994); Marie Romero Cash and Siegfried Halus, *Living Shrines: Home Altars of New Mexico* (Santa Fe: Museum of New Mexico Press, 1998).

27. On religion and spirituality among Catholics in colonial New Mexico, see Gutiérrez, *When Jesus Came*; Charles Montgomery, *The Spanish Redemption: Heritage, Power and Loss on New Mexico's Upper Rio Grande* (Berkeley: University of California Press, 2002). On spiritual spaces, altars, and worship, see "Borderlands—Altars and Shrines" at www.spirithouses-shrines.ucdavis.edu. For one official Catholic stance on the faith traditions of New Mexico, see the message "Seeds of Struggle, Harvest of Faith: Four Hundred Years of Catholicism in New Mexico," January 1, 1998, by Archbishop Michael J. Sheehan, at www.archdiocesesantafe.org.

28. Agustín Gurza, "Our Lady of Controversy," *Los Angeles Times* (May 27, 2001), www.latimes.com.

29. See the women, many Catholic, who wrote to decry this aspect on the website tracking of the e-mail correspondence, articles, and scholarship produced during and after the controversy: www.almalopez.com.

30. Television and movie concerns, about which any protest whatsoever is rarely raised, include alarming statistics about the amount of violence, woman hating, and sexually explicit content children are watching. See "Children and TV Violence" at www.aacap.org.

31. A number of works in Chicana studies have cited Yolanda M. López's *Walking Guadalupe* (1978) on the cover of the June-July 1984 issue of *Fem*. See Karen Mary Dávalos, *Yolanda M. López* (Los Angeles: UCLA Chicano Studies Research Center Press, 2008), 22. For other interesting linkages in the case being made for women priests, for example, see the discussion of Yolanda M. López's Virgen de Guadalupe series at www.womenpriests.org.

32. See www.almalopez.com.

33. On www.almalopez.com, see Chicano dissent against the depiction: "In the year 2001, some people, mainly from California, with the aid of California artist, Alma López, and the administrative staff of the New Mexico Museum of International Folk Arts, tried to kill La Virgen de Guadalupe, the apparition that became sacred to the people of Mexico, just as Tonantzin, the indigenous goddess, had been sacred, and whom the Catholic Spaniards had also tried to kill, and failed.—Octavio Romano (5/26)."

34. On several debates surrounding teachers' efforts to assign the primary and only textbook in the discipline of Chicana/o studies, see "Is Teaching 'La Causa' Grounds for Firing?" (December 3, 1998), www.rethinkingschools.org; on other teachers similarly accused or dismissed, see "LA School Teacher Fired for Being Too 'Afrocentric'; Arizona Bill Proposes to Prohibit Teachings Critical of Western Civilization," *Democracy NOW!* (Pacifica Radio, June 18, 2008), www.democracynow.org.

35. Examples include the following comments: "Like you, although other issues are clear and obvious, I believe the real problem is that many men can't tolerate independent, self-assured women."—Freda Elliot (May 22, 2001); "Your strong images of La Virgen de Guadalupe has influenced a lot on my Chicana Lesbian identity."—Chary Olmedo (May 22, 2001), both at www.almalopez.com.

5

Art Comes for the Archbishop

THE SEMIOTICS OF CONTEMPORARY CHICANA
FEMINISM AND THE WORK OF ALMA LÓPEZ

Luz Calvo

T
HE VIRGIN OF GUADALUPE is omnipresent in Chicano/a
visual space.[1] She is painted on car windows, tattooed on
shoulders or backs, emblazoned on neighborhood walls,
and silk-screened on T-shirts sold at local flea markets. Pe-
riodically, her presence is manifested in miraculous apparitions: on a tree near Watsonville, California; on a water tank, a car bumper,
or a freshly made tortilla. She is the sorrowful mother, a figure who embodies
the suffering of Chicano/a and Mexican populations in the context of colonization, racism, and economic disenfranchisement.

The Virgin of Guadalupe is a polyvalent sign, able to convey multiple and
divergent meanings and deployed by different groups for contradictory political ends. For example, the Catholic Church deploys the image of the Virgin
of Guadalupe in service of its regressive sexual politics. However, progressive
movements have also carried the image of the Virgin of Guadalupe to signify
resistance to colonization and economic exploitation, as in the War of Mexican Independence and in the United Farm Workers' struggle for economic
justice. Chicano/a cultural workers—from graffiti artists to novelists—use the
Virgin of Guadalupe as a sign of racial solidarity, for she is imagined to have
brown skin,[2] or as a sign of transnational solidarity, for she is the patron saint

of Mexico. Chicano/a artists have reproduced and reinterpreted the Virgin of Guadalupe in their *retablos*, paintings, murals, posters, films, performance, and literature. Almost without exception, Chicano/a films include the image of Guadalupe in their sets, nodding to her importance in Chicano/a visual space. And merchants in Chicano/a neighborhoods use the Virgin of Guadalupe to sell their product: it is commonplace to see a mural devoted to the Virgin on the outside of a neighborhood liquor store or to find Virgin of Guadalupe auto "air fresheners" at the car wash.

Because of her ubiquity and her polyvalence, the image of the Virgin of Guadalupe is a sign that is especially available for semiotic resignification and cultural transformation. Alma López, a Chicana lesbian artist, has seized this semiotic possibility, creating a series of digital images that break open and transfigure previous interpretations and uses of the Virgin. López's images make manifest the sexuality and desire that are embedded in Chicano/a attachments to the image of the Virgin of Guadalupe. As might be expected, López's work has been quite controversial. Her 1999 digital collage *Our Lady* incited demonstrations, community meetings, and letters to the editor when it was displayed at the Museum of International Folk Art in Santa Fe, New Mexico.[3] Angered by López's image, a vocal group of Chicano and Catholic activists called for its removal from the museum. Rhetorically reducing the image to the language of fashion, these activists repeatedly described López's piece as a depiction of "the Virgin of Guadalupe in a bikini." The demonstrators gained the support of Santa Fe archbishop Michael J. Sheehan, who called the piece "insulting and sacrilegious," asserting that in López's image the Virgin is "shown as a tart or a street woman."[4] Chicano nationalists tried to maintain control over the meaning of the Virgin of Guadalupe and contain her within the semiotic structure of the Catholic Church.

The protests that surrounded *Our Lady* caused considerable consternation and debate within Chicano/a communities in New Mexico and beyond.[5] Ultimately, however, López's defenders successfully deployed First Amendment arguments and the New Mexico museum's Committee on Sensitive Materials decided that the work would remain on display. Undoubtedly, free speech arguments have strategic value—that is, they protect a space for the public articulation of queer desire and the display of images that contest fixed and static ideas about cultural identity. However, First Amendment arguments cannot begin to account for the kind of cultural work achieved by queer and feminist Chicano/a art. Speaking from the position of a queer Chicana cultural critic, I argue that rights-based arguments assume that we (artists and critics of color, queers, and other disenfranchised people) already have what we seek to defend, namely, equal footing with the imagined subject of Western liberal democracy. In my view, López's art poses a critique and challenge that is about more than free speech or even equal rights.

López's art breaks open a public, cultural space for the articulation of queer Chicana desire. This desire is at once sexual and political. Her images seduce the spectator into new desiring positions by exposing Chicano/a libidinal investments—conscious and unconscious—in the Virgin of Guadalupe. Her images mobilize and disturb these investments, channeling Chicano/a desire in queer directions. Significantly, *Our Lady* refuses to indulge in the disavowal of the body that informs conventional, religious representations of the Virgin. Instead, *Our Lady* represents the interlinkage of racial identities and sexual and political desires while, at the same time, pointing to the constitutive ambivalence at the heart of Chicano/a—and other—identity formations.

Working in digital collage, as well as in other media, López—a relatively young artist—has already produced a sizable oeuvre, much of which is displayed on her website, www.almalopez.com. López is a public artist and the Internet allows her work to circulate beyond the confines of the museum or art gallery. When López's work appears in art exhibits and galleries, most of her prints are relatively small, and the three images I discuss in this essay are all 14" × 17". López's images are more commonly viewed on computer screens, as individual users visit her website. The scale of López's work is most important in her large digital murals, which have been installed on the outside walls of buildings in East Los Angeles and at San Francisco's Galleria de la Raza. In these works, López locates herself within the Mexican and Chicano/a mural tradition, which changes community space by producing art on the walls of housing projects, public buildings, local businesses, and so forth. As another way of circulating her art, López has produced art for the cover of a number of important books in Chicano/a cultural studies and for a number of important Chicano/a conferences. The book covers and posters circulate her art in bookstores, universities, living rooms, and dormitories.[6] Through her diverse artistic interventions, López is having a significant impact on Chicano/a visual space.

In *Our Lady*, López reconfigures the Virgin of Guadalupe, opening up her feminist and queer potential. *Our Lady* makes reference to the "original" image of La Virgen de Guadalupe, which hangs in the basilica in Mexico City.[7]

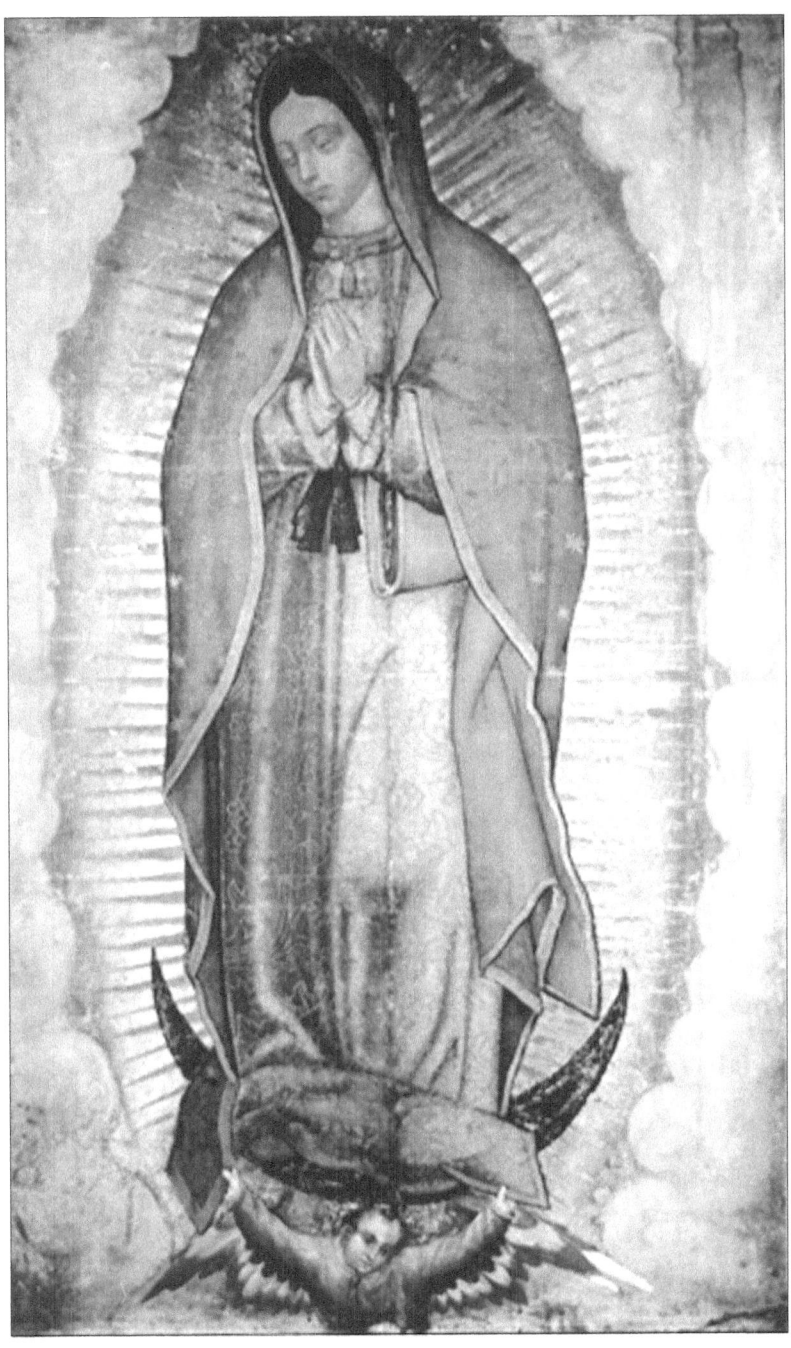

5.1. Original Virgen de Guadalupe image, Mexico City, circa 1531.

In the original image, the Virgen is posed with hands in prayer and eyes cast down. She wears a long-sleeved gown, which covers her from neck to toe. Over her gown, a blue mantle drapes her head and the back of her body. The mantle is adorned with gold stars. She stands upon a dark crescent moon, held aloft by a little angel.

López's *Our Lady* presents significant changes to the original version: In her image, López draws attention to the brown female body by exposing more of it. López's image features a photograph of Latina performance artist Raquel Salinas, her legs, arms, and midriff bare. Salinas is clothed only in roses, a symbol of the "proof" of the Virgin's 1531 apparition in Mexico. López modifies some other characteristics of the traditional image: the patterned rose-colored gown, which usually obscures the Virgin's body, is here rendered as background. The Virgin's traditional starry blue shawl is now draped and folded on a platform at the bottom of the frame. A modified blue gray cloak covers the model's shoulders—this one filled in with the image of the Aztec goddess Coyolxauhqui, the rebellious daughter. The angel who holds up the moon in the traditional image has been replaced with a bare-breasted (and pierced) Latina (Raquel Gutierrez) superimposed over a butterfly. Finally, and importantly, López changes the stance of the Virgin of Guadalupe, who traditionally stands demurely with eyes cast downward and her hands together in prayer. In López's image, the model has her hands on her hips and her gaze cast forward defiantly, toward the spectator.[8]

López draws from earlier Chicana feminist artistic engagements with the Virgin of Guadalupe by artists such as Ester Hernández and Yolanda M. López. Hernández's *La Virgen de Guadalupe Defendiendo los Derechos de los Xicanos* (1976) and Yolanda M. López's *Guadalupe Triptych* (1978) also refigure the pose of the Virgen. These images represent the Virgin of Guadalupe in active stances and with contemporary Chicana identities: practicing karate or running a marathon, as a seamstress or an *abuelita* (grandmother). In other images, these two artists explore the sexual potential of the Virgin: Hernández's *La Ofrenda* (1988) depicts a tattoo of the Virgin on the back of a Chicana lesbian, while Yolanda M. López's *Walking Guadalupe* (1978) portrays the Virgin walking in a dress and open-toed heels. Like Alma López's *Our Lady*, these two images were received with threats and, in some cases, violence.[9]

The level of controversy that attends to feminist and queer revisions of the Virgin of Guadalupe reveals the high stakes of Chicano/a cultural identity—and its constitutive ambivalence. Images—such as the Virgin of

Guadalupe—that purport to represent identity are inevitably locked in a paradoxical position in that they can never fully achieve their goal: this is the gap between the signifier and the signified and the ambivalence at the heart of representation and identity. To use an example, the declarative utterance "I am Chicana" can never capture the complexity of the subject, who both exceeds the declaration (is more than that) and inevitably falls short (can never be Chicana enough). As in this example, there is always a disjuncture between representation and the subject. Attempts to disavow this gap anchor the meaning of ethnic identity in static, fixed, and often retrograde ways, resulting in what Emma Pérez—drawing on Michel Foucault—names a "fascist militancy."[10] Pérez productively considers Foucault's provocation: "How does one keep from being a fascist, even (especially) when one believes oneself to be a revolutionary militant?"[11] Emma Pérez is correct in warning us of the potential political danger posed by those who try to control, police, and anchor the meaning of Chicano/a identity—or, by extension, the meaning of the Virgin of Guadalupe.

Reading contemporary Chicano/a politics as a space where "power polices desire," Emma Pérez argues: "We are threatened once again by a reemergence of uncompromising nationalist movements in which feminisms are dismissed as bourgeois, in which queer voices are scoffed at as a white thing, in which anyone who does not sustain the 'family values' of modernist, patriarchal nationalism is not tolerated and is often silenced."[12] In the case of the controversy surrounding Alma López's *Our Lady*, Emma Pérez is exactly on point, for it has been precisely those elements of the Chicano community that remain invested in "patriarchal nationalism" (namely, the church and male nationalist activists) who have been most vigorous in their attempts to silence the Chicana lesbian artist.[13]

The controversy surrounding López's art exposes the danger of fascism that arises from attempts to erase ambivalence. The Virgin of Guadalupe has the potential to be the sign of this fascist impulse. In a psychoanalytic reading, Emma Pérez argues: "The nationalist imperative is to move back in time, a regression, a return to the mother, but the mother cannot be Malinche. She must be La Virgen de Guadalupe; she cannot be sexual."[14] Nationalists mobilize Oedipus to structure Chicano/a identity in a heterosexual direction, embedding it in relations of patriarchal power and the incest taboo. However, as lesbian scholars such as Teresa de Lauretis have argued, the meaning of Oedipal structures is never as static—or heterosexual—as it might first appear.[15]

In Alma López's art, the Virgin of Guadalupe is claimed by Chicana lesbians, troubling the heterosexual matrix of Chicano/a nationalism. The nationalists root their politics in a mythic past and an image of totality that insists on the mother's heterosexual desire. However, Chicana feminism also mobilizes a notion of totality, although differently inscribed. In Chicana feminist art, the image of the Virgin signifies plentitude and omniscience: she is *nuestra madre* (our mother) who watches over us in the context of racism, sexual violence, economic injustice, and, even, homophobia.

Postcolonial critic Homi K. Bhabha, explaining the working of identification, argues that "identity is never an a priori, nor a finished product; it is only ever the problematic process of access to an image of totality."[16] In Chicano/a contexts, the Virgin is the sign of such totality, hence her significance to the production of Chicano/a identifications. While Chicano nationalists assume that identity is unified, fixed, and needs to be guarded from outside influence (such as queer sexualities), postcolonial critics such as Bhabha and Emma Pérez understand identity as something produced by always ambivalent and never stable psychic processes. What Bhabha means when he writes of "access to an image of totality" is a plentitude and fulfillment that can never be fully achieved: it is the desire for an impossible object, whether it be the mother or complete freedom.

The psychoanalytic concept of identification provides a tool for understanding identity as an open-ended process, never complete and always fraught with ambivalent desires. Identification is the process by which a subject introjects an object from the outside. Introjection takes an object from outside (another subject or an image) and incorporates it into one's own ego. The relationship between young Chicana fans and late pop star Selena is an excellent example of the way that identification works in Chicana contexts. This identification is the subject of *Corpus: A Home Movie for Selena*, a 1999 documentary by Lourdes Portillo. Her film opens with a scene of young Chicana fans lip-synching the songs of the recently deceased Selena. The young women emulate Selena's style, body gestures, and dance moves. In this identification with Selena, the girls introject Selena into their own egos, or sense of self. The young girls are able to deal with the loss of their idol (in Freudian terms, their "ego-ideal") by keeping her alive inside themselves. Sigmund Freud provides a more trivial example of this process of introjection: "A child who was unhappy over the loss of a kitten declared straight out that now he himself was the kitten, and accordingly crawled about on all fours, would not eat at the table, etc."[17] This example of the lost kitten illustrates the relationship between identification and loss. The child's pain over the loss of the kitten leads the child to incorporate the pet into his own ego (his sense of self): the child, in order to keep the kitten alive, becomes the kitten. In psychoanalytic terms, the "ego" (a psychoanalytic term for identity) is comprised entirely of identifications with objects that have been lost.

When Chicana girls (and, not incidentally, Chicano drag queens) impersonate Selena, it is a melancholic identification that constitutes the ego/identity along the axis of loss (Selena's death) and plentitude (Selena's Chicana body). Chicano/a identification with Selena is—like all identifications—ambivalent and aggressive: her death, while experienced as an intense loss, is also an opportunity to replace Selena, that is, the opportunity to be the next pop star, to be adored and to be loved. In a footnote to her discussion of Selena's death, Emma Pérez reports a conversation she had with Teresa de Lauretis.[18] The two scholars watched a 1995 Univisión interview with Yolanda Saldívar, Selena's murderer and the president of her fan club. They speculate that Saldívar was less likely to be motivated by lesbian desire (this rumor circulated widely) than by the desire to be Selena: "a psychological condition experienced by obsessed fans who want to become the star."[19] Like the infamous Aimée discussed by Jacques Lacan, Saldívar's aggression, notes Emma Pérez, "has linked herself in memory, in history, to Selena."[20] As is often the case in psychological phenomena, this extreme form of fandom shares a similar psychical structure to the more benign forms of fan desire: in both cases, identification with the star masks an aggressive component.

For her fans, Selena's brown female body signifies a plentitude in the context of a racial imaginary that devalues, degrades, and disparages female and brown bodies. In hegemonic U.S. cultural texts, brown female bodies are simultaneously sexualized and repudiated, desired and found disgusting. The brown female body is invested with particular social meanings resulting from her position at the intersection of racial and sexual categories; her body becomes the repository for U.S. cultural anxieties about both sexual and racial difference. In the case of Selena—as with the Virgin of Guadalupe—the brown female body is the cultural sign that encourages Chicana identification, even though, on the surface, these two figures appear to be very different. Selena's body is exposed, celebrated, and commodified, while the Virgin's body

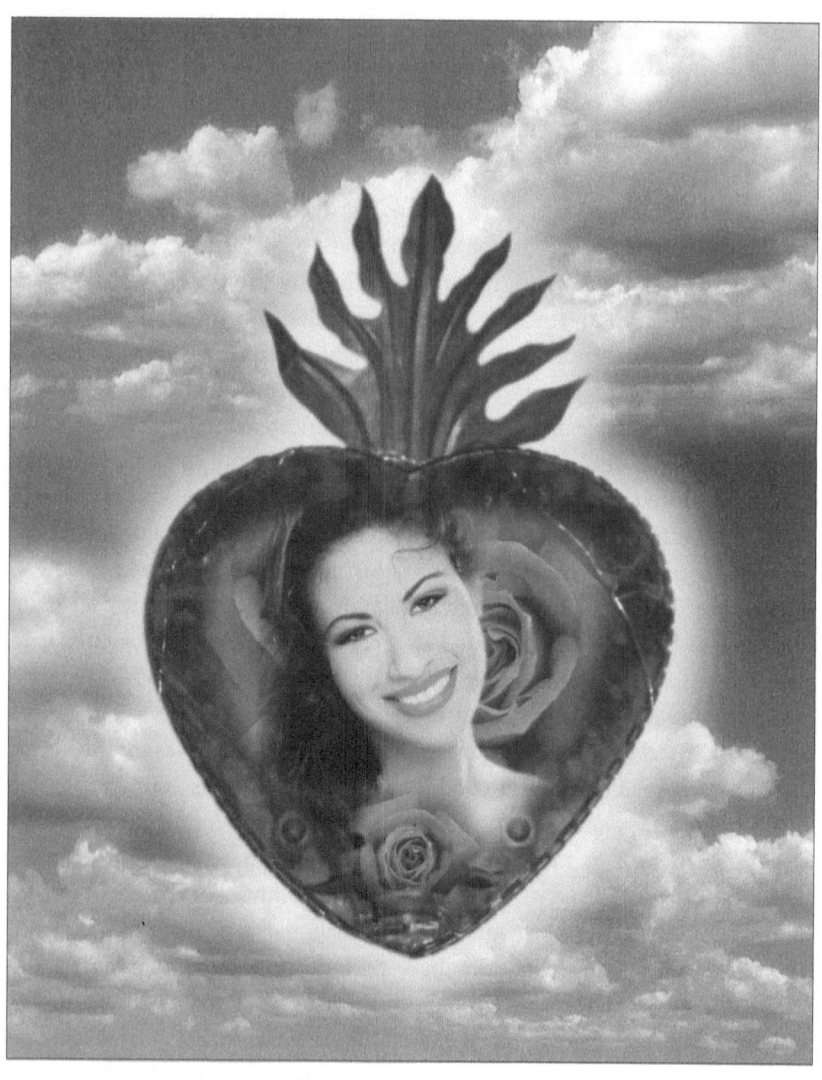

5.2.   *Selena in the Sky with Roses.* Digital print by Alma López, © 2000.
       Courtesy of Alma López.

is hidden and disavowed. Politically, however, identification with Selena and the Virgin both allow for a certain recuperation of the brown female body, a possibility that can occur with public figures, either religious or pop.

Sandra Cisneros, in her essay "Guadalupe the Sex Goddess," directly addresses the issue of Chicana investment in the representation of brown female bodies. Cisneros's essay powerfully engages the slippery, mutually embedded categories of racial and sexual difference. Writing of her relationship to the Virgin of Guadalupe, Cisneros reveals a desire to lift the Virgin's dress, to see her underwear and her sex: "When I see La Virgen de Guadalupe I want to lift her dress as I did my dolls' and look to see if she comes with chones, and does her panocha look like mine, and does she have dark nipples too? Yes, I am certain she does."[21]

Cisneros's desire to see the Virgin's body underscores the complexity of the nexus of racial and sexual difference in the formation of Chicana subjectivity. Within a cultural context where brown bodies and female bodies are undervalued, Cisneros wants to see her own image of her body (her "body-ego," in Freud's terms) reflected in a sacred icon. Perhaps paradoxically, she also constructs her self or body-ego in relation to a pornographic film featuring a white woman.

Cisneros writes: "Once, watching a porn film, I saw a sight that terrified me. It was the film star's panocha—a tidy, elliptical opening, pink and shiny like a rabbit's ear. To make matters worse, it was shaved."[22] If the sight of the Anglo porn star's genitals evoked in Cisneros feelings of horror, it was because of a difference that was at once racially and sexually coded. Here, the Lacanian concept of lack has application not (only) to the lack of the phallus but to the lack of the "white slit" that Cisneros witnessed in the pornography film. Cisneros interprets the porn star's genitals in relation to her own self-image: "I think what startled me most was the realization that my own sex has no resemblance to this woman's. My sex, dark as an orchid, rubbery and blue purple as a pulpo, an octopus, does not look nice and tidy, but otherworldly."[23] Cisneros uses figurative language to describe her genitals ("an orchid," "an octopus"). The image of her Chicana body is constructed through language, including the language of pornography, religious iconography, and poetic metaphor. In short, her brown, Chicana body is not an essential characteristic but rather a position within a grid that figures racial and sexual difference inside particular social symbolic structures.

Cisneros's description of her horror at the sight of the porn star's genitals recalls a scenario imagined by Freud: the scene of castration anxiety. In Freud's scenario, a young boy is surprised to learn that his mother does not have a penis. The scene of castration constitutes the boy as threatened: his penis could be taken away. At the same time, the scene reveals to the boy that he is "endowed"; that is, he realizes that he has something his mother does not.

A few notes of caution for those who would reject Freud's account outright. First, this is an allegory of sexual difference and should not be read literally. Second, this account of the constitution of male subjectivity is firmly entrenched in historically situated, patriarchal social relations; it is not ahistorical. Finally, the male subjectivity that is constituted in this scenario is thoroughly ambivalent. In her Lacanian reading of this scenario, Judith Butler argues that being endowed with the penis (or, in other terms, "phallus") is "a symbolic position . . . which is only partially and vainly approximated by those marked masculine beings who vainly and partially occupy that position within language."[24] The scene of castration constructs a masculinity that is in perpetual crisis.

David L. Eng makes productive use of Freud's allegory of castration in his book *Racial Castration*. He argues that feminist and queer theories that deploy "psychoanalytic theory to deconstruct naturalizing discourses of sexual, and in particular heterosexual, difference must be rethought to include viable accounts of race as well."[25] Eng thoughtfully undertakes this project by reading race back into psychoanalysis, finding in the case of castration that "castration is always racial castration."[26] Drawing on Eng's theoretical intervention (which I can only gloss here), I read Cisneros's essay in terms of racial castration anxiety.

For, in some sense, Cisneros's fantasy of lifting the Virgin's dress is also a search for the penis—that is, for a symbol of cultural power denied to Chicana subjects. Here, "the" penis would figure both sexual and racial difference. Cisneros's claim that she is searching for a "panocha like hers" hides another desire, that is, to find the Chicana mother's penis. This claim, of course, takes Freud's scenario in a different direction. However, if we read castration to be about the binary of presence/absence, then, perhaps, it is productive to consider "race" (imagined as manifested on or through the body) in these terms. The enigma of the meaning of "race" for racialized subjects produces a number of questions, captured in Cisneros's allegory of lifting the Virgin's dress—which can only be interpreted as a scenario to find the social symbolic meaning of her sexed and raced body. What she finds is an ambivalent position: while she claims to find her body under the Virgin of Guadalupe's gown, Cisneros's rhetorical consideration of pornography demonstrates that the Chicana body is overdetermined by the cultural binary of virgin/whore and presence/absence.

López's *Our Lady* provides yet another response to the binary of virgin/whore, presenting the materiality of the brown female body as a site of desire. While Cisneros explores Chicana identification (implicitly heterosexual, because of the author's explicitly heterosexual—though queer-friendly—public identity) with the Virgin's brown body, López presents the brown body of the Virgin as desirable, perhaps even as seductress, thus encouraging and inciting a queer reading. The queer potential of the Virgin of Guadalupe is made explicit in *Encuentro*, which depicts the celestial meeting of La Sirena and La Virgen de Guadalupe, and in *Lupe & Sirena in Love*, which depicts the two in a sexual embrace.

Encuentro introduces three iconic elements that recur throughout López's work: La Virgen, La Sirena (the mermaid), and La Mariposa (the butterfly). The Viceroy butterfly—an orange butterfly with black markings—is a recurring motif in López's images. In an artist statement, López discusses her choice of the Viceroy butterfly, which resembles, and indeed mimics, the better-known Monarch butterfly. The Monarch butterfly, unlike the Viceroy, is poisonous to its predators. López explains: "The Viceroy pretends to be something it is not just to be able to exist. For me, the Viceroy mirrors parallel and intersecting histories of being different or 'other' even within our own communities. Racist attitudes see us Latinos as criminals and an economic burden, and families may see us as perverted or deviant. So from outside and inside our communities, we are perceived as something we are not. When in essence we are very vulnerable Viceroy butterflies, just trying to live and survive."[27]

There is a play of recognition and misrecognition suggested by the metaphor of the Viceroy butterfly. Ultimately, this butterfly (the queer Chicano/a subject) must forego the possibility of recognition; in order to survive, she must mimic the Monarch (someone less vulnerable than herself). In *Our Lady*, the placement of the bare-breasted, pierced Chicana superimposed on the Viceroy butterfly sustains the metaphor equating the butterfly with the queer Chicano/a subject. Like Cisneros, López uses figurative language and images to represent Chicana subjectivity and bodies.

To represent the Virgin of Guadalupe's love interest, López chooses the mermaid from the popular Mexican game *lotería*. In *lotería*, as in bingo, players hold a card with a grid. In the Mexican version, the grid is filled not with numbers but with images that map a Mexican national imaginary and construct Mexican identity.[28] In this way, the game figures identity in much the same way as I have discussed it in this essay, as a grid in which one finds one's (albeit ambivalent) place. The categories of people depicted on the *lotería* cards reflect (often problematic) national, class, racial, and gendered categories.

Perhaps the most problematic cards are those that figure race: there is a card picturing a black dandy entitled "El Negrito,"[29] and another picturing an Indian wearing a feather headdress and carrying a bow and arrow, entitled "El Apache." Similarly, racialized gender is reproduced in a conventional fashion. In a card entitled "La Dama," a slender, light-skinned woman wears a ladies' suit and carries a matching handbag. Masculinity is portrayed on a card entitled "El Valiente," portraying a mestizo working-class man wielding a machete, and on another even less flattering card entitled "El Borracho," which portrays a drunk mestizo man with a bottle stumbling on a sidewalk. "El Catrín," in contrast, shows a light-skinned, upper-class effete man dressed in a tuxedo. Within the grid of *mexicanidad* mapped by *lotería*, La Sirena stands out as a hybrid subject: she is part woman, part fish. This Sirena appears to be of mestiza heritage because instead of the usual blonde hair this mermaid has long, wavy black hair. She is yet another figural representation of Chicana subjectivity.

As we have seen, *Encuentro* is structured by the combination of three elements—*lotería*'s mermaid, the traditional Virgin of Guadalupe, and a butterfly. Semiotics holds that meaning is derived from two axes: selection (the paradigmatic axis) and combination (the syntagmatic axis). Meaning is constructed from the manner in which elements are selected and combined. The string of symbols on the *lotería* card is an excellent example of what semioticians call a "paradigmatic axis." Out of a set of possible *lotería* characters, the artist selects one, La Sirena. Just as the artist selects La Sirena instead of, say, El Apache, she chooses the Viceroy butterfly instead of the Monarch butterfly and La Virgen de Guadalupe instead of an image of Tonantzin (a pre-Columbian goddess). And yet, because these other—unchosen—elements exist in what Victor Burgin calls the "popular preconscious," these elements linger in the field of meaning evoked by López's image, the "pre-text."[30] The popular preconscious is defined by Burgin as "those ever-shifting contents which we may reasonably suppose can be called to mind by the majority of individuals in

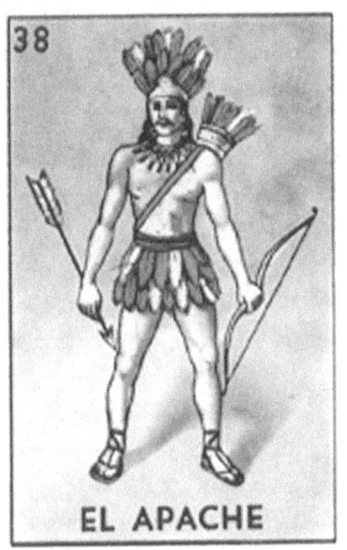

EL APACHE

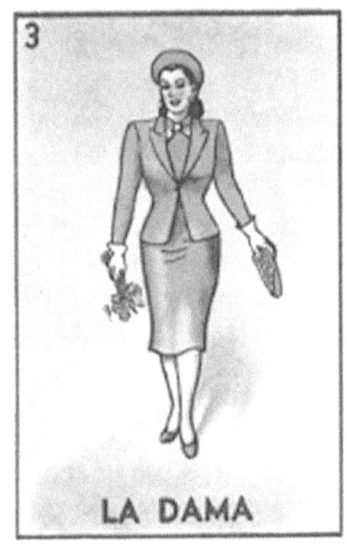

LA DAMA

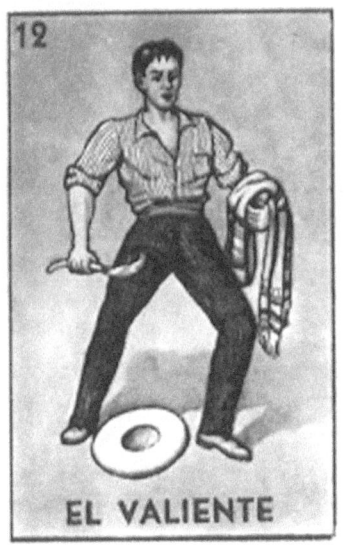

EL VALIENTE

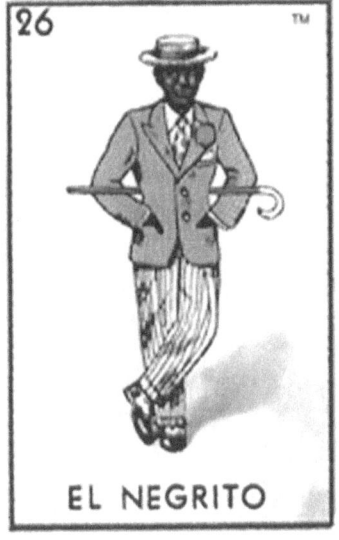

EL NEGRITO

5.3. *Lotería* cards.

a given society at a particular moment in history; that which is 'common knowledge.'"[31] Burgin, however, does not account for the different knowledges of those not in "the majority." In the case of the elements in López's work, the pre-text is not common knowledge for hegemonic U.S. subjects, while it most likely is recognized by Chicanos/as. Of course, this does not mean that the image is unreadable to non-Chicanos/as but simply that the pre-text will yield a different set of images along the paradigmatic chain. For example, the composition of López's *Encuentro* recalls Michelangelo's portrayal of the creation of Adam on the Sistine Chapel ceiling, a scene that is in the preconscious of many, but not all, educated in Western cultural traditions. Thus, it should be clear that chains of association are open-ended, which means that a "meaning" of any particular image is never fixed or sealed. Rather, there are multiple meanings, and the same image will register differently (produce another set of associations) with each spectator, depending in large part on their cultural location.

Subaltern artistic practice makes use of a postcolonial preconscious, which is distinct from the "common knowledge" of the society at large. The subaltern's specialized knowledge produces a particular kind of viewing pleasure for those who "get it." For example, a chain of linguistic associations along the paradigmatic axis suggests queerness: mariposa (butterfly) is connected to the words *"marimacha"* (dyke) and *"maricón"* (fag) through the prefix *"mari"* (and the prefix is etymologically linked back to María, the Virgin Mary). Moreover, queer meaning is also constructed along the syntagmatic axis, that is, by the combination of two female forms in a sexual relationship.

In *Lupe and Sirena in Love*, the three iconic elements of *Encuentro*—the mermaid, the Virgin of Guadalupe, and the Viceroy butterfly—are combined with more images: the cityscape of Los Angeles; the wall at the Mexico-U.S. border replete with a mural of the traditional image of La Virgen, superimposed with "1848," the year of the signing of the treaty of Guadalupe-Hidalgo; and a photograph of a man being chased by an agent of the *migra* (U.S. Immigration and Naturalization "Service"). Three blond cherubs holding a gold ribbon and bouquets of roses frame this scene. In this image, there is a depth of field and layering of images, which contrasts with the relative flatness of *Encuentro*.

Finally, both *Encuentro* and *Lupe and Sirena in Love* suggest a Chicana lesbian primal scene: the fantasy of *nuestra madre* (our mother) in a sexual embrace with another woman.[32] This imagined scene stages the conception of queer desire in explicitly Chicano/a terms. In *Lupe and Sirena in Love*, queer desire is inseparable from its racial and cultural context and from its geographic location in the Mexico-U.S. borderlands. Moreover, the sense of place mapped in López's images reflects geography more akin to psychic space than physical space.[33] By placing the Los Angeles cityscape and the fence at the Mexico-U.S. border in one frame, López begins to map Chicana psychic geography as a transnational formation. Moreover, its geography is not that of the rational, imperialist cartographer but rather the layered space of the unconscious, where past and present, here and there, can exist in one image.

Collage, by self-consciously recycling images, enacts the postmodern notion that one cannot begin from outside of existing image regimes. Instead, cultural workers intervene by reworking preexisting images and remapping existing fantasies. Collage as an art form takes existing images and through a process of selection and combination shifts the terms of their meaning. Collage is not unlike the process of the constitution of the postmodern subject, who must piece together a self, however fragmented and shifting, by sampling bits and pieces from different histories, iconographies, and relationships. López uses the digital format to make transparent the process of assembly and juxtaposition. Digital collage differs from traditional collage because digital images are endlessly available and cut-and-paste technology allows artists to resize, blend, and create images that appear "seamless." López's images, however, are not seamless; instead, they call attention to the cut-and-paste technique used by the artist to piece together her statement.

Ironically, one of López's most vociferous detractors, New Mexican artist Pedro Romero Sedeño, astutely reads her work as "a hodge-podge of ideas digitally mixed." He compares López's art to Mary Shelley's Dr. Frankenstein, who, "in his lab, assembled human body parts, and was able to fabricate or interpret his own kind of being."[34] While Romero Sedeño intended this interpretation pejoratively, I think that his analogy is evocative, suggesting both Chicano/a and postmodern aesthetic practices, and the possibility of assembling new subject positions from a "hodge-podge." The form of López's work draws attention to the process of fabrication and thus to the hybridity of Chicana identity. Her work challenges Chicano/a nationalist ideologies that disavow mixedness in favor of a fantasy of "pure" Chicano/a identity.

There is, I think, a further similarity among collage, postcolonial hybridity, and the Chicano/a aesthetic stance called "*rasquachismo*."[35] Tomás Ybarra Frausto has described *rasquachismo* as a "stance rooted in resourcefulness and adaptability, yet ever mindful of aesthetics."[36] Poverty fuels the practice of *rasquachismo*, for it is a "making do," a piecing together, selecting from bits and pieces recovered from other uses or cheaply acquired. Ybarra Frausto finds that such "utilization of available resources makes for syncretism, juxtaposition, and integration."[37] However, reliance on things at hand does not mean that a highly developed code does not exist, or that items are selected at random. Rather, *rasquache* aesthetics provide an apt example of a language structured by rules of selection and combination. In *rasquachismo*, the rules of selection run counter to bourgeois sensibilities, and, indeed, this is part of their pleasure.

Like *rasquachismo*, digital art uses selection and combination to create new meanings. López does not attempt to create a queer Chicana viewing pleasure from scratch; instead, she culls from existing images of Mexican and Chicana women. She chooses from popular art forms rather than from so-called high art; she selects her "bits and pieces" from the existing repertoire of working-class Chicano/a visual culture. While López, as an artist working in digital media, has access to high technology, she uses that technology to develop a digital *rasquachismo*. Like many Chicano/a artists, López does not reject the popular cultural practices; instead, she deploys *rasquachismo* as an aesthetic stance. She selects and combines images from popular and available sources, she uses layering and bright colors, and she juxtaposes religious iconography with photographs of her friends.

In both its popular practice and its academic production, *rasquachismo* exhibits a particularly nonnormative—indeed, queer—pleasure, as in the following definition proffered by Ybarra Frausto: "In the realm of taste, to be rasquache is to be unfettered and unrestrained, to favor the elaborate over the simple, the flamboyant over the severe. Bright colors are preferred to somber, high intensity to low, the shimmering and pattern filling all available space with bold display."[38] In this vivid account, a queer camp aesthetic is embedded in a distinctly Chicano/a artistic practice through the "unrestrained," "the flamboyant," and "the shimmering." *Rasquachismo* is not an essential characteristic of either gay or Chicano/a communities but rather an aesthetic stance that is historically and culturally produced.

In its rejection of bourgeois sensibility, *rasquachismo* is a cultural practice that does not care what the neighbors think, wears too-bright colors and a flower in its hair. An example of Chicano/a *rasquache* aesthetics is depicted in the novel *The Miraculous Day of Amalia Gomez*, by gay Chicano author John

Rechy. In his introduction to the second edition, Rechy describes his encounter with a woman who becomes Amalia, the protagonist of his novel:

[At Thrifty's Drugstore] I . . . encountered one of the most resplendent women I've ever seen, a gorgeous Mexican-American woman in her upper thirties, a bit heavier than she might like to think, but quite lush and sexy. She wore high-heeled sling shoes—and a tight red dress, to show off proud breasts, but she had added a ruffle there to avoid any hint of vulgarity, a fashion that defied all fashion except her own. She had a luxuriance of black shiny hair, and into its natural waves she had inserted . . . a real red rose.[39]

Throughout this novel, Amalia is constructed as an icon of Latina suffering and working-class beauty, by an author most widely known for his portrayals of gay hustlers. Amalia's style is staunchly *rasquache*, produced by a gay author in admiration for such women. This novel stages an extradiegetic identification of the gay Chicano author with the working-class, *rasquache*, Chicana protagonist. Rechy's brilliant staging of this identification reveals an intersection of queer and Chicano/a working-class desire.

Mobilizing a similar *rasquache* aesthetic—with its embedded queer potential—López has revised and recontexualized Chicana fascination with the Virgin of Guadalupe. In *Encuentro* and *Lupe and Sirena in Love*, López stages a primal fantasy, that is, a fantasy that constitutes a desiring subject. As in other primal fantasies that produce cultural locations and incite all kinds of desires (sexual, political, and racial), López's art focuses attention on Chicana feminist and queer Chicana subject formation. López depicts a scene of lesbian seduction as a founding moment of Chicana subjectivity. In so doing, she places a queer Chicana love story on the same symbolic terrain as the apparition of the Virgin of Guadalupe and thus transfigures the Virgin of Guadalupe. Making productive use of the visual image of everyday Chicano/a life, López's images begin to create a Chicana feminist and queer iconography. Far from starting from something completely "new," López's art reworks (and reveals) the political-sexual desire that is latent in the omnipresent image of the suffering Virgin. By mobilizing the semiotic processes of selection and combination and occupying the Chicano/a aesthetic stance of *rasquachismo*, López's images successfully invite and sustain queer interpretations of the Virgin of Guadalupe and open polymorphous and perverse spaces for sexuality and desire in Chicano/a imaginaries.

In conclusion, reading López's artistic reimaginings of the Virgin of Guadalupe through Sandra Cisneros's desire to see the Virgin's brown body has revealed the constitutive lack that fuels all Chicano/a identifications with the Virgin of Guadalupe. It becomes clear that the imagined brownness of the Virgin has always structured Chicano/a allegiance to her. Chicano/a desire for a brown-skinned Guadalupe is formed in and through the social and historical institutionalization of racial hierarchies, a direct result of the colonization of the Americas and its enduring racial legacies. However, the imagined collective allegiance to a sexless brown mother has come at considerable cost: women's active sexuality. The cultural work of Cisneros and López stretches Chicano/a collective imaginaries, shifting the terms by which Chicano/a subjects understand themselves, desire others, and act on the social world.

CHIASTIC AFTERWORD

Reconsidering López's work, several years after the controversy in Santa Fe and after the original publication of my essay "Art Comes for the Archbishop" in 2004, I have a few additional thoughts on the historical and figurative meanings of López's art. The passage of years often adds historical clarity and such is the case with my thinking about López's *Our Lady*. I now see the importance of being even more mindful of the political context of Bush-era attacks on queer lives and of the challenging chiasmus posed by López's art.

A trope is a figure of speech—it is a form or a formal element of communication in which words or images are used in a way that change their "original" meaning. Original is in scare quotes here because the original itself is already twisted from previous meanings: meaning is always changing—in that it is alive, embedded in social processes, not static. Some have compared the project of semiotics to the practice of peeling an onion. We peel back meaning layer by layer. But unlike the chef, this peeling-back process can go on more or less indefinitely. Semiotics is important to the project of Latino/a art criticism because it directs our attention away from the notion of discovering the ultimate or real meaning of a text; rather, semiotics instructs us to think about *how meaning is produced*.

Thus, we undertake an examination of tropes because they are one important way that meaning is produced. From the Greek word *tropos*, trope means "to turn or twist," so that a trope twists the meaning of a word or phrase or image—in this case, Alma López's *Our Lady* twists the meaning of the Virgin, taking her in a new direction. At the 2008 National Association of Chicana and Chicano Studies Annual Conference, I was part of the panel that explored López's work in relation to chiasmus, a trope structured by repetition and reversal. If the first part of the chiasmus is structured as AB, the second is structured as BA—as in the Chicano/a slogan "We didn't cross the border, the border crossed us," or the Queer Nation slogan "You say don't fuck, we say fuck you." By rearranging the original phrase, the author, artist, or activist radically disrupts previously stable visions of reality. Chiasmus, by reversing the original, allows us to see reality in a new light; we create a new way of seeing and hopefully a new way of being in the world. This particular trope provides the rhetorical ground for us to make new political claims on the social world. Perhaps chiasmus is the perfect trope for radical cultural workers—for it reverses the order of things.

The iconic figure of the Virgin of Guadalupe has always relied on the power of the trope. In greater Mexico, the image of the Virgin of Guadalupe functions as the very trope of the suffering nation. She is the mother who cares for her oppressed children—those who suffer at the hands of colonization, genocide, US capitalism, and racist immigration policy. Her meaning is already twisted or "troped" from the image of the Virgin Mary, the Spanish image of the Virgin of Guadalupe, and various pre-Columbian goddess figures such as Tonantzin. As I have argued, the Virgin of Guadalupe—precisely because she is always already a polyvalent sign—is especially available for retooling and radical reconfiguration by Chicana artists.

In retrospect, it is very clear that the controversy surrounding López's *Our Lady* was complexly situated among a number of different historical and ideological processes—including but by no means limited to the meaning of Chicano/a, Mexicano/a, and Hispano/a identity; the representation of female sexuality; the workings of faith; the cultural ownership of symbols and icons; the politics of art; and the policing of desire, ritual, tradition, and cultural change. It is important to remember that the *Cyber Arte* exhibit opened five short weeks after the inauguration of George W. Bush. Even though Bush did not win the popular vote (and indeed by most accounts stole the election), his rise to power demonstrated the enormous power of a hate-based political message—one aimed to appeal to and construct the religious right as a voting bloc. This newly formed Republican message held tremendous rhetorical power—constructing a very effective counterattack on the gains made by feminist and queer activists of the 1990s. Bush's election signifies the rise of a U.S. nationalism that is explicitly gendered—a consolidation of hetero-patriarchy—a wresting of the nation away from queers, feminists, and feminist queers.

The national political context has received scant attention in analyses of the controversy. There is a tendency to accept the terms of the debate as insider versus outsider, local versus global, rural versus cosmopolitan; however, these binaries problematically construct New Mexican Hispano culture as something that exists outside of history—and immune to the pressures of national and transnational change. While I understand the political impetus behind calls to be respectful of local articulations and understandings, it is equally important to understand the way that local is embedded in transnational relations of power. As museum curator Tey Mariana Nunn reveals in her essay on the controversy—the Santa Fe "local" was aided and abetted by global religious conservatives. Indeed, part of the protest against *Our Lady* included participation—welcomed by the local detractors—of the Philadelphia-based group American Society for the Defense of Tradition, Family and Property. This transnational organization is a Catholic group that articulates what we might recognize as "religious right" politics. It was founded in Brazil, where it made efforts to outlaw the samba.[40]

It strikes me that we—Chicana theorists—have not paid enough attention to the religious right. Too often, we fail to situate analysis of Chicano/a issues within and in relation to U.S. political forces—as if (with the possible exception of immigration and education policy) our communities are somehow immune to—or outside of—hegemonic discourses and as if our communities were only involved in internal struggles. How do we—Chicanas, queers, and queer Chicanas—resist the religious right? Indeed, what is our analysis of the religious right and how do we develop a politics to contest the hate and exclusion that they preach? While Chicana academics have been mostly silent on this issue, Chicana artists have been waging the rhetorical battle over the meaning of religious symbols and the relationship of the female body to both U.S. and Chicano attachments to nation.

In her article "Chiasmus—Art in Politics/Politics in Art," art critic Freida High discusses Yolanda M. López's Guadalupe series from the 1970s. She writes that López's series depicts "three generations of Chicanas symbolized as icons of suffering and despair, hope, faith, and power: chiasmus: Chicana women in La Virgen and La Virgen in Chicana women."[41] Like Yolanda M. López's Guadalupe series, Alma López's *Our Lady* confronts the very meaning of Chicano/a identity, and the intersection of two core components: gender and nation. López's *Lady* produces a female gendered subject, not one who suffers for the nation or one who nurtures those who suffer; rather, in López's *Lady*, the woman emerges as a complex political subject, with feelings, with desire, with demands for autonomy. López's *Our Lady* disarticulates the nation's claim on Chicana bodies, producing a critique of the religious right—with its hatred of queers and its explicit mission of controlling female sexuality of all kinds.

NOTES

I would like to thank Catrióna Rueda Esquibel, Thuy Linh Nguyen Tu, Tomás Ybarra Frausto, and the anonymous readers at Meridians for their productive and generous critiques of my essay. Originally published in *Meridians: Feminism, Race, Transnationalism* 5.1 (2004): 201–224. This version includes different artwork and a new Afterword.

1. The 1993 discovery of an image of the Virgin of Guadalupe on a tree near Watsonville is referenced by Cherríe Moraga in her poem "Our Lady of the Cannery Workers" (1996) and her play "Watsonville: Some Place Not Here" (2002).

2. In this essay, I use the term "brown skin" to signal a collective cultural belief about Chicano/a bodies and not to reify some bodies or skin colors as more or less authentic. Indeed, "brown" Chicano/a bodies come in all shades. Brownness is a position within a social symbolic structure and is, I argue, constructed through language and fantasy; it is not, as some might assume, an essential or biological characteristic.

3. *Our Lady* was part of *Cyber Arte: Tradition Meets Technology*, an exhibit that ran from February 25 to October 28, 2001.

4. Office of Communications, Archdiocese of Santa Fe, "Archbishop Michael J. Sheehan on *Our Lady* of Guadalupe Portrayal," Archdiocese of Santa Fe website, November 25, 2002, www.archdiocesesantafe.org.

5. López has documented this debate, collecting e-mails from detractors and supporters, newspaper articles from around the world, and letters to the editor on her website, www.almalopez.com. This site is an invaluable resource for researchers.

6. For example, López has designed the covers of *Puro Teatro: A Latina Anthology*, edited by Alberto Sandoval-Sánchez and Nancy Saporta Sternbach (Tucson: University of Arizona Press, 2000); *Chicano/a Renaissance*, edited by David R. Maciel, Isidro D. Ortiz, and María Herrera-Sobek (Tucson: University of Arizona Press,

2000); and *Velvet Barrios: Popular Culture & Chicana/o Sexualities*, edited by Alicia Gaspar de Alba (Basingstoke: Palgrave Macmillan, 2003). She also designed posters for the "Otro Corazón: Queering the Art of Aztlán" conference (February 10, 2001, University of California, Los Angeles) and for the National Association of Chicana and Chicano Studies Conference (April 2–6, 2003, Los Angeles).

7. The original image of the Virgin of Guadalupe is thought to reference a statue of the Virgin Mary in Extremadura, Spain, which was also known as the Virgin of Guadalupe. Others understand the Virgin of Guadalupe to be a refiguration of a pre-Columbian goddess. As in all representation, the notion of an original referent is complicated.

8. López always names and thanks her models in public descriptions of her work. This gesture draws attention to the fact that her photographs depict particular subjects, with names, histories, and a relationship to the artist.

9. These images and their reception have been widely discussed by Chicana visual theorists, such as Angie Chabram-Dernersesian (1992), Yvonne Yarbro-Bejarano (1995), Alicia Gaspar de Alba (1998), Laura Elisa Pérez (1999), and Deena González (2003).

10. Emma Pérez, *The Decolonial Imaginary: Writing Chicanas into History* (Bloomington: Indiana University Press, 1999), 124.

11. Quoted in ibid., 123.

12. Ibid., 124

13. While the men were the most vocal detractors of López's art, some Chicana and Nuevomexicana women also joined in the public critique. Such women present a challenge to my argument, and I hope that future research might be done—perhaps an ethnographic study—to explore their political and cultural formation.

14. Pérez, *The Decolonial Imaginary*, 122.

15. Teresa de Lauretis, *The Practice of Love: Lesbian Sexuality and Perverse Desire* (Bloomington: Indiana University Press, 1994).

16. Ibid., 51

17. Sigmund Freud, "Group Psychology and the Analysis of the Ego," *The Standard Edition of the Complete Psychological Works of Sigmund Freud*, edited by James Strachey (London: Hogarth Press, 1924), vol. 18, 109.

18. Pérez, *The Decolonial Imaginary*, 158.

19. Ibid.

20. Ibid.

21. Sandra Cisneros, "Guadalupe the Sex Goddess," in *Goddess of the Americas/La Diosa de las Américas: Writings on the Virgin of Guadalupe*, edited by Ana Castillo (New York: Riverhead Books, 1996), 54.

22. Ibid., 50–51.

23. Ibid., 51.

24. Judith Butler, *Bodies That Matter: On the Discursive Limits of "Sex"* (New York: Routledge, 1993), 63.

25. David L. Eng, *Racial Castration: Managing Masculinity in Asian America* (Durham, N.C.: Duke University Press, 2004), 5.

26. Ibid.

27. Alma López, "Mermaids, Butterflies, and Princesses," in *Aztlán: A Journal of Chicano Studies*, 25. (Spring 2000): 189–191.

28. The signifying system of *lotería* is further complicated by a series of verbal descriptions of each card. In many versions of the game, instead of the caller simply yelling out "La Sirena," she will instead provide a popular saying. For example, for the mermaid card, the saying is "Con los cantos de sirena no te vayas a marear" (Don't get dizzy with the siren song). Thus, the meaning of *lotería* images is anchored not only to the descriptive title of each card but also to the popular saying that accompanies them.

29. ALLGO, a queer Latino/a organization in Austin, Texas, has created a queer version of *lotería*. In a smart rhetorical move, they recast "El Negrito" as San Martín de Porres, a popular black saint from Peru and renamed the card "El Santo" (the saint). See ALLGO, "Lotería Jotería," Austin Latino/Latina Lesbian, Gay, Bisexual & Transgender Organization website, www.allgo.org; November 30, 2002.

30. Victor Burgin, *In/Different Spaces: Place and Memory in Visual Culture* (Berkeley: University of California Press, 1996), 60.

31. Ibid., 58.

32. See de Lauretis, *The Practice of Love*, 81–142, for her recasting of the primal scene as a site of lesbian desire; and Pérez, *The Decolonial Imaginary*, 110–114; and Luz Calvo, "Lemme Stay, I Want to Watch: Ambivalence in Borderlands' Cinema," in *Latino/a Popular Culture*, edited by Mary Romero and Michelle Habell-Pallán (New York: New York University Press, 2004), 74, for discussions of the primal scene of colonialism and the formation of Mexican and Chicano/a subjectivities.

33. Gloria Anzaldúa also maps this psychic space in her theorization of "the borderlands" in *Borderlands/La Frontera: The New Mestiza* (San Francisco: Aunt Lute Books, 1987).

34. E-mail from Sedeño to Alma López, February 12, 2002, www.almalopez.com.

35. Thanks to Tomás Ybarra Frausto for his helpful suggestions regarding *rasquachismo*.

36. Tomás Ybarra Frausto, "The Chicano Movement/The Movement of Chicano Art," in *Beyond the Fantastic: Contemporary Art Criticism from Latin America*, edited by Gerardo Mosquera (Cambridge, Mass.: MIT Press, 1996), 174.

37. Ibid.

38. Ibid.

39. John Rechy, *The Miraculous Day of Amalia Gómez*, 2nd ed. (New York: Grove Press, 2004), vii–viii.

40. Tey Marianna Nunn, "The *Our Lady* Controversy: Chicana Art, Hispanic Identity, and the Politics of Place and Gender in Nuevo México," in *Expressing New Mexico: Nuevomexicano Creativity, Ritual, and Memory*, edited by Philip B. Gonzales (Tucson: University of Arizona Press, 2007), 176; Chapter 2 here.

41. Freida High, "Chiasmus: Art in Politics/Politics in Art Chicano/a and African-American Image, Text, and Activism of the Nineteen Sixties and Seventies," in *Voices of Color in the Americas*, edited by Phoebe Ferris-Duphrene (Atlantic Highlands, N.J.: Humanities Press, 1997), 154.

6

Queering the Sacred

LOVE AS OPPOSITIONAL CONSCIOUSNESS
IN ALMA LÓPEZ'S VISUAL ART

Clara Román-Odio

A SIGN OF TRANSNATIONAL SOLIDARITY, La Virgen de Guadalupe is the patron saint of Mexico and the Americas, as well as a political banner for Chicano and Mexican populations subjected to colonization, racism, and economic dispossession. Indeed, she has many meanings that, as Luz Calvo suggests in "Art Comes for the Archbishop," are often "deployed by different groups for contradictory political ends."[1] This multiplicity of meanings reflects the history and political agendas of Mexican and Mexican American communities, and examples of her legacy abound. In the colonial period, *criollos* appropriated the image to justify the conquest and to glorify Mexico.[2] The Mexican independence movements also began and culminated under her banner, first in 1810 with Father Miguel Hidalgo y Costilla, and a century later, in the 1910 Mexican Revolution with Pancho Villa and Emiliano Zapata. Beyond the U.S.-Mexican border, Chicano communities have also claimed social, religious, and national rights in her name, as César Chávez's social activism in the 1960s and contemporary Chicano/a writers and artists demonstrate. Yet, the polyvalence of the icon is nowhere else made more visceral than in the exhibit *Cyber Arte: Tradition Meets Technology*, launched by the Museum of International Folk Art (MOIFA), in Santa Fe, New Mexico, in 2001.

The show consisted of works by four artists—Teresa Archuleta-Sagel, Elena Baca, Alma López, and Marion C. Martínez—who used computers to compose traditional images and to explore connections between tradition and technology. Among the eight pieces that López included in the show, *Our Lady* (1999) portrays a 14" × 17.5" digital image of Our Lady of Guadalupe as a young, self-confident Latina (Raquel Salinas) wearing a mantle not of stars but of stone, with a garland of roses covering her chest and hips.[3]

With her hands on her hips, her head held high, and her weight solidly grounded on her right foot, she stands on a crescent moon and looks straight at the spectator. The traditional angel holding up Our Lady is replaced by a bare-breasted young Latina (Raquel Gutiérrez) emerging from the wings of a Viceroy butterfly. Beneath the butterfly lies the traditional mantle of stars. There is no maternity band on this brown body, but the traditional robe, identified by the nagvioli flower, is used as the background, with roses adorning the lower area of the canvas.

Like other Chicanas, Chicanos, and Mexicans before her, López recasts the sacred image, reinterpreting its original attributes.[4] However, the controversy created by *Our Lady* largely overshadowed the work of the other artists in the exhibit. Archbishop Michael J. Sheehan of New Mexico accused the artist of portraying the religious icon as a "tart" and insisted the work be removed. Catholics protested and organized prayer vigils against the digital collage, which they viewed as a desecration. In a response to the demands and letters the artist and the museum received, López explained:

> Even if I look really hard at "Our Lady" and the works of many Chicana artists, I don't see what is so offensive. I see beautiful bodies: gifts from our creator. Maybe because my mother breastfed me as a baby, I see breasts as nurturing. Maybe because I love women, I see beauty and strength. I also see the true representation of Mary. Mary was an awesome woman and mother with a difficult task. She had a child that was not her husband's, she kept her son safe from a murderous king, she suffered her son's struggles and death, and most of all she raised her son to have love and compassion for everyone, including female prostitutes. I think Mary was a lot like some of our mothers.[5]

Hence, the discrepancy between the artist's intention and the protestors' reaction begs the question of what lies behind the controversy. In an interview with Nancy Warren in which López reflected on what seemed inappropriate and sacrilegious to the men leading the protests, she added: "The image in Santa Fe is very much about a strong woman standing there with an attitude and wearing flowers. It has nothing to do with sex or sexuality."[6]

However, the Santa Fe Catholic community's sense of indignation remained. Calvo offers an insightful perspective on how gender politics shaped the controversy: "[Alma López's] images seduce the spectator into new desiring positions by exposing Chicano/a libidinal investments—conscious and unconscious—in the Virgin of Guadalupe. Her images mobilize and disturb these investments, channeling Chicano/a desires in queer directions."[7] In other words, López's images are disturbing because they redirect Chicano/a community's psychic energy associated with sexual desire in surprisingly anomalous directions, which is unsettling because within the Chicano/a imaginary the Virgin of Guadalupe has represented everything from patriotism to unconditional love except for sexuality and desire.

Calvo's interpretation also highlights the power of images to arrest and expose the subconscious in ways that can be disturbing. In the case of López's images, they depict the Virgin showing alternative identities to illustrate lived realities of Chicanas (including the queer). But in doing so, they also offer visual reminders of what male-dominated culture promotes in order to hold power: the representation of women as sexual objects or as objects of sexual violence. Hence, even though López's intention in *Our Lady* was not to address sexuality, her work brings to the forefront gendered power relations that can be uncomfortable and, consequently, that are interpreted as sacrilege.

Another assumption that substantiates the *Cyber Arte* controversy is that López was using the image ironically, as iconoclasts do, in order to unmask patriarchy's mandate of female abnegation and passivity and compulsory heterosexuality. In this chapter, I will nuance this assumption to show that López's engagement with the Virgin of Guadalupe is quite complex, including a desire to reclaim the artist's full spiritual and bodily self. Based on my conversations with Alma López and several other Chicana artists, I contend that it is essential to explore other frameworks, including Chicana spirituality and Chicana conceptualizations of Aztlán, in order to understand the scandal and to propose an alternative interpretation of López's art. By looking at *Our Lady* within these frameworks and in relation to other works created by the artist in the same series, we shall see that López's engagement with the Virgin of Guadalupe is intimately connected to a personal spirituality and to a particular conceptualization of love that critics have overlooked, perhaps because sexuality has monopolized the attention of both Catholics and agnostics.

The notion of queering the sacred implies, on first approximation, an apparent degradation (and, to some, even desecration) of a religious icon. Chicana visual artist Alma López is known for, and her artwork gives rise to, substantial controversy because of the ways in which she alters the visual representation of the Virgin of Guadalupe. However, in the present work I will argue that, far from being a "desecration" of the iconography, López's artwork represents an effort to deploy it for a purpose of feminist empowerment. López challenges traditional notions of love and the sacred through a methodology that Chela Sandoval has named "differential consciousness," through which the artist is able to create a crossroads or an open space wherein she resists and disrupts dominant narratives of gender, race, class, sexuality, and nation-state. By underscoring López's use of tropes to queer the iconography of the Virgin, in this chapter I will show that the artist makes a gesture of loving resistance whereby previous meanings of the sacred Mother are taken in a new direction by a daughter seeking to disrupt normative discourses of gender, race, nation, and compulsory heterosexuality.

OPPOSITIONAL CONSCIOUSNESS

According to Chicana theorist Chela Sandoval, U.S. feminists of color who were active across diverse social movements during the 1968–1990 period practiced a method of "oppositional consciousness" that Sandoval names "differential consciousness." This methodology, Sandoval explains, is the expression of a new subject position that permits functioning within, yet beyond, the demands of dominant ideology.[8] In other words, differential consciousness represents a strategy of oppositional ideology that seeks to transform power relations through a process of shifting location, where the subject is both within and outside dominant ideology. The method was used by U.S. feminists of color as a strategy to seek empowerment and to unmask gender, sexual, racial, and social inequalities within the United States by pointing out "the so-called third world in the first world."[9] Feminists of color also used differential consciousness to draw attention to white feminists' inconsistencies on these same issues. Much of white feminist theory up to the late 1970s ignored the experiences of women of color in the United States. White feminists failed to fully understand the unique positioning of women of color in the United States not because of their lack of commitment to addressing their experiences but, as Chicana theorist Aida Hurtado explains, because their class origin and their relationship to white men's patriarchal power prevented them from fully understanding the simultaneous sources of oppression for women of color.[10] Exclusion and appropriation from U.S. mainstream feminism kept feminists of color at bay. White feminists exercised power through a universal category of "woman" and other discursive homogenizations that did not take into account the pluralities and locations of U.S. women of color.[11] Consequently, the tropes of transculturalism, global-local tensions, and the border became dominant in Chicana cultural criticism, and *mestizaje* emerged as a thematic and formal marker of identity.[12] As a transgressive trope, the Chicana body became a site from which a history of dislocation, violence, and economic exploitation emerged.[13] Yet, from the Chicana body also emerged an alternative way of knowledge, represented by Gloria Anzaldúa's new mestiza consciousness, as well as by a feminist spirituality standing over and against the patriarchal Indo, Hispanic, Anglo nation-state.

In Sandoval's Chicana political theory, the notion of oppositional consciousness constitutes part of "the methodology of the oppressed," a process by which dominant ideologies are challenged and resisted by those who are marginalized and oppressed. This methodology is deployed via five technologies of resistance, working individually or in concert: (1) "semiotics," or sign reading; (2) "de-construction," or the act of separating a material form from its dominant meaning; (3) "meta-ideologizing," or the appropriation and transformation of dominant ideological forms; (4) "democratics," a moral commitment to equality; and (5) "differential movement," a "re-appropriation of space" and boundaries to impress dominant powers—where the self shifts in order to survive and according to the requisites of power.[14] These technologies of resistance function as cognitive strategies to reinterpret, deconstruct, redefine, and transform cultural signs that control or limit the agency of the oppressed. For instance, Chicana critic and writer Gloria E. Anzaldúa reappropriates the notion of "borderlands" to generate new knowledge and nuanced identities that cannot be essentialized or overgeneralized. Within her theoretical work, the term *borderlands* refers to a specific geographical locale, the U.S-Mexico border, and the specific history of American citizens of Mexican descent. But Anzaldúa also distinguishes between borderlands, conceived as a territorial and cultural category, and *nepantla*, the spiritual result of residing in that location.[15] Borderlands also serves as a metaphor that describes "liminal stages of transition," in other words, how identity becomes an ongoing activity and a framework for a complex composition that melds disparate selves and the collective dreams and experiences that are held together by memory.[16] Hence, through Anzaldúa's resignification, borderlands points to "disassociations of identity, identity breakdowns and buildups and to intercultural impingement."[17] This process of resignification enables challenging conventional labeling and epistemological categories, which explains why for Anzaldúa borderlands is both a process of and a quest for decolonization, a counternarrative to globalization, a technology for border crossing, and an alternative epistemological approach to dominant ideologies.

Like Anzaldúa's borderlands, Alma López's artwork exemplifies the methodology of the oppressed and finds resonance in a group of Chicana visual artists, including Ester Hernández, Yolanda M. López, Consuelo Jiménez Underwood, Marion C. Martínez, and Santa Barraza, among others, who have engaged with the iconography of the Virgin of Guadalupe with the aim of equalizing gender power, countering racism, and helping galvanize the political feminist spirit of the Chicana social movement. Their sign readings, deconstructions, and ideological reappropriations are vital to their ethical commitments and political agendas. In their own particular ways, all of these Chicana artists seek to make visible subjects who have been erased or devalued by mainstream U.S. America. They engage in re-creating the self and in mapping their own identities. They also debate and produce new conceptualizations of Aztlán in response to the entrenched sexism of the Chicano movement. And they explore spiritualism as a method of transmutation.

For instance, Ester Hernández ruptures ideology by turning the *mestiza* body into a site where the material conditions of neocolonial histories are played out. Yolanda M. López empowers the bodies and daily realities of Chicana women by taking symbols of the Virgin of Guadalupe's power and virtue and transferring them to women she knows. Jiménez Underwood's artwork deploys tactics that resist conflating the local and the national to dismantle narratives that render invisible poor and immigrant populations in the borderlands. Marion C. Martínez's "tech-media" art locates the damaging effects of capitalist globalization within the United States by making visible the politics of racialization in the Southwest of the United States. And Santa Barraza reappropriates pre-Columbian codices, colors, and designs to stir historical memory and to reconnect to a cultural ideology that is rooted in the Mexican past.

Like these Chicana artists, Alma López reappropriates the iconography of the Virgin of Guadalupe while engaging with the image as a sign of a special kind of love, which the artist uses to resist two myths or conceptualizations of the nation that exclude the feminist experience: the U.S. Manifest Destiny myth of conquest, and the Chicano cultural homeland myth of Aztlán.

ALMA LÓPEZ'S ART AND THE 2001 CYBER ARTE EXHIBIT: NEW MEXICANS, AN ENDANGERED CULTURE?

Toward an understanding of the sociopolitical context, it is important to recall that seven years after the *Cyber Arte* scandal, at the 2008 National Association for Chicana and Chicano Studies (NACCS) Roundtable, "Irreverent Apparitions: Chiasmatic Interpretations of Alma López's *Our Lady*," Luz Calvo argued—rightly so—that the Virgin of Guadalupe has always been a twisted/troped icon: "The iconic figure of the Virgin of Guadalupe has always relied on the power of the trope. In greater Mexico, her image functions as the very trope of the suffering nation. She is the mother who cares for her oppressed children—those who suffer at the hands of colonization, genocide, U.S. capitalism, racist immigration policy. Her meaning is already twisted/troped from the image of the Virgin Mary OR the Spanish image of the Virgin of Guadalupe OR various pre-Columbian goddess figures."[18] Given the polyvalence of the icon, it is necessary to ask, Who is the Virgin of Guadalupe for the subculture represented by the New Mexican Catholics who objected to López's image?

Miguel León-Portilla's notion of "endangered cultures" offers a useful perspective for an interpretation of the *Cyber Arte* controversy from the point of view of the protestors. According to León-Portilla, "endangered cultures" are societies, nations, or communities "whose value systems, languages, worldviews, internal structures, or in a word, whose very cultural identities exist in a state of crisis or at risk of total disappearance."[19] As a "culture of the vanquished," a characteristic feature of this community would be "the subjugation to permanent contact with more powerful hegemonic entities."[20] Some of these communities, which are faced by aggression and forced acculturation, have partially developed effective defense mechanisms that enable them to cling determinedly to their cultural identities. The community of New Mexicans involved in the *Cyber Arte* controversy can be considered an endangered culture.

As Deena González has shown in *Refusing the Favor*, Santa Fe was and continues to be the center of a multiethnic frontier with a complex history of subjugation: "Conquest and colonization impoverished the majority of the residents of Santa Fe and perhaps much of the New Mexican North. It disempowered women, who had previously exercised certain rights guaranteed by Spanish law. And it made most Spanish-Americans dependent on wages, earned in jobs."[21] Sustained colonization—as in the case of Santa Fe—can result in a permanent danger of losing cultural identity. Consequently, beliefs, symbols, values, and the moral orientation of the community become crucial for securing the internal structure of the group.

For many citizens of Santa Fe, it is conceivable that the traditional image of Our Lady of Guadalupe came to signify everything that held them together—the shared experience of losing their land to the conquerors, pride in their traditions, a cultural ideology rooted in a Spanish and a Mexican past, as well as a spiritual faith that had been maintained for centuries. Hence, it is plausible that when a Santa Fe journalist renamed López's image the "Bikini Virgin," the catchy phrase charged the work with new meanings that became offensive even for those who never attended the exhibit. Arguably, the community's strong sense of tradition, which helped it resist and survive colonization, was a major force driving the protest. The irony, of course, is that the very tradition that it was trying to uphold—Catholicism—is part of the colonialist agenda, first of the Spaniards and later of the Anglos, that conquered Santa Fe.[22]

From my conversation with Alma López, and also from reading the statements she issued at the time of the controversy, it is clear to me that she never intended to be disrespectful to the Santa Fe community or to the image of the Virgin of Guadalupe. In a phone interview, I specifically addressed the controversy: "Alma, do you agree that the Hispanic Catholic community in Santa Fe misrepresented what you were trying to do with *Our Lady*? If so, in what ways?" López's reply illuminates how the framework used by both the protestors and the artist determined their respective reactions:

> They found *Our Lady* offensive because they were unable to separate between the church—a place for prayer—and the museum—a place for art exhibits. They looked at the image sexually. The archbishop called *Our Lady* a "tart," that is, a streetwalker. What I intended was very different. I wanted to answer Sandra Cisneros's question: Does the Virgen de Guadalupe have a

body like mine? She's brown, but does she have a body like mine? Does she have breasts and vagina and does she look like me? Is she real? I wondered what she would look like if I lifted her dress. My answer was flowers, roses, because roses were the proof of the Virgen's apparition. The proof that she was real is the roses in the story and the myth. That's why, when I worked on *Our Lady*, I covered her in roses. It wasn't about her being naked. It was about her being covered in roses. She was proving that she was real, that her myth or story was real. I think that quite a few people missed that point. They saw some other stuff that wasn't there.[23]

In a previous conversation, when I asked López about using the image to represent lesbian desire, she replied: "Raquel Salinas and Raquel Gutiérrez are my friends; I don't see them as lovers."[24] And returning to Cisneros's essay as the point of departure for her image, López added:

Sandra's essay, I think, is incredibly powerful because it speaks about the dangers of being a young woman; not knowing our bodies and how the Virgen de Guadalupe is very much part of that cult: the cult of the cover-up, of not knowing who you are, not knowing your body, not knowing your sexual power. Ultimately, I feel that she (as I am) is trying to find a deep and significant connection to the Virgen de Guadalupe, a deep understanding that is very different perhaps from traditional religious understanding or connection.[25]

Alma López's explanation of the origin of the piece makes it clear that the protestors' reaction had more to do with their own framework, the feeling of being culturally endangered, than with the artist's intent. Arguably, the sociopolitical context of Santa Fe determined the meanings that *Our Lady* generated and the direction viewers' interpretations took.

In what follows, I will consider two different but equally important frameworks for interpreting Alma López's artwork: spirituality, and the Chicana conceptualization of Aztlán. Within the context of Chicana art, the term *spirituality* incorporates several ideas: first, the merger and appropriation of Western and non-Western spiritual traditions; second, a healing force that resists oppression; and third, a politics that generates social justice for the dispossessed and marginalized.[26] As we shall see, López's spirituality is personal and sui generis but also historical inasmuch as it criticizes Christianity for reproducing Eurocentrism, patriarchy, and compulsory heterosexuality. In discussing the artist's interpretation of her place of origin, I will look at her reappropriation of the cultural myth of Aztlán, including the role played by La Virgen, in works from both her 1848 series and her Lupe and Sirena series, which were produced between 1997 and 1999, and 1999, respectively. López's images signal a departure from the gendered and highly controlled Mother and Virgin in the Chicano imaginary of homeland. Her images incorporate other subjectivities, including women and children from the community as well as queer and lesbian friends of the artist in order to transform sexism and homophobia in the dominant ideology of Chicanismo. Ultimately, López's Lupe and Sirena series will shed light on and enable a new interpretation of *Our Lady* in which the queering of the sacred image is viewed as a technology of resistance, one that, as we shall see, is comparable to the experience of love.

THE ORIGINAL NARRATIVE OF OUR LADY, OR THE *NICAN MOPOHUA*

In the case of the Virgin of Guadalupe, alterations of iconography, like those López makes, trace back to a piece of Nahuatl literature known as the *Nican Mopohua*, which was put in writing by Antonio Valeriano in 1556 and published for the first time in 1649 by Luis Lasso de la Vega, chaplain of the Guadalupe sanctuary in Mexico City.[27] The text tells about four apparitions of Tonantzin to the Indian Juan Diego on the hill of Tepeyac in 1531, ten years after the Aztec empire was conquered by the Spaniards. She identifies herself as the mother of the Giver of Life, Ipalnemohuani, and asks him to obtain permission from the archbishop of Mexico, Juan de Zumárraga, to build a temple in her name at the bottom of the hill. In exchange, she promises to love, protect, and defend anyone who seeks her love and help.

The Indian is profoundly surprised, thinking that he is in the Flowering Land, Xochitlalpan, in the Land of Our Sustenance, Tonacatlalpan, in the Celestial Land of which the elders used to speak. Juan Diego goes twice to the archbishop but is unable to persuade him of the mission entrusted to him by the Lady whom, by now, he knows as Tonantzin Guadalupe. The best he gets from the archbishop is the suggestion that the Lady give him a sign that will convince him, the archbishop, of her existence. The sign is the roses that the Lady asks Juan to cut at the top of Tepeyac, where only *nopales* and mesquites used to grow. Juan Diego picks them, puts them in his *tilma* (his cactus-fiber shawl), and brings them to Zumárraga. When the Indian opens his *tilma*, the flowers fall out, and the story concludes by telling that, at that moment and before the astonished eyes of the archbishop and others who were with him, the image of Our Lady appeared imprinted on the Indian's *tilma*.

The image became a catalyst for the conversion of over six million Aztecs in the next nine years. It hangs in the Basílica de Guadalupe in Mexico City and has hardly deteriorated since it was placed there in the sixteenth century. As Miguel León-Portilla, Virgilio Elizondo, and other scholars have established, there are numerous studies by *guadalupistas* and *anti-aparicionistas* (antiapparitionists) that debate the origin of the image and story.[28] It is not my intention to take part in this debate since, in matters of miracles, history cannot prove or disprove anything. What is certain is that the story contains vestiges of both Nahuatl and Christian thought that have served to integrate groups, communities, and entire populations from the Americas over the last five centuries.

SPIRITUALITY AND THE PLACE OF ORIGIN
IN ALMA LÓPEZ'S DIGITAL ART

The narrative of the Virgin of Guadalupe ties directly to spirituality and place of origin as central themes in López's artwork. In *Santa Niña de Mochis* (1999), for example, the artist creates a complex visual narrative by juxtaposing Los Angeles skyscrapers, the U.S.-Mexico border, the memory of a child "clothed in light and standing on a crescent moon," and the Virgin of Guadalupe. Regarding the origin of the piece, López has stated:

> This image came at a time when I was trying to decide what to do with my career. I remember that a *santero* told me: "Your ancestors want you to be happy; seek their guidance." And I thought: "My mom is an orphan since she was ten, where do I go?" So I plan a trip to Los Mochis, where my grandmother was buried. I traveled with my mom, sister, and a niece. It was el Día de los Muertos. We were at the cemetery, where many Mexican families go at this time of the year, and I saw this girl dressed like an angel, and I ask her parents if I could take her picture. She moved like an angel. And she came to represent the spirit of my grandmother—of that energy the *santero* talked about. As people in Tijuana made Juan Soldado a saint for helping so many

people cross the border, I made my grandmother a saint (the Santa Niña de Mochis) for answering the prayer or the question I had about what to do with my career. The piece is a tribute to my grandmother. I wanted to thank her. Also, the piece belongs to the series 1848 Chicanos in the U.S. after the Signing of the Treaty of Guadalupe. The space portrayed was created after the treaty. The U.S. Manifest Destiny myth of conquest has attempted to erase, to make invisible, those who were/are in that land, and I make them visible. So it is a counternarrative that has a political theme.[29]

The artist's anecdote speaks of a spiritual quest, the need to come back home to find family and community and migration, while underscoring the importance of elders in the Hispanic community and the value of nonorganized religiosity in Chicano/a pop culture. López also refers to the Treaty of Guadalupe and, in so doing, she speaks of her cultural place of origin: Aztlán, the Chicano imaginary homeland that came into being in 1848, with the Treaty of Guadalupe.

In "There Is No Place Like Aztlán: Embodied Aesthetics in Chicana Art," Alicia Gaspar de Alba identifies a place-based aesthetic in Chicana/Chicano art that she calls "Aztlán aesthetics," which I want to use to shed light on López's manipulation and reinterpretation of Aztlán. According to Gaspar de Alba, this aesthetic practice expresses attachment to place, "but place means more than geographical location. For Third World people in the United States, place means race, religion, community, and (as we shall see later) body, as well. Central to all these practices is the concept of *homeland*, the idea that the land of the artist's place of birth or the place of origin of the artist's people/group/race, as well as the history and cultural beliefs and practices of the land—all inform the content and theme of the art."[30]

López's political engagement with both her place of origin and La Virgen can be interpreted through Aztlán aesthetics, which Gaspar de Alba characterizes as "a representation of both territorial dispossession and cultural reclamation."[31] According to Gaspar de Alba, "territorial dispossession" and its correlate—the sense of loss—became effective with the 1848 Treaty of Guadalupe by virtue of which Mexican citizens who chose to remain in the conquered north of Mexico "lost their citizenship, their country, their land and eventually their language."[32] The other aspect of the myth—"cultural reclamation"—emerged 120 years later in the concept of Aztlán, a cultural myth of Chicanismo that galvanized the movement, as expressed in its first manifesto, "El Plan Espiritual de Aztlán."

Gaspar de Alba maintains that "El Plan" was written "as both rebuttal and response to the ideology of Manifest Destiny" and shared with this ideology many points of contact:

> As opposed to the "chosen children of God," whose destiny and divine right it was to move toward the frontier, to conquer and civilize "the West," we have "the people of the sun" (a reference to the Aztec sun god, Huitzilo-pochtli, by the way) whose destiny is to move into the streets, the fields, and the classrooms to reclaim and civilize the Mexican North. Both are driven by their male desire to control the land and by the "call of [their] blood"; be it white or brown, race is still the driving force, the power behind their movement.[33]

The problem with this construction of Chicano cultural nationalism, Gaspar de Alba rightly contends, is that its patriarchal ideology reduces female models to "virgins" and "mothers" whose only acceptable role is "holding the family, the house, and the culture together."[34] Therefore, the Virgin of Guadalupe is used to represent the maternal mystique of the movement, "the beating heart of Aztlán."[35] As Gaspar de Alba shows, Chicanas politicize their identity through a politics of "disidentification" that enables them to produce an alternative aesthetics, which the critic calls "embodied aesthetics": "Instead of dispossession, ownership or reclamation of a place outside the self, embodied aesthetics uses the body as the signifier for place. As such the body functions as site of origin, bridge between worlds, and locus of liberation."[36]

In *Santa Niña de Mochis*, from López's 1848 series, we find an expression of a politicized Chicana identity, which the embodied aesthetics made possible. The central figure in *Santa Niña* is a girl wearing what looks like a First Communion dress, rubber sandals, and the translucent wings of a butterfly. As López has indicated in several interviews, the Viceroy butterfly represents the Chicano/Latino migration path between the United States and Mexico as well the community's ability to adapt as a means of survival: "For me, the image of the butterfly is about migration, but also about memory. The child of the butterfly is the one traveling back because there is a genetic need to return home, a need for making and finding community."[37]

Cultural, racial, and class identity are marked by the girl's body ornamentations. She wears the attributes of her religion (a white First Communion dress), her underprivileged social class (marked by her rubber sandals), and she symbolically displays her ability to survive across the border through her butterfly wings. The 1848 map of Mexico at the bottom of the composition and the delineation between the two national territories suggest that the body of the girl is out of place because she has lost her home, the land of her ancestors—Aztlán. Through its attributes, the child's body parallels the Virgin's, who seems to enable the restitution of cultural memory. The body of Aztlán continues to be subjected to persecution and dispossession, as the Border Patrolman in López's image suggests.

But, in striking contrast, a spiritual desire for origin and presence is embodied by the girl/Virgin. We have an expectation of how the story will develop. The northern territory of Mexico (as represented by the myth of Aztlán) was obviously lost to the United States, first in 1848 with the Treaty of Guadalupe and, a few years later, in 1854, with the Gadsden Purchase of southern New Mexico and Arizona. And, as the narrative of the Border Patrol implies, there is no return possible.

Then again, the vulnerable child's ability to survive gives the story another possibility. By resisting both the U.S. Anglo nation and the Chicano imaginary of Aztlán, the artist creates her own place of origin, using the body of the child as a signifier for place of origin. Therefore, *Santa Niña* confirms Gaspar de Alba's hypothesis for it depicts the power of the border body, of the subject who does not need the founding myth of the nation but exists in in-between liminal spaces and survives.

The other important narrative represented in *Santa Niña* is the U.S. Manifest Destiny myth of conquest: the Anglo's moral and divine mission to conquer the land all the way to the western frontier for the sake of progress and civilization. On December 27, 1845, John O'Sullivan, the editor of *The Review* summarized this ideology as follows: "Our manifest destiny [is] to overspread and to possess the whole continent, which providence has given us for the development of the great experiment of liberty . . . In everything which makes a people great, the supremacy of the Anglo-American is the most prominent factor of this age."[38]

The myth of the frontier and the myth of Aztlán have several points of contact, including a gendered dynamics that depicts the place of origin or the homeland as both virgin and vanquished mother, as Gaspar de Alba has shown.[39] In *Santa Niña de Mochis* these plots are disrupted by unmasking the exclusion of *real* women and children from the land, women and children whose oppression, destitution, and lack of egalitarian social relations remain invisible. López moves away from the foundational power of these nation-building narratives by connecting instead with something else, an alternative system of knowledge, which I call the *spiritual* not only because the composition points to that which is spectral (La Virgen de Guadalupe and the spirit of the grandmother represented through the body of the child) but also because the body of the girl/Virgin functions as a healing force that enables remembering, envisioning, and inscribing the Chicana body. The girl's body exists in a liminal space, torn between ways, unable or unwilling to return to the native culture or to assimilate into the new culture. Therefore, the composition suggests that the girl/Virgin survives not because of her innocent and virginal qualities but because of her ability to live on the border without the founding myth of the nation.

In summary, *Santa Niña de Mochis* represents an alternative to two contending narratives of the nation: the U.S. Manifest Destiny myth of conquest, and the Chicano myth of Aztlán. By rejecting both of them, the work speaks about the power of the border body, of the subject with at least double vision, and of the importance of the Mother, who teaches survival. The Virgin of Guadalupe is invoked through the girl both as an anchor of memory that enables the inscription of the Chicana brown body and as Tonantzin Guadalupe, who spoke of the spiritual Land of Our Sustenance, Tonacatlalpan, and of her loving body as a "locus for liberation," as Gaspar de Alba has put it.

The Mother is again evoked in another piece from López's 1848 series, *María de los Ángeles* (1997), where the icon of the Virgin of Guadalupe is expanded to include other myths. In this case, La Virgen is connected to several generations of women and to their spiritual ancestors: the Aztec goddess Coatlicue, mother of all creation and the gods; and her daughter Coyolxauhqui, the warrior Aztec goddess of the moon. These women seem to be in the Flowering, Celestial Land that is mentioned in the *Nican Mopohua*. They are in and, at the same time, represent the Land of Our Sustenance.

The Guadalupana Mother is the central figure, but then again, the body of the Mother is not one but many, including real mothers and daughters from the Estrada Courts housing project in Los Angeles, as López indicated in one of our conversations:

> *María de los Ángeles* is one of six public-art digital murals I worked on, when I was starting to make digital art in 1997. At the time, I was working for a nonprofit art organization in California called the Social and Public Art Resource Center (SPARC). I was also working part time at UCLA as a research

assistant for Professor Judy Baca. I assisted her to coordinate a project that consisted of the creation of six murals in the Estrada Courts community, a housing project in L.A. I led two of those projects that had to do with women; one of them was *María de los Ángeles*. The mural represents mothers and daughters of the Estrada Courts community who are linked to other mothers and daughters from the Aztec goddesses Coatlicue and Coyolxauhqui, to the postconquest mother, the Virgen of Guadalupe. The piece was named after an activist resident of the community, María de los Ángeles, and seeks to convey the message that this place has cultural and community roots that go really far back, which are connected through mothers.[40]

In *María de los Ángeles*, as in *Santa Niña de Mochis*, grandmothers, mothers, daughters, and their religious icons speak not only of the memory of place but also of identity formation. They represent the self as Anzaldúa describes it, that is, as "a city made up of various communities" inhabited by numerous

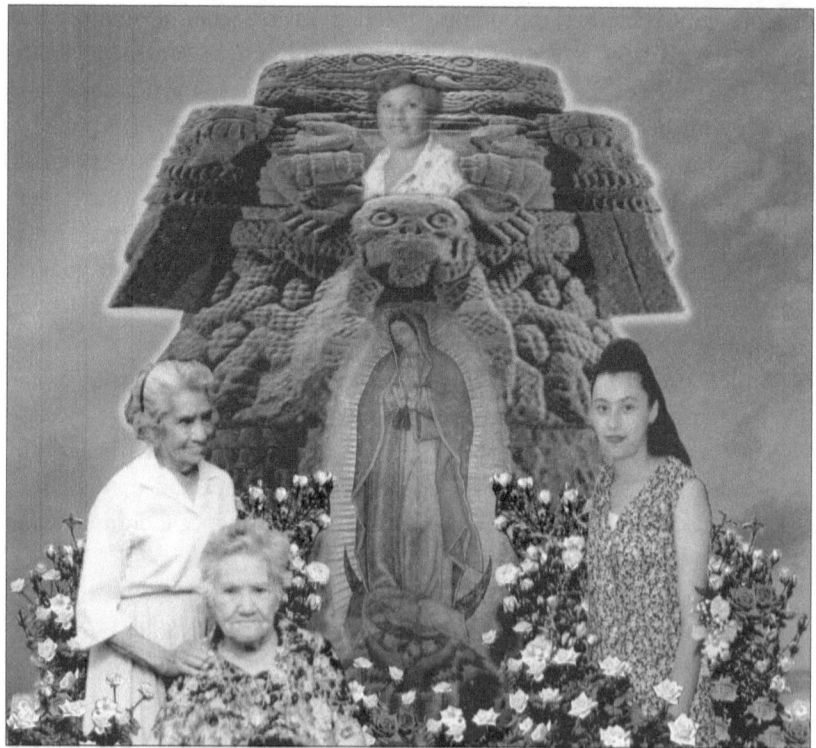

6.1.   *María de los Ángeles*. Digital print by Alma López with the SPARC/César Chávez Digital Mural Lab, © 1997. Courtesy of Alma López and the SPARC archives.

people, "an amalgam of body, mind, emotions, spirit" and "the stories we tell to ourselves about ourselves."⁴¹ In the case of *María de los Ángeles*, López resists equating unequivocally the notion of the Sacred Mother with the Virgin of Guadalupe. Instead, we find the Sacred Mother represented by older women, younger women, warriors, virgins, cultural ancestral mothers, women with many roles to play: the Tonantzin–Guadalupe–Coatlicue–Coyolxauhqui–Real Chicana mothers of the community, who are also women.

Important as well is the connection between place, identity, and community in *María de los Ángeles*. By stirring historical memory and cultural pride, López reclaims an urban community of colonized Aztlán. But the heroic iconography of *her* Aztlán originates in women's bodies, which are linked to a spiritual female ancestry from the pre- and postconquest era. Therefore, *María de los Ángeles* counters the racist appropriation of space in Los Angeles, produces political empowerment, and returns to the Estrada Courts community the memory of its female cultural roots.

LOVE AS OPPOSITIONAL SOCIAL ACTION IN ALMA LÓPEZ'S ARTWORKS

In *December 12* (1999) from her Lupe and Sirena series, López reenacts the story of the miraculous apparition of Our Lady to Juan Diego, but this time the artist herself is the messenger of the miracle. Several elements from the *Nican Mopohua* are transformed in this composition. The place of origin is located, once again, in the Chicana body. As another aspect of the Tonantzin Guadalupe story, López layers the identity of Coyolxauhqui—the Aztec moon goddess who was dismembered by her brother Huitzilopochtli. With Coyolxauhqui, the artist unearths the spiritual female ancestry of Tonantzin Guadalupe to privilege the active female warrior who resists patriarchal ideology, represented by Huitzilopochtli. In *December 12* López transposes her image from *Lupe and Sirena in Love* (1999) onto the *tilma*, or the mantle, "to show that what appears to the Juana Diega is not just Our Lady of Guadalupe but Guadalupe embracing the *sirena*,"⁴² says López, thus making it a queer apparition "of unconditional love for the queer body of Juana Diega." Luz Calvo interprets the meaning of the *sirena*, an image from the popular game *lotería*, as follows: "Within the grid of *mexicanidad* mapped by *lotería*, La Sirena stands out as a hybrid subject: she is part woman, part fish. This Sirena appears to be of mestiza heritage because instead of the usual blonde hair this mermaid has long, wavy black hair. She is yet another figural representation of Chicana subjectivity."[43]

Alma López further explains the image as a hybrid figure, symbolizing the miracle of bringing together in love two radically different natures. As she explains it: "The apparition, the miracle of unconditional love, is no longer of the Virgen, but it is also of the couple. This is a miraculous love because Lupe and Sirena come from different worlds, air and water, but they come together in love."[44] Through the *sirena*'s hybrid nature (part human, part fish), López provides a visual language to represent lesbian love. As Yarbro-Bejarano has shown, the scarcity of lesbian images in Chicano/a art history stems from "a conflicted history of racial and sexual representations as well as an attachment to *certain* embodiments of the identity of Chicana/o."[45] In the case of *December 12*, the artist disrupts the cultural-nationalist representations of Guadalupe as mother/motherland by queering the story of La Virgen's apparition. Moreover, her *sirena* challenges heteronormativity (racism, sexism, and homophobia) since she at once embodies the fetishistic fantasy object (the hypersexual brown female) and queers the Chicano/Mexican imaginary that constructs her, for the brown beautiful female is, in fact, lesbian. By transforming the *sirena* from a heterosexist fantasy to a representation of lesbian spiritual and erotic love, López engages the spectator in Sandoval's meta-ideologizing. This is the appropriation and transformation of the dominant ideology of heterosexism.

From the standpoint of the original narrative/icon of the Virgin of Guadalupe, *December 12* represents a radical transformation that points to Sandoval's methodology of the oppressed. As we saw earlier in this chapter, the method was developed to challenge dominant ideologies via five technologies of resistance: semiotics, deconstruction, meta-ideologizing, democratics, and differential movement. López avails herself of these technologies and reads the Guadalupe story as a sign of a dominant ideological apparatus that excludes any expression of love that is not heterosexual and white. The artist deconstructs this ideology by breaking down the original icon to include other protagonists: the artist herself as the messenger; Coyolxauhqui, or the warrior moon goddess who resists patriarchy; and the lesbian couple representing unconditional love. By appropriating and transforming the signifier, López engages in meta-ideologizing and points to how ideology shapes our conception of reality. Moreover, her visual transformation of the icon can be considered an oppositional social action, for it intervenes on behalf of lesbian

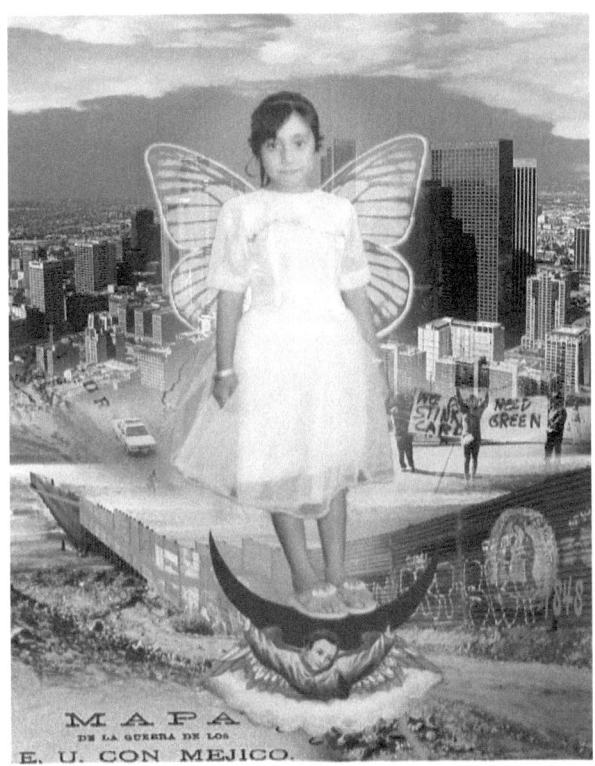

Santa Niña de Mochis. Digital print by Alma López, © 1999. Courtesy of Alma López.

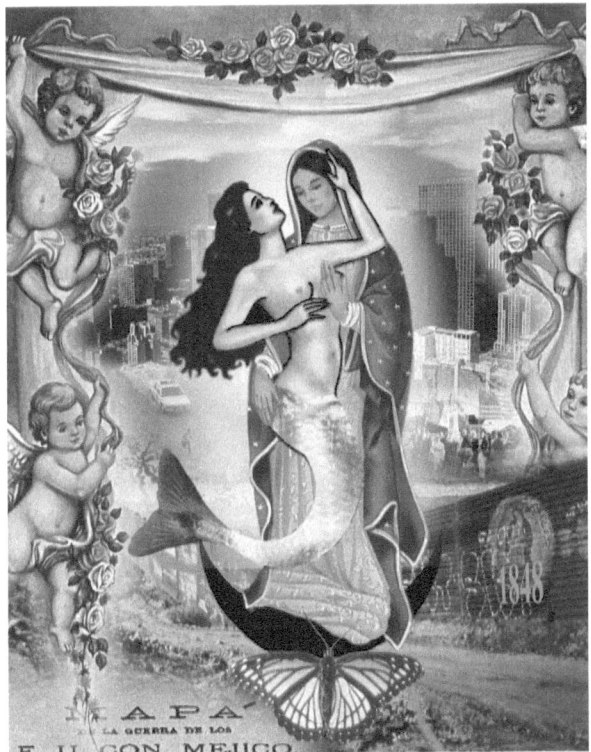

Lupe and Sirena in Love. Digital print by Alma López, © 1999. Courtesy of Alma López.

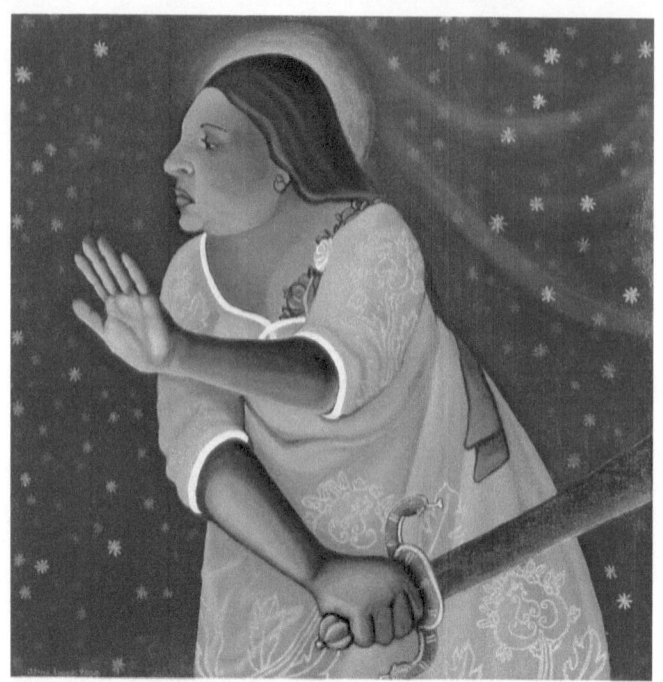

Coyolxauhqui Returns as Our Lady Disguised as La Virgen de Guadalupe to Defend the Rights of las Chicanas. Acrylic on canvas by Alma López, © 2004. Courtesy of Alma López.

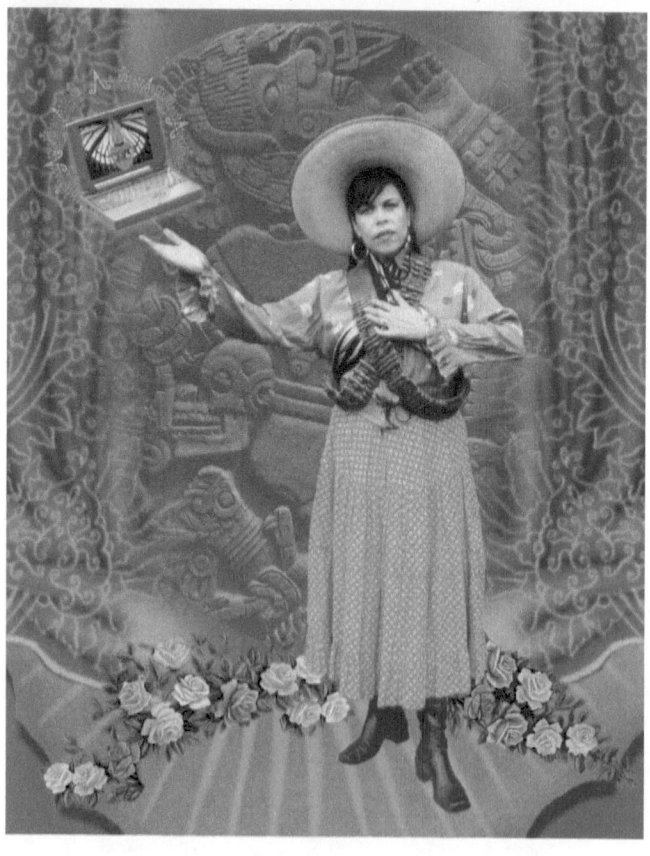

Adelita. Digital print by Alma López, © 2001. Courtesy of Alma López. Special thanks to Diane Rodríguez.

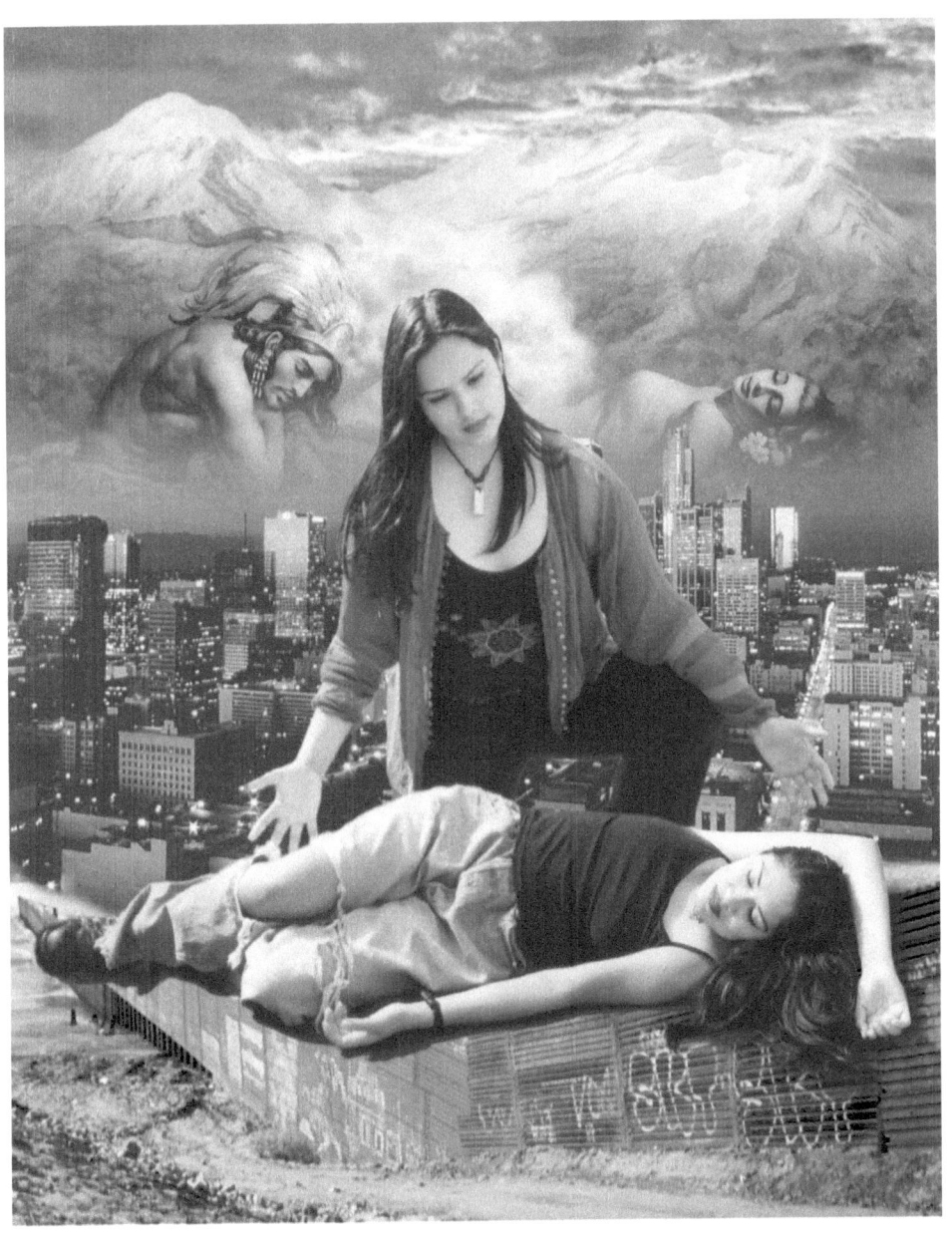

Ixta. Digital print by Alma López, © 1999. Courtesy of Alma López.
Special thanks to Cristina Serna and Mirna Tapia.

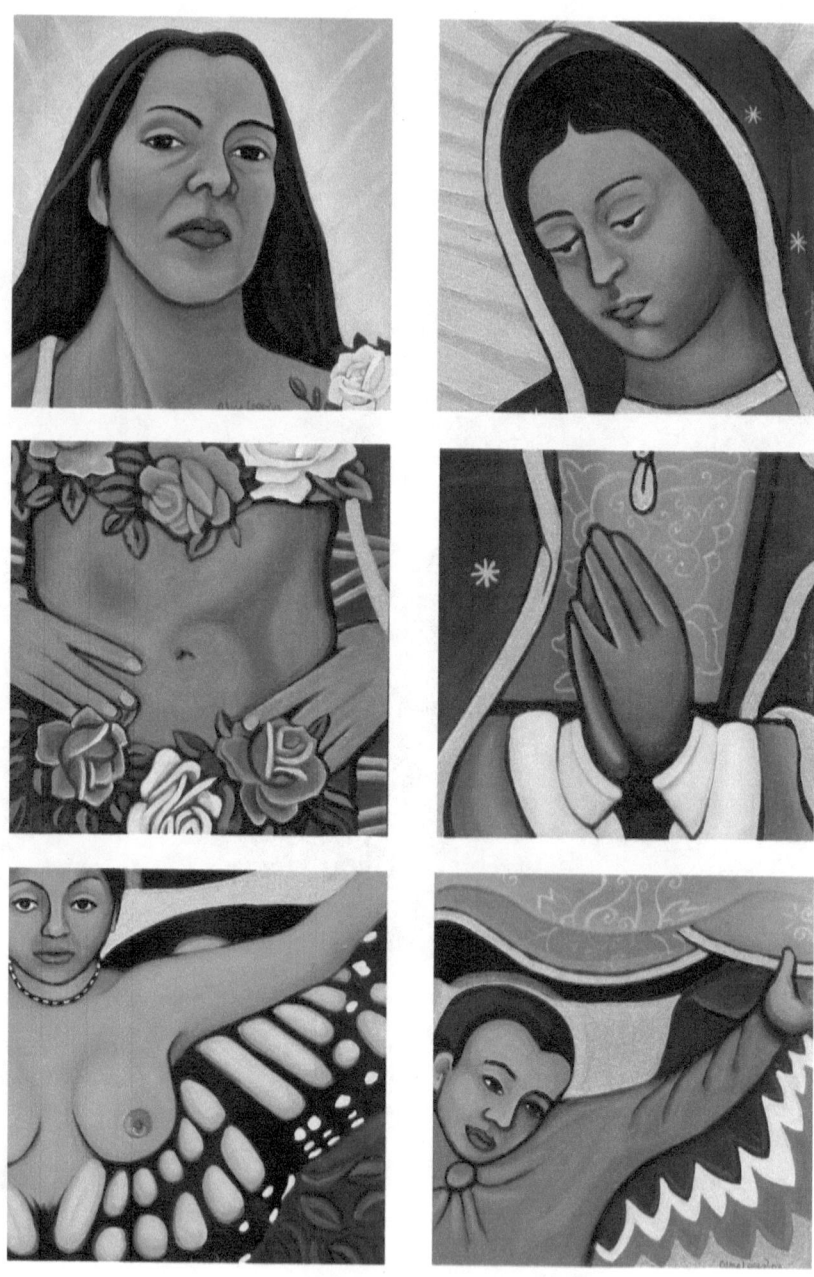

Virgen/Lady. Acrylic on canvas by Alma López, © 2001–2009. Courtesy of Alma López.

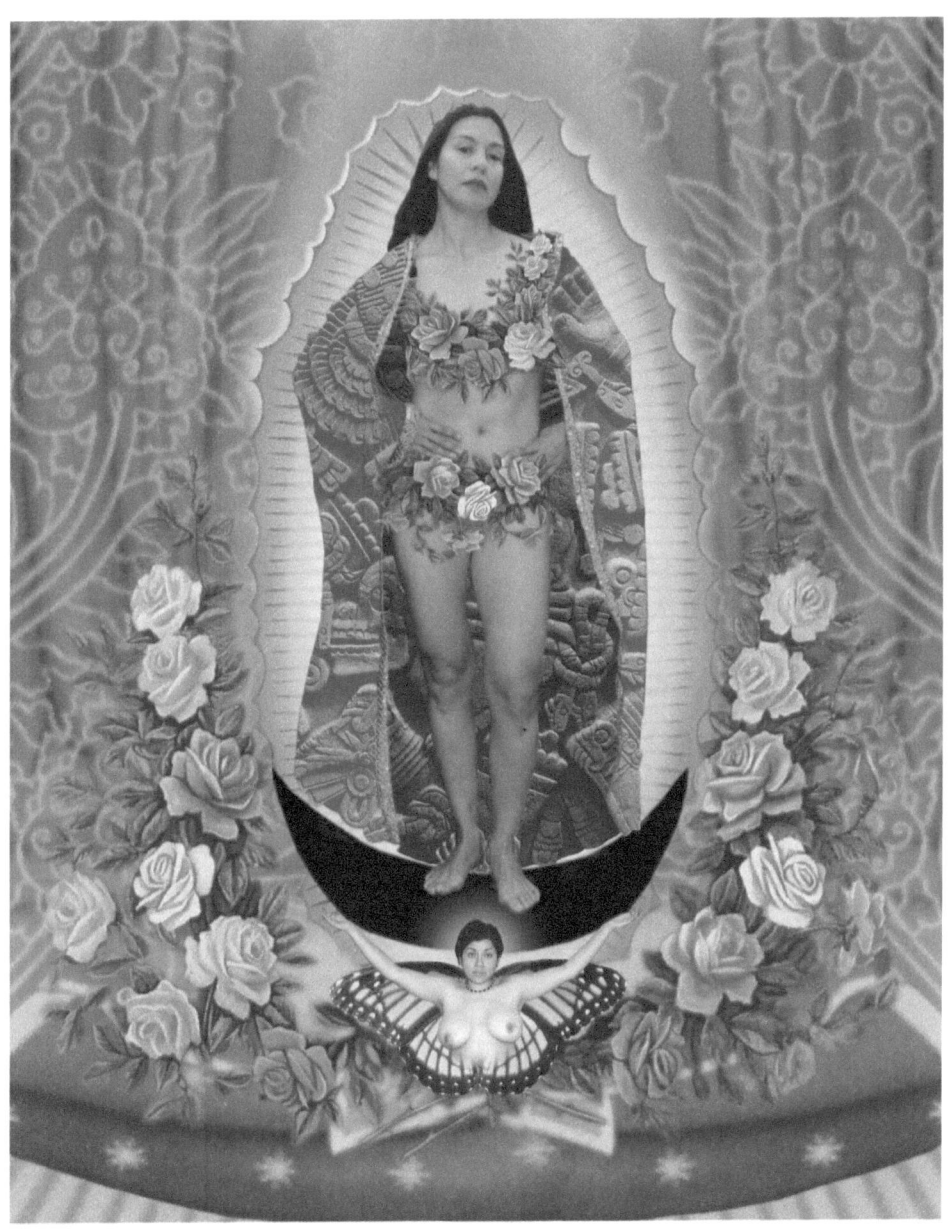

Our Lady. Digital print by Alma López, © 1999. Courtesy of Alma López.
Special thanks to Raquel Salinas and Raquel Gutiérrez.

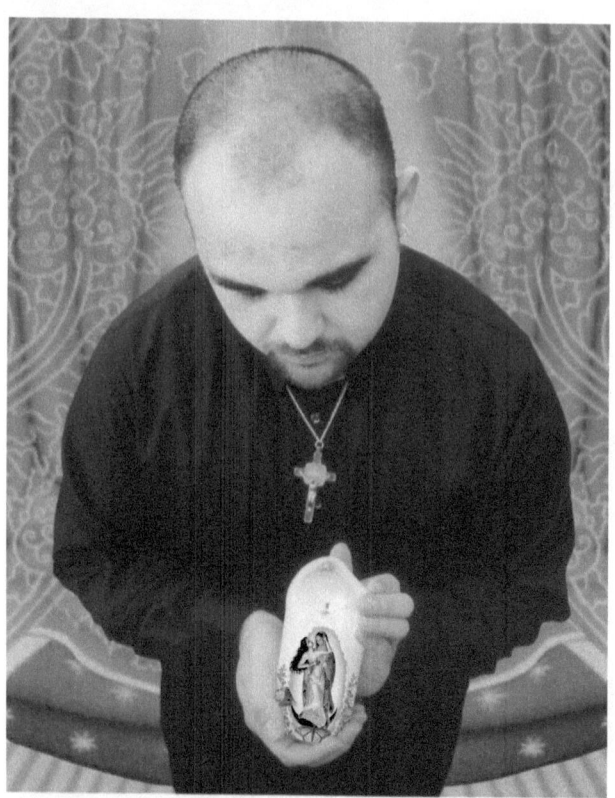

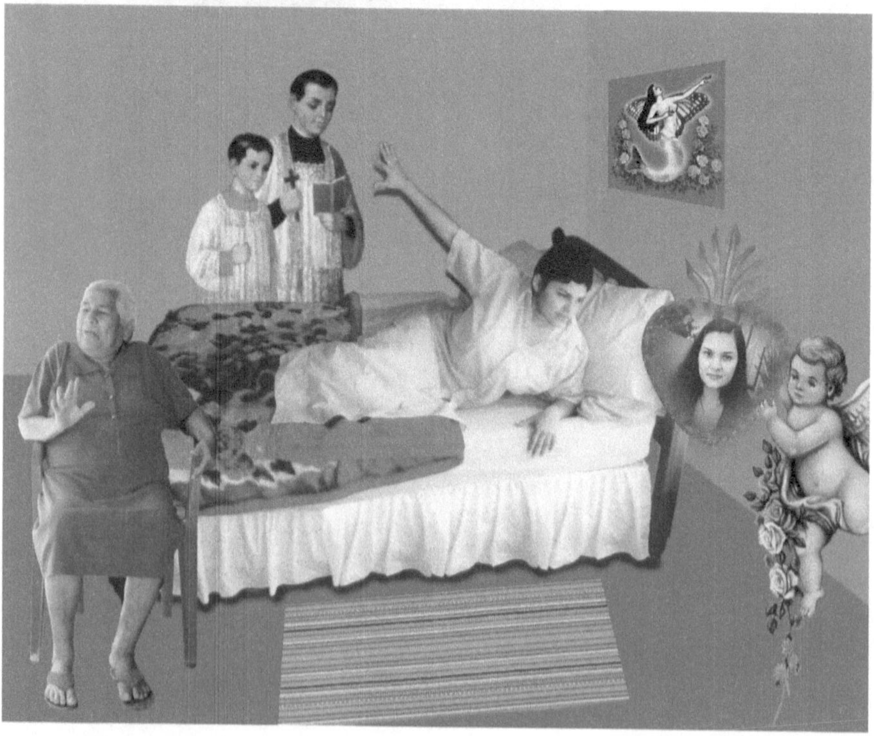

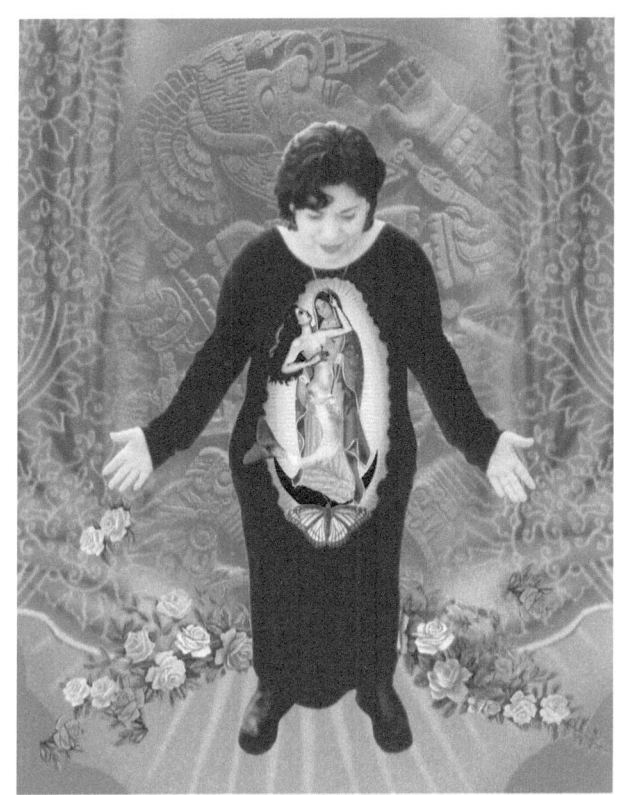

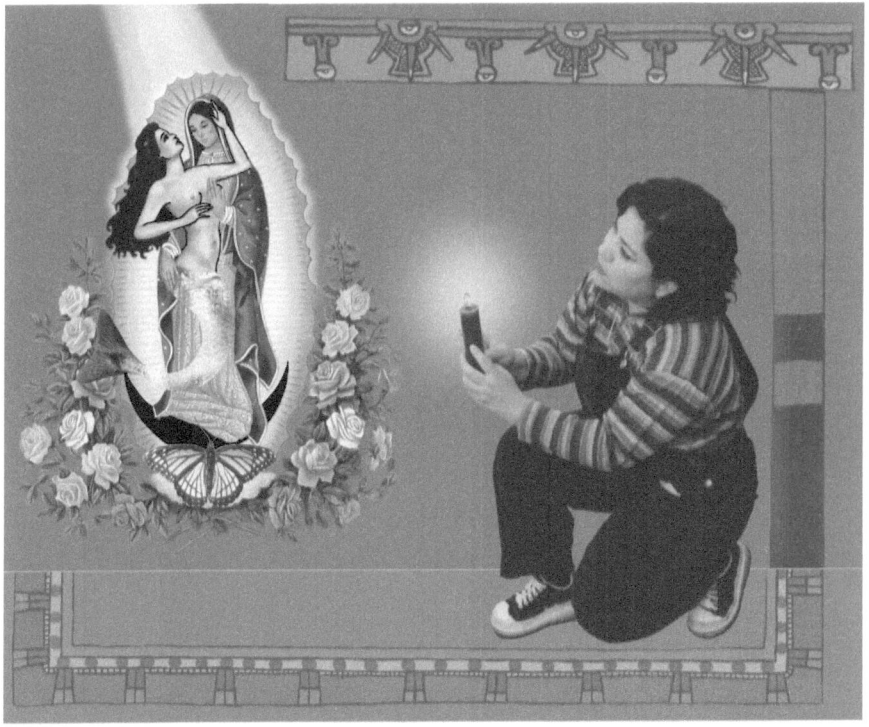

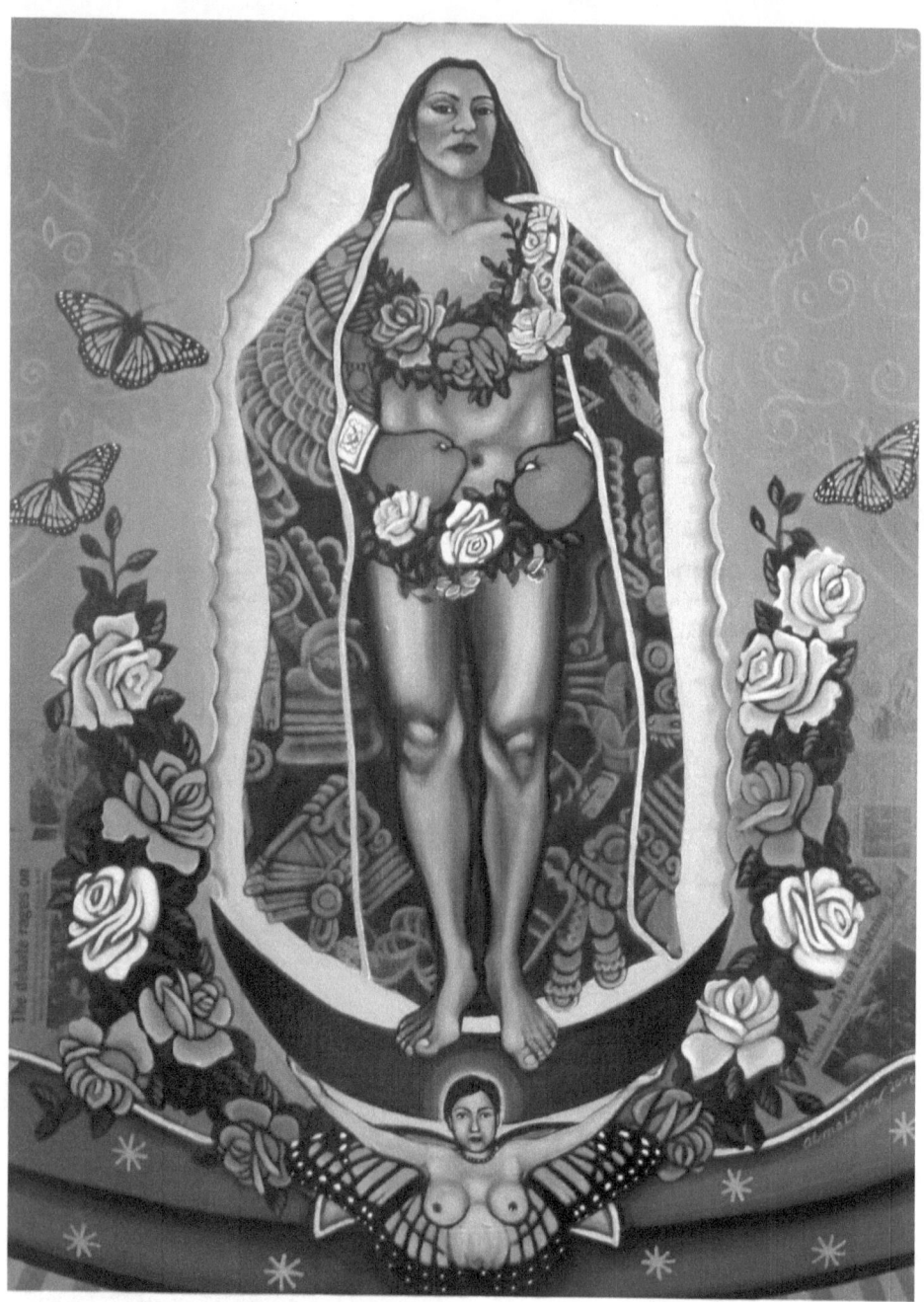

Our Lady of Controversy II, Alma López, 2008.

love, complying with the love imperative (a moral commitment to equality) in the democratics technology. Ultimately, *December 12* exemplifies Sandoval's technologies of resistance in the methodology of the oppressed, for the piece invites the spectator to operate both within and outside religious/racial/ gender/class ideologies and transforms power relations through a process of shifting location that mobilizes identities and thrives in oscillation.

Through these technologies working in concert, *December 12* points to a complex kind of love, a hermeneutic, or a way of approaching and interpreting reality that breaks through the ideological apparatus to remake community. Evoking Roland Barthes's language in *A Lovers' Discourse*, Sandoval compares this social approach to the language of lovers, which breaks through social narratives representing the law: "The language of lovers can puncture through the everyday narratives that tie us to social time and space, to the descriptions, recitals, and plots that dull and order our senses insofar as such social narratives are tied to the law. The act of falling in love can thus function as a 'punctum,' that which breaks through social narratives to permit a bleeding, meanings unanchored and moving away from their traditional moorings."[46] In other words, love releases consciousness from its grounding in dominant language, identities, and powers because, engulfed by love, we experience a zero degree of all meaning; we submit, drift, and pass into another kind of knowledge, the erotics, the sensuous apprehension and expression of love, where the one who gathers the narrative is undone. Within this experience, subjectivity becomes freed from ideology or from master narratives deeply indebted to racism and colonialism. Alma López's images function as a "punctum" because they bleed out social narratives that divide communities by gender, race, sexual orientation, class, and place of origin. In *December 12* López dislodges meanings that have been attached to the traditional icon and makes us look behind it to propose an alternative love story that embraces the experiences of the subaltern and the marginalized, including the queer female immigrant experience.

In another important composition from the Lupe and Sirena series entitled *Diego* (1999), López retells the story of the apparition from the point of view of Diego, who looks down at a small candle that intertextually represents the originating piece from the series. Alterations to the original narrative of the Virgin of Guadalupe are crucial here insofar as they imply a nonessentialist notion of identity. In the *Nican Mopohua*, we read that Juan Diego was a poor *macehual*, a simple man, "an unhappy laborer," "whose destiny was to obey,

to serve, to be taken," in sum, "a burden."[47] Tonantzin Guadalupe's message
was for the *macehuales*, the vanquished of the conquest represented by Juan
Diego, those who after the conquest had ended up in the position of the dispossessed and the marginalized. And the message was one of love and hope.
As López explains, in *Diego* she appropriates this message of unconditional
love: "When the Virgen de Guadalupe first appeared to Juan Diego, she told
him, 'I love you, you can trust me, I am you and you are me. This is a story
about unconditional love because you are me and I am you.' Diego is the
recipient of that love and also the witness of the queer love that Lupe and La
Sirena represent. Diego is wrapped around the love of the Virgen; her mantle
surrounds him. The image relates to *December 12*, where the apparition, the
miracle of unconditional love, is no longer of the Virgen, but it is also of
the couple."[48] As in the original story, López's Diego is the recipient and the
witness of love, yet he represents not one who is destined "to obey and to
serve, "to be taken," or to be "a burden" because of class or race but, rather,
one who loves through alliance and affinity, across lines of difference. Thus,
the language of love embedded in the original story is lifted and deployed by
López to puncture class, race, gender, and sexual narratives that dominant
ideologies enforce. The notion of *mestizaje* that *Diego* embodies points not to
bloodlines but to lines of affinity that occur through attraction or empathy in
spite of difference, as represented by the relationship between Diego and the
queer couple. Diego is a mestizo who loves and accepts the "third meaning"
enacted by Lupe and the *sirena*, the queer couple.[49]

QUEERING THE SACRED THROUGH TROPES

This notion of *mestizaje* as lines of affinity and alliance that occur through
unconditional love is central in *Our Lady*. In this section I will argue that in
Our Lady López queers the image of the Virgin of Guadalupe through the use
of tropes that question social and cultural norms and that decenter notions
of gender and reproductive sexuality. Of all the tropes, synecdoche (from the
Greek, meaning "act of taking together," or "understanding one thing with
another") strikes me as a particularly powerful tool for understanding the
subversive quality of López's artwork since synecdoche captures meanings
that might be assumed without being expressed.[50] Kenneth Burke emphasizes that in ancient metaphysical doctrines of macrocosm and microcosm
the individual (read male not female) is seen as recapitulating the nature and

structure of the universe.[51] This is particularly relevant in López's case since the artist relies on the power of the synecdoche to dismantle assumptions about Chicana bodies, female sexuality, and spirituality by queering them in relation to both the U.S. and the Chicano nation.

As I mentioned earlier, in *Our Lady* López disrobes the sacred image, covering parts of the body with roses and a stone cape representing Coyolxauhqui, the warrior Aztec goddess of the moon. The cape functions as a synecdoche that signals Aztec spiritual female ancestry, and the roses point both to the postconquest Guadalupana and the *xochitl*, or flower, the Aztec symbol of beauty and truth. These discrete elements express an identity that includes several cultures, spiritualities, and bloodlines (at least Mexican, Chicana, Spanish, and indigenous). The dismembered body of Coyolxauhqui that the cape brings to the foreground is reconstructed on the body of Raquel Salinas. This synecdochic manipulation suggests that *Our Lady* represents the Aztec warrior who is returning to defy gendered power relations in the U.S./Chicano nation. Accordingly, in *Our Lady*, the sacred image becomes flesh in order to challenge assumptions about the Latina brown body.

In López's image, Our Lady does not wear the maternity band that marks the original icon. This new turn in meaning points to a body that goes beyond the cultural mandate of sexual reproduction to become a site of beauty and truth, meanings that are encoded by both the Aztec and the Christian symbols of the rose. As López has stated, for her, the rose signals that which is *real* or the evidence of being real. Hence, in *Our Lady* the roses covering the body can be interpreted as a synecdochic expression of the *real* beauty and truth of Latina bodies. Also important, the bare-breasted young Latina angel emerging from a Viceroy butterfly serves as synecdoche for queer identity.

The queer butterfly angel, then, contests canonical Catholic spirituality in two ways: first, it uncovers the female body, while Catholicism dictates that the naked female body is sinful; and second, as a synecdoche for queerness, it makes queer identity a type of pedestal for *Our Lady*, thus underscoring the queer message, that is, the message of loving difference, represented by the entire image. In López's own words: "The Viceroy butterfly mimics the Monarch, it looks like the Monarch, but on its secondary wing it has a horizontal line. So the Viceroy butterfly looks the same; it is part of the same community, but it is a little different; it's queer. We face the same difficulties of migration, the same issues, are part of the same community, but we are a little different."[52] In that very sense, the Chicana butterfly in *Our Lady* points to the technologies of resistance we saw in *December 12* as well as to the notion of *mestizaje* that is embodied in *Diego*, for it speaks on behalf of those in the community who suffer similar oppression but who are, in the words of the artist, "a little different."

As these examples demonstrate, more than reversing terms or attempting merely to destroy meanings, López engages in a differential analysis that highlights the instability inherent in the notions of race, class, gender, and sexuality, often regarded as something natural and innate in both the United States and the Chicano nation. Through synecdochic manipulations, López queers the sacred image of the Virgin of Guadalupe, transgressing the borders between the "proper" and the "improper," and producing a visual strategy that represents what Nikki Sullivan calls a "queer practice," that is, a critical approach that emphasizes "the constructed, contingent, unstable and heterogeneous character of subjectivity, social relations, power and knowledge."[53]

TONANTZIN-GUADALUPE-COATLICUE-COYOLXAUHQUI-CHICANA: A MESTIZA-INSPIRED SPIRITUALITY

Given the controversy surrounding *Our Lady*, we must consider the question of what the Virgin of Guadalupe means to López. In the last analysis, for Alma López, La Virgen de Guadalupe represents a kaleidoscopic cultural experience including the body of the Mother, who is not one but many. She is a multiplicity of spiritual Mothers linked through a cross section of bloodlines, mythologies, spiritualities, and communities, as represented in *María de los Ángeles*. She is the Land/Body of Sustenance, who teaches survival to the subject of colonized Aztlán, as in *Santa Niña de Mochis*, where La Virgen enables remembering and inscribing the Chicana body. And in *December 12* and *Diego*, she is the miracle of an unconditional love—one that embraces alliance and affinity across lines of difference by resisting and deflating dominant ideologies. To summarize, in López's Lupe and Sirena series, La Virgen represents a mestiza-inspired spirituality that honors the Chicana body, builds alliances with the colonized (including those who are oppressed by their own families and communities because of their sexuality), and seeks social justice by conceptualizing a more democratic and loving maternal imaginary for the Chicano/a community.

The examples analyzed above also demonstrate that for Alma López queering the sacred image of Guadalupe is a political *movida* (move) seeking to dislodge racial, gender, sexual, and spiritual meanings that are normative within both the United States and the Chicano nation. As López herself states, her imagery intervenes politically in these narratives because "I am not interested in reproducing something that has been done. I am interested in investigating and asking how does this image relate to my reality? Clearly, I am not alone; many women like me are affected by racism, homophobia, and a gendered socialization. I use images that I know and help me understand where I am standing with respect to many issues: social, cultural, gender, racial, sexual."[54]

As Luz Calvo, Alicia Gaspar de Alba, and many other critics and historians have demonstrated, the sacred image of the Virgin of Guadalupe has always been a sign of political and spiritual solidarity. Key symbols from the *Nican Mopohua*, such as roses, goddesses, the *tilma,* and the community of the vanquished, repeatedly find expression in Alma López's artwork and bring colonized Aztlán into focus. But instead of reclaiming the lost land through the nationalist tropes used by Chicano artists, López reclaims her full spiritual and bodily self through Gaspar de Alba's "embodied aesthetics," where the body functions as a site of origin and liberation. The Lupe and Sirena series and, in particular, *Our Lady* represent not an essentialist notion of the sacred but a provisional political sacred that spoils and denaturalizes heteronormativity and at the same time manipulates and subverts the nationalist tropes of the Aztlán aesthetic. López disrupts U.S. and Chicano nation-building narratives and connects instead to an alternative system of knowledge, which I call "spiritual" because its content functions as a healing force that enables an existence in liminal spaces that are contingent, unstable, and heterogeneous. Her artwork points to a complex kind of love practiced by U.S. Third World feminists of color, in which love is understood as a hermeneutic, or a set of practices and procedures that lead to a differential mode of consciousness. By deploying that hermeneutic the artist is able to summon abstruse meanings beyond dualistic thought, meanings that shimmer behind all we know.

NOTES

Most of the Alma López images discussed in this chapter are located in the color plate section of the book.

1. Chap. 5, this volume.
2. For example, the engraving by Samuel Stradanus, *Indulgence for Alms towards the Erection of a Church Dedicated to the Virgin of Guadalupe*, ca. 1615–1620, copper, 12⅞ × 8¼ inches (Metropolitan Museum of Art, New York, gift of H. H. Behrens, 1948 [48.70]), represents miracles that occurred to the governing Creole class. In the upper-left section we see the miraculous healing of Don Luis de Castilla, a rich Spaniard, and to the right, the intervention of the Virgin of Guadalupe for the son of the Spanish conqueror, Don Antonio de Carvajal, who fell from his horse. Stradanus's engraving is also important for what it excludes. As Jeanette Favrot Peterson explains: "None of the ex-votos represents a miracle worked by Guadalupe on behalf of her native constituency, including her cure of Juan Diego's uncle in 1531" ("The Virgin of Guadalupe: Symbol of Conquest or Liberation?" *Art Journal* 51.4 [1992]: 39–47; quotation on 40). For other in-depth discussions of contradictory uses of La Virgen's image, see also Jacques Lafaye, *Quetzalcóatl and Guadalupe: The Formation of a Mexican National Consciousness, 1531–1813*, translated by Benjamin Keen (Chicago: University of Chicago Press, 1976); and William Taylor, "The Virgin of Guadalupe in New Spain: An Inquiry into the Social History of Marian Devotion," *American Ethnologist* 1 (1987): 9–33.
3. The images examined here are reproduced with the permission of the artist, Alma López, who holds the copyright. These images cannot be reproduced by any informational system without permission from the artist. I am immensely grateful to López for her permission to reproduce them in this publication.
4. See, for example, Ana Castillo, *Goddess of the Americas/La Diosa de las Américas: Writings of the Virgin of Guadalupe* (1996); Sandra Cisneros, *Woman Hollering Creek and Other Stories* (1991); Yolanda M. López, *Victoria F. Franco: Our Lady of Guadalupe* (1978); idem, *Margaret F. Stewart: Our Lady of Guadalupe* (1978); idem, *Portrait of the Artist as the Virgin of Guadalupe* (1978); idem, *Nuestra Madre* (1985–1988); idem, *Madre Mestiza* (2002); idem, *Virgin at the Crossroads* (2002); and Ester Hernández's artwork, which I address in "La Virgen de Guadalupe y el feminismo transnacional de Ester Hernández," in *Confluencias en México: Palabra y Género*, edited by Patricia González Gómez Cásseres and Alicia V. Ramírez Olivares (Puebla, Mex.: Fomento Editorial, Benemérita Universidad Autónoma de Puebla, 2007), 299–315. For a discussion of Castillo's *Goddess of the Americas*, see my "Disrobed: The Virgin of Guadalupe and Social Activism in Chicanas' Writing," *Pembroke Magazine* 40 (2008): 187–200. These works offer new ways of

understanding gender, body, and spirituality and challenge an Anglo-European feminist discourse, which has maintained a minimalist and dualistic discourse about Hispanic feminisms with the formula "marianismo/machismo."

5. Alma López, "Silencing Our Lady: La Respuesta de Alma," *Aztlán: A Journal of Chicano Studies* 26.2 (2001): 254–255.

6. Nancy Warren, "Some Like a Virgin, Some Don't: Alma López Generates Controversy in New Mexico," Special to SF Gate, April 27, 2001, www.sfgate.com.

7. Calvo, Chap. 5 here.

8. Chela Sandoval, *Methodology of the Oppressed* (Minneapolis: University of Minnesota Press, 2000), 43.

9. Ibid., 191.

10. Aida Hurtado, "Relating to Privilege: Seduction and Rejection in the Subordination of White Women and Women of Color," *Signs* 14.4 (1989): 833.

11. For instance, Chicana critic and writer Gloria E. Anzaldúa describes her experience with exclusion in the Feminist Writers' Guild Community from the San Francisco, Oakland, and Berkeley area: "When it was my turn to talk, it was almost like they were putting words into my mouth. They interrupted me while I was still talking or after I had finished, they interpreted what I just said according to their thoughts and ideas. They thought that all women were oppressed in the same way, and they tried to force me to accept their image of me and my experiences . . . They didn't understand what we were going through. They wanted to speak for us because they had an idea of what feminism was, and they wanted to apply their notion of feminism across all cultures" (Karin Ikas, "Interview with Gloria Anzaldúa," *Borderlands/La Frontera: The New Mestiza*, 2nd ed. [San Francisco: Aunt Lute Books, 1999]: 231–232).

12. Chicana critics Norma Alarcón, Gloria Anzaldúa, Laura Pérez and Chela Sandoval have theorized about the role of the Virgin of Guadalupe in Chicanas' spirituality and Chicana *mestizaje* as a method for liberation. Specifically, see Norma Alarcón, "Traddutora, Traditora: A Paradigmatic Figure of Chicana Feminism," *Cultural Critique* 13 (1989): 57–87; Gloria Anzaldúa, *Borderlands/La Frontera: The New Mestiza (San Francisco: Aunt Lute Books, 1987)*; and Laura E. Pérez, *Chicana Art.*

13. I explored this issue in "Decentralizing Globalization: Cultural Politics, Transnational Feminisms, and Religious Iconography in Chicana Artistic Productions," National Association for Chicana and Chicano Studies, Austin, Texas, March 19–22, 2008, where I examined works by Ester Hernández, Consuelo Jiménez Underwood, Alma López, and Marion C. Martínez.

14. Chela Sandoval, "Re-entering Cyberspace: Sciences of Resistance," *Dispositio/n* 19.46 (1994): 89.

15. The Mesoamerican concept of *nepantla*, a Nahuatl word referencing "the land in the middle," was originally used by Nahuatl-speaking people in the sixteenth century to define their situation vis-à-vis the Spanish colonizer. According to the legend, Fray Diego Durán, a Dominican missionary who was writing an ethnographic history of the Nahuatl speakers, asked one of them what he thought about the difficult cultural situation created for them by the Spanish invasion. The informant is said to have responded: "Estamos en nepantla," that is, "We are in between." According to Anzaldúa, the state of being in *nepantla*, "prompts you to shift into a new perception of yourself and of the world. Nothing is fixed. The pulse of existence, the heart of the universe is fluid. Identity, like a river, is always changing, always in transition, always in nepantla" ("Now Let Us Shift . . . the Path of Conocimiento . . . Inner Work, Public Acts," in *This Bridge We Call Home: Radical Visions for Transformation*, edited by Gloria E. Anzaldúa and Analouise Keating [New York: Routledge, 2002]: 556).

16. Gloria E. Anzaldúa, "Nepantla: Creative Acts of Vision," *Collected Papers (1942–2004)*, Benson Latin American Collection, University of Texas, Austin, 1.

17. Gloria E. Anzaldúa, "Border Arte: *Nepantla*, el Lugar de la Frontera," in *La Frontera/The Border: Art about the Mexican/United States Border Experience* (San Diego: Centro Cultural de La Raza/Museum of Contemporary Art, 1993): 110.

18. Luz Calvo, "It's Not about the Gender in My Nation, but the Nation in My Gender," paper presented at the "Irreverent Apparitions: Chiasmatic Interpretations of Alma López's 'Our Lady,'" NACCS Roundtable. I am grateful to Luz Calvo for sharing the text of her talk via an e-mail on November 8, 2008, from which this citation comes.

19. Miguel León-Portilla, *Endangered Cultures* (Dallas, Tex.: Southern Methodist University Press, 1990), 13.

20. Ibid., 13.

21. Deena J. González, *Refusing the Favor: The Spanish-Mexican Women of Santa Fe, 1820–1880* (Oxford: Oxford University Press, 1999), 3.

22. I am grateful to Alicia Gaspar de Alba for offering this insightful observation.

23. Alma López, phone interview with the author, November 13, 2008.

24. Alma López, interview with the author, March 21, 2008, Austin, Texas.

25. Alma López, phone interview with the author, November 13, 2008.

26. For an in-depth analysis of Chicana spirituality, see Laura Pérez, *Chicana Art: The Politics of Spiritual and Aesthetic Altarities* (Durham, N.C.: Duke University Press, 2007).

27. See León Portilla's useful discussion of Valeriano's manuscript in *Tonantzin Guadalupe: Pensamiento náhuatl y mensaje cristiano en el 'Nican Mopohua'* (Mexico City: Fondo de Cultura Económica, 2000), 19–47. For another account of the origin and impact of the *Nican Mopohua*, see Richard Nebel, *Santa María Tonantzin: Virgen de Guadalupe* (Mexico City: Fondo de Cultura Económica, 1995), 167–269.

28. León-Portilla, *Tonantzin Guadalupe*, 19–47.

29. Alma López, phone interview with the author, November 13, 2008.

30. Alicia Gaspar de Alba, "There Is No Place Like Aztlán: Embodied Aesthetics in Chicana Art," *New Centennial Review* 42.2 (2004): 114.

31. Ibid.

32. Ibid., 123.

33. Ibid., 123–124.

34. Ibid., 125.

35. Ibid., 125.

36. Ibid., 127.

37. Alma López, phone interview with the author, November 13, 2008.

38. Elizabeth "Betita" Martínez, *500 Years of Chicana Women's History: Años de la Mujer Chicana* (New Brunswick, N.J.: Rutgers University Press, 2008), 27.

39. Gaspar de Alba, "There Is No Place Like Aztlán," 123.

40. Alma López, phone interview with the author, November 13, 2008.

41. Anzaldúa describes this idea in "Nepantla: The Theory and the Manifesto," *Collected Papers (1942–2004)*, Benson Latin American Collection, University of Texas, Austin.

42. Alma López, phone interview with the author, 14 October 2009.

43. Luz Calvo, "Art Comes for the Archbishop," 215.

44. Alma López, phone interview with the author, November 13, 2008.

45. Yvonne Yarbro-Bejarano, "Laying It Bare: The Queer/Colored Body in Photography by Laura Aguilar," in *Living Chicana Theory*, edited by Carla Trujillo (Berkeley, Calif.: Third Woman Press, 1998), 291, original emphasis.

46. Sandoval, *Methodology of the Oppressed*, 140.

47. León-Portilla, *Tonantzin Guadalupe*, 68, my translation.

48. Alma López, phone interview with the author, November 13, 2008.

49. *Editorial note*: Further queering the sacred text of the *Nican Mopohua* and the Guadalupe story is the fact that Diego is represented by Los Angeles queer artist Rigo Maldonado, suggesting another radical reinscription of the recently canonized saint Juan Diego.

50. Robert Evans, "Synecdoche," *Princeton Encyclopedia of Poetry and Poetics* (Princeton, N.J.: Princeton University Press, 1974), 840.

51. Kenneth Burke, "Four Master Tropes," *A Grammar of Motives, and a Rhetoric of Motives* (Cleveland, Ohio: World Publishing Co., 1945), 503.

52. Alma López, phone interview with the author, November 13, 2008.

53. See Nikki Sullivan, *A Critical Introduction to Queer Theory* (New York: New York University Press, 2003), esp. 42–43.

54. Alma López, phone interview with the author, November 13, 2008.

7

The Decolonial Virgin in a Colonial Site

IT'S NOT ABOUT THE GENDER IN MY NATION,
IT'S ABOUT THE NATION IN MY GENDER

Emma Pérez

> Chicano/a desire for a brown-skinned Gua-
> dalupe is formed in and through the social and
> historical institutionalization of racial hierar-
> chies, a direct result of the colonization of the
> Americas and its enduring racial legacies.
> However, the imagined collective allegiance to
> a sexless brown mother has come at consid-
> erable cost: women's active sexuality.
>
> LUZ CALVO, "Art Comes for the Archbishop"

ALMA LÓPEZ'S DIGITAL PRINT titled *Our Lady* offers a decolonial methodology for Chicanas who have reclaimed La Virgen de Guadalupe and reinscribed her with queer desire and
pleasure. The epigraph exemplifies a decolonial critique of
traditional gender roles pervasive in colonial, patriarchal ideologies. The ideology is one that promotes a virgin/whore dichotomy that remains integrated in Latino/a culture. And because López's digital print com-
plicates the virgin/whore binary, a controversy ensued in the Chicano nation.

In "Art Comes for the Archbishop: The Semiotics of Contemporary Chicana Feminism and the Work of Alma López" (Chap. 5 here), Chicana feminist theorist Luz Calvo reasons that the making of La Virgen de Guadalupe
depended on a colonial moment in the Americas, a coloniality that perpetu-
ates the Chicano nationalist desire for demure, passive brown women who
emulate the nation's brown Virgin.[1] Calvo's premise contests the ideology

espoused in colonial patriarchal culture. Commenting on Alma López's digital collage, *Our Lady*, the feminist theorist maintains that controversy pursues
López's representation of La Virgen de Guadalupe precisely because women,
especially Latinas and Chicanas, are not permitted to be active, sexed subjects
of their own lives. History and its colonizing institutions have not allowed
brown women to be active subjects. If, however, women break out of a passive, sexless role, they are deemed "bad" women. There are, after all, only
two types of women: the "bad" woman in the street with whom a man may
carouse and spend the night, and the "good" woman at home to whom he
is married. Good women should not be in the street carousing. Instead, they
must be condemned to virginal goodness and greet their husbands cheerfully
regardless of the latter's extramarital exploits.

With Spain's invasion of the Americas, a colonial mind-set that mirrored
Eurocentric gender roles was installed. I have argued that the Chicano/a
community inherited the virgin/whore binary that was imposed on the
"new world" through a religious icon, La Virgen de Guadalupe, and through
La Malinche, or Malintzin Tenepal, known historically as Hernán Cortés's
whore.[2] Shortly before Cortés journeyed to Tenochtitlan in 1519, Malinche
had already been sold as a slave by her parents. Offered as a gift to Cortés
along with twenty-one other Indian maidens, the young woman became an
indispensable interpreter for the Spanish conqueror. By 1521, the conquest of
Tenochtitlan was complete, and ten years later the brown Virgin appeared to
the Indian Juan Diego on Tepeyac hill. Scholars have noted that the growing
mestizo population of the "new" world rejected Spain's white Mary, compelling the Catholic Church to offer the newly colonized people a brown Virgin
with whom they could identify.[3] Interestingly, the virgin/whore dichotomy
emerged in colonial Mexico's sixteenth century as a colonial construction that
would inhabit the lives of mestizos and mestizas into the twenty-first century.
It has taken Chicana feminists to undo this colonial binary that continues to
trouble contemporary gender roles.

The Chicana lesbian artist Alma López has provided a window into de-
constructing the meaning of a paramount cultural icon in Chicano/a communities that has been used to perpetuate problematic gender expectations.
When López deliberately departs from a traditional depiction of Our Lady,
she submits knowingly an intervention that calls on audiences to revitalize
the image with new meanings. In this instance, the Virgin stands in a rather
provocative floral bikini compelling spectators to think about her as a real,

living, loving, sexed, desiring woman. Spectators, especially Chicana lesbian spectators, take pleasure in gazing on López's rendering. And that pleasure, pronounced unabashedly, is as improper as it is offensive to the patriarchal Chicano nation.

I would like to examine some of the protest language sparked by *Our Lady* when Santa Fe's Museum of International Folk Art (MOIFA) exhibited the digital artwork in 2001. What the discourse of protest shows is that the New Mexican Chicano/a community, which opposed the piece, believed that only they controlled the "true" meaning of the Virgin. Ironically, their discursive turn demonstrated how the protestors themselves, not the artist, were the ones who inflicted an overly sexualized Virgin on the people's imagination. By "putting sex into discourse" and "speaking of it ad infinitum,"[4] the protesters attempted to guard La Virgen from sexuality. Virgins, after all, must remain virgins. But while the protestors' language called for the Virgin's protection against sexual innuendo, women in general were also addressed. A close look at the discourse reveals how women were once again prohibited from being sexual, desiring subjects. As a result, the discourse that emerged from the exhibit sought to silence a specific Chicana lesbian but also to control women in general.

When examining the protestors' letters to the artist, I was not surprised that the most vociferous, persistent dissenters were men; however, the women who practiced devout community, regional Catholicism representative of Nuevomexicana tradition and history, also criticized López's *Our Lady*. As a result, the artwork itself cannot be seen as an intervention for Chicanas who challenge how the Chicano nation has marked them as colonial objects with no agency, no desire, and no right to be "desiring subjects." Instead, the "imagined collective allegiance to a sexless brown mother," as Calvo points out, was grasped and enforced.

My analysis probes the necessity of decolonizing the mind of a community ruled by historical colonial relationships that continue to stamp contemporary life and culture. How do we decolonize our community's perspectives about La Virgen de Guadalupe? Public ownership is seemingly patriarchal, I would argue, and as a result a patriarchal order of things is enforced not only by men but also by women. But the manner in which men and women prop up a patriarchal order is distinct. Moreover, particular Chicano nationalist politics is far more invested in sustaining traditional, colonial perceptions of La Virgen than in decolonizing those images.

My own relationship to La Virgen de Guadalupe is not complex. Like López, I am a Chicana lesbian who honors my mother and her plight within patriarchal institutions that dictate limitations for women. I think this specific understanding allows mothers and daughters to respect each other's methods of revering La Virgen. When my aunts and mother visit my home and see La Virgen de Guadalupe in various forms and shapes hanging on walls, sitting on windowsills and placed in niches throughout the house, they express contentment. They do not question why La Virgen appears as a tattoo on the back of a Chicana with a "punk" haircut in Ester Hernández's serigraph *La Ofrenda*, which is on view in my hallway. Nor do they remark on the amorous embrace between La Sirena and La Virgen de Guadalupe in Alma López's digital collage on my bathroom wall. I think they prefer to focus on the more traditional representations of La Virgen displayed on walls and windowsills. What I also sense is that they do not want to seem disrespectful of the less-than-traditional images in my home. But what I know about my family is that while the women are exceedingly Catholic, these same women have a sense of humor. Privately, I imagine one of them would probably have said of the angel in *Our Lady*: "¡Ay, pero qué chichona!" while another would have noted: "Pero qué bonitas flores" without judging or imposing censorship. Of course, no one made such remarks. Not publicly anyway.

Ada María Isasi-Díaz invites us to observe the difference between what Catholic Chicanas and Latinas might declare publicly and what they may say privately. Isasi-Díaz argues that Latinas are subversive in subtle, constructive practices: "Hispanas/Latinas temporarily adapt and pretend, or do not think or feel the way they are 'supposed' to."[5] For the feminist-liberation theologian, these women may not oppose dominant power structures successfully; however, they assert "quiet but effective forms of resistance."[6] In this case, I would contend that although women publicly protested López's digital representation of La Virgen by holding vigils and going to the museum to call for the removal of the art, they did not persist and sustain their protests in the same manner that three specific Chicano male ideologues did. In other words, the women did not seem as invested in writing unending complaints as were these three men. However, women came forward and wrote to López, calling her epithets like "disgraceful bitch,"[7] and as the following excerpt shows, a New Mexican woman labeled the artist *sinvergüenza*, shameless: "I was moved to tears when I saw the digital photograph of Our Lady. The artist, if she is Catholic and Hispanic as well seems to have lost all respect for our culture and most especially for what our culture holds in highest esteem. I am sure she did not learn this at her mother's knee. SINVERGUENZA."[8]

This next protestor is not as harsh even if she does offer advice to the artist: "This isn't very nice for catholics who praise our lady of guadalupe. have a little more respect for our lady and for yourself."[9]

I found that no one woman arose as a persistent critic in the same way certain men performed dogged condemnation. While I am not arguing that the protests were split along clear-cut gender lines, I am arguing that an explicit patriarchal, Chicano nationalist voice would not go away. It was as if these three men decided that they held the burden of policing and disciplining the artist—a Chicana lesbian—because her representation of La Virgen endangered the very survival of the Chicano nation. I would also add that according to the e-mails sent to López from 2001 to 2008, many Chicanas and Chicanos as well as women and men from other ethnic and racial groups unswervingly defended the artist.

Why are these nationalist men so invested in policing women's bodies, women's desires, and women's sexualities? In *The History of Sexuality*, Michel Foucault puts forth his notion of the repressive hypothesis to demonstrate why those with power practice power within the realm of sexuality. As he explains, the issue is not whether one says yes or no to sex; the real question is who gets to speak about sex and "which institutions prompt people to speak about it."[10] Moreover, he posits that various social and legal institutions may object to "wayward or unproductive sexualities," but their purpose is to conflate pleasure and power. He warns of "the pleasure that comes of exercising a power that questions, monitors, watches, spies, searches out, palpates, brings to light: and on the other hand, the pleasure that kindles at having to evade this power, flee from it, fool it, or travesty it."[11] The theorist compels us to rethink how repression operates to illuminate sexuality, but as it does so, the alleged repression also performs "perpetual spirals of power and pleasure."[12] Ultimately, the repression itself creates the endless cycle of fixation with sex and sexuality. It is an interesting dance in which power and pleasure become incontestable, fused, and ever-present.

In the same way, the male-centered ideologues took over the discursive protests, and what transpired was a language of sex that reinforced rigid gender roles within heteronormative relationships. The nationalists made statements that smacked of misogyny and homophobia as they defended historical and ecclesiastical traditions.

When women voiced disapproval, on the other hand, they expressed it once and went on with their lives. Yet these three men would not let up. Deeming themselves as either leaders or spokesmen for a single Chicano nation, José Villegas Sr., Pedro Romero Sedeño, and Ernesto Cienfuegos were probably the most vociferous dissenters on paper. The women may have publicly protested but they did not participate in the e-mail complaints that lasted for years after the exhibit closed. Taking the artist to task for misrepresenting "our madre," the dissenters each had their own agenda.

Villegas, a native of New Mexico, was the first to declare objections in a letter to López dated March 17, 2001. Pedro Romero Sedeño, who adamantly pointed out that he held a Master's in Fine Arts, challenged López's art, calling the piece anything but art. López, who also holds a Master's in Fine Arts, engaged in a lively debate with Sedeño as she defended her stance and her right to her own artistic method and imagination. In 2004, when the city of Fullerton in Southern California prepared to put *Our Lady* on display, Cienfuegos came forward as the voice speaking for a single Chicano nation while objecting to the "decadent" Chicana lesbian artist's digital print.

OUR LADY AS MOTHER-SEDUCER

Freudian psychoanalysis grants women the power of seducing and of being seduced, being . . . sexed and desiring subjects.

TERESA DE LAURETIS, *The Practice of Love*

Before I deconstruct passages from the letters to Alma López, let me back up and offer my critique of La Malinche as "phallic" mother of the Chicano nation.[13] Elsewhere, I argue for the construction of decolonial motherhood by way of Malintzin Tenepal, more popularly known as La Malinche. I argue that ideologues of the Chicano nation despise Malinche as the betrayer of her people and Cortés's whore. But for Chicanas, Malinche bore a new race. She is the all-powerful, phallic mother who is feared and despised by the heteronormative Chicano nation. La Virgen, on the other hand, is forever "virginal" and must remain sexless, nurturing, and always forgiving. The virgin/whore dichotomy continues to rear its head in contemporary society. The nation's phallogocentric discourse insists on inflicting a dichotomy that authorizes patriarchal institutions so they may continue to have power over women, both real and imagined.

Chicano nationalist discourse constructs its own discursive trappings by reinforcing the good woman/bad woman binary. Women should not aspire to be Malinche, the whore, but at the same time women can never be as holy and pure as La Virgen de Guadalupe. The challenge is that they must try to be. There are no in-betweens. No real women need apply since sexualized women are by definition already whores.

EXAMPLES OF MALE-CENTERED DISCOURSE

What is particular to modern societies, in fact,
is not that they consigned sex to a shadow existence,
but that they dedicated themselves to speaking of it
ad infinitum, while exploiting it as the secret.[14]

Chicano activist and New Mexico resident José Villegas wrote a scathing letter of protest to artist Alma López a few weeks after the exhibit with *Our Lady* opened in Santa Fe. I have included a few revealing paragraphs from the e-mail to demonstrate how Villegas was obsessed with "sacred images" of the Virgen and other Catholic icons. He was quick to point out that for him, López had crossed "sacred boundaries" and disrespected over "five hundred years" of traditional values. Ironically, Villegas imposed a colonial mind-set that believed in customs that had been the weapons of colonization. He eagerly noted "the Immaculate Conception" to instruct the artist about religious traditions that she had overlooked:

March 17, 2001

Dear Ms. López:
As you know or aware of, our local Santa Fe newspaper wrote a story "Skimpily Attired 'Our Lady' Protested." So far, the community reaction to this story is very unfavorable towards your Cyber Arte exhibit and you may find yourself in some serious trouble with our raza in Northern New Mexico
. . .
Some people say it is alright to do your own onda in art expression, however, when you cross the sacred boundaries of our gentes traditional values of over five hundred years, you cannot impose and/or provoke thought on an issue that will inflame emotions against your own gente.

A point of clarification, Our Nuestra de Guadalupe picture really consti-tutes Guadalupe. It is taken as representing the Immaculate Conception . . .

Our Indio-Chicano-Mexican religious beliefs, customs, traditions, prin-ciples, and value system is part of an entire Nuestra de Guadalupe story. Our sacred images and religious symbols is the foundation of our faith and belief systems in place and should not be taken advantage of . . . Again, these sa-cred images belong to the indigenous people of the Americas, not you and/ or your new-age ideology that your exhibit portrays as "CyberArte Tradition Meets Technology."

Que Viva La Raza!

Que Viva La Causa!

Que Viva Los Brown Berets!

Que Viva Cesar Estrada Chavez!

José L. Villegas, Sr.

Chicano Activist

Villegas uses Chicano nationalist liberatory slogans to assure how much he himself believes in Chicano liberation. By writing "Que Viva La Raza," "Que Viva La Causa," and "Que Viva Los Brown Berets," the Chicano ideologue re-confirms a nation that practices colonial, heteronormative exclusionary acts by deciding who is and who is not a real Chicano or Chicana. In his mind, López's feminist image opposes all things Chicano. And it is his antifeminist vision of the nation that he inserts into gender roles.

When a López supporter challenged Villegas's antifeminist and antilesbian stance, the critic defended himself: "At no time did I personally attack Alma because of her sexual orientation and/or gender due to this type of art. And I will not even go there! Orale! On a personal note, it was my mother's love that created the man that I am. It is my mother's sangre and tears that has molded me to what I am today. I have never disrespected my elders and thier [sic] elders, especially 'la mujer' in my barrio."[15] Again, what is reaffirmed in this message is the nationalist shift to place woman on a pedestal and, as the good woman she is, desexualize and reify her as Holy Mother. For these na-tionalist men, you simply do not mess with their vision of the Holy Mother.

Artist Pedro Romero Sedeño wrote numerous e-mails to López because he seemed convinced he had a lesson to teach her about "true" art. For Sede-ño, López's art was not art at all, and his messages articulated a patronizing, patriarchal posture. At no time did he say that he respected López the artist.

Instead he asserted that he, Pedro Romero, was the authentic artist, and López's art should never have been exhibited in any museum: "I reiterate here
that Alma López has every right to make whatever, and if this Museum wants
to prop the notion that what she made is of artistic merit, I, Pedro Romero,
have every right to question the merit of the 'work.'"[16]

Sedeño decided to offer his expertise as one who had the right to interpret
La Virgen de Guadalupe. For him, López's daring interpretation was culturally and historically wrong. Only he could really know the genuine cultural
and historical meaning of Our Lady. In Sedeño's mind, López was neither
artist nor intellectual; therefore she was not entitled to her own historical rendering of famous female icons. But what I find intriguing is Sedeño's personal
attack on López. He feared that López believed women were unforgiving and
retaliatory when in fact women should "bestow compassion." His revealing
assertion proves how yet another Chicano nationalist ideologue insists that
women must restrict themselves to specific gender roles, and those roles call
for ongoing forgiveness regardless of men's "sins":

> Alma's concept of feminine strength is that of a woman ready to retaliate,
> not one prepared to bestow compassion. Depicted are princesses of destruc-
> tion, not the Queen of creation . . . Alma López' and her supporters' mistake
> is to claim that her piece is an interpretation of Guadalupe, much less a valid
> one. The work is more about the myth of the ego of Alma López, an ego
> that deceives her to believe "retaliate, don't forgive," an anti-myth made to
> stand up to the creation of compassion. This analysis can be applied also to
> the La Lupe series as a whole. Guadalupe does not cavort with La Sirena,
> who does not exist, except in myths and loteria cards and in the myth, in my
> opinion, that Alma López actually cares about the feelings of respect or value
> a viewer may have for Guadalupe-Tonantzin, our compassionate Mother.[17]

In a message sent a week earlier, Sedeño emphasized that women were best
represented in rigid gender roles. "I think feminist art comes into its full
power when it acknowledges and upholds, rather than ignores, the maternal
values of womanhood."[18]

Through May of 2002, Sedeño sustained his objections and wrote more e-
mails to illustrate how his was the correct conviction while "a Chicano ideology that seeks to repudiate the image of Our Lady of Guadalupe as a Catholic and European invention, a 'colonizing' instrument, as Alma López puts

it,"[19] was erroneous. Never mind scholarship that has shown the colonizing effects of Christianity in the Americas.[20]

Other male critics who protested *Our Lady* wrote electronic mail from 2001 to 2005, illustrating more male-centered discourse with a deep desire to discipline the female artist. For example, seventy-two-year-old Carlos Martínez, a resident of Santa Fe, wrote that he was "extremely offended" by López's rendering of "the blessed Virgin Mary the mother of our Savior Jesus Christ in a bikini" and that he was disappointed to discover the artist was "Hispana" and therefore "should know better than to show utter disrespect" for the "Mother of the Americas."[21]

The following e-mail from a Euro-American man is exceedingly offensive:

Dear Birdbrain,
You state that your intentions were not to offend the Blessed Mother. Now tell me, in what state of mind (abnormal), could you justify degrading the most sacred woman to ever grace this planet. Your feminist, twisted-sisters, don't care who they offend as long as their cause is carried forward. You not only insult our Mother, but her Son also, by portraying His Mother in such a vile manner.[22]

And another letter from yet another Euro-American man is equally offensive: "This is blasphemy & deadly to your Soul."[23] Note the manner in which "birdbrain," and "feminist twisted-sisters" are conflated in the first letter to show disdain for women as thinking, critical beings. The author proclaims that López must know feminists are stupid and have no right to intellectual discourse.

While Villegas and Sedeño spoke as the entitled, truthful Chicano voices hailing from New Mexico, Ernesto Cienfuegos anointed himself the Chicano voice of Aztlán in southern California.

HOMOPHOBIA IN AZTLÁN

The letter by Ernesto Cienfuegos is perhaps the most disturbing since he authors a contemporary online newsletter/magazine that advertises spiteful misogyny and homophobia. Single-handedly, Cienfuegos attacked López repeatedly, focusing on her sexuality and naming her and her work "sexually deviant." By "putting sex into language," Cienfuegos laid bare his own pervasive discourse about the "Guadalupe in a bikini," "the lesbian artist," the "Sapphic pose," "the lesbian lover," "the sexually deviant lesbian connotations," "homosexual and lesbian lifestyles" and wrote an editorial titled "Chicana Lesbians Denigrate La Virgen" in another issue of his online journal. Sample paragraphs from his letter represent Cienfuegos's disdain for López:

To: Joe Felz, Director, Fullerton Museum Center
August 1, 2004

Dear Mr. Felz:

Our news publication, *La Voz de Aztlan*, has received your press release concerning the planned exhibit "The Virgin of Guadalupe: Interpreting Devotion" to open on August 28. Your press release mentions that as part of the exhibit, you will be including the highly offensive "Guadalupe in a Bikini" by the decadent lesbian artist Alma López.

Sir, you may not be aware but the image has extremely sexually deviant symbolism and has already been condemned by millions of Mexicans here in the USA and in Mexico.

Firstly, the person in the sapphic pose representing the "Mother of Jesus" is nothing less than Raquel Salinas, the lesbian lover of the so called artist Alma López. Raquel Salinas calls herself "La Chuparosa" which Alma López often depicts on her abominable images. For a full description of the sexually deviant lesbian connotations of "Chuparosa" and of other symbolisms in López' rendering of "La Reina de Mexico," please read our editorial "Chicana Lesbians Denigrate La Virgen de Guadalupe" which can be read on our website on the Internet at http://aztlan.net/lupe.htm

Mr. Felz, we would like to think that you are merely ignorant of the facts and not involved in an anti-Mexican effort to destroy our most revered spiritual beliefs and cultural values. We would like to believe that the City of Fullerton's intentions for "The Virgin of Guadalupe: Interpreting Devotion" exhibit is to extend the hand of friendship to the large and growing Mexican population of Orange County and not to, like many anti-Mexicans xenophobes, to denigrate the values of our community in collusion with those in the homosexual and lesbian lifestyles and of those others who have a deep hate against us.

We are requesting that you refrain from exhibiting these and other offensive and abominable renderings of the Mexican "Holy Mother." Please, let us know before the City of Fullerton City Council's meeting of August 3, of your decision to refrain from destroying the faith based beliefs of the youths who attend Fullerton's educational system and of those others in our community.

Respectfully, Ernesto Cienfuegos, Editor-in-Chief, *La Voz de Aztlan*.

Cienfuegos was successful. His rhetorical turn alerted the director of the Fullerton Museum Center, who probably did not want the same kind of controversy in his museum that had already occurred in Santa Fe. The museum, however, did exhibit other artwork by López.

Four years later, in 2008, Cienfuegos was still perpetuating alarming homophobia in *La Voz de Aztlan*. Reporting the gay and lesbian protest marches in Los Angeles, *La Voz de Aztlan* noted that "it now appears that the issue of sodomite marriages may be headed back to the California Supreme Court."[24] The editor of the online news magazine further noted that a black youth declared to the *Los Angeles Times* that "the so-called 'gays' are asking for major trouble" and a Latino youth remarked: "It may be time to send the homosexuals back into the closet."[25]

Remarkably, Cienfuegos is a self-appointed ideologue of the Chicano nation. Naming his online "news" mag-rag *La Voz de Aztlan* is an exceedingly arrogant declaration. He has led himself to believe that his misogynist, homophobic voice, which is out of touch with multiple, diverse perspectives in the growing Chicana/o communities, is the voice of the Chicano nation. Yet *La Voz de Aztlan* has been operating under his name for over a decade. While the online journal reports news and opinions about anti-Mexican immigration and Ku Klux Klan racism, provides biographical features on important Chicano/a leaders like César Chávez and Dolores Huerta, and presents think pieces by Chicano professors like Rodolfo Acuña and Armando Navarro, for the most part, the journal spouts an explicit patriarchal dogma that can be found in the criticism against artists like Alma López. Cienfuegos has repeatedly criticized Chicana lesbians, and I suspect he will continue to express his reactionary views as long as he publishes his online diary.

PRO-ARTE

Our Lady represents the interlinkage of racial identities and sexual and political desires while, at the same time, pointing to the constitutive ambivalence of the heart of Chicano/a—and other—identity formations

LUZ CALVO, "Art Comes for the Archbishop"

In *La Lucha Continues*, Ada Maria Isasi-Díaz argues that the community's Catholic women are always reinscribing their own brand of Catholicism to fit their needs. Although the parish priests may not condone women's practices, the women perform their type of Catholicism despite patriarchal objections.

So, how do we decolonize our community's perspectives about La Virgen de Guadalupe? What I have attempted throughout this chapter is to show that the answer lies in decolonizing the minds of a community ruled by historical, colonial relationships that continue to colonize, even in the twenty-first century. To decolonize the community, members of that kinship must question and challenge the very myths and symbols that define their communal sense of identity, whether *familia* or nation. In my discussion on how diasporic, displaced, or immigrant subjectivities rewrite the histories of their nations as they carry their cultural memories through space and time, I argue that the concept of a nation and its culture is not written in stone:

> The diasporic subject reminds us that Aztlán, the mythic homeland, shifts and moves beneath and around us. The mythic homeland is longed for, constructed, and rewritten through collective memories. Time is traversed, and a mythic past entwines with a future where a decolonized imaginary has possibilities. . . . The culture of an imagined nation such as Aztlán is not a linear, horizontal thing that can be traced through time, its movement and lineage tracked from the old world to the new. . . . The "imagined community" of Aztlán was initially given an "essentialist identity," but if it is rethought as traveling culture, then its identity depends upon its social construction, in which memory and forgetting are as much a part of the history as the myth.[26]

Our Lady is an example of how a cultural myth as iconic as La Virgen de Guadalupe can "travel" from a past in which the nation constructed and colonized the female gender to a future in which the female gender forgets its own colonization and so rewrites the nation. The controversy over *Our Lady* showed us to what degree the issue was not how the artist's gender or sexuality had disrupted the nation by altering the Virgin of Guadalupe; rather, it was how the nation kept wanting to reassert control over the artist's and *Our Lady's* gender.

By offering up her art, López has pushed the parameters of gender debates and compelled Santa Fe's women and men to take a position about *Our Lady*. When residents of New Mexico wrote to local newspapers, marched in protest, and confronted each other, they began a debate that forced them to reconsider women's traditional roles through representations of La Virgen. By writing e-mails to López and engaging in a discussion, colonial mind-sets were put in motion and challenged the very thing that has held women in traditional roles—a patriarchal Catholic Church. López propelled the shift to decolonial mind-sets when she put flesh on La Virgen de Guadalupe and freed *Our Lady* from the chains of patriarchal vision and expectations.

The following examples prove that there are those eager to change for the betterment of the community rather than hold on to a colonial past that has only reinforced a virgin/whore dichotomy, which has been detrimental to all women and all men: "In our community, images of La Virgin, San Judas Tadeo, even Jesus Christ himself have been cultural icons for decades. I wonder if there exist 'less than appropriate' representations of these icons in gardens and stores, on jewelry, clothing, or even dishes in Santa Fe? I would not be surprised. How would Mr. Villegas explain the usage in this case?"[27] Another resident of New Mexico objected to Villegas in the following manner: "On your website, I read Jose Villegas' email to you, and I was sorry that he had the nerve to speak for all of Northern New Mexico."[28] A pointed criticism from another local woman demonstrated that not all New Mexicans agreed with Villegas: "I suspect that what is infuriating all these caballeros in Northern New Mexico is NOT the costume, but the loss of the all-loving, all-forgiving, all-nurturing mom."[29]

The following quotation from a Chicano shows how there were men from the community who were willing to see another perspective. "The image of 'Our Lady' forces me to take a second look at my own indoctrination where an exposed female body is seen as promiscuous and unholy."[30]

Finally, a daughter elucidated the life of her eighty-three-year-old New Mexican mother, who spoke about her own mother's life in early-twentieth-century New Mexico and by doing so clarified the value of López's art. The quotation is in the daughter's voice: "She then proceeded to tell me what a feminist her own mother was working on the farm along the Rio Grande in NM. Gramma bought men's shoes so she could work outside, she wore Grampa's overalls and she cut her hair. She worked outside and raised 10 children inside. Mom said she was a modern thinker. Your piece keeps affecting people's lives and their thinking."[31]

Artist Alma López's digital print *Our Lady* represents a transformative move toward decolonization in which the virgin/whore binary is disrupted and women are honored for their multiple ways of being. Because the male ideologues could not see the work as art, they refused to acknowledge the intervention by a Chicana lesbian artist who compelled the Chicano nation to quit marking women as colonial objects. Through *Our Lady* López declares that Chicanas and Latinas are subjects who live, love, and desire. We refuse to be colonized any longer.

NOTES

I want to thank Luz Calvo for allowing me to use her clever title.

1. Luz Calvo, "Art Comes for the Archbishop: The Semiotics of Contemporary Chicana Feminism and the Work of Alma López," *Meridians: Feminism, Race, Transnationalism* 5.1 (2004): 201–224; Chap. 5 here.

2. Emma Pérez, *The Decolonial Imaginary: Writing Chicanas into History* (Bloomington: Indiana University Press, 1999), 121–122.

3. See, for example, Jeanette Rodríguez, *Our Lady of Guadalupe: Faith and Empowerment among Mexican-American Women* (Austin: University of Texas Press, 1994); D. A. Brading, *Mexican Phoenix: Our Lady of Guadalupe: Image and Tradition across Five Centuries* (London: Cambridge University Press, 2003).

4. Michel Foucault, *The History of Sexuality: An Introduction*, vol. 1 (New York: Vintage Books, 1980), 11, 34.

5. Ada María Isasi-Díaz, *La Lucha Continues: Mujerista Theology* (Maryknoll, N.Y.: Orbis Books, 2004), 54.

6. Ibid.

7. "This is a sin and it is morally wrong, I think that you are a disgraceful bitch who has no respect for the one who crushes the serpent," Edna Best, e-mail to Alma López, October 4, 2001, www.almalopez.com.

8. Mary Rivera Griswold, *The New Mexican* (March 2001), www.almalopez.com.

9. Esperanza, e-mail to Alma López, November 25, 2002, www.almalopez.com.

10. Foucault, The History of Sexuality, 11.

11. Ibid., 45.

12. Ibid.

13. The epigraph is from Teresa de Lauretis, *The Practice of Love: Lesbian Sexuality and Perverse Desire* (Bloomington: Indiana University Press, 1994), 155.

14. Foucault, *The History of Sexuality*, 34.

15. José Villegas, e-mail to Alma López, March 18, 2001, www.almalopez.com.

16. Pedro Romero Sedeño, e-mail to M. V. Sedano, February 9, 2002, www.almalopez.com. See the numerous messages in February 2002 that show the contrasting views of Sedeño and López.

17. Pedro Romero Sedeño, e-mail to M. V. Sedano, February 12, 2002, www.almalopez.com.

18. Pedro Romero Sedeño, e-mail to Alma López, February 2, 2002, www.almalopez.com.

19. Pedro Romero Sedeño, e-mail to AztlanNet Listserve, May 10, 2002, www.almalopez.com.

20. As an example of scholarship that challenges the European model, refer to Walter Mignolo, *Global Histories, Local Designs* (Princeton, N.J.: Princeton University Press, 2000). For an intriguingly fresh look at the violence emerging from European colonization, see Nelson Maldonado-Torres, *Against War* (Durham, N.C.: Duke University Press, 2008). For an excellent feminist revision of Catholicism as a patriarchal institution, see Isasi-Díaz, *La Lucha Continues*.

21. Carlos Martínez, e-mail to Alma López, March 25, 2001, www.almalopez.com.

22. Mike Gratz, e-mail to Alma López, May 22, 2001, www.almalopez.com.

23. Kevin Sorbanelli, e-mail to Alma López, September 29, 2005, www.almalopez.com.

24. See "LOS(T) ANGELES: Homosexuals Sodomize Image of Jesus Christ," *La Voz de Aztlan* (November 13, 2008), www.aztlan.net. Proposition 8, the anti–gay marriage bill, passed in California.

25. Ibid.

26. Pérez, *Decolonial Imaginary*, 78–79.

27. Consuelo Flores, e-mail to Alma López, March 26, 2001, www.almalopez.com.

28. Yolanda Rael, e-mail to Alma López, December 11, 2001, www.almalopez.com.

29. Elvira Segura, e-mail to Alma López, October 30, 2002, www.almalopez.com.

30. Héctor Álvarez, e-mail to Alma López, October 6, 2001, www.almalopez.com.

31. Helen López, e-mail to Alma López, April 27, 2001, www.almalopez.com.

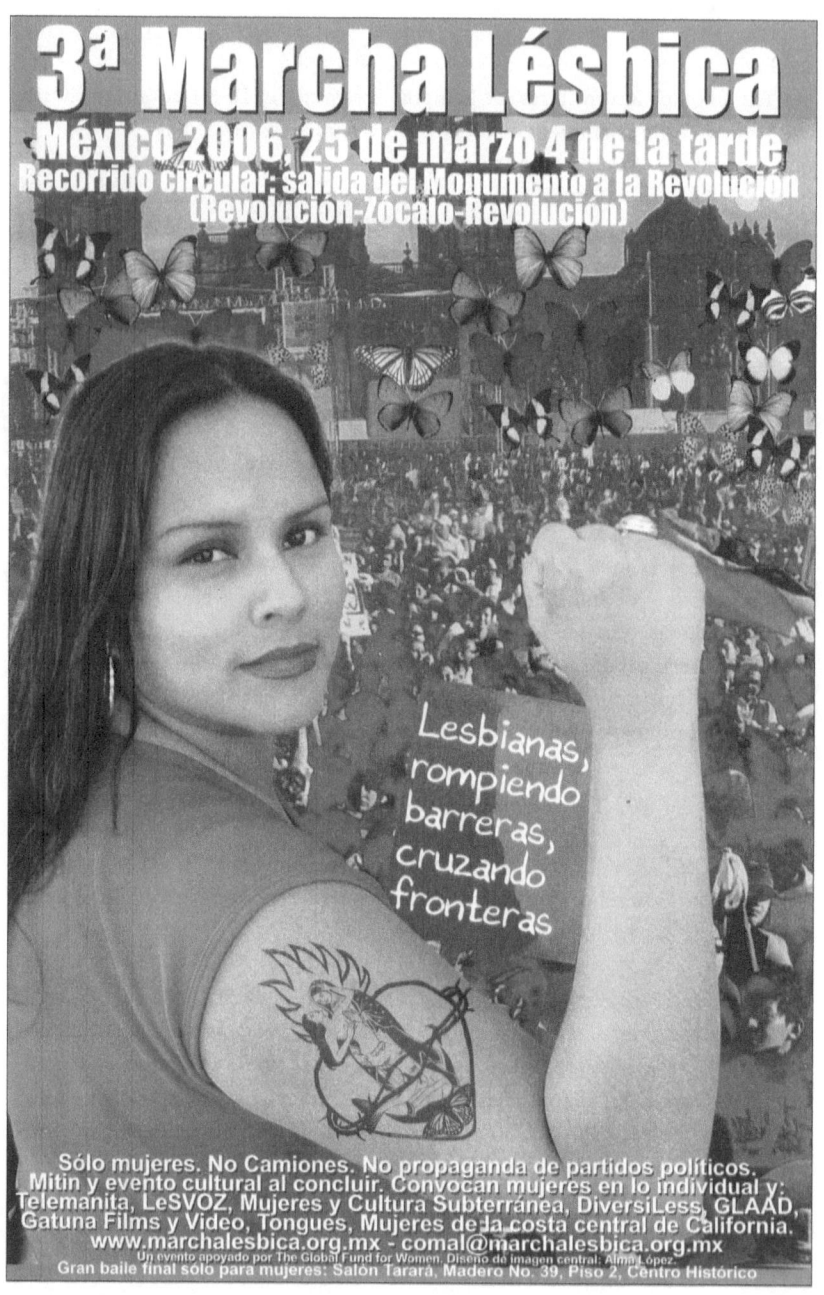

8.1. *Marcha Lésbica*. Digital print by Alma López, © 2006. Courtesy of Alma López. Special thanks to Cristina Serna.

It's Not about the Virgins in My Life, It's about the Life in My Virgins

Cristina Serna

O N MARCH 25, 2006, while millions of her undocumented children marched for immigrant rights in cities across the United States, Mexico's Virgen de Guadalupe broke out of her ecclesiastical closet to join an impassioned group of Chicana, Latina, and Mexicana lesbians and queer allies as we marched in the third Mexico City Marcha Lésbica. Like our friends and families across the border, we marched to demand recognition as equal members of our communities and societies, deserving of the basic human rights to live and love free from the threat of discrimination or violence. The chants we shouted as we advanced toward the *zócalo*, the central plaza which houses the National Palace and the Metropolitan Cathedral, the symbolic centers of church and state power in Mexico, conveyed the irreverent spirit of the march. While some decried the less-than-holy trinity of church, state, and Pro-Vida forces that proclaimed itself the guardian of Mexican morality, others evoked an alternative political and cultural landscape peopled by our own contingent of queer role models and heroes. Among these public acts of reclamation, not surprisingly, one of the most contentious was Alma López's repositioning of La Virgen de Guadalupe in her design for the 2006 Marcha Lésbica poster.

López's poster design posed the lesbian protagonists of her emblematic *Lupe and Sirena in Love* (1999) within a stylized Sacred Heart tattoo that was inscribed on a working-class Chicana lesbian's body, making it a double, or triple, mark of transgression.[1] Her eroticized inscription of the Virgin of Guadalupe in a sapphic pose with the sensuous Sirena roused threats against march organizers and acts of vandalism against the image, which was posted in public places throughout the city.

In response to these attempts to censor public expressions of lesbianism, and inspired by Alma López's artistic vision, the activists who participated in the 2006 Marcha Lésbica reappropriated the symbol of La Virgen de Guadalupe from a church and National Action Party (PAN) that co-opted her image to legitimize their failing moral and political authority. Instead, they turned "Lupe la lesbiana," as she was baptized in the marchers' queered rendition of the hymn "La Guadalupana," into a symbol of an alternative and "decolonial imaginary" that celebrates love and sex between women and offers redemption and healing to the socially maligned.[2]

Taking an interstitial position that was disrespectful of borders and disciplinary morality, the 2006 Marcha Lésbica organizers brought activists together across various borders of nation, race, language, sexuality, and class under a common banner that heretically refigured the most sanctified Catholic symbol of the feminine ideal.[3] This cross-border activist moment was also significant in that parallel histories and trajectories of queer Chicana and Mexicana art and activism converged and overlapped with each other as the marchers collectively reclaimed the religious and political symbolic landscapes of Mexico-Tenochtitlan.

The 2006 Marcha Lésbica witnessed the converging of various cycles of history, artistic vision, and activism. López's Marcha Lésbica poster brought a Chicana Virgen de Guadalupe back to Mexico City, the site of the Virgin's apparition to Juan Diego and of her cult at Tepeyac. It is also significant that this image came to Mexico in the context of political activism and attempts to build cross-border solidarity among working-class Chicana, Latina, and Mexicana activists and their allies. The occupation of the *zócalo*, which was part of the march, was similarly important because this historic plaza is the symbolic center of Mexican state and religious power, the location from which hegemonic inscriptions of La Virgen de Guadalupe's image are dictated and policed.

The inclusion of a Chicana representation of La Virgen de Guadalupe in a Mexican march prompts me to ask how Alma López's Chicana feminist artistic vision dialogues with works by Mexican artists who have also explored and questioned the ideological and political functions of her symbol, albeit from a distinct social location. An examination of Mexican and Chicana reinterpretations of La Virgen de Guadalupe and the disciplinary responses that are directed toward these works reveals that there are important similarities and divergences between these two cultural and artistic paradigms. One of the most notable distinctions is the creative and constructive vision of Chicana feminist artists, who do more than critique and deconstruct oppressive symbols; they offer us new ones.

Through her refigurations of the Virgin of Guadalupe, Alma López presents us with a new postapocalyptic vision in which the socially abject—the lesbians and queer women who are cast out of a metaphorical social paradise—are revindicated and portrayed through the eyes of love. Only through the loving and erotic gaze of a queer woman could Guadalupe be portrayed in such a loving manner. Her body, violated by misogyny, is redeemed and seen through the eyes of divinity and decolonial desire.[4]

As a queer Chicana, I am moved by López's vision because she sees the beauty others will deny and acknowledges our strengths and vulnerabilities, and the traumas we survive, because she knows them personally. She sees the beauty in those that our own families, communities, and nations denigrate and cast out. She sees hope in the love we have for other women and each other.

The image of the Virgin of Guadalupe that is said to have appeared to Juan Diego in 1531 was based on an apocalyptic vision of the Virgin Mother, perhaps because she appeared at a moment when the world itself, *el ombligo del universo*, seemed to be crumbling and the way of life of the Nahua peoples seemed poised to come to an end.[5] But La Virgen de Guadalupe that Alma offers us as she takes on a role *as una nueva mensajera*, a new intermediary, a Juana Diega for a new millennium, is not an image of apocalypse but one of hope and redemption. She offers us a new vision and a new imaginary. That which the world finds horrifying and demonizes is revealed as beautiful in Alma López's art. As a harbinger of hope and healing for women, Alma López performs the kind of "decolonizing, *curandera*, or healing work" that Laura E. Pérez finds in much Chicana aesthetic, political, and spiritual practice.⁶ Her art presents us with an alternate paradigm through which we can view ourselves through a lens of love and self-acceptance that can help heal the wounds of past violences, giving us a larger capacity from which to fight to make our social visions a reality.

CHICANA FEMINIST RE-VISIONINGS: REARTICULATING THE CATHOLIC VIRGEN DE GUADALUPE

> There is no pure, authentic, original history.
> There are only stories—many stories.
>
> **EMMA PÉREZ**, *The Decolonial Imaginary*

Alma López's feminist re-visionings in *Our Lady* (1999) and *Lupe and Sirena in Love* (1999) are part of a larger movement in Chicana art that has offered radically imaginative reinterpretations of La Virgen de Guadalupe since at least the 1970s.⁷ Her art dialogues with, and builds on, the work of Chicana artists and writers like Ester Hernández, Yolanda M. López, Cherríe L. Moraga, Sandra Cisneros, Ana Castillo, and Gloria E. Anzaldúa, to name but a few of the many who have contributed to this dynamic body of work. In their reinterpretations of this symbol, Chicana artists historicize the Virgin's icon by making her social and political legacies and functions visible. They also renarrativize her and give her new life and meaning as a symbol that is used to represent feminist and decolonial struggles, both in Mexico and in the United States.

In *Our Lady* and *Lupe and Sirena in Love*, Alma López extends the creative refigurations of Ester Hernández and Yolanda M. López, who were some of the earliest to depict La Virgen de Guadalupe as a real, living, breathing woman. These images serve as counterdiscourses to heteropatriarchal and Eurocentric perspectives that uphold a narrow, colonialist vision of La Virgen de Guadalupe's icon.⁸ López's art is informed by a decolonizing feminist politics that recovers the indigenous associations embedded within the Virgin of Guadalupe's lineage, often by strategically transposing or superimposing images of Coyolxauhqui or Coatlicue on the traditional icon of La Virgen.⁹ In this way she coincides with other artists and intellectuals who recognize the Virgin of Guadalupe as a figure whose cult and meaning is transculturally linked to that of the indigenous Tonantzin.¹⁰ But perhaps most significantly, López is part of a line of feminist reclamation that has sexualized and queered La Virgen de Guadalupe, most notably, Ester Hernandez's *La Ofrenda*

(1988), which was one of the earliest Chicana visual works to place the Virgin of Guadalupe in an openly lesbian frame of reference and context. These are only a few of the multiple layers of reclamation through which Chicana artists contest and redefine the hegemonic meanings ascribed to the Virgin of Guadalupe's symbol.

Like these aforementioned Chicana writers and artists, Alma López creates art which seeks to "re-member" and heal the colonizing splits that were imposed on/between our spiritual and sexual bodies while offering a countervision to the male-dominated aesthetics of religious and nationalist cultures.[11] And, like other Chicana artists, she deliberately voices her critiques and reconceptualizations through familiar metaphors and visual vocabularies.[12]

La Virgen de Guadalupe is a familiar image for Chicanas and Latinas who have grown up Catholic; it is intimately tied to memories of childhood and to our earliest socializations in religious, cultural, gendered, and sexual norms. As a Mexican incarnation of the Christian Virgin Mother, we associate her with the gender and sexual roles that are taught through Catholic and cultural doctrine. As the supreme representation of woman and mother in Mexican and Chicana/o ideological structures, Chicana feminists recognize the Virgin of Guadalupe as a symbol that prescribes an idealized model of womanhood that is meant to enforce limiting, dichotomizing gender and sexual roles for women.

Yet, in spite of her function as an instrument of heteropatriarchal morality and values, Chicana feminists refuse to relinquish her symbol to the nationalist and religious authorities that claim sole proprietorship of her image. The Virgin of Guadalupe's profound significance in Chicana/o and Mexican political and spiritual histories makes her a compelling symbol for Chicanas, one which they appropriate, alter, and transform into a decolonizing tool of self-empowerment, politicized love, and social redemption.

Despite the Catholic Church's attempts to anchor the meaning and image of La Virgen de Guadalupe within the bounds of ecclesiastical doctrine, it has not been able to fully contain the power of her symbol within one unitary narrative structure. Chicana feminists contribute to the multivocality of her image through a complex body of work that explores and expands her meaning and function in Mexican and Chicana/o cultural imaginaries. From visual and literary works, the Virgin of Guadalupe emerges as a powerful and transcendental symbol that evokes a multiplicity of meanings. To some the Virgin of Guadalupe is a childhood memory; to others she is an indigenous warrior "goddess." Within Chicana feminist and decolonial imaginaries, Guadalupe is an empowering "sex goddess" as well as a compassionate, forgiving mother. The Virgin of Guadalupe is thus a multilayered and malleable figure whose meaning is forged in a continual process of reappropriation and contestation.

THE POLITICAL FUNCTIONS OF THE VIRGEN DE GUADALUPE ICON

Though various interpretations of the authenticity of her apparition abound, the Virgin of Guadalupe is popularly believed to have appeared on the American continent in 1531, a decade after the center of the Aztec universe, México-Tenochtitlan, fell to the Spanish invaders.[13] According to postconquest narratives, this brown-skinned Virgin appeared to a recently converted Nahua Indian by the name of Juan Diego. This encounter between a Christianized Indian and the Virgin of Guadalupe took place on the hill of Tepeyac, an ancient pilgrimage site in Central Mexico dedicated to the sacred earth mother, Tonantzin. Both colonial-era reports by Catholic missionaries and contemporary studies of "Indianized" Catholicism reveal that elements of indigenous philosophy and practice survive within the Virgin of Guadalupe's modern-day cults.[14]

The varied and often contradictory meanings and functions associated with the Virgin of Guadalupe's symbol reflect the multiethnic, socially stratified nature of Mexican society, in which distinct social and political groups have used her symbol to represent their particular needs and interests. Throughout the seventeenth and eighteenth centuries, for example, *criollo* elites in Mexico used La Virgen de Guadalupe to legitimize their incipient nationalist consciousness, often at the cost of erasing indigenous people from that consciousness.[15] In reinterpreting the Virgin of Guadalupe symbol, Chicana artists thus intervene in a long, primarily male, tradition of utilizing her image either to subvert hegemonic religious structures or to give visual shape to politically and socially invested visions. However, one of the most distinctive representational strategies of Chicana artists is the way in which they refigure and transform the traditional icon to present their own models of identity and self-representation.[16]

Chicana artists have brought the Virgin of Guadalupe into the realm of the ordinary by giving her a humanized embodiment, thus refusing the colonial dichotomy that arbitrarily designates a separation and hierarchy between

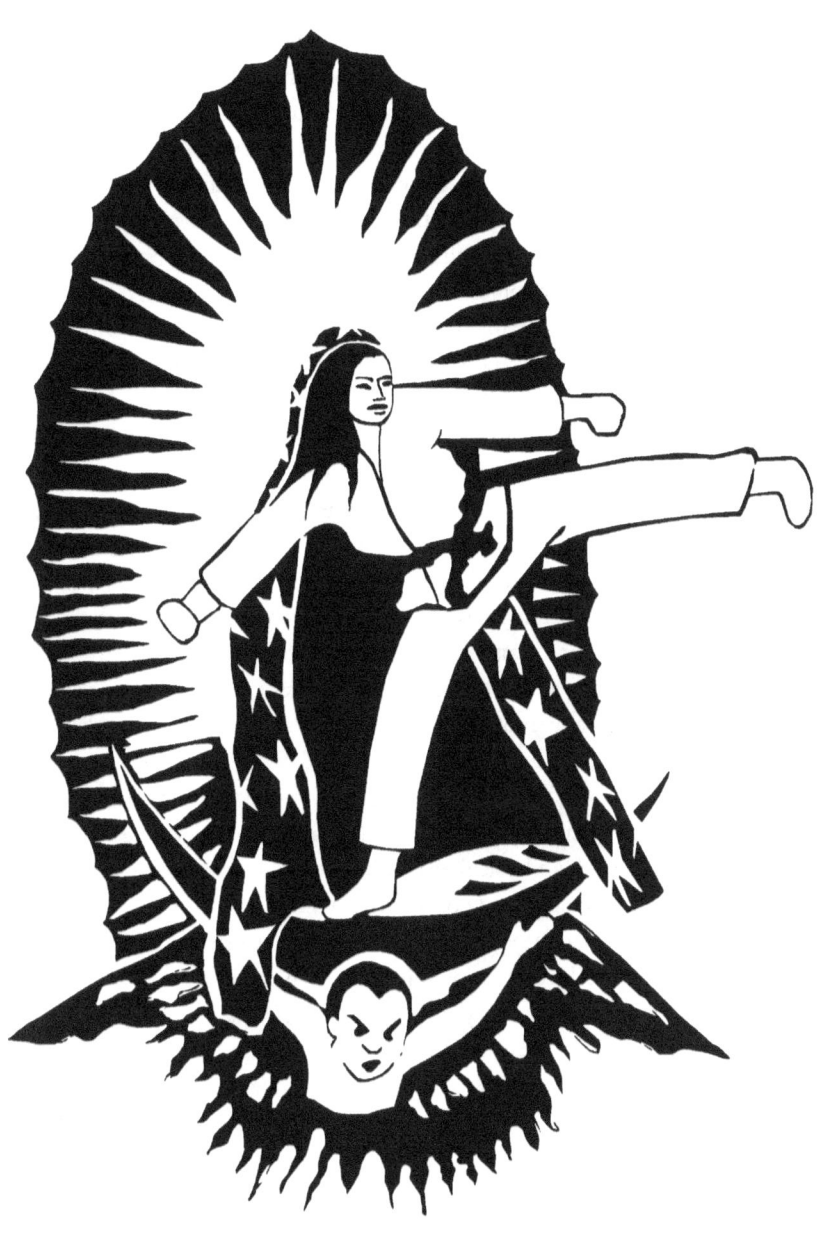

8.2.   *La Virgen de Guadalupe Defendiendo los Derechos de los Xicanos*. Etching
       by Ester Hernández, © 1976. Courtesy of Ester Hernández.

spiritual and material, or "profane," realms. They have also used her image to articulate feminist critiques of patriarchal norms and practices in Chicano culture and politics. Ester Hernández's 1976 etching, *La Virgen de Guadalupe Defendiendo los Derechos de los Xicanos*, first presented the Virgen as a contemporary woman, depicting her as a social activist and warrior. Hernández politicized and transformed the traditional icon into an active and empowered rendition of La Virgen of Guadalupe as a karate black belt who was poised to defend the rights of her pueblo. This image reinstates La Virgen de Guadalupe as a social activist and warrior who is willing to fight against injustice rather than accept her culturally sanctioned role as a passive and suffering mother.

In her Guadalupe series Yolanda M. López further expanded the Virgin of Guadalupe symbol by presenting her in a wide range of guises. During the 1970s, motivated by the omnipresence of the Virgin of Guadalupe's icon in the visual culture of the Chicano movement, Yolanda M. López chose to interrogate her to introduce a more varied repertoire of images of women within the movement. In this foundational series, López alternately depicted her as an ordinary working-class woman, a mother, a grandmother, and in *Nuestra Madre* (1978) as a transculturated symbol that represented the survival of indigenous identity and spiritual consciousness. López's goal was to recognize the power and worth of ordinary women by eliminating the distinction between the Holy Mother of God and everyday women as she transposed them through her venerated figure. This is a move that also informs Alma López's *Our Lady*, which poses Raquel Salinas as La Virgen de Guadalupe, thus giving La Virgen a physical embodiment and humanized identity by articulating her through the body of a "real" woman.

The Virgin of Guadalupe that Chicana artists have envisioned is a contemporary image that reflects their own reality as Chicanas, but she is also a symbol of the survival and recovery of indigenous spirituality and consciousness in Chicana cultural and historical memory. Like other cultural workers and scholars, Alma López recognizes the Virgin of Guadalupe as a symbol of an indigenous and more fluidly gendered spirituality that has survived in the face of colonization and heterosexual patriarchy. "We may know her as the Virgin of Guadalupe," wrote Ana Castillo in 1996, "but She was known by many other names, before and after the Conquest of Mexico."[17] This sentiment and this symbolism, which are rendered through a wide variety of visual and literary works, also find their way into Alma López's digital oeuvre as she transposes the figure of the fallen rebel daughter Coyolxauhqui with that of the

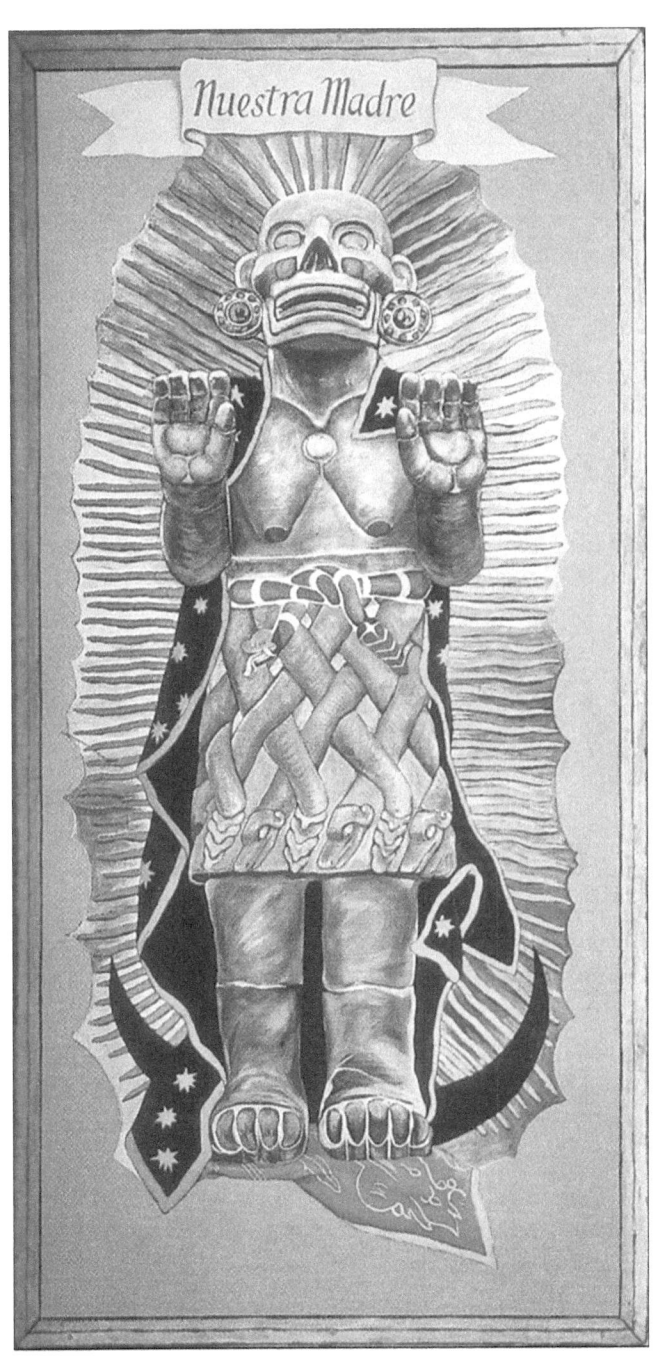

8.3.
Nuestra Madre. Acrylic
painting on Masonite by
Yolanda M. López, ©
1981–1991. Courtesy
of Yolanda M. López.

Virgin of Guadalupe in *Our Lady* in order to assert the survivor-warrior spirit of her newly figured icon.

But the most radical reconceptualizations of the Virgin of Guadalupe's symbol are those that sexualize and, more significantly for me as a Chicana lesbian, those that queer her, evoking her symbol to signal a resacralization of women's sexual bodies or, alternately, of lesbian love and eroticism. Works by Ester Hernández, Gloria Anzaldúa, Ana Castillo, Sandra Cisneros, and Carla Trujillo, among others, contribute to this conversation within Chicana art. In her often-quoted essay, "Guadalupe the Sex Goddess," which strongly influenced the vision behind López's *Our Lady*, Sandra Cisneros echoes Anzaldúa's call to "re-member" the body and reintegrate sexuality into our conceptions of the feminine divine. The Virgin of Guadalupe Cisneros seeks to recuperate from the erasures of colonial histories is "the she before the Church desexed her." As Cisneros writes of this new Virgen: "She is Guadalupe the sex goddess, a goddess who makes me feel good about my sexual power, my sexual energy, who reminds me I must . . . write from my *panocha*."[18]

In her striking print *La Ofrenda*, Ester Hernández similarly refutes the Euro-Christian division between the sexual and spiritual planes, as she places the Virgin of Guadalupe within the realm of Chicana lesbian desire.[19] This is accomplished through the double positioning of the Virgin's image, which Carla Trujillo notes: "The placement of the Virgin on a woman's back on a Chicana lesbian book interrupts and redefines previously configured historical and religious uses and views of the icon. *La Ofrenda* transfigures the icon and places her into the daily lives and existence of the Chicana lesbian. . . . Here we see not rejection of the Virgin Mary, but in recognition of her power and cultural significance, a reclamation and reconstruction of La Virgen in our own way and not as historically ascribed."[20]

Through their re-presentations of the Virgin of Guadalupe, all of these Chicana artists deconstruct Euro-Christian colonial ideologies that impose a false dichotomy and hierarchy between the sacred and the ordinary, the masculine and the feminine, the sex and the spirit, and between the human and the divine. At the same time, they offer counternarratives to colonialist histories and visions that deny the presence of the indigenous, the female, the differently gendered, and the queer. But perhaps most significant, they also offer alternate and decolonial visions of other social realities that are possible.

ALMA LÓPEZ AS A NEW JUANA DIEGA

In her 1999 digital print *December 12*, Alma López presents herself in the guise of Juan Diego, the recently converted native who is supposed to have witnessed the original apparition of La Virgen de Guadalupe in the hills of Tepeyac. López evokes a pose that is common in popular representations of Juan Diego, recalling the moment in which the native messenger drops the roses he has gathered at La Virgen de Guadalupe's request to reveal the icon that has been divinely imprinted on his *tilma*. In her reenvisioned apparition narrative, López bears the imprint of her own irreverent apparition on her body. Like Ester Hernández in *La Ofrenda*, López presents her "lesbian body-as-altar,"[21] giving up her body as a sacrificial offering to those who will surely persecute and punish her for this heretical act.

With a downward gaze and arms outstretched, López appears as a new Juana Diega to offer her own miraculous apparition to the viewer—a Guadalupe refashioned in her own image as a Chicana lesbian. The Virgen de Guadalupe she presents has been freed from ecclesiastical constraints and lovingly and provocatively embraces the Sirena figure.

December 12 forms part of the larger digital series titled Lupe and Sirena in Love in which López, like various Chicana artists, "manipulates the visual language of Catholicism to a variety of ends."[22] By depicting the erotic embrace of Lupe and Sirena in the form of an *acheiropoietos*—an "image not made by human hands"—López posits it as a divine apparition. The artist here draws on the same Catholic tropes that were once used to authenticate divine iconography in order to make her own queer, feminist interventions into Mexican and Chicana/o cultural and religious ideologies.

In fashioning her refigured icon of La Virgen, López retains most of the recognizable iconographic elements of the original. The Virgin of Guadalupe, rebaptized as Lupe in the series title, wears her traditional star-spangled blue mantle and pink, flower-adorned robe. She stands on a black crescent moon as the sun's rays form a bright yellow mandorla behind her. This image of La Virgen de Guadalupe, which the artist borrowed from a religious *estampa* (prayer card), is repositioned with an image of the *lotería*'s Sirena, placing them on the same mythic plane in a sexualized embrace. The proximity of their bodies, the placement of Guadalupe's hands around La Sirena's torso and breast, in addition to the series' title, facilitate a homoerotic reading of their intimate encounter. Through this bold and defiant image, López confronts and challenges the sexual politics of Catholic doctrines that enforce heteropatriarchal norms, thus offering her own "theological queering" in playful and satirical form.[23]

At Lupe and Sirena's feet, replacing the traditional image of a male cherub, is a Viceroy butterfly, which López utilizes to reference the migrations and dislocations experienced by Mexicans and Chicanos, as well as their experiences of "being different or 'other.'"[24] Behind López's portrait, providing an almost theatrical backdrop, hangs the draped blue fabric of the Virgin's robe on which the artist has superimposed an image of the monumental stone carving of the Aztec warrior moon "goddess" Coyolxauhqui.

The meanings and associations that López ascribes to Coyolxauhqui in this image are constructed in reference and dialogue with the work of Cherríe Moraga, Irene Pérez, and other Chicana artists and writers. In addition to serving as a symbol of a recovered Xicana indigenous spirituality, Coyolxauhqui, as a female warrior who was killed by her brother, is also used by Chicanas to present a critique of patriarchal betrayals within Mexican and Chicano cultures. In her rewriting of the Coyolxauhqui myth, Chicana lesbian writer Cherríe Moraga reminds us that within Chicana feminist imaginaries, Coyolxauhqui "is la fuerza femenina, our attempts to pick up the fragments of our dismembered womanhood and reconstitute ourselves . . . She is the female god we seek in our work, la Mechicana before the 'fall.'"[25] In Chicana cultural production, Coyolxauhqui's story is thus an allegory for a rebellious female warrior spirit that is punished, through death and dismemberment, for challenging her brother's militaristic and patriarchal rule. Alma López attempts to re-member Coyolxauhqui's mutilated body, not by piecing her back together, as Irene Pérez does in *Maestrapeace* (1994), but by imagining her through the lens of her own feminist countermemory, which recognizes Coyolxauhqui as a symbol of female empowerment and as a venerated goddess of the moon.[26]

In *December 12* and *Retablo*, two pieces in her digital oeuvre that include a self-portrait, López also subverts the established conventions of a masculine, Western tradition of self-portraiture. Her use of the self-portrait articulates a form of Chicana authorship that stands in stark contrast with those of male and European-descended artists. *Retablo*, another print in the Lupe and Sirena in Love series, reaffirms this point. Meant to evoke the visual narrative of a votive or ex-voto painting, López presents herself genuflecting and holding up a candle in veneration of the Lupe and Sirena apparition that hovers above her. López depicts herself wearing the overalls that serve as her work clothes,

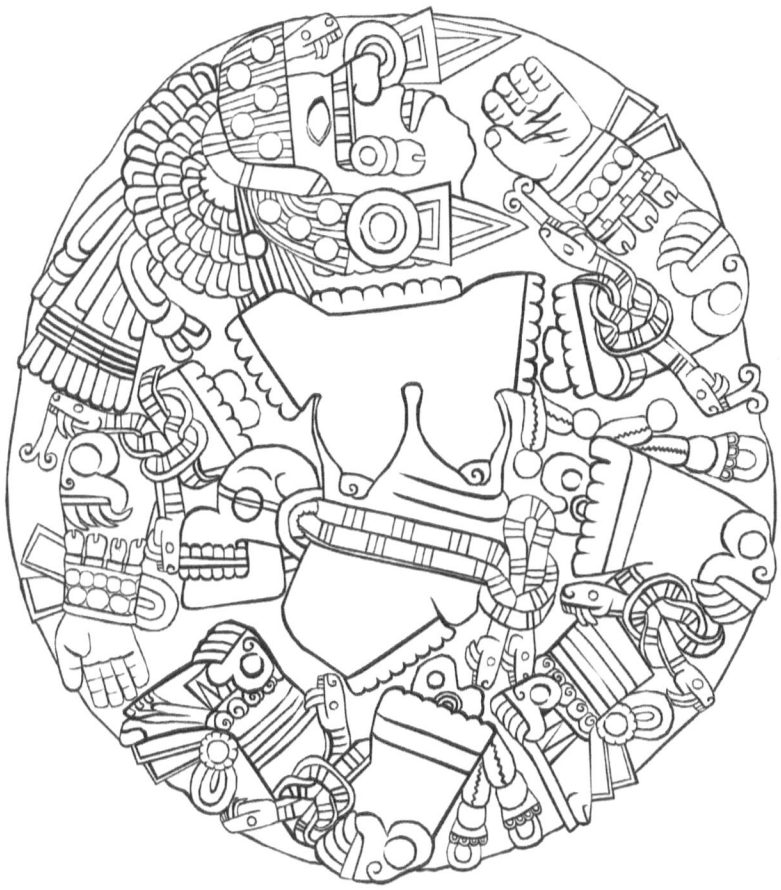

8.4.   *The Coyolxauhqui Stone.* Digital drawing by Alma López, © 2009.
Courtesy of Alma López.

thus denoting her labor and craft as an artist. This provides an interesting distinction from male Renaissance artists, who imaged themselves in a distinguished, elitist pose and dress, purposely distancing themselves from views of the artist as a skilled worker or artisan. In stark contrast to an artist like Albrecht Dürer, who, in his famous *Self-Portrait* (1500), transformed the Christ's *vera icon* into a self-portrait that was meant to elevate him and claim a higher social status for himself as an artist, López alternately represents herself as a humble native messenger (*December 12*) or as an artist and devotee dressed in her work clothes (*Retablo*).

In *Lupe and Sirena in Love*, Lupe and Sirena are also depicted in a context that sheds light on the transnational geographies they occupy in López's de-colonial imaginary. The print, which catalyzed the series, reflects Chicana/o experiences of migration and dislocation. *Lupe and Sirena in Love* also speaks to the historical and present-day relationships that Mexicans and Chicana/os have with territory that today forms part of the United States. While assert-ing a place for queer sexuality in Mexican and Chicana/o cultural imaginar-ies, this print simultaneously evokes the tactical "mobility" of cultural prac-tices, ideologies, and narratives as they move from one location, in Mexico, to another in the United States. This mobility does not result solely from move-ment through physical space (migration) but also from shifting paradigms that result when inhabiting a territory that is colonized and incorporated into a new national imaginary. Both the city of Los Angeles—the artist's home—and the territories "ceded" by the 1848 Treaty of Guadalupe Hidalgo speak to this shifting sense of location and dislocation.

Holding up the Lupe and Sirena is a recurrent visual metaphor in López's work: the symbol of the Monarch lookalike butterfly. In various interviews and essays López has articulated the meaning she attributes to the Monarch butterfly, which migrates yearly between Mexico and the United States: "The most remarkable aspect of this migration is that on its flight back to Mexico or the northern United States, it is no longer the original butterfly, but it is the child returning, guided by genetic memory. Like the Monarch butterfly, in-digenous peoples of this continent have migrated between both countries."[27] The butterfly she represents in her artwork, however, is the Viceroy butterfly, which relies on its semblance to the Monarch to avoid its predators. López likens the life of the Viceroy to the precarious existence of immigrants in the United States and to the even more perilous experiences of queer people within Latino communities. "For me," she writes, "the Viceroy mirrors par-allel and intersecting histories of being different or 'other' even within our own communities."[28] The Monarch/Viceroy butterflies in López's work thus stand generally for Mexicans and Chicana/os who inhabit and negotiate from the "third spaces" of multiple, and often hostile, environments.

In *Retablo, December 12*, and *Lupe and Sirena in Love*, Alma López turns Ca-tholicism's own discourse and visual tropes on themselves in order to disrupt the gender and sexual politics she finds problematic. She also forges a space for the type of non–church sanctioned, culturally hybrid, politicized spiritu-ality that informs numerous Chicana creative works.[29] Moreover, because the Virgin of Guadalupe is also a cultural and nationalist symbol, the act of "queering" her allows the artist to voice her critique of heteropatriarchal structures within Chicano and Mexicano nationalisms.[30]

At the same time, López manipulates Catholic-based theological and visual tropes to articulate and authenticate the counternarratives she is authoring. For example, she validates her feminist and queer interrogations of institutional Catholic doctrine by depicting Lupe and Sirena's embrace as a divinely imprinted *acheiropoietos* in *December 12*, and as an apparition and self-fashioned "icon of devotion" in *Retablo*.[31] Here she references the visual mechanisms through which the divine nature of Christian iconography was established via popular religious worship. In *Retablo*, López also draws on the mechanism of devotional votive images, alluding to a vernacular practice of Catholic devotion when she depicts herself offering a candle and kneeling before the icon of Lupe and Sirena's apparition. Simultaneously, López challenges Catholic views of the artist and worshipper as passive receptacles of divinity when she presents herself as both author (in her role as artist) and devotee of these newly "sacralized" images.

In her Lupe and Sirena series, López's digitalized oeuvre recodes Catholic, Mexican, and Mesoamerican symbols, reformulating their associations with heterosexist, colonialist, and/or patriarchal ideologies as she invests them with new, subverted, and decolonial meanings. Utilizing a hybrid pictorial vocabulary, López redefines these ideologically loaded cultural symbols through a decolonizing and expressly queer Chicana feminist lens.[32] Moreover, as art historian Guisela Latorre suggests, through these acts of authorship the artist is also "creating an icon of love and devotion that fits her own subjectivity as a lesbian woman of color."[33]

How does the art of queer Chicana and feminist artists like Alma López dialogue with the work of artists in Mexico who similarly interrogate nationalist, cultural, and religious ideologies and discourses in their art? In what ways does an artist's social location within or between various nations inform her or his use of nationalist, cultural, or religious symbols and the responses to her or his work?

CENSORING *EL REAL TEMPLO REAL* AND *OUR LADY*

On February 18, 1988, a popular demonstration took over the *zócalo* in Mexico City. At a time of growing economic crisis and discontent, the protestors voiced their opposition to the recently passed Pacto de Solidaridad Económica, which heralded the beginning of a neoliberal era in Mexico.[34] Just a few days later, a coalition of conservative political and religious groups staged a separate and seemingly unrelated march in defense of the Virgin and the flag, in response to the "blasphemous" offenses of Mexican artist Rolando De la Rosa. This Marcha de Desagravio convened in the same plaza as the earlier march and concluded with a pilgrimage to the Basílica de Guadalupe, where a group of enraged Guadalupanos held a mass to denounce the "sacrilegious" art that had been exhibited in the Museum of Modern Art.[35] De la Rosa's altar installation, El Real Templo Real (the real royal temple), was censured for depicting La Virgen de Guadalupe with the face of Marilyn Monroe and for posing a pair of cowboy boots trampling the Mexican flag. The early removal of De la Rosa's installation from the museum and the forced resignation of the museum director did not deter the protestors from staging a very intentional public spectacle in "defense" of the Virgin and the flag on the eve of a highly contentious presidential election.[36]

Over a decade later, in 2001, a similar controversy erupted over Alma López's Our Lady while on exhibition at the Museum of International Folk Art in Santa Fe, New Mexico. In this heated manifestation against the art of a Chicana lesbian artist, heteropatriarchal privilege played a more pronounced role. Liberated from the mantle that covers the traditional Virgin of Guadalupe figure, López's Our Lady bares her flesh while wearing a bathing suit of roses. Through her assertive and confrontational stance she challenges the gaze of those who seek to control and police her body, sexuality, and spirituality.

In Santa Fe, a primarily male-led campaign was organized against the Chicana artist and the curator. Male Chicano activists, Catholic priests, and the local Catholic archbishop galvanized public manifestations and legal attacks against the artist, curator, and museum, all of whom took a stand in defense of the exhibition.[37] In both Santa Fe and Mexico City, state officials supported calls made by religious groups to censor the offending works. In both cities there were also coalitions of artists, intellectuals, community activists, and citizens who took active stances in defense of the artists' right to free expression.[38]

What do these campaigns against the art of Rolando De la Rosa and Alma López have in common? What do they expose about the political stakes involved in the cultural battles that are waged over public art exhibitions depicting powerful religious and national symbols in neoliberal states?

DISMANTLING *EL REAL TEMPLO REAL*, MEXICO CITY

In 1987, Rolando De la Rosa's *El Real Templo Real* was selected for inclusion in the Alternative Art section of the Salón Nacional de Artes Plásticas. De la Rosa's altar installation juxtaposed a series of images and icons taken from Mexican and U.S. national, religious, and popular cultures to provoke critical reflection about the contradictory gender, religious, cultural, and sexual politics that inform the visual universe and values of Mexican society. This visual universe is one in which images of Jesus Christ, the Virgin of Guadalupe, and other religious icons coexist along with mass culture icons like the Mexican charro and ladies' man Pedro Infante, the American sex symbol Marilyn Monroe, and a barrage of advertisements that commodify and sexually objectify women's bodies. De la Rosa was also questioning the gendered norms and models that are taught to Mexican men via media images that depict a masculinity based on macho womanizing and alcoholism. The artist also drew attention to the contradictions of a Catholic culture in which many Mexican men are taught to view women, with the exception of their mothers and sisters, as whores. De la Rosa's piece thus interrogated the inconsistencies of a patriarchal society that deploys a Catholic moral authority while simultaneously condoning or engaging in these types of hypersexual macho roles.[39] Yet another important theme informing his installation was the artist's critique of U.S. economic and cultural imperialism in Mexico, which in this moment of impending economic liberalization (the late 1980s) was increasingly visible.

In keeping with his satirical appropriation and interrogation of Catholic discourse, De la Rosa presented his installation in an altarlike structure comprising three *nichos* irreverently dedicated to "La Virgen Marilyn," "Cristo Infante," and "Fútbol-Sexo-Alcohol." In the first shrine, De la Rosa composed an image of the Virgin of Guadalupe with the face and breasts of Marilyn Monroe. Two vertical phrases framing the image read: "Ni mi madre," "Ni mi hermana."[40] The second *nicho* was a rearticulation of Leonardo da Vinci's *Last Supper* in which Pedro Infante, celebrated icon of Mexican masculinity, appeared as Christ with a large bottle of beer on the table in front of him. In other images De la Rosa similarly juxtaposed symbols of popular culture, like soccer balls and magazine cutouts of nude or scantily clad women, with religious and national symbols that included Catholic saints, the Mexican flag, and various commodity items. Besides the Virgin Marilyn the piece that most infuriated protestors was a Mexican flag laid out on the floor with a pair of cowboy boots trampling on it. This symbolized the artist's critique of the way in which American "foreign incursions are trampling the nation."[41]

De la Rosa's altarpiece relied on the polyvalent meanings and associations of the symbols he used. Like various Chicana artists, he utilized the symbol of the Virgin of Guadalupe to critique the virgin/whore dichotomy as it plays out in contemporary popular culture. In another parallel with the work of Chicana artists, De la Rosa referenced the connection between the Virgin of Guadalupe and her indigenous precursor, Tonantzin, privileging the latter as a symbol of a precolonial or decolonized Mexican identity. Relying on the Virgin of Guadalupe's function as a Mexican nationalist symbol, he also used her to critique the ways in which foreign cultural and capital incursions impacted cultural and consumption practices and aesthetics in Mexico. In an interview De la Rosa explained, for instance, that he used the image of Marilyn Monroe, which was widely circulated in Mexico, to comment on women's hypersexualized gendered roles while questioning the incursion of U.S. cultural hegemony and its accompanying white ideals of beauty into Mexico.[42]

Regardless of his intention to provoke critical self-reflection, *El Real Templo Real* was met with a series of protests sparked by the incendiary coverage of several newsweeklies that portrayed the installation as a "demonic" offense to the Virgin and the flag.[43] As tends to be the case in this type of museum "controversy," the media helped decontextualize and narrow De la Rosa's intended cultural critiques while inciting particular responses from the public. The crusade against the installation was taken up by a coalition of conservative political and religious groups such as Comité Nacional Provida, Unión Nacional de Padres de Familia, and the Unión Nacional Sinarquista. These organizations coordinated an aggressive physical attack on the Museum of Modern Art (Museo de Arte Moderno, MAM) during which protestors pressured museum officials to remove the most "offensive" pieces from De la Rosa's installation—those utilizing the Virgin of Guadalupe and the Mexican flag.[44]

Who were the social actors with a stake in censoring this artwork? The leaders of the crusade against De la Rosa's installation—Comité Nacional Provida, Unión Nacional de Padres de Familia, and the Unión Nacional Sinarquista—are powerful interest groups that work in coalition with Catholic Church officials and conservative politicians in Mexico. These influential groups restrict public debates on sexual and reproductive freedom to questions of morality, reifying the moral authority of the church and presenting significant obstacles to democratization.

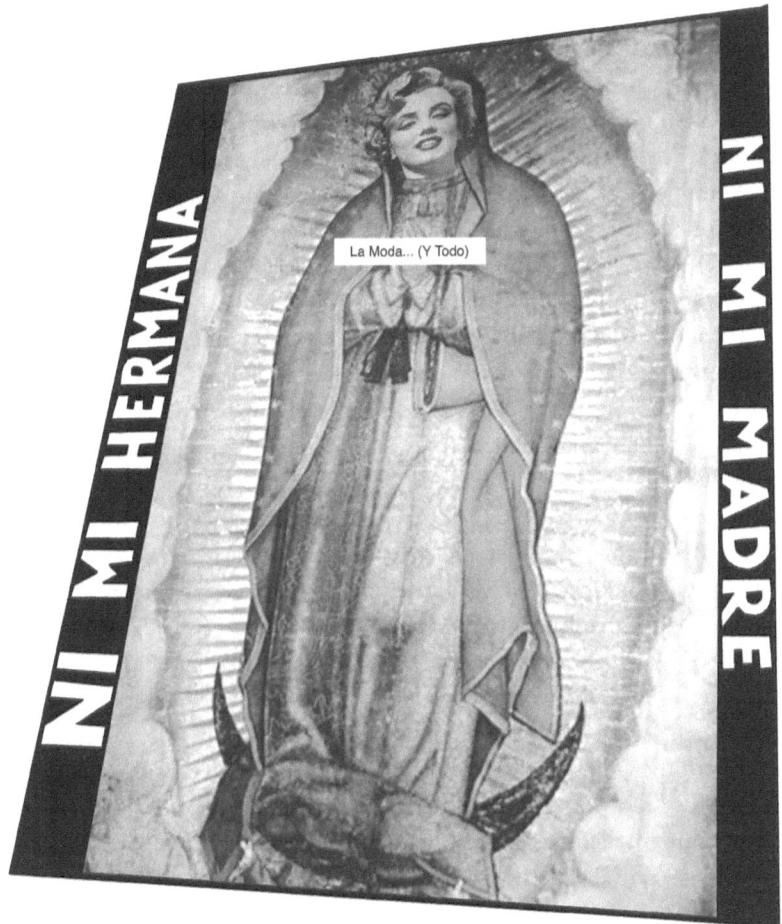

8.5. *La Virgen de Guadalupe con la Cara de Marilyn Monroe.* Mixed-media collage by
Rolando De la Rosa, © 1988. Digitally restored by Alma López. Courtesy of
Rolando De la Rosa/*La Jornada*/México.

These interest groups presented charges against the National Institute of
Fine Arts (Instituto Nacional de Bellas Artes, INBA) and the subsecretary of
education and cultural affairs, which led the institutions to ask Jorge Alberto
Manrique, then director of the MAM, to resign.

Another entity with a position to defend in 1988 was the ruling government
of the Institutional Revolutionary Party (Partido Revolucionario Institucional,

PRI), whose position as "standard bearer and gatekeeper of Mexican national-ism and national identity" was significantly weakening.[45] Since 1968, Mexico had been experiencing a transition from one-party rule to a multiparty sys-tem as a result of increasing discontent with the repression, corruption, and violence of the state. Also, in the late 1980s, social movements were on the rise because of increasing economic displacement and the failure of the state to ameliorate the hardships of the most affected sector, the working poor. Ap-propriately, there was also an accompanying move by progressive and activist artists to exert a more "powerful challenge to the symbolic underpinnings of official nationalist discourse." The PRI thus faced a challenge to its previous hegemony over the "symbolic vocabulary of *mexicanidad.*"[46]

In 1988, there was also a decisive presidential election in Mexico as the coun-try faced a neoliberal privatization agenda during the presidency of Carlos Salinas de Gortari. In 1988, Salinas de Gortari was the PRI candidate with the lowest level of support in PRI history.[47] According to social-movement scholar Edward McCaughan, this election was a turning point in Mexican politics as "a broad coalition of opposition parties and social movements supported the candidacy of progressive nationalist Cuauhtémoc Cárdenas."[48] Salinas de Gor-tari scraped by with 50.25 percent of the vote in an election that is widely rec-ognized as having been won as a result of widespread and blatant fraud.[49] As a further sign of the PRI's declining hegemony, Cuauhtémoc Cárdenas formed the Party of the Democratic Revolution (Partido de la Revolución Democráti-ca, PRD) the following year, bringing an end to one-party rule.

The impact of leftist, feminist, gay, and lesbian movements of the 1970s on Mexican cultural politics also shaped the context of De la Rosa's work and the reaction to it. In his insightful study of art in Mexican social movements, McCaughan affirms that these movements were instrumental in "challenging the configurations of power, national identity, and citizenship in ways that recognize the centrality of gender, sexuality, and subjectivity."[50] McCaughan also notes that one of the themes in the work of feminist, gay, and lesbian art-ists in the late 1980s was "a reappropriation of national symbols, myths, and forms of popular culture."[51] This use of Mexican symbols, he argues, differs from that of earlier Mexican artists and activists, who tended to dismiss them as irredeemably hegemonic. The Virgin of Guadalupe is one symbol that was previously dismissed by Mexican artists, who saw her as a symbol belonging to the hegemonic official nationalist culture that they associated with poli-cies of repression and exploitation. Like many Chicana and Chicano artists, progressive Mexican artists of Rolando De la Rosa's generation were more willing to use national symbols and reappropriate them in order to articulate counterhegemonic discourses through familiar forms. This reappropriation also signified the artists' unwillingness to cede the power of defining national symbols to corrupt regimes and religious institutions.[52]

A more recent example of a Mexican artist's appropriation of Guadalupe as a national symbol for a popular and decolonial cause is Polo Castellanos's *La Comandanta Lupita* (2006), which depicts the Virgin of Guadalupe as a Zapatista. It is not only artists but also other social movement actors who are reclaiming La Virgen. Subcomandante Marcos's March 24, 1995, communiqué on Guadalupan Zapatistas and the Virgin of Guadalupe also claims La Virgen as a symbol belonging to the people. In fact, the Zapatista Army of National Liberation (Ejército Zapatista de Liberación Nacional, EZLN) used an image of La Virgen with her face covered by a handkerchief and held aloft by a masked angel to advertise their 2008 Festival Mundial de la Digna Rabia (World Festival of Dignified Rage).

These reclamations of La Virgen are especially meaningful when read in contrast to PAN president Vicente Fox's highly publicized and criticized waving of the Virgin of Guadalupe's banner during his presidential campaign.[53] In contrast, the aforementioned works attempt to democratize and reclaim the Virgin of Guadalupe from the church and the state, turning her into a symbol of decolonial struggle. As Polo Castellanos affirmed after his work was censored by the Museo del Carmen in Mexico City, "Es una virgen que nos pertenece a todos: zapatistas, panistas, priístas, es de todos."[54]

THE LOVE AFFAIR OF CHURCH AND STATE IN NEW MEXICO

In 2001, members of the Santa Fe Catholic community as well as Chicano and Hispanic activists waged a similar inquisition against Alma López's *Our Lady* in the *Cyber Arte: Tradition Meets Technology* show at the Museum of International Folk Art. The media and conservative discourses leveled against Alma López's reenvisioned icon of the Virgin of Guadalupe recalled the attacks against Rolando De la Rosa and the debates about the National Endowment for the Arts (NEA) funding of exhibitions by Andrés Serrano and Chris Ofili in the United States. As occurred in Mexico, the artist, curator, and museum were aggressively attacked and threatened by outraged religious and conservative groups of Nuevomexicanos in Santa Fe. Similar charges of "sacrilege," "blasphemy," and "obscenity" were circulated in the press and via legal channels to pressure the museum to take down the offending piece.[55] The defamations against the artist, curator, and museum came not only from religious conservatives but also from self-proclaimed Chicano activists, who voiced a narrow, homophobic, and masculinist vision of Aztlán. The Museum of International Folk Art was able to keep the exhibition open for several months despite various threats, but it was eventually forced to close it early in the face of escalating legal action.[56]

The most vocal and visible critics were male Catholic and Chicano activists, who organized rallies, inflamed public opinion via various media outlets, and directed vocal opposition at several museum-sponsored community meetings. When the museum refused to close the exhibition, they filed appeals and lawsuits against the museum.[57] The exhibition curator, Tey Marianna Nunn, reported that the New Mexico State Legislative Finance Committee threatened to cut the museum's funding due to the charges brought by the church. The committee, astoundingly, cited "no separation of Church and state in New Mexico."[58] The artist and curator received the brunt of the protestors' outrage and were the target of various personal attacks, defamations, and threats. Nunn recounted that local law enforcement officials cancelled one of the community meetings because they feared an escalation of the already violent atmosphere. Both women were escorted out of the building amid chilling cries of "burn her, burn them."[59]

At the heart of these reactions was the discomfort and outrage provoked by a queer Chicana artist whose artwork challenged the dominant moral, sexual, and religious orderings of this New Mexican community. In *Our Lady*, López reenvisioned the traditional sixteenth-century icon of the *Virgin of Guadalupe*, presenting her as a contemporary woman with a real body. Through the authorship she exercised in reworking this image, Alma López subverted the cultural authority of the Catholic Church and of Mexican and Chicano patriarchal ideologies that police and malign women's sexual bodies.

In her analysis of Virgen de Guadalupe imagery in Chicana art, feminist scholar Laura E. Pérez notes that "the work of denaturalizing gendered and sexed expectations of negatively racialized women is at the heart of the enormous body of Virgin of Guadalupe art by Chicana feminist artists."[60] To this end, Alma López "manipulates the visual language of Catholicism" to challenge the dominant definitions imposed by the Catholic Church,[61] the U.S imperial state, and those who, like the Chicano male activists leading the protests, wish to impose essentialist visions of Aztlán. López's work can also be seen as a feminist attempt to "discover, uncover, and recover the power of the Mother of God or her image" from interpretations that use her as a "prescriptive sign authorizing male privilege and female abnegation and submission before it."[62]

It is precisely these moves that make the work of Alma López and of other feminist artists that employ similar revisionist and creative strategies so threatening. These moves, in which artists take existing symbols and rearticulate them to produce new meanings, follow the disordering logic of what Laura Pérez, building on Ybarra-Frausto and Mesa-Bains, describes as a *rasquache* aesthetic. Like other artists, Alma López draws from existing signs that convey particular hegemonic meanings "in order to project them back into the everyday world under the guise of the familiar, but functioning to introduce the unfamiliar, and the normally marginalized or unspeakable."[63] What López introduces through the body of the refigured Virgin of Guadalupe in *Our Lady* is her vision of an emancipated Chicana subject that gives meaning to her own symbols, constructs her own reality, and contests the definitions imposed by dominant religious and political orders.

As Chicana feminist scholars remind us, the reality of a Chicana/o "community of practiced, co-existing differences" is continuously denied in favor of the fantasy of a Chicano nation situated in a patriarchal and heterosexual imaginary.[64] By reinterpreting ideologically charged cultural symbols like La Virgen through a queer Chicana feminist lens, López's art thus "breaks open a public, cultural space for the articulation of queer Chicana desire."[65] In doing this she continues a long tradition of Chicana lesbian feminist disordering practices that "were part of the *foundational* struggle over how to *undefine* Aztlán."[66]

The types of responses that *Our Lady* elicits reflect the marginalized status of queer and feminist movements within the larger U.S. society and within Chicana/o communities, including those that self-identify as activist or progressive. The controversy surrounding *Our Lady* revealed an ideological struggle in which certain Catholic and Chicano nationalist groups "tried to maintain control over the meaning of the Virgin of Guadalupe and contain her within the semiotic structure of the Catholic Church."[67] As López affirms, it was primarily the Catholic Church and male Chicano activists who were attempting to enforce their patriarchal privilege by insisting on the exclusive right to interpret this image.

The presence of oppositional Chicana feminist works like *Our Lady* in public museums is also significant in the context of the gendered narrative, subject, and gaze that are often presented and constructed in modern art museums. The subject and holder of the gaze has traditionally been presumed to be white, male, and heterosexual. Female bodies are overwhelmingly portrayed as figures with little identity other than their sexuality and availability for male spectatorship.[68] The presence of López's *Our Lady* in a public museum can therefore also be viewed as an encounter between a queer Chicana feminist artist/subject engaged in self-representation and a masculine, Western art historical tradition that does not acknowledge how race, gender, sexuality, and colonialism inform its own artistic and exhibition practices.

Important insights can be gained from examining these two campaigns and the aggressive, and often violent, disciplinary actions directed against the work of these Mexican and Chicana artists. There are various parallels between the case of Alma López in Santa Fe and the case against Rolando De la Rosa in Mexico City, as the reaction to their work was so similar. Not coincidentally, both are critical and social activist artists who have utilized the Virgin of Guadalupe icon to dismantle, or at the very least question, the religious and nationalist ideologies that are enforced by those who attempt to control and restrict the meaning and power of the Virgin's image. In Mexico, the Catholic Church has a prominent role in official nationalist culture, and the partnership between church and state is something conservative politicians no longer pretend to hide. But in the United States, which proclaims itself a secular democracy, we nonetheless witness similar alliances between right- or left-wing groups and conservative religious forces that often get played out in the realm of culture.

The massive demonstration against Rolando De la Rosa filled the *zócalo* with tens of thousands of enraged Guadalupanos, the loving children of God who stood in front of the Metropolitan Cathedral and the Basílica de Guadalupe ready to lynch—or crucify—him for his heretical acts. While it may not seem surprising that individuals who see La Virgen as a sanctified image of purity and chastity would be affronted by these representations of the Mother of God, what should make us take pause and reflect is the fact that some of the most morally corrupt religious and state officials are often at the forefront of the crusades against these artists, who, unlike them, make no claim to represent or uphold Catholic morality or doctrine.

The fact that both of these moralistic persecutions occurred in response to exhibitions in public art museums is also important. Why does the secular museum need to uphold a particular religious vision? These pilgrimage protests against Rolando De la Rosa and Alma López are significant because they reveal the power of art, which can move people to extreme reactions.[69] But more important, they reveal the fact that these public acts of discipline and spectacle are the visible cultural front of much larger social and political battles.

Critical and politically motivated art by Mexican and Chicana artists offers viewers a way to question and think beyond what they have previously been allowed to envision. López's stance with *Our Lady*, however, was much more radical than Rolando De la Rosa's approach in that it went beyond deconstruction and critique to the construction of a new reality. This reality is one in which a woman's body is not automatically perceived as sinful but is understood as belonging to a complete human being who does not need to disassociate her sexuality from her spirituality in order to exist. López's depiction of Raquel Salinas in *Our Lady* is an attempt to redeem that which is socially marginalized and cast as unrepresentable or abject when viewed through patriarchal, Euro-Christian paradigms.

The experiences of Alma López, Rolando De la Rosa, and other artists who have been castigated for daring to articulate themselves through La Virgen de Guadalupe's icon reveal the degree to which religious and nationalist heteropatriarchal forces feel that they have sole ownership of an image that has been reclaimed and resignified as a symbol of hope, decolonial struggles, and social redemption by so many. It also highlights the multiple contradictions and hypocrisies of a church and state alliance that claims to speak through the authoritative voice of God and justice yet polices these supposedly altruistic ideals through Inquisition-like threats of expulsion, defamation, and violence.

NOTES

1. All of the Alma López images discussed in this chapter are included in the color plate section of this book.

2. Emma Pérez, "Irigaray's Female Symbolic in the Making of Chicana Lesbian Sitios y Lenguas (Sites and Discourses)," in *Living Chicana Theory*, edited by Carla Trujillo (Berkeley, Calif.: Third Woman Press, 1998), 87–101; and idem,

The Decolonial Imaginary: Writing Chicanas into History (Bloomington: Indiana University Press, 1999). Emma Pérez describes the "decolonial imaginary" as an interstitial and decolonizing "third space." As Laura E. Pérez, Irene Lara, and others point out in their analyses of decolonizing strategies in Chicana art, this decolonial imaginary is a space where colonial binaries and repressions, including those of sexuality and spirit, are challenged. See Laura E. Pérez, "Spirit Glyphs: Reimagining Art and Artist in the Work of Chicana Tlamatinime," *Modern Fiction Studies* 44.1 (1998): 36–76; and idem, *Chicana Art: The Politics of Spiritual and Aesthetic Altarities* (Durham, N.C.: Duke University Press, 2007). And see Irene Lara, "Goddess of the Américas in the Decolonial Imaginary: Beyond the Virtuous Virgen/Pagan Puta Dichotomy," *Feminist Studies* 34.1–34.2 (2008): 99–127; and idem, "Tonanlupanisma: Re-Membering Tonantzin-Guadalupe in Chicana Visual Art," *Aztlán: A Journal of Chicano Studies* 33.2 (2008): 61–90.

3. The theme of the 2006 Mexico City Marcha Lésbica was "Lesbianas, rompiendo barreras, cruzando fronteras" (Lesbians, breaking barriers, crossing borders) coined by the contingent from Santa Cruz, California, during the previous year's march. I specifically use the term *interstitial* (E. Pérez, "Irigaray's Female Symbolic," 89) to mark the interstitial countersites from which Lesbian March participants negotiated our "differential politics" in relation to hegemonic and normative conceptions of nation, culture, gender, sexuality, and citizenship.

4. In *The Decolonial Imaginary*, Emma Pérez posits "desire as a medium for social change, desire as revolution, desire as love and hope for a different kind of future—a postcolonial one" (xix). In sexualizing and "queering" an ideologically loaded religious and cultural symbol like the Virgin of Guadalupe, Alma López thus enacts and gives visual form to her "decolonial desire" (125). López's queer desire is decolonial in that it aims to disrupt sex-spirit repressions based on Euro-Christian, colonialist ideologies.

5. In her iconographic and stylistic analysis of the traditional Virgin of Guadalupe icon, art historian Jeanette Favrot Peterson finds that the sixteenth-century Guadalupe icon is modeled on descriptions and engravings of the apocalyptic woman of Revelation 12:1. See "The Virgin of Guadalupe: Symbol of Conquest or Liberation?" *Art Journal* 51.4 (1992): 40.

6. L. Pérez, *Chicana Art*, 8.

7. Numerous scholars of Chicana literature and art have documented and analyzed this trajectory of Chicana cultural production. See, for example, Gloria E. Anzaldúa, *Borderlands/La Frontera: The New Mestiza* (San Francisco: Aunt Lute Books, 1987); Angie Chabram-Dernersesian, "I Throw Punches for My Race, but I Don't Want to Be a Man: Writing Us—Chica-nos (Girl, Us)/Chicanas— into the Movement Script," in *Cultural Studies*, edited by Lawrence Grossberg, Cary Nelson, and Paula Treichler (New York: Routledge, 1992), 81–95; Peterson,

"The Virgin of Guadalupe"; Yvonne Yarbro-Bejarano, "Turning It Around: Chicana Art Critic Yvonne Yarbro-Bejarano Discusses the Insider/Outsider Visions of Ester Hernández and Yolanda M. López," *Crossroads* 31 (1993): 15, 17; idem, "The Lesbian Body in Latina Cultural Production," in *Entiendes?: Queer Readings, Hispanic Writings*, edited by Emilie L. Bergmann and Paul Julian Smith (Durham, N.C.: Duke University Press, 1995), 181–197; Ana Castillo, "Introduction," in *The Goddess of the Americas/La Diosa de las Américas: Writings on the Virgin of Guadalupe*, edited by Ana Castillo (New York: Riverhead Books, 1996), xv–xxiii; Alicia Gaspar de Alba, *Chicano Art Inside/Outside the Master's House: Cultural Politics and the CARA Exhibition* (Austin: University of Texas Press, 1998); Carla Trujillo, "La Virgen de Guadalupe and Her Reconstruction in Chicana Lesbian Desire," in *Living Chicana Theory*, edited by Carla Trujillo (Berkeley, Calif.: Third Woman Press, 1998), 214–231; Laura E. Pérez, "El Desorden, Nationalism, and Chicana/o Aesthetics," in *Between Woman and Nation: Nationalisms, Transnational Feminisms, and the State*, edited by Caren Kaplan, Norma Alarcón, and Minoo Moallem (Durham, N.C.: Duke University Press, 1999), 19-46; idem, *Chicana Art*; Charlene Villaseñor Black, "Sacred Cults, Subversive Icons: Chicanas and the Pictorial Language of Catholicism," in *Speaking Chicana: Voice, Power, and Identity*, edited by D. Letticia Galindo and María Dolores González (Tucson: University of Arizona Press, 1999), 134–174; Teresa Eckmann, "Chicano Artists and Neo-Mexicanists: (De) Constructions of National Identity," LAII Research Paper Series, no. 36 (Albuquerque: University of New Mexico, 2000); Reina Alejandra Prado Saldívar, "Goddesses, Sirenas, Lupes y Ángel Cholas: The Work of Alma López," *Aztlán: A Journal of Chicano Studies* 25.1 (2000): 195–203; Luz Calvo, "Art Comes for the Archbishop: The Semiotics of Contemporary Chicana Feminism and the Work of Alma López," *Meridians: Feminism, Race, Transnationalism* 5.1 (2004): 201–224; Lara, "Goddess of the Américas"; idem, "Tonanlupanisma"; and Guisela Latorre, "Icons of Love and Devotion: Alma López's Art," *Feminist Studies* 34.1–34.2 (2008): 131–150. This is not, by any means, a comprehensive list.

8. L. Pérez, *Chicana Art*.

9. For a discussion of decolonial feminism and decolonizing spiritualities in Chicana art, see L. Pérez, "Spirit Glyphs"; and idem, *Chicana Art*.

10. Lara, "Tonanlupanisma," 2008.

11. For more on decolonial strategies of "re-membering" and healing sexual-spiritual dichotomies through Chicana art and spiritual practice, see L. Pérez, "Spirit Glyphs"; idem, *Chicana Art*; Lara, "Goddess of the Américas"; and idem, "Tonanlupanisma."

12. For expanded analyses of the Chicana/Latina strategies of representation discussed in this chapter, see Yvonne Yarbro-Bejarano, "The Lesbian Body"; E. Pérez, "Irigaray's Female Symbolic"; L. Pérez, "El Desorden"; and idem, *Chicana Art*.

13. Although 1531 is the year claimed in Catholic Mexican popular narratives as the date of the Virgin of Guadalupe's apparition, scholars and theologians continue to engage in debate. For an overview of apparitionist and historical (antiapparitionist) interpretations, including where Chicana feminist artists fit within these debates, see Socorro Castañeda-Liles, "Our Lady of Guadalupe and the Politics of Cultural Interpretation," in *Mexican American Religions: Spirituality, Activism, and Culture*, edited by Gastón Espinosa and Mario T. García (Durham, N.C.: Duke University Press, 2008), 153–179. For an in-depth examination of the iconography of the Virgin of Guadalupe *tilma* image and the thesis that this image was painted by the native artist Marcos Cipac de Aquino, see Jeanette Favrot Peterson, "Creating the Virgin of Guadalupe: The Cloth, the Artist, and Sources in Sixteenth Century New Spain," *The Americas* 64.4 (April 2005): 571–610.

14. Castillo, "Introduction"; Yolanda Broyles-González, "Indianizing Catholicism: Chicana/India/Mexicana Indigenous Spiritual Practices in Our Image," in *Chicana Traditions: Continuity and Change*, edited by Norma E. Cantú and Olga Nájera-Ramírez (Urbana: University of Illinois Press, 2002), 117–132.

15. Peterson, "The Virgin of Guadalupe."

16. Eckmann, "Chicano Artists and Neo-Mexicanists," 6.

17. Castillo, "Introduction," xv.

18. Sandra Cisneros, "Guadalupe the Sex Goddess," in *Goddess of the Americas/La Diosa de las Américas: Writings on the Virgin of Guadalupe*, edited by Ana Castillo (New York: Riverhead Books, 1996), 49.

19. Yarbro-Bejarano, "The Lesbian Body," 184–185.

20. Trujillo, "La Virgen de Guadalupe," 219.

21. Yarbro-Bejarano, "The Lesbian Body," 184.

22. Villaseñor Black, "Sacred Cults," 134.

23. See Marcella Althaus Reid for more on the concept of "indecent" and queer liberation theologies, *The Queer God* (New York: Routledge, 2003). I thank Laura E. Pérez for this reference.

24. Alma López, "Mermaids, Butterflies, and Princesses," *Aztlán: A Journal of Chicano Studies* 25.1 (2000): 190.

25. Cherríe Moraga, "El Mito Azteca," in *The Goddess of the Americas/La Diosa de las Américas: Writings on the Virgin of Guadalupe*, edited by Ana Castillo (New York: Riverhead Books, 1996), 69.

26. Alma López, telephone interview with the author, January 16, 2005.

27. López, "Mermaids," 189.

28. Ibid., 190.

29. L. Pérez, "Spirit Glyphs"; and idem, *Chicana Art*.

30. Calvo, "Art Comes for the Archbishop."

31. Latorre, "Icons of Love and Devotion."

32. In her analyses of Chicana art, Laura E. Pérez ("Spirit Glyphs" and *Chicana Art*) argues that Chicana artists articulate a politicized and culturally hybrid "decolonizing spirituality" through a mixing of diverse artistic languages drawn from Mesoamerican, European, Native American, African, and other cultural and spiritual traditions.

33. Latorre, "Icons of Love and Devotion," 135.

34. *La Jornada* (February 19, 1988).

35. Jorge Alberto Manrique, "Ataque al Museo de Arte Moderno," *Luna Cornea* 11 (1997): 78.

36. In 1988, Carlos Salinas de Gortari obtained the Mexican presidency through an election that is widely considered to have been the result of massive fraud.

37. Alma López, "Silencing Our Lady: La Respuesta de Alma," *Aztlán: A Journal of Chicano Studies* 26.2 (2001): 249–267.

38. Ibid.; Comité Nacional para la Defensa de la Libertad de Expresión y las Manifestaciones Artísticas y Culturales, "Contra la manipulación de la religiosidad del pueblo mexicano," *La Jornada* (February 27, 1988), www.jornada.unam.mx.

39. *La Jornada* (January 28, 1988); Manrique, "Ataque al Museo de Arte Moderno."

40. "Not my mother nor my sister": *La Jornada* (January 24, 1988).

41. Ibid., my translation. *Editor's note*: The cowboy boots are also an allusion to the takeover of Texas by Anglo-American so-called freedom fighters in 1836, which led to the Battle of the Alamo and, ten years later, to the U.S.-Mexico War, which resulted in the loss of half of Mexico's territory to the United States.

42. Ibid.

43. Manrique, "Ataque al Museo de Arte Moderno," 78

44. *La Jornada* (January 24, 1988), www.jornada.unam.mx.

45. Edward J. McCaughan, "Gender, Sexuality, and Nation in the Art of Mexican Social Movements," *Nepantla: Views from the South* 3.1 (2002): 105.

46. Ibid., 106 and 110.

47. Michael J. Twomey, "A Falta de Pan, Tortillas: Mexican Economists on the Current Crisis," *Latin American Research Review* 24.3 (1989): 245.

48. McCaughan, "Gender, Sexuality, and Nation," 128.

49. *La Jornada* (March 17, 2004), www.jornada.unam.mx.

50. McCaughan, "Gender, Sexuality, and Nation," 118.

51. Ibid.

52. Ibid., 107-135.

53. *La Jornada* (September 13, 1999), as cited in Eckmann, "Chicano Artists and Neo-Mexicanists," 5

54. "She is a Virgin that belongs to all of us: Zapatistas, PAN adherents, PRI adherents, she belongs to all of us": *La Jornada* (December 8, 2006), www.jornada.unam .mx.

55. Tey Marianna Nunn, "The Cyberarte Exhibit: A Curator's Journey through Community and Controversy," paper presented at the Research and Museums Conference (Smithsonian Institution, Washington, DC, November 20–23, 2002); and idem, "The *Our Lady* Controversy: Chicana Art, Hispanic Identity, and the Politics of Place and Gender in Nuevo México," in *Expressing New Mexico: Nuevomexicano Creativity, Ritual, and Memory*, edited by Phillip B. Gonzales (Tucson: University of Arizona Press, 2007), 162–183.

56. Nunn, "The Cyberarte Exhibit," 9.

57. López, "Silencing Our Lady."

58. Nunn, "The Cyberarte Exhibit," 9.

59. Nunn, "The *Our Lady* Controversy," 175.

60. L. Pérez, *Chicana Art*, 258.

61. Villaseñor Black, "Sacred Cults," 134.

62. L. Pérez, *Chicana Art*, 262.

63. L. Pérez, "El Desorden," 34.

64. Ibid.

65. Calvo, "Art Comes for the Archbishop," 203–204.

66. L. Pérez, "El Desorden," 24.

67. Calvo, "Art Comes for the Archbishop," 202.

68. Carol Duncan, *Civilizing Rituals: Inside Public Art Museums* (London: Routledge, 1995), 111.

69. For more about how the protest became transformed into a pilgrimage in Santa Fe, see Alicia Gaspar de Alba, Chap. 10 here.

9

Do U Think I'm a Nasty Girl?

Catrióna Rueda Esquibel

INTRODUCTION

I'm sure that many queer folks have memories of confronting a sexuality for which one does not yet have words. I remember those moments in northern New Mexico in the 1980s, like watching *Some Like It Hot* with my mom for the first time. On the one hand, I was dumbfounded by Marilyn Monroe's *je ne sais quoi*. On the other hand, I totally identified with Jack Lemmon and Tony Curtis, in drag and feeling hidden, caught, exposed, and overwhelmed. This same reaction was provoked by pretty much anything having to do with Prince, who seemed the epitome of gender nonconformity. His music, his movie, his protégées. Sheila E., Apollonia, Vanity 6—who made their mark with "Nasty Girl":

> Tonight we're living in a fantasy
> Our own little nasty world.
> Tonight, don't you want to come with me?
> Do you think I'm a nasty girl.

The songstresses' bold come-on promised experience, insatiability, all that.

That's right, I can't control it.
I need seven inches more.
Tonight, I can no longer hold it.
Get it up, get it up, I can't wait any longer.

The sexual intensity was balanced by the comedic ending. The girls are "too much" for the presumed heterosexual male of the song, and he cannot measure up to the desire.

Is that it?
Wake me when you're done.
I guess you'll be the only one having fun

As if the song itself is not enough, in the music video the trio is dancing in sexy lingerie: camisoles, baby dolls, teddies (all very eighties). This was 1982, and while MTV had come to New Mexico, we were still bowled over by the explicit sexuality.

I had no words to express my fascination with the song and the video. Even now, I can't address the articulation of female sexuality and agency, which exceeded the limits of heterosexuality. I can intellectualize, but the truth is, I was feeling both like and unlike a teenage boy—the self-same teenage boy who is unable to satisfy these ladies. My friends and I bought each other black panties, nightgowns, stockings, and modeled them. We sang "Do you think I'm a nasty girl," and I felt like both the speaker and the audience.

In the course of this chapter, I will be discussing Alma López's 1999 *Our Lady* and arguing against a 2001 reactionary Catholic reading of this artwork as a sexualization of La Virgen de Guadalupe and a blasphemy against Mexican culture and spirituality. Why then, do I reference this Vanity 6 song in my title? I think because the artwork, like the song, casts me in different and simultaneous positions: identification with the model (standing in for *Our Lady*), and the position outside as the spectator.

LA VIRGEN

La Virgen de Guadalupe is inexplicably tied to cultural conquest, *la otra conquista* (the other conquest). She is a syncretic mixture of religious figures, combining the "old" mother goddesses of indigenous Mexico (Tonantzin,

Coatlaxopeuh, Cihuacoatl) with the new Catholic Virgin Mary. Catholicism began to enjoy real success in the Americas only after the 1531 apparition of "una azteca, vestida en ropa de India."[1] She appeared to the Indian Juan Diego, a recent convert to Catholicism, on the hill of Tepeyac, a site sacred to Tonantsi, an Azteca-Mexica earth goddess.

Like La Malinche, La Virgen de Guadalupe has gone through several transformations. During the Independence period, her image was carried as a battle standard by *criollos*, *indios*, and mestizos against the Spanish *peninsulares*. Her image was also prominent in the Mexican Revolution. Yet, as Guillermo Gómez-Peña points out, Guadalupe is the signifier for contradictory signifieds: "a fundamentalist Catholic movement operating out of fear of modernity and change," and yet protector of the undocumented farmworkers; a symbol of the Partido Revolucionario Institucional, PRI (Institutional Revolutionary Party) to "guard our identity, our national character, and our sovereignty,"[2] and yet a loving mother who embraces all her children—low-riding *cholos*, Chicana lesbians, and student activists alike—with unconditional love. La Virgen is never stern or condemning but always loving and accepting.

The challenge La Virgen poses to Chicana feminists is her link to a patriarchal religion in which she has consistently been used to enforce women's self-abnegation in a culturally approved Marianismo: "the model for the ideal woman . . . derived from the religious cult of the Virgin Mary" and based on humility and self-sacrifice.[3] La Virgen is an impossible ideal that no flesh and blood woman can live up to.

Yet Chicana writers and artists have put the flesh and blood back on the young woman of the apparition "to find God in myself and love her, love her fiercely."[4] It is through the Chicana feminist rebellion against an ossified Virgen de Guadalupe that La Virgen truly comes to life. It is through their identifying La Virgen with a human woman—their own grandmother, their own mother, their own selves—that Chicana artists in particular have made peace with her.

In doing so, however, they have made the opposite of peace with the Catholic Church, conservative Guadalupanos, and Mexican and Chicano patriarchy. Chicana artists have had their icons of La Virgen met with bomb scares, death threats, and defacement. By putting a human face on La Virgen, Chicana artists have assailed her position as the Virgin Mary, "alone of all her sex."

I am reminded of a similar issue of representation in Chicano/a *teatro* when El Teatro Campesino puts on its biennial Christmas performance, *La Virgen*

de Tepeyac, the longest-running play in their repertory. As Yolanda Broyles-
González shows in her oral histories of the women of El Teatro Campesino,
casting decisions consistently divided women by age, experience, and skin
color. Actresses Socorro Valdéz and Olivia Chumacero complained that La
Virgen—who ought to have been the most important character in the play—
was reduced to a statue, a figurehead through casting decisions that restricted
the role to the youngest, least-experienced actresses: "[The directors] see the
Virgen of Guadalupe as a soft, demure, peaceful, saintly ingénue type."[5] Coincidentally, casting for La Virgen was restricted to light-skinned actresses and
has largely excluded Indian-featured women. While the actresses have challenged the casting practices, their criticisms have been discounted, frequently
in illogical ways. Socorro Valdéz was told: "You don't look like La Virgen.
Your teeth are too big." Valdéz replied: "¿Apoca estaba molacha La Virgen de
Guadalupe? That is the stupidest thing I ever heard."[6] The implication that a
demure, light-skinned woman with small teeth would better represent the
sixteenth-century apparition than an outspoken or indigenous-featured Chicana is laughable. Of course what is meant is that the first actress agrees with
the director's preconceived notion of La Virgen, and the second actress challenges that notion. The question of which woman actually looks more like La
Virgen will only be settled when La Virgen shows up herself to prove it.

Any challenge to a conservative iconography of La Virgen is recast as an
assault on the values of Mexican/Chicano culture. When reactionary organizations proclaim that "Lesbians insult La Virgen de Guadalupe," the intent to
identify lesbians with Malinche (i.e., a cultural traitor) becomes clear. Yet just
as they have reclaimed La Malinche, Chicana feminists and queer Chicanas refuse to abandon Guadalupe to either conservative movements or the Catholic
Church. Through art and literature they reiterate the unconditional nature of
La Virgen's maternal love. In La Madre's words: "I will give all my love and
motherly compassion to those who seek my aid."[7]

THE EPISCOPAL SHELL GAME

Through her title, "Art Comes for the Archbishop,"[8] Luz Calvo constructs a
semiotic link between Alma López's *Our Lady* (condemned by the archbishop
of Santa Fe) and the history of religious colonialism in both Mexico (1520–
1531) and New Mexico (the 1800s). In 1531, Bishop Zumárraga of Puebla
refused to believe in the apparition of Guadalupe. In the nineteenth century,
French archbishop Lamy taxed poor New Mexican villages in order to build

his European-style cathedral: both of these are examples of a prelate disre-
garding a local community and instead asserting his own authority. Both of
those earlier tales are of the faulty judgment of a prelate: his inability to appreciate what is sacred and holy, his dismissal of racial and ethnic minori-
ties, and his ethnocentrist view of faith. In these earlier historical periods, the
ecclesiastical authority represents a racist and dismissive position.

Through her linkage with the apparition of López's *Our Lady* in New
Mexico, Calvo remembers these histories. In doing so she also reveals the
archbishop's political stakes: at the end of the twentieth century, the Catholic Church faced a crisis of its own making, and by attacking a lesbian, gay,
bisexual, transgender (LGBT)–identified artist, the church, using a reliable
ecclesiastical strategy, was able to shift from defending its own policies to attacking the lavender menace.

The *Nican Mopohua* recounts Juan Diego's four encounters with La Virgen
de Guadalupe in 1531, as well as his three encounters with the "new bishop
[of New Spain], D. Fray Juan de Zumárraga."[9] Juan Diego goes to the bishop to describe the miraculous apparition and to deliver La Virgen's powerful
message. His encounters with the bishop are in sharp contrast with those with
La Virgen: she is caring, motherly; he is distant and patriarchal; she recognizes
their sameness; the bishop has no interest in the Indian convert. Juan Diego
has a struggle each time he wishes to see the bishop, as race, class, status, and
hierarchy conspire to keep him from the bishop's presence. In contrast, La
Virgen communicates directly with Juan Diego without an intermediary and
without recognizing the need for one. Instead, it is the bishop who needs an
intermediary—Juan Diego—to receive Our Lady's word. But rather than valu-
ing Juan Diego for his role, he interrogates him and then has him spied on.

The *Nican Mopohua* rationalizes that it was not the bishop but those who
served him who were at fault. When Juan Diego eludes the spies, they return,
angry, to the bishop: "They went to inform the lord bishop, creating in him
a bad attitude so that he would not believe [Juan Diego]; they told him that
[Juan Diego] was only deceiving him; that he was only imagining what he
was coming to say; that he was only dreaming; or that he had invented what
he was coming to tell him. They agreed among themselves that if he were to
come again, they would grab him and punish him harshly, so that he would
not lie again or deceive the people."[10]

Popular depictions of Zumárraga are not so forgiving. On El Día de la
Virgen (December 12), the apparitions of La Virgen are often reenacted as
part of the celebration of her feast day. Sometimes these reenactments follow

a script of the *Nican Mopohua*, but just as often they can be scripted plays or unscripted *actos* (short ensemble performances, often unscripted). In El Teatro Campesino's (ETC's) *La Virgen de Tepeyac*, the bishop himself speaks harshly to Juan Diego. Audiences of ETC and of other folk pageants across Latino America are likely to hear the bishop disparage Juan Diego as a "stupid Indian." The scenes of the encounter between Juan Diego and Zumárraga contrast the wealth of the bishop and his court with the poverty of Juan Diego and his family, and when compared with Juan Diego's encounters with La Virgen, contrast again the gentleness of La Virgen with the harshness of the bishop.

Thus, popular dramatizations of the story inscribe the bishop's rejection of Juan Diego and his vision as determined by racist belief that the Indians are not capable of truly absorbing the Catholic faith and have reverted to paganism. Still less does Zumárraga believe it possible that the Mother of God would appear in Mexico as a lowly Indian.

In 2001, the archbishop of Santa Fe presented himself as rushing to the defense of Our Lady of Guadalupe and rallying Catholics with his call. However, comparing the New Mexico controversy with the apparitions of Guadalupe at Tepeyac demonstrates that the archbishop of Santa Fe, like the bishop of Mexico, was the powerful attacking the powerless, in this case, a queer Chicana/Mexicana artist, to consolidate his own power. He claimed that only the Catholic Church's interpretation of Guadalupe as the "Virgin Mary" was valid and that López's feminist vision was invalid and blasphemous. Before addressing why such a power play by the archbishop of New Mexico would be necessary, I turn to a history specific to New Mexico and the role (and rule) of the Catholic Church.

The second connection Calvo makes, with Archbishop Lamy of New Mexico, may need more elaboration for those unfamiliar with New Mexican history. From the end of the Spanish colonial period through the American colonial period, New Mexican Catholicism was kept alive by native Hispano priests and by lay organizations such as Los Hermanos.[11] Contemporary with the Anglo takeover of New Mexico, the Catholic Church imposed French archbishop Jean Baptiste Lamy on the New Mexican people in an attempt to restore control to Rome and reestablish orthodoxy. This story is depicted in a racist and one-sided fashion in such texts as *History of New Mexico*, and Willa Cather's *Death Comes for the Archbishop*.[12] Lamy is represented as the "Great Man" (one might say "Great White Hope"), and Taos priest Antonio

José Martínez, who was prominent in fighting for Hispano rights in the New Mexican territory, is depicted as an evil, corrupt demagogue. Since the 1970s, Chicano historians and theologians have worked to rescue the reputation of Padre Martínez, including an effort to lift the order of excommunication laid on him by Archbishop Lamy in 1858.

In Hispano communities, the oral tradition remembers Lamy for his obsession with building a cathedral in the New Mexico highlands and his attack on Los Hermanos in northern New Mexico. To pay for the construction of his European-style cathedral, Lamy reestablished tithing, which had been abolished in the era of Mexican independence. When poor communities did not comply, Lamy directed local priests to deny the sacraments to their parishes until such time as they paid the full tithe.

Before the publication of Alberto Pulido's *The Sacred World of the Penitentes*,[13] it was difficult to find reliable discussions of Los Hermanos. Pulido's study focuses on their theology and values and their role in their community. Outsider representations of the group have frequently depicted it in hyperbolic and sensationalist detail as a cult practicing sadomasochism and defying the authority of the church. The brotherhood was excommunicated in 1880. The prurient fascination with Los Hermanos continues. In the 1960s, for example, Anglo spectators would turn up at the small chapels, or *moradas*, in which Los Hermanos worship, and shine their headlights into the chapels to watch the goings-on. In some communities, Los Hermanos and their defenders responded with a show of arms. In spite of their conflicted history with the Catholic Church, Los Hermanos have outlasted one bishop after another, one pope after another. Their excommunication was eventually revoked after a decades-long process which culminated when Archbishop Roberto Sánchez professed himself to be one of Los Hermanos.

That much-earlier archbishop, Jean Baptiste Lamy, is remembered as being out of touch with the poor Hispano villagers and unsympathetic to their plight, concerned only with his own power and status, and establishing the authority of the Catholic Church in the new Anglo government. His attacks on Los Hermanos and on Padre Martínez are part of that legacy.

What, then, do these historical bishops have to do with Archbishop Sheehan and his attack on Alma López and *Our Lady*? At least part of the answer lies in the pedophilia scandals of the Catholic Church at the end of the twentieth century and the role New Mexico played in the ecclesiastical cover-up in the United States.

A DUMPING GROUND

> Just as New Mexico is the nuclear waste dumping ground of the United States, it is also the ecclesiastical dumping ground of the Catholic Church.

BRUCE PASTERNAK

In the Archdiocese of Santa Fe, Michael J. Sheehan succeeded the immensely popular Roberto Sánchez, the first U.S. Latino to be raised to bishop.[14] Sánchez is credited with healing the long-standing rift between Los Hermanos and the Catholic clergy. He had long been active in the movement to make the U.S. Catholic Church more inclusive of and respectful toward the traditions of Mexican America.[15] Sánchez's 1993 resignation, although triggered by revelations that he had had consensual sexual relations with at least five women over the course of his priesthood, was ultimately a result of his role in the archdiocese's cover-up of child sexual abuse in New Mexico.

The historical context of the U.S. Catholic Church at the end of the twentieth century was dominated by the pedophilia scandals. Sexual molestation of children in New Mexico by priests was reported as early as the 1960s. New Mexico was the silent center of this controversy because it was home to a religious facility that claimed to rehabilitate troubled priests. The facility's area of specialization was alcoholism, but church officials heard only what they wanted to hear with regard to the efficacy of rehabilitating child molesters. For thirty years, priests accused of sexual molestation of children were routinely sent to the facility. While in residence there, many became active in local parishes. Thus, even while undergoing therapy for molesting children, these priests were able to continue their abuse. In addition, priests who completed their treatment were welcomed into the archdiocese.

This is the most recent legacy of the Catholic Church in New Mexico, and the one which Sheehan—an Anglo outsider replacing a Hispano insider—inherited. In his attack on artist Alma López, we can see an effort to salvage the image of church officials. Thus, using smoke and mirrors, the archbishop deflected attention from the crisis within the Catholic Church (both local and national) by rallying public opinion against López and her unorthodox portrait. This strategy is similar and related to the "threat" of gay marriage, which is frequently documented with faulty readings of the Christian Bible. As Peter Gomes says: "Gay marriage is seen to threaten heterosexual marriage to such an extent that constitutional amendments must be designed to prevent it, although no one seems prepared to propose similar legislation to prohibit divorce, which is a far greater threat to marriage and the family, and on which subject Jesus himself had distinct views. On homosexuality, he had nothing to say."[16] Similarly, Nancy Wilson argues that homophobia is a reliable and lucrative practice: "The fact is that the radical or religious right breaks the Ninth Commandment every day, using ignorance and fear of homosexuality and homosexuals to raise millions and millions of dollars. But they are not alone. The whole church and other religious bodies have born false witness about gays and lesbians for at least a millennium."[17]

In his description of *Our Lady* the archbishop seemed eager to compare her to a prostitute. In this, we can see the common contrast of the Virgin (Mary) and the whore (Mary Magdalene). The archbishop seemed to accuse López of taking our Virgin and making her a whore. As feminist viewers, we recognize that the model (Raquel Salinas) is making eye contact with the viewer because she is the subject of the artwork. She is a person. The archbishop's description relied on a traditional sexist interpretation in which, by definition, a woman was the object of the artwork; thus, he could only interpret her direct gaze as a sexual come-on. He saw only a "nasty girl."

SCARED, SCARRED, AND SACRED

Patrisia Gonzales and Roberto Rodríguez engage the controversy over *Our Lady* by going straight to the body at the center, looking for the voice and the story behind the woman's body:

> Her body is beautiful, brown and strong like the earth. Yet, you can't get
> Raquel Salinas to say much about herself without causing her to choke
> up with emotion. For nearly half her life, she was ashamed of her body—
> burdened with guilt for having been raped. Today her body is the subject of a
> raging controversy in Northern New Mexico because Los Angeles artist Alma
> López depicted her as *Our Lady*—a rose-covered woman personifying pre-
> Columbian moon and earth entities and vestiges of the Virgen de Guadalupe.
> She is one body of the sacred feminine as redefined in recent Chicana art.[18]

Gonzales and Rodríguez discuss Salinas's concept of La Virgen de Guadalupe and what that image means today:

The image Salinas depicts is that of "a heroine, of a strong woman . . . That's who I believe Guadalupe is . . . a symbol of struggle," said Salinas . . . To those opposed to the image, Salinas' body offends. It is violating and sacrilegious. On the surface, the controversy is about sacredness vs. the freedom of expression. When these ideals clash, there can be no winners. Yet look through the eyes of Salinas and you see something else raging: a desire for justice in a world that hungers for it and a desire to honor the sacred feminine in a world that daily dishonors women.[19]

They argue that Salinas's artistic modeling, which culminates in/as *Our Lady*, is part of her long healing process from a rape and the subsequent reaction of our rape cultures, which blame the woman, inculcating *vergüenza* (shame) in her about her body, her sexuality, her self. Without personal support following her attack, Salinas learned to hate her self and her body. Only through emotional and spiritual work did she build a new relationship with her body. Gonzales and Rodríguez show the terms of the debate about sacredness vs. freedom of expression as a false dichotomy. Like religion vs. homosexuality, the dichotomy implies that the homophobes have an unquestionable claim to "sacredness" and "religion." Through her embodiment of *Our Lady*, Salinas reclaims the body that has been abused in our racist sexist cultures, and the artwork is an affirmation of loving one's own female body as beautiful and sacred.

LESBIAN, LESBIAN, WHO'S GOT THE LESBIAN?

Ironically, of course, *Our Lady* is not in any conventional sense a lesbian image. It is an image of one woman standing alone, not two women together. It is not titled *Our Lady of Lesbians*, or *Our Lesbian Lady*. The main model does not noticeably transgress norms of female attractiveness: she sports no butch haircut, reveals no piercings, tattoos, or other body modifications. She neither invites the viewer's gaze nor coyly avoids it. Her attitude is perceived as transgressive not in and of itself but within the context of representation of La Virgen, which, the Catholic Church argues, allows only the one—orthodox—reading. Protestors and media made frequent reference to López's other artwork *Lupe and Sirena in Love*, but Lupe and Sirena were not appearing in the New Mexico museum. The attack was clearly provoked by linking Salinas's body with López's sexuality. The angel in *Our Lady* is by no means the first bare-breasted angel in the history of sacred art. Thus, in and of itself, the angel is neither "lesbian" or transgressive. Nor is the angel's position in relation to Our Lady depicted as in any way sexual.[20]

If I return, then, to Gonzales and Rodríguez's approach of going to the body at the center of the controversy, it becomes clearer that, ironically enough, the body at the center is not Salinas's body but López's. López is the lesbian at the heart of *Our Lady*, and it is this queerness, this otherness, that was being challenged, as anti-Catholic, anti-Nuevomexicana, anti-Latina. The archbishop thus effectively mobilized against López by switching their positions and portraying the archdiocese as culturally sensitive to New Mexican traditions and the Chicana artist as the interloper/lesbian/heretic.

Our Lady is transgressive in the same sense described by the women of El Teatro Campesino: La Virgen is being restrained to an image that is "a soft, demure, peaceful, saintly ingénue type," not outspoken, not confident, not capable.[21]

BEFORE ORTHODOXY: A FABLE TO KINDLE HOPE

This "traditional" position claimed by the archdiocese and Chicano nationalists is, in fact, the position of empire. Before Christianity became the church of the Roman Empire, it enjoyed heterodoxy: one can accurately refer to the many Christianities of that time rather than to a unified and orthodox Christianity.[22] Scholars of the history of religion and liberal theology bring to us the different gospels, theologies, and movements of those times, because this diversity can provide encouragement in the twenty-first century for we who are looking for a God who is too big for any one religion to contain, and for those of us raised in Christian traditions who have been alienated by doctrines of exclusion.

I find Gnostic gospels and specious saints to be fascinating material to draw from as I construct my own personal theology, even as I appreciate their influence on literature in general and Chicano literature in particular. Linda Coon discusses dominant tropes in the lives of women saints in particular.[23] Women saints had to be cast quite literally as either virgins or whores. The virgins were martyred when they refused pagan marriage. The whores lived lives of sin and pleasure, which they ultimately renounced to embrace salvation through Christianity. This latter trope is a popular means of discrediting female religious figures, the most obvious example of which is Mary Magdalene. By in effect grafting the story of the repentant woman onto the life of Mary of Magdala, she was demoted from disciple to prostitute, from an active participant in the shaping of Christianity to an object of scorn.[24] Coon focuses particularly on Saint Pelagia of Antioch and Saint Mary of Egypt. On the surface, both women look like stock figures of "God's Holy Harlots,"[25] but in fact both are resistant figures because of their later transgendered presentation and the challenges they posed to church authorities. Both women became hermits in the tradition of the desert fathers rather than the more gender-conforming "anchorite," women who spent their lives secluded in a small walled-up cell.[26]

I find Saint Pelagia a powerful figure in the study of the controversy over *Our Lady* precisely because of the way her story focuses on the female body, on the reaction of churchmen, and for its implications for the sacred feminine. In the vita of Saint Pelagia of Antioch we see another bishop encounter the female body, and this encounter, with another attitude toward the female body, shapes his understanding of Christianity.

Pelagia, the most famous actress in the city, in a parade heading to her performance, passed by a group of bishops at the church door. Scandalized, the bishops covered their faces with veils so that they would not look upon Pelagia's beautiful form. (An interesting gender twist, since usually women are veiled to shield them from the gaze of men. In this instance, the bishops must veil their eyes because they cannot otherwise control them.) All of the bishops, that is, but one: the Holy Bishop Nonnus gazed intently at Pelagia as she and her entourage passed by, and he continued to stare after her for some minutes. He immediately asked of his fellow bishops:

> "Were you not delighted by such great beauty?" They are still scandalized and do not respond.
>
> "Were you not delighted by her great beauty?" Still they did not answer, so "Indeed," he said, "I was very greatly delighted and her beauty pleased me very much!"[27]

Nonnus remains focused on Pelagia's beauty, which, he points out, must require hours of preparation "in order to lack nothing in beauty and adornment of the body; she wants to please all those who see her." He admonishes his fellow bishops: "When we are going to see the great and glorious face of our Bridegroom which has a beauty beyond compare . . . why do we not adorn ourselves and wash the dirt from our unhappy souls, why do we let ourselves lie so neglected?"[28]

Pelagia has bathed and clad her body in jewels and enticing garments; she is arrayed in beauty and perfume. In contrast, Nonnus points out, those who profess their love for Christ walk around with their souls hairy-legged, dry-skinned, smelly, and in need of exfoliation and massage. In effect, he challenges the other bishops to throw the misogynous veils from their eyes and learn to accept the beauty and sacredness of the feminine.

The archbishop of Santa Fe—like the petty bishops of Pelagia's tale—calls down condemnation on the woman who is beautiful and who is displaying her beauty. His description of the woman in *Our Lady* as a "tart or a street woman" reiterates a disgust for women and the female body and fails to acknowledge either the beauty and sacredness of women and women's bodies or the possibility that his own religious interpretation might be finite, that his box is too small for either God or *Our Lady*. Rather than embracing *Our Lady*, rather than seeing in it the call to beautify our souls, and rather than perceiving the apparition of the divine feminine, he condemns the work as a blasphemy.[29] Such a response may be orthodox, but it highlights the limitations of a rigid theology of exclusion versus a loving theology of inclusion.

COYOLXAUHQUI

As I look at *Our Lady*, I can see López's references to the violated Chicana body through the Virgin's cloak. In a traditional icon of La Virgen, the cloak is a night sky of stars. In *Our Lady*, the cloak is a cutout filled in with the stone circle of Coyolxauhqui. Coyolxauhqui has become an important icon in Chicana *muxerista* activism and theory.[30]

Coyolxauhqui is the daughter of Coatlicue. Her downfall was that she tried to prevent the entry of war into the land of her people. Her mother was pregnant and about to give birth to the god of war (Huitzilopochtli). Coyolxauhqui led a rebellion among her siblings, the four hundred stars, intending to kill the god before he could be born. She was too late: "At the moment of his birth [Huitzilopotchli] murders Coyolxauhqui, cutting off her head and completely dismembering her body. Breast splits from hip splits from thigh from knee from arm and foot. Coyolxauhqui is banished to the darkness and becomes the moon, la diosa de la luna."[31]

Cherríe Moraga resists the conformity (and presumed collaboration) of La Virgen by turning her attention to Coyolxauhqui. She is interested in the rebellious daughter rather than the loving mother.

Huitzilopochtli is not my god. And although I revere his mother Coatlicue, Diosa de la Muerte y la Vida, I do not pray to her. I pray to the daughter, La Hija Rebelde. She who has been banished, the mutilated sister who transforms herself into the moon. She is la fuerza femenina, our attempt to pick up the fragments of our dismembered womanhood and reconstitute ourselves. She is the Chicana writer's words, the Chicana painter's canvas, the Chicana dancer's step. She is motherhood reclaimed and sisterhood honored. She is the female god we seek in our work, la Mechicana before the "fall."[32]

The killing of Coyolxauhqui was the central metaphor of Aztec worship in that the sacrificial victims had their hearts torn from their chests and then their bodies thrown down the steps of the Templo Mayor, the rolling of their bodies symbolizing the circular shape of the stone of Coyolxauhqui and the moon.

Our image of Coyolxauhqui comes from this stone, discovered in Mexico City in 1978. The return of the repressed Mexicana body, the stone is cracked from side to side, further symbolizing the fractured legacy of Coyolxauhqui. In fact, we have no originary whole Coyolxauhqui to whom we can refer. We have only the image of her body dismembered, after the fall.

Chicana feminism has reclaimed Coyolxauhqui, and artists, activists, and scholars are literally putting her back together, re-membering her dismembered body. Remembering Coyolxauhqui. Re-membering Coyolxauhqui means putting the flesh back on the body, like Isis piecing her lover Osiris back together after he has been dismembered; like the survivors of the Acteal massacre in Chiapas in 1997, who took the "broken image" of La Virgen, which they "pieced back together as their shrine," the Virgin of the Massacre.[33] This remembering is a resurrection of sorts, and the circular stone of Coyolxauhqui's dismemberment becomes like a cross with the crucified Christ.

So what is this rebellious daughter doing in the cloak of *Our Lady*? Other Chicana artists have referenced Aztec goddesses in their depictions of La Virgen de Guadalupe, precisely because she is identified with a pre-Columbian mother figure. Yolanda M. López's *Nuestra Madre* provides a drawing of Coatlicue wearing La Virgen's dress and mantle. But Alma López is not dressing Coyolxauhqui as La Virgen; Coyolxauhqui is the garment that clothes *Our Lady*. She is cloaking the model, shielding her from the danger. She quite literally "has her back." Coyolxauhqui embraces *Our Lady* as the real (embodied) woman. *Our Lady*'s cloak is not only the flesh of Coyolxauhqui, it is also quite literally stone, ready to deflect the slings, arrows, and bullets of judgment and intolerance.[34] Coyolxauhqui accompanies La Chicana in the resurrection of the body and the life to come. When she returns, *Coyolxauhqui Returns As Our Lady Disguised as La Virgen de Guadalupe to Defend the Rights of las Chicanas*.[35]

Unlike some spectators of *Our Lady*, I do not look at the image and see an outsider. She is not the Other. Instead, the image calls me in and makes me engage with the meaning of La Virgen and my own queer Chicana identity. When I look at *Our Lady*, I am not the same shy teenager unable to name my own desire, nor do I identify with that inept teenage boy in the Vanity 6 MTV video who doesn't have the goods to satisfy all those "nasty girls." Like Nonnus, I am amazed at the beauty of Pelagia, "living in a fantasy" of sacred possibility.

NOTES

1. "An Aztec woman, dressed in the garments of an Indian" (Gloria Anzaldúa, *Borderlands/La Frontera: The New Mestiza*, 2nd ed. [San Francisco: Aunt Lute Books, 1999]), 50.

2. Guillermo Gómez-Peña, "The Two Guadalupes," in *Goddess of the Americas*, edited by Ana Castillo (New York: Riverhead Books, 1996), 175.

3. June Macklin, "'All the Good and Bad in This World': Women, Traditional Medicine, and Mexican American Culture," in *Twice a Minority*, edited by Margarita B. Melville (St. Louis: C. V. Mosby Company, 1980), 129.

4. Ntozake Shange, *For Colored Girls Who Have Considered Suicide When the Rainbow Is Enuf* (New York: Macmillan, 1977).

5. Yolanda Broyles-González, "Women in El Teatro Campesino: ¿Apoca Estaba Molacha La Virgen de Guadalupe?" in *Chicana Voices: Intersections of Class Race and Gender*, edited by Teresa Córdoba (Austin, Tex.: Center for Mexican American Studies, 1986), 127–128.

6. "Now you're telling me La Virgen had no teeth?" (ibid., 178).

7. Andrés Gonzales Guerrero, *A Chicano Theology* (New York: Orbis Books, 1987), 97.

8. Luz Calvo, "Art Comes for the Archbishop: The Semiotics of Feminism and the Work of Alma López," *Meridians: Feminism, Race, Transnationalism* 5.1 (2004); reprinted as Chap. 5 here.

9. Virgilio Elizondo et al., eds., *The Treasure of Guadalupe* (New York: Rowman & Littlefield, 2006), 109.

10. Ibid., 114.

210 CATRIÓNA RUEDA ESQUIBEL

11. Although they are commonly identified as Los Penitentes, I was taught that this term is disrespectful, and so I will use Los Hermanos.

12. *History of New Mexico: Its Resources and People* (Los Angeles: Pacific States Publishing Co., 1907); Willa Cather, *Death Comes for the Archbishop* (New York: Knopf, 1927).

13. Alberto López Pulido, *The Sacred World of the Penitentes* (Washington, DC: Smithsonian Institution Press, 2000).

14. The epigraph is quoted in Elinor Burkett and Frank Bruni, *A Gospel of Shame: Children, Sexual Abuse, and the Catholic Church* (New York: Viking/Penguin, 1993), 126.

15. Demetria Martínez, "To Hispanics, Sanchez Is 'Pastoral Giant,'" *National Catholic Reporter* 20.29 (1993).

16. Peter J. Gomes, *The Scandalous Gospel of Jesus: What's So Good about the Good News?* (New York: Harper Collins, 2007), 106.

17. Nancy L. Wilson, *Our Tribe: Queer Folks, God, Jesus, and the Bible* (San Francisco: Harper, 1995), 26.

18. Patrisia Gonzales and Roberto Rodríguez, "The Body of the Sacred Feminine," *United Press Syndicate*, www.networkaztlan.com.

19. Ibid.; third ellipses mine.

20. This is in contrast to, for example, the book jacket of *Santora: The Good Daughter*, by Resurrección Cruz (a pseudonym), in which a contemporary Chicana appears in the aura of La Virgen and is supported by a male devil figure who is smoking a cigarette and looking up her skirt.

21. Cherríe Moraga makes a similar argument in her play "Watsonville: Some Place Not Here" in *Watsonville/Circle in the Dirt*. (Albuquerque: West End Press, 2002). Moraga's character, Juan Cunningham (the queer mixed-race former priest), argues against the church's interpretation of an apparition of La Virgen de Guadalupe on a tree outside of Watsonville. The local parish priest tells Dolores, the bereft mother to whom La Virgen appears, that it was a sign that "she must open her heart, forgive her husband his offenses." Cunningham charges that "that's all the Church ever tells these women" and counters with "Do you remember the words of the Virgin Mary when she says 'The mighty will be put down from their thrones. / And the lowly will be lifted up in their place. . . . [And the hungry will be fed] . . . And the fat and over-content will be sent away empty . . .' Well those are the words of an angry woman . . . Not some passive long-suffering santa" (71–72).

22. Elaine Pagels, *The Gnostic Gospels* (New York: Random House, 1979).

23. Lynda L. Coon, *Sacred Fictions: Holy Women and Hagiography in Late Antiquity* (Philadelphia: University of Pennsylvania Press, 1997).

24. And, although it is clear from the Christian Bible that Jesus scorned neither of these women, religious traditions frequently present them negatively.

25. The term is Coon's. I take the "holy harlot" part of the narrative with a grain of salt, as more of a sign that we do not know the history of any particular woman before this point rather than as evidence that she was a prostitute or promiscuous.

26. In fact, Pelagia in particular became a desert father, Pelagius, but that comes later.

27. Benedicta Ward, *Harlots of the Desert: A Study of Repentance in Early Monastic Sources* (Kalamazoo, Mich.: Cistercian Publications, 1987), 67.

28. Pelagia, converted by Bishop Nonnus's Christian attitude, renounces her ways and follows Nonnus as her spiritual mentor. She then takes his robe, flees to the desert, changes her gender and name, and becomes Pelagius, one of the desert fathers.

29. According to the New Mexican theology expressed in both Jo Carrillo's *Maria Littlebear* and Leslie Marmon Silko's *Garden in the Dunes*, the viewer's reaction to the apparition is a clear sign of the state of his or her soul. Spectators who see Jesus or La Virgen are saved, while those who see the devil had better give away all their possessions and change their lives.

30. *Muxerista*, also *mujerista* from *mujerista* theology: "In the mujerista, God revindicates the divine image and likeness of women." See Ada María Isasi-Díaz, "Mujeristas: A Name of Our Own," *Christian Century* (May 24–31, 1989): 560.

31. Cherríe Moraga, "El Mito Azteca," in *The Goddess of the Americas/La Diosa de las Américas: Writings on the Virgin of Guadalupe*, edited by Ana Castillo (New York: Riverhead Books, 1996), 68.

32. Ibid., 69.

33. Patrisia Gonzales, "Lupe and the Buddha," *Column of the Americas*, www.almalo pez.com.

34. In *Bulletproof Faith: A Spiritual Survival Guide for Gay and Lesbian Christians* (San Francisco: Jossey-Bass, 2008), Candace Chellew Hodge coins the term "Bulletproof Faith" to describe the shield gays and lesbians need in the face of hostility in the guise of Christianity. Of course, I especially like the Wonder Woman reference.

35. This is the title of another Alma López painting, which she painted in 2004 and which graces the cover of my book, *With Her Machete in Her Hands: Reading Chicana Lesbians* (Austin: University of Texas Press, 2006).

10

Devil in a Rose Bikini

THE SECOND COMING OF OUR LADY IN SANTA FE

Alicia Gaspar de Alba

> I see the Devil.
>
> **JOSÉ VILLEGAS**

> Blasphemy is in the eye of the beholder.
>
> **DANIEL DEL SOLAR**

O N SUNDAY, APRIL 1, 2001, *Journal North*, a Santa Fe newspaper, published a very telling cartoon by Jon Richards. The cartoon shows a caricature of Archbishop Michael J. Sheehan standing next to an Ayatollah Khomeini–like figure, the image of Alma López's *Our Lady* in the background. The men appear to be looking at the image on the wall of the museum, and the Sheehan character asks: "So just how do you go about issuing a fatwa?" The cartoon is alluding to the infamous diktat of the Ayatollah's in which he called for the assassination of Salman Rushdie for having allegedly blasphemed against the prophet Mohammed in his 1988 novel, *The Satanic Verses*. Calling the fatwa a "religious duty for Muslims" because of the novel's great offense against Islam, the Ayatollah deputized any Muslim in the world to "send [the writer] to Hell."[1] Given its publication date, the cartoon could be taken as a sardonic April Fool's comment on the cultural climate in Santa Fe at the time of the *Our Lady* controversy, but I think it aptly illustrates the zealotry with which the archbishop and his holy army of protestors attacked the constitutional rights of Alma López and sought to punish her for her alleged offense against the Mother of God.

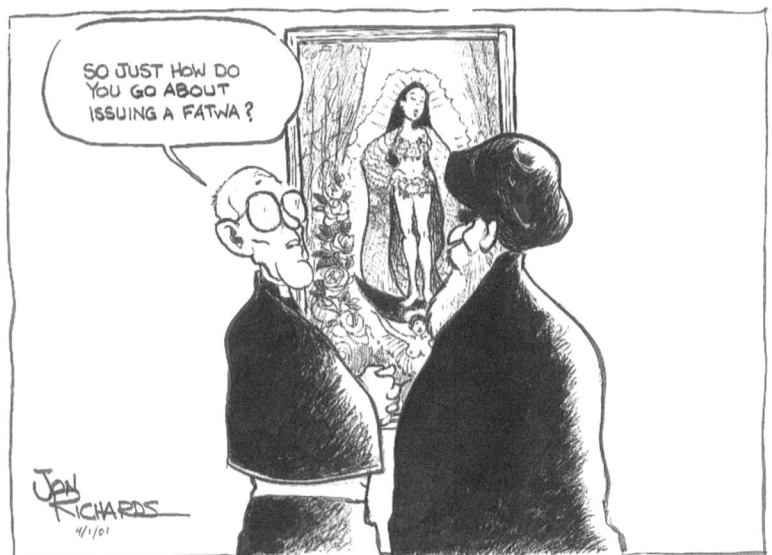

SO JUST HOW DO YOU GO ABOUT ISSUING A FATWA?

10.1.   Fatwa cartoon, *Journal North* (April 1, 2001), by Jon Richards, © 2001.
        Courtesy of Jon Richards.

I want to look more closely at the popular reception of *Our Lady*, the social discourse that surrounded and indeed engulfed the piece in waves of gossip, scandal, and religious fanaticism. Some saw the work as evil incarnate and protested vehemently against displaying it in a state-funded museum. Some saw evil incarnate in the protestors and found unacceptable their demand for censorship in the name of religion. What is interesting to me in examining the protest over this 14" × 17.5" digital photo collage is how an action of disapproval and denunciation by hundreds of "faithful" Catholics was converted or, rather, inverted into a procession and then a pilgrimage, such as those that follow miraculous appearances on a tree or a tortilla. At the heart of the protest was the miracle of the appearance of the Virgin of Guadalupe to a lowly Aztec in 1531, a story that has won the hearts and souls of millions across the centuries and that is credited for single-handedly converting the "bloodthirsty heathens" in Mexico to Christianity and the Catholic faith.

My contention in this chapter is that in their apocalyptic protest of an artwork that they saw as profaning the miraculous image of Our Lady of Guadalupe, the protestor-pilgrims, as I will refer to them throughout, virtually witnessed a second miracle, transforming Alma López's *Our Lady* into an irreverent apparition to which a multitude of believers and disbelievers flocked in witness.

The dictionary defines "apparition" as "1. Anything that appears unexpectedly or in an extraordinary way; esp., a strange figure appearing suddenly and thought to be a ghost. 2. The act of appearing or becoming visible." The second meaning presupposes that what has suddenly become visible used to be invisible or could not be seen. This quality of the unseen and the invisible suggests something else, that what has become visible was not really there in the first place but came into being at the moment it was "seen." To see, however, is not just to perceive something visually but also to understand, to learn, and to believe. To see an image of the Virgin Mary in the charred cornmeal of a tortilla or on the bark of a cottonwood is more than just to observe the form in an unusual location; it is also, and more significantly, to witness a miracle, something that not everyone can perceive or believe. Thus, miracles and apparitions are created by the eye / I of the believer.[2] The viewer's subjective beliefs inscribe the image with connotative meaning, be it sacred or sacrilegious.

While clamoring for the censorship of López's "sacrilegious" image from the *Cyber Arte* exhibition at the Museum of International Folk Art (MOIFA) in Santa Fe, the protestor-pilgrims—most of whom did not even witness *Our Lady* with their own eyes but were spurred by the technology of *"chisme"*— actually created an apparition; that is, they perceived something that was not visible. They did not see *Our Lady*, a photo-based digital collage of a rose-clad woman named Raquel Salinas created by Alma López. They saw something that was not there. Some saw their mother. Some saw the Virgin Mary or the image on Juan Diego's *tilma*. José Villegas, the first instigator of the protest, saw "the Devil" with "her bosoms sticking out," while Archbishop Michael Sheehan saw a "tart and a call girl." One outraged letter to the editor in the *Albuquerque Tribune* spells it out: "Sacrilege consists in profaning persons, places, and things consecrated to God. No one of God's creatures is more totally consecrated to God than the most holy virgin mother of God, Mary Immaculate. Thus, to portray the mother of God in bikini attire is to desecrate her in a most outrageous and sacrilegious manner."[3] In essence, this argument is based on the miraculous transubstantiation of Raquel Salinas into the Mother of God. And so what started as a protest became a collective witnessing of a miraculous, albeit unholy, transformation that sparked a procession and then a pilgrimage of believers, skeptics, and holy inquisitors.

Another interesting transformation occurred at the level of the museum, which in some of the protestor-pilgrims' eyes had been turned into a "cyber-chapel," as it was called in some of the e-mails; a "New Age chapel," a "parody of a chapel," and, most intriguing of all, an "occult" or "Satanic chapel." In a hand-delivered memo to his "excellency," Archbishop Sheehan, Henry Casso entreated the archbishop to seek the return of all sacred art that was in the custody of the Museum of International Folk Art. Casso's objection was that MOIFA desecrated sacred art, as could be seen, he argued, in the way that the museum had parodied the holy architecture of a chapel in the installation of the *Cyber Arte* exhibition:

> Given the pervasive use of symbols that parody a Catholic Chapel it would be fair to say that the Museum has designed the Cyber Arte exhibit as an Occult Chapel. The "chapel" consists of 13 pictures to the side in parody of the Stations of the Cross. Although there are 14 Stations of the Cross the number 13 is favored among occultists. . . . There is a prie-dieu (a kneeler), and an altar. On the "altar" is a computer monitor. The computer monitor is situated on the "altar" in parody of the Tabernacle. Above the tabernacle on the wall is an image of a cross with a black snake wrapped around it. At one time during the exhibit there was a sign asking visitors to leave their "Ofren-das." . . . We are very much aware of the pagan revival and the animosity of the occult movements toward the Catholic Faith and the People of God. . . . Indeed the extensive use of parody raises suspicions of a Satanic Chapel.[4]

Casso's memo falls short of accusing the museum of staging satanic masses, but the implication is clear: if the installation itself is a satanic space, then *Our Lady* must be the equivalent of its reigning anti-Christ, its Devil in a rose bikini, and viewers who support the work and the exhibit are probably devil worshippers themselves.

What did that make the artists, I wonder? Particularly since their work summoned those demonic technologies that issued from the unholy com-puter/tabernacle in the occult virtual universe known as cyberspace. Indeed, part of the outcry was directed at the perceived threat of new millennium technologies and irreverent art practices on the redemptive, protective, and revered image of the their "Nuestra de Guadalupe," as she was called in José Villegas's first e-mail to the artist, on March 19, 2001: "Some people say it is alright to do your own onda in art expression, however, when you cross the sacred boundaries of our gente traditional values of over five hundred years, you cannot impose and/or provoke thought on an issue that will inflame emotions against your own gente . . . Our Nuestra de Guadalupe does not belong to the new age interpretation of the millienum [*sic*] century and never will."[5]

If she does not belong to the New Age artist, if she has nothing to do with computer technology, how can we have Virgin of Guadalupe websites through which we can send e-cards emblazoned with different images of La Virgen,[6] and hear a virtual mass from within the Basílica de Guadalupe in Mexico City? Are the video homages on YouTube any more or less "holy" than Alma López's *Our Lady*? Or was there something else about *Our Lady* that inflamed the emotions of the Catholic "gente" of New Mexico and spurred them to perform a particularly virulent brand of "disruptive religion"?[7]

MIS/READING AND META-IDEOLOGIZING THE SIGN

In "Whose Lady? Laying Claim to the Virgin Mary," freelance journalist Hollis Walker summarizes the controversy as an insider/outsider conflict that was also riddled with class and sexuality issues. While on the surface the controversy was a about a piece of art that offended the devout, it was more complex than that. Protestors repeatedly and consistently posited their argument as one of outsider/Anglo versus native/Hispano (though this argument ignored the fact that the exhibit's curator and all four exhibiting artists were Hispana). Another "underground" issue was López's sexuality. She is openly lesbian, and her website depicts imagery that is decidedly lesbian. Protest leaders used those images to incite opposition. The controversy also posed as class conflict, in which museum officials were elite, wealthy, and educated while protestors were uneducated peasants.[8]

As Hollis Walker's title asks, whose lady is *Our Lady*? Does she belong to the offended community of protestor-pilgrims? Does she belong to the Catholic Church, which has used the image to disseminate a miraculous legend of conversion and colonialism since the sixteenth century? Does she belong to the native people of Mexico and their descendants, for whom she represents the syncretized face of their Aztec creation goddess, Tonantzin? Does she belong to Alma López and any other Chicana/Mexicana/Latina artists who choose to represent her in ways that signify their own lives? Does she belong in a museum? Ultimately, these are semiotic questions of interpretation, of the perception, reception, and negotiation of meanings inherent in cultural signs. Even more, however, these are also questions about power.

For people of color, women, and other oppressed and marginalized groups, says Chela Sandoval in *Methodology of the Oppressed*, "the semiotic perception of signs in culture as structured meanings that carry power is a basic survival skill necessary to subordinated and oppressed citizenry."[9] We will see that it was Alma López's exploration of the way her own life fit into the structured meaning of the Virgin of Guadalupe which led her to "meta-ideologize" the image and create a different sign with an altered meaning that most challenged the powers that claim ownership of the sign.[10]

Sandoval defines meta-ideologizing as "the operation of appropriating dominant ideological forms, and using them whole in order to transform them."[11] Although Alma López did not appropriate the exact image of the sign known as the Virgin of Guadalupe, she did appropriate key elements of the sign such as the Virgin's brocade gown and the folds of her starry cloak in the background, the black crescent moon upon which the Virgin stands, the aura of rays around the Virgin's body, the cherubic angel at her feet, and most important, the roses that are said to signify the miracle of her apparition.

"In Encoding/Decoding," Stuart Hall posits that there are "three hypothetical positions from which decodings of a [visual] discourse may be constructed,"[12] three sets of codes by which a cultural text is coded and in which it can be read, or received: the dominant, the negotiated, and the oppositional. We could say that, despite their ethos and pathos of opposition, José Villegas, Deacon Trujillo, Archbishop Sheehan, and their congregation of protestor-pilgrims were reading *Our Lady* within the dominant reference code of a patriarchal, misogynistic Catholicism that teaches not only that the Virgin of Guadalupe is the immaculately conceived "Mother of God" but also that, as a pure vessel of love, she is an abnegated, submissive, all-suffering, all-forgiving, asexual maternal figure to which all "good girls" and "respectable women" should aspire and which men have the authority to control. In this reference code, a woman who stands ostensibly naked in front of a camera and covered only in roses does not constitute a pure vessel. Nor does she suggest the archetypal Eve in the Garden of Eden before the Fall but rather, the fallen Eve, the shameful, sinful, disobedient Eve who listened to the serpent and partook of the secret knowledge that God the Father had forbade her to learn, and who tempted Adam to his own fall from grace. Thus, *Our Lady* is that same shameful, sinful, disobedient woman who leads men into temptation and who was reincarnated as Mary Magdalene and then as La Malinche.

The archbishop's objection to *Our Lady* was "not on the basis of morals," he said in a statement to the *Ottawa Citizen*: "My objection is on the basis of the insult to the religious beliefs of a very large number of people that look at the Virgin Mary as being very holy. She is depicted in a floral bikini as if she were a tart."[13]

The idea that *Our Lady* is dressed in a "floral bikini" did not originate with the archbishop. Rather, as Hollis Walker points out, a March 17 article in the *Albuquerque Journal North* by staff writer Morgan Lee describes the artwork as "the Virgin of Guadalupe in a floral bikini."[14] This description sensationalized the image and "helped fuel Villegas' complaints into a firestorm; the image was thereafter referred to in media accounts as "the Bikini Virgin."[15] Never mind that the rose wreaths are neither "itsy-bitsy" nor "teeny-weeny," "or even a two-piece bathing suit," says Hollis Walker; it "may as well have been a G-string as far as some people were concerned."[16]

These sensationalized sentiments were echoed in some of the comments left in the museum's comment books. Although there were more comments in support of *Our Lady* than in opposition to it, some viewers called the work "trash," "offensive," a "centerfold picture," "sacrilegious," and "blasphemy," and two offered to pray for the artist and the curator:

> I pray for the soul of Alma López, Dr. Wilson and Dr. Nunn, may the Lord have mercy on you! I can only hope the regents of this museum rightly take it down and *send it back to California*. (Emphasis added)

> You should not show Jesus' mother like that. Would you dipict [sic] your own mother in such a manor [sic]? It was very disrespectful. Mary was a virgin not a stripper!![17]

This, then, constitutes the dominant domain or reference code in which *Our Lady* was decoded and in which the protest took root and flourished, bringing hundreds of angry spectators to the door of the "master's house" to express their outrage at the museum's decision to display what they saw as an intentionally disrespectful rendering of "their" Virgin of Guadalupe by an outsider. For this contingency, Margaret Montoya explains, Guadalupe "is not anatomically correct; she has no breasts, no nipples, no pubic hair, no vagina, and no erogenous zones."[18] Still, the protestor-pilgrims saw all of that in *Our Lady*. Out of their subjective perception of what was not actually on the walls of the museum, the protestor-pilgrims were able to transmute an absence (of faith) into a presence (of body) while at the same time justifying the reactionary bludgeoning of an artist's constitutional right to represent the meaning of the Virgin of Guadalupe in her own life. In this bizarre turn of events, the act of censorship can be likened to a sacrifice, and, indeed, Alma López was racked, pinioned, and crucified under the scrutiny of the archbishop.

The Mexican-born Sinaloense artist from the El Sereno barrio of northeast Los Angeles occupies the other end of the spectrum, the oppositional reference code, which "deconstructs and decontextualizes the dominant code and reinterprets the message through an alternative context."[19] For Alma López, that alternative context is the positionality of a Mexican immigrant, Chicana, lesbian, feminist working-class artist who opposes all of the misogyny of the dominant code and instead sees the beauty of the female form, the nurturing breasts, the fearless stare, and the strength of women's collective survival in patriarchy. Says the artist in the statement she delivered at MOIFA on April 4, 2001, at the first meeting of the museum's Board of Regents, which was stormed by protestors:

> Even if I look really hard at my work and the works of many Chicana artists, I don't see what is so offensive. I see beautiful bodies that are gifts from our creator. I see nurturing breasts. I see the strong nurturing mothers of all of us. I am forced to wonder how men like Mr. Villegas and the Archbishop are looking at my work that they feel it is "blasphemy" and "the Devil." I wonder how they see bodies of women. I wonder why they think that our bodies are so ugly and perverted that they cannot be seen in an art piece in a museum? . . . This museum, like other museums, is a site of learning. Museums are not churches or sites of spiritual devotion. . . . If my work is removed, that means that I have no right to express myself as an artist and a woman. It means that there must be something wrong and sexually perverted with my female body. It means that it's okay for men to look at our bodies as ugly. It means that as Chicanas we can only be sexualized or only be virgins. It means that only men can tell us how to look at La Virgen. It means that we cannot look upon La Virgen as an image of a strong woman like us.[20]

Well aware that *Our Lady* contested La Virgen's "structured meanings" of docility, modesty, and humility to signify the sacred feminine, and choosing to depict her instead as a strong, liberated, revolutionary image, which challenged the "power" of men to confer negative and abusive meanings on women's bodies, Alma López catalyzed and harnessed the oppositional consciousness of a social movement.

As the museum's comment book shows, month after month, from March to August 2001, visitors left messages applauding the museum's decision to show *Our Lady*, entreating people to "stop fearing art" and to "censor censorship," expressing dismay and surprise at the "ruckus" and the "fuss" being stirred up over this "beautiful," "respectful," and "innocuous" image, which none of them saw as dressed in a bikini:

> Thank you for bringing this most creative & thought provoking show. If it hadn't been for the protest *against* art I might have missed this wonderful exhibit!!!

> Local Catholics acting too much like Taliban!!! Miss Guadalupe is dressed with more modesty than young "ladies" in public places today.

> As a devout Catholic & New Mexican, I believe we exhibit our faith individually. "Censorship in the name of God" is unacceptable.

> Guadalupe is shown with love, with respect, with humor. "Thank God" the museum allows that vision to reach the good people of New Mexico. My tax money has been spent well, very well. Viva Guadalupe y Viva el Museum de International Folk Art.

> I gave my rosary to the computer altar as a symbol of my appreciation for this great show. I believe that Alma López is expressing all her respect for women's bodies and the Lady of Guadalupe cult in her work. Congratulations to the museum for this instigative exhibition.

> Blasphemy is in the eye of the beholder.

> Me da berguenza [*sic*] pensar que todavía estamos en la epoca de la Inquisición![21]

In addition to these viewer comments were the many positive reviews that appeared in the local New Mexican newspapers and national periodicals like the *New York Times*, the *Los Angeles Times*, *Ms.* magazine, *Art Papers*, and *Art in America*. At least two-thirds of the nine hundred e-mails Alma received in support of her vision of Our Lady,[22] which inspired her to create a website specifically devoted to the controversy, attest to the power of oppositional discourse. Other forms of what Chela Sandoval calls "the politics of the Other-in-opposition" include the militant feminist artworks of *Las Malcriadas*,[23] an exhibition that opened in Santa Fe in July 2001, organized by New Mexican artist Delilah Montoya in response to the threat of censorship experienced by Alma López.[24] In a speech to the American Women Artists organization, which was hosting its annual show in Santa Fe in June 2001, Judy Chicago, creator of the famous installation *The Dinner Party*, called for solidarity with Alma López in the maelstrom of this male-led crusade against *Our Lady*, urging the women artists in the room to stage counterprotests to "'support the right of women artists to create the art they want to make.'"[25] Taken together, all of these actions and the numerous other tactics and strategies of oppositional consciousness deployed by individuals and organizations like the American Civil Liberties Union and the National Coalition against Censorship in support of Alma López and *Our Lady* since the exhibition constitute the equivalent of a "differential social movement," which Sandoval defines as a "global decolonizing alliance of difference in its drive toward egalitarian social relations and economic well-being for all citizenry."[26]

What were the negotiated readings of this "miracle" that was created by the protest? The negotiated discourse is the tricky middle ground between the dominant and the oppositional registers of meaning. "A negotiated reading occurs when the viewer acknowledges and even, on an abstract level, adopts the message of the dominant code, but also contradicts that message by restricting or applying it to what Stuart Hall calls 'situational logic,'"[27] the logic of any given situation that has the power to invert or subvert the meaning of a cultural text. We can say that the Museum of New Mexico itself applied that negotiated reading when, in response to the initial community outcry against *Our Lady*, and after meeting with city officials, community members, and representatives from the Catholic Church after the show's opening, the museum agreed to hold a community forum to allow both protestors and supporters to express their views about the piece. The gathering was originally scheduled to take place at the museum on April 4, at the meeting of the museum's Board of Regents, and it was at the press conference that followed the meeting that Alma López presented the statement quoted above.

Hundreds of protestor-pilgrims showed up, too many to be safely contained within the museum without posing a fire hazard. The forum had to be postponed and rescheduled for a week later in the Sweeney Center in downtown Santa Fe, which could accommodate up to twelve hundred people. Sack lunches, bottled water, and even day care were provided for those in attendance, supporters and protestor-pilgrims alike. According to some reports, between six hundred and one thousand people attended this second attempt at democratizing the protest. If the old adage about putting your money where your mouth is tells us anything, the fact that the museum spent $12,000 on the forum and only $4,500 on the exhibition should indicate its sincerity at trying to assuage the inflamed emotions of the community.

Summoning the curative qualities of the traditional Virgin of Guadalupe and her compassionate interventionist skills, Museum of New Mexico director Thomas Wilson stated in a press release that the forum could have a "healing" effect for all of the stakeholders:

> We have an opportunity to be a national model of what can work when a community explores its differences from a standpoint of cooperation. The format we have proposed will allow all sides to hear and understand each other's points of view . . . I also want to take this opportunity to apologize to anyone who has been hurt by the contemporary depiction of Our Lady of Guadalupe in the *Cyber Arte* exhibition. The museum meant no disrespect, and I regret any distress that this issue has caused . . . This forum can be just the first step toward healing in a way which leaves no one out.[28]

While acknowledging the religious concerns raised by the protestor-pilgrims, and even issuing an apology to the community for any pain that the exhibition may have caused inadvertently, Tom Wilson, along with MOIFA director, Joyce Ice, and Tey Marianna Nunn, the exhibition curator, applied the situational logic of the museum's "mission to present changing ideas and concepts, a mission shared with other museums accredited by the American Association of Museums and one that is central to the educational responsibility of museums in today's world."[29]

Nevertheless, the museum made some compromises. It posted bilingual warning signs outside the exhibit stating: "Some objects in this exhibit may be disturbing to certain viewers." And instead of extending the run of the show by four months, museum officials decided to close the show on October 28, 2001, as had been originally scheduled.

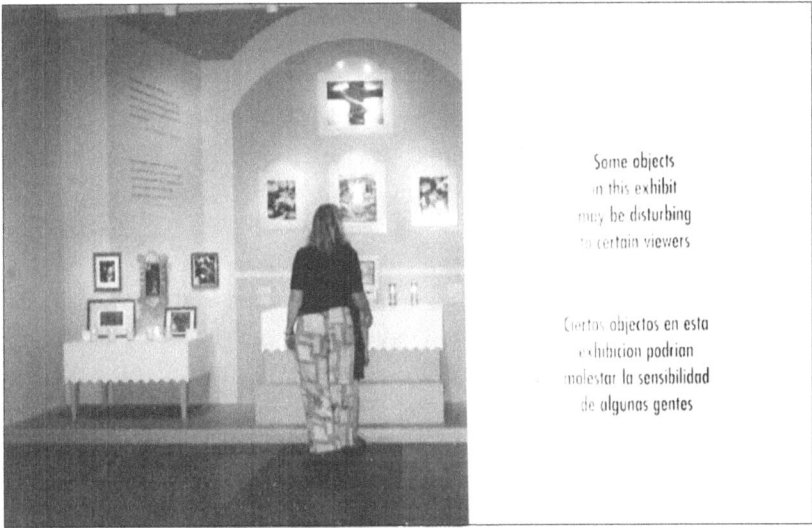

Some objects
in this exhibit
may be disturbing
to certain viewers

Ciertos objectos en esta
exhibicion podrian
molestar la sensibilidad
de algunas gentes

10.2.   Warning signs outside *Cyber Arte* exhibit. Photograph by Alma López, © 2001.
Alma López private papers.

Why were Catholics so deeply disturbed by this image? "Perhaps, time and place play prominent roles in this controversy," said Alma López in her April 2, 2001 statement (Chap. 1 here). "This is Lent, a time of devotion between Ash Wednesday and Easter. Santa Fe is a place with deep spiritual and traditional roots, and the Museum of International Folk Art is the place where many images of saints reside."[30] Lent in Santa Fe, a time of sacrifice and pilgrimage for the Catholic community, a time of *penitente* reenactment of the Passion of Christ from flagellation to crucifixion, is the "situational logic" of the controversy. As one viewer comment expressed in defense of the protestors' call for the removal of *Our Lady*: "We are not censoring! We are protesting sacrilegious rendering in the land of the penitente, the matachine, and Chimayo."

Here are the three ruling planets that align over northern New Mexico: the brotherhood, or *hermandad*, of Jesus of Nazareth emulators, "credited with preserving the sacred traditions of New Mexico and southern Colorado as early as the eighteenth century . . . [t]hrough acts of caridad (charity), oración (prayer), and el buen ejemplo (the good example),"[31] for whom the performance of corporeal penitence constitutes a form of sacrifice akin to Christ's; the northern Mexican and New Mexican native *matachine* dancers, who perform their most sacred dance reenacting the conquest of the Aztecs,

complete with a Malinche figure, in December, in honor of Our Lady of Guadalupe; and the Santuario de Chimayó, located twenty-five miles north of
Santa Fe, considered the "the most important Catholic pilgrimage center in
the United States." Wikipedia tells us that, because of its "reputation as a
healing site (believers claim that dirt from a back room of the church can heal
physical and spiritual ills), it has become known as the 'Lourdes of America,'
and attracts close to 300,000 visitors a year, including up to 30,000 during
Holy Week (the week prior to Easter)."[32] It is in that logic of the Lenten season, in the convergence of the penitent, the conquered, and the miraculous,
and the consequent drama of their interaction, that the inversion occurs, the
chiastic transformation of a protest into a procession and a pilgrimage.

PROTEST AS PERFORMANCE ART

In *Symbol and Conquest: Public Ritual and Drama in Santa Fe*, Ronald Grimes
explains the difference between processions and pilgrimages, two popular
forms of public spectacle in Santa Fe. Although both forms are "ritualistic
movement[s] through space,"[33] their difference is dictated by their purpose.
Whereas "[t]he typical activities involved in processions are walking, carrying, showing, viewing, praying, singing, and being seen" through the city
streets and,[34] typically, through the center of the city as a way of reenacting
the status quo, pilgrimages are more "goal-oriented" in that their ultimate
purpose is to reach a particular site in which something miraculous or holy
has been manifested. Processions are more spectator-driven. Their objective
is not to reach a particular location but rather to display the journey itself as
a ritual reinforcement of the community's beliefs and values. "One way to
interpret a procession," writes Grimes, "is by selecting and reciting a story—a
historical or mythical narrative."[35]

I attended the 2009 Virgin of Guadalupe procession held in East Los Angeles and had the opportunity to take hundreds of pictures of La Virgen's
devout followers on their mile-long journey down historic César Chávez Avenue. Their destination was the football stadium at East Los Angeles College
(ELAC), where a mass would be offered by a number of priests and bishops
complete with smoking copal incense and Communion wafers for the multitude. The theme of this year's procession was "No Tengas Miedo," or "Don't
Be Afraid," taken from the myth narrative of the miraculous apparition of an
indigenous Mother of God to the Aztec convert to Christianity Juan Diego.

According to the myth, the Lady's apparition frightened Juan Diego, and the Divine Mother reassured him by saying: "Don't be afraid, aren't I who am your mother here with you?" Several floats in the procession—dioramas and installations staged on the back of pickup trucks—echoed this theme as did the clumps of women walking under a variety of standards of the Guadalupana and praying the rosary or singing praises to the Virgin. They were followed by barefoot *matachine* dancers with elaborate feathered headdresses, women and girls enacting Native American dances and wearing face paint and pleated red skirts emblazoned with sequined Guadalupes, charros on horseback carrying huge Mexican flags adorned with Guadalupe images in the place of the Mexican eagle, masked figures that could have been *brujos*, or wise men, in baroque costumes and crowns, children in miniature Juan Diego *tilmas* with hand-drawn and colored pictures of Guadalupe, people in wheelchairs and on crutches, high school students in matching blue Guadalupe T-shirts—all paying homage to their Holy Mother. Parishes across Los Angeles were represented, and the flags of all of the Americas were present. The ELAC stadium was almost full as the bilingual mass was kicked off on the fifty-yard line.

The historical or mythical narrative that the protestor-pilgrims in Santa Fe had selected for their community action was also the Virgin's apparition to Juan Diego, a "miracle" that catalyzed the conversion of nine million native people only ten years after the Spanish invasion and conquest of Mexico. It was this miracle that they felt was being defiled by *Our Lady*, and this story that was on the lips and in the minds of the protestor-pilgrims who had come as if on procession to the center of Santa Fe. For, as Grimes notes, "processions inevitably pass through the central plaza of the city . . . Passing through this center usually symbolizes, and requires as a prerequisite, the sanction of civil authorities, many of whom actually participate in the processions."[36] Indeed, all but two of the New Mexico state legislators agreed with the protestor-pilgrims that *Our Lady* blasphemed the holy image and myth of the Virgin of Guadalupe.

On March 31, José Villegas organized a procession in the parking lot of the museum. In the video *Bikini Virgen on Trial*, by Cynthia Buzzard—a compilation of video clippings about the controversy and footage of the protests—the protestor-pilgrims are seen arriving in cars and buses and starting to assemble for the procession. Although small in comparison to the mob that showed up on April 4 to manifest their anger at the museum and at the artist,

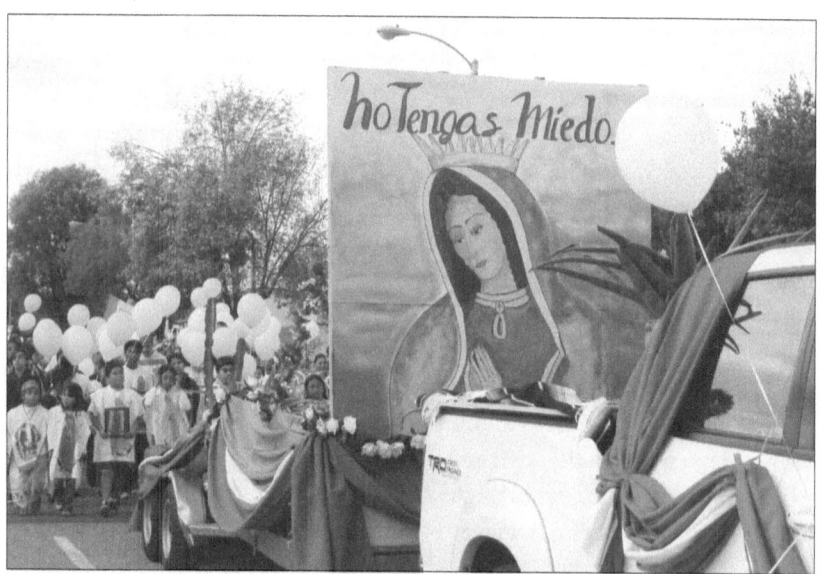

10.3.   *No Tengas Miedo*, Virgin of Guadalupe Procession, East Los Angeles. Photograph
by Alicia Gaspar de Alba, © 2009. Courtesy of Alicia Gaspar de Alba.

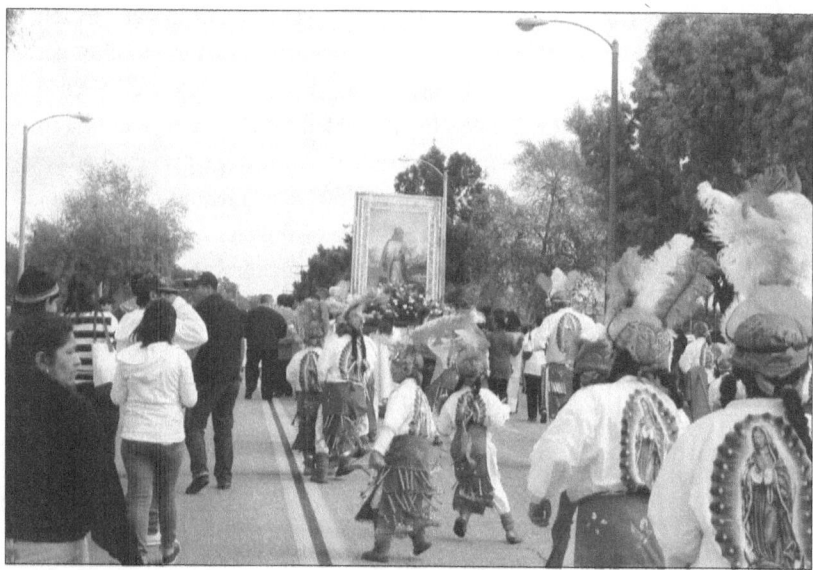

10.4.   *Following Juan Diego*, Virgin of Guadalupe Procession, East Los Angeles. Photograph
by Alicia Gaspar de Alba, © 2009. Courtesy of Alicia Gaspar de Alba.

the gathering has all the trappings of a procession, and indeed is called a procession by its organizer. Heading the procession is a shrine to the Virgin of Guadalupe carried on a small palanquin, followed by the faithful carrying placards demanding: "Stop Blasphemy now!" and "Honor thy Mother!" The standards of other saints are also being carried, the most visible of which is a life-size image of the resurrected Christ in his flowing white robe. The Virgin shrine is placed on a table at the steps leading up to the museum, and an altar is quickly assembled. On the altar, the Virgin is flanked by an archangel and surrounded by votive candles and blue containers of generic salt. Perhaps the salt is intended to "protect" the Virgin from the "evil" the protestor-pilgrims perceive as emanating from the museum. Henry Casso, the author of the letter to Archbishop Sheehan about how the *Cyber Arte* show was installed like a satanic chapel, sits at the head of the media table next to the "real" Guadalupe. Musicians are playing guitars and tambourines, and people are praying the "Hail Mary." Speeches are given, petitions are signed, and off to the side, five women docents of the museum are gathered in support of the artist.

By April 4, the peaceful procession had given way to a more threatening presence of hundreds of protestor-pilgrims demanding to be let in to the auditorium where the museum's Board of Regents had agreed to open its meeting to a civil debate that did not happen. The facilitator of the meeting called it a "dangerous situation," as more and more people jammed the museum grounds. "Alma López was taken away by security as soon as the meeting ended because museum officials feared for her safety," stated a reporter for Santa Fe's Channel 13 News.

When Frank Ortiz, the only museum board member who opposed *Our Lady*, announced that the meeting had been cancelled and would be rescheduled in a larger venue, a "small group of musicians started playing harmonicas, and prayers in Spanish along with clapping and cheers broke out among the crowd."[37]

But there were more than prayers and *alabanzas* in praise of the Virgin Mary being uttered by the protestor-pilgrims. Soapbox speeches rang out from the microphone and chants of "Burn her! Burn them!" were heard at both gatherings.[38] A writer for the *Santa Fe Trend* described the protest "event" at the Sweeney Center as a "mix between a crudely produced public access television talk show and a bad open-mike poetry reading . . . the participants . . . delivering common folk testimonials normally relegated to infomercials."[39]

Praying, singing, chanting, testimonials bearing witness to the sacred healing and life-saving interventions of the Virgin of Guadalupe—was this activism or performance art? In "Staging Prisons: Performance, Activism, and
Social Bodies," Peter Caster distinguishes between "activist performance"
and "staged activism." Activist performance is theater that unambiguously
defines itself as theater and "associates itself with a particular social project"
and "makes its alliances explicit." Staged activism "employs theatrical strategies of representation," yet the event is considered "really real"—it is not performed by actors, but by activists. Indeed, says Caster, "one of the fundamental goals of staged activism is *telling the difference* between the two [experience
and performance], as oppressed people describe their positions in their own
words, communicating as fully as possible the circumstances and actualities
of their oppression."[40]

I argue that the protestor-pilgrims engaged theatrical modes of representation both to communicate "the actualities of their oppression" by the Museum of New Mexico and an irreverent apparition and also, paradoxically, to
enforce imperializing right-wing ideologies, or "structured meanings," about
the Virgin of Guadalupe and the role of women in relation to both church
and state. Indeed, one journalist described the protestors as "elderly men . . .
standing like St. Peter fending off evil-doers from the pearly gates" and dem-
onstrating "the kind of fervor reserved for abortion clinics against this female
artist's appalling depiction of 'their' Virgin Mary."[41]

This analogy reminds me of what Peggy Phelan has written in *Unmarked:
The Politics of Performance* about the tactical uses of performance art in anti-
abortion demonstrations, whose purpose is "making a spectacle *for* the sake
of publicity."[42] Staging rescues of fetuses that need to be saved from the maws
of abortionists, male rescuers at a demonstration play the part of the unborn
"baby" crawling around on all fours and "yell[ing] out in a strange falsetto,
'Mother, please don't murder me,'"[43] while a choir of women nearby chant
and pray with their arms in the air. "The spatial separation between the men
and the women rescuers mimics the situation often found in mainstream
Western theatre: speaking men and observing women."[44]

This describes exactly the protest against *Our Lady*, men like Villegas, Trujillo, Casso, and the archbishop taking the microphone, and women observing their submissive role in patriarchy, doing the praying, the chanting, and
the crying. Because the protest was ultimately about determining not just
who owns the Virgin of Guadalupe, who has the power to dictate what the

Mother of God looks like but, more important, how faith will be exercised and how women are supposed to behave within the faith, it was men who initiated the protest against *Our Lady* and took center stage in the spectacle. Like the "speaking fetuses" of Operation Rescue, the male defenders of the City of Faith wanted to manifest their predetermined right to control women's bodies, particularly the body of the woman they were all claiming as their mother: "In excessively marking the boundaries of the woman's *body*, precisely in order to make it thoroughly visible, patriarchal culture seeks to make *her* subject to legal, artistic, and psychic surveillance."[45]

By casting themselves in the role of the oppressed children of a maligned mother, the protestor-pilgrims performed the social discourse of a people clamoring for salvation and in need of deliverance from evil, which in turn created both a physical and a virtual community of offended Catholics and angry taxpayers demanding that their faith be respected. "Social protests that either deliberately or inadvertently draw on the conventions of theatre produce the unity through political investment that makes the audience a social body joined in affect," writes Peter Caster.[46] In other words, in both staged activism and activist performance, a social body, a "we," is produced which recognizes its responsibility to act.

Although this staged activism originated as a protest meant to express the Catholic community's indignation about and offense at what it saw as a vilification of a sacred symbol, the protestor-pilgrims turned the "cyber chapel" of the exhibition into a pilgrimage site, as visitors flocked to the museum in droves in a crusade that continued for months. MOIFA records estimate that over 14,000 viewers came to see *Cyber Arte* and that attendance averaged 344 people per day after the March 17 article by Morgan Lee, which launched the Helen of New Mexico or, rather, the "Bikini Virgin."[47] As Ronald Grimes reminds us, pilgrimages "are usually characterized by images rather than relics, and . . . [pilgrimage sites] are liminally located beyond the centers of cities and towns and beyond the centers of economic, political, and ecclesiastical power."[48] All of those visitors; the constant gathering of protestor-pilgrims outside the Museum of International Folk Art, located miles away from the downtown plaza, in the periphery of the city off Old Santa Fe Trail and Camino Lejo; the pilgrimages taken by Catholics from outside of New Mexico, namely, the America Needs Fatima group that came from Philadelphia (a group that stands for tradition, family, and property) to bring word of the "true" image of Mary;[49] and all of the protestor-pilgrims who walked and drove and were bused in from towns outside Santa Fe—all contributed to transforming MOIFA and the *Cyber Arte* show into a pilgrimage site: "Pilgrimage sites are not necessarily established only through the official sanction of a church or a religious tradition. Rather, pilgrims may in fact 'create' a pilgrimage site simply by flocking in large numbers to a place believed to be imbued with the sacred."[50] In the case of the *Our Lady* controversy, however, the Museum of International Folk Art was believed to be imbued with the opposite, the antisacred. Ironically, the protest was inverted into its opposite, a pilgrimage, spurred by the social body's miraculous transformation of a photo-based digital collage into an irreverent apparition.

In a final performance of the controversy, six long months after the hullabaloo erupted, on October 28, 2001, the last day of the *Cyber Arte* show at MOIFA, Deacon Anthony Trujillo of the Guadalupe parish "staged a mock burial ceremony" of *Our Lady*:

> Trujillo instructed the 20 or so people who turned out to write down on pieces of paper whatever animosity [about the work or the exhibit] they wanted to bury, and place it in a hole he dug outside the church . . . Trujillo also participated in the burial, throwing into the mock grave court documents from his attempts to stop the exhibit . . . A mariachi band was joined by a church choir that sang before the ceremony began. After the burial, the paper-filled hole was covered with dirt.[51]

A photo accompanying the article shows a woman and a child casting their notes into the small hole, which has been dug beside a sign that reads "Our Lady of Guadalupe Parish." How nice of Trujillo to have "buried" *Our Lady* in hallowed ground.

What were the actual gains of these different manifestations of staged activism? For one critic of the protest (and there were many, as the articles, editorials, and letters to the editor collected in the *Cyber Arte* archives show), all that the "idolaters" protesting *Our Lady* actually did was call attention to themselves, so that, instead of letting the issue slip quietly into oblivion, the ruckus they made brought more and more people to see the show and lured the spotlight of sensationalism directly over Santa Fe, and perhaps they even broke a commandment or two: "If the Catholics and other Christians protesting this piece of art were truly devout, they would understand that God made a complete ban of all art in the second commandment. They would not, therefore, have icons of any kind that depict angels, Christ, or the Madonna . . . I would even suggest that they are, by their protest, also breaking the third commandment against taking the Lord's name in vain; that is, they are using the Lord's name as a means to bring notoriety and/or power unto themselves."[52]

One more performative protest event deserves some attention, as it shows the nationalistic rather than the religious side of the controversy. Pedro Romero Sedeño, a Santa Fe artist who left his own Chicano cultural nationalist comment in the museum's comment book early on, organized in June what he called a "performance art intervention" titled the *Santa Fe Ofrenda Project*, which was to be staged every Sunday beginning June 2 at MOIFA.[53] The purpose of the intervention was didactic as well as nationalistic. Said Sedeño: "We as human ofrendas [offerings] enrobed with the Mexican flag, will offer the Museum of New Mexico, its docents and Alma López . . . education as to the profound cultural significance of, and devotion to, the traditional image of Our Lady of Guadalupe to the Mexican people, and its sovereign place as the banner for Mexican cultural identity."[54] Completely stripping his "human ofrendas" project of religious overtones, Sedeño's performance art of protest nonetheless had ideological dogma embedded in its intention. Rather than point fingers at how Alma López had desacralized the image of Our Lady of Guadalupe, Sedeño assumed that the artist (not to mention the museum staff) was ignorant of the "cultural significance" of the Virgin as a symbol for "Mexican cultural identity."

Sedeño was not the first or the only Chicano who fixed the Virgin of Guadalupe's meaning in the realm of Mexican history and Mexican national identity politics and claimed her as a sign of Chicano cultural nationalism. Chicano protest processions have been using the banner of La Virgen to champion their cause since the 1960s. The most historically significant, said to have launched the Chicano civil rights movement, was the 250-mile farmworker march from the fields of Delano to the steps of the capitol in Sacramento in 1966, which was led by United Farm Workers (UFW) leaders César Chávez and Dolores Huerta and photographed by Jon Lewis.

As a volunteer for the UFW, Jon Lewis helped put a national face on César Chávez and his farmworker movement through his photos of the march to Sacramento, especially his use of the Virgen in his photos.[55] The Guadalupe standard was one of four flags that were carried in the march, the other three being the U.S. flag, the Mexican flag, and the UFW flag, to signify the

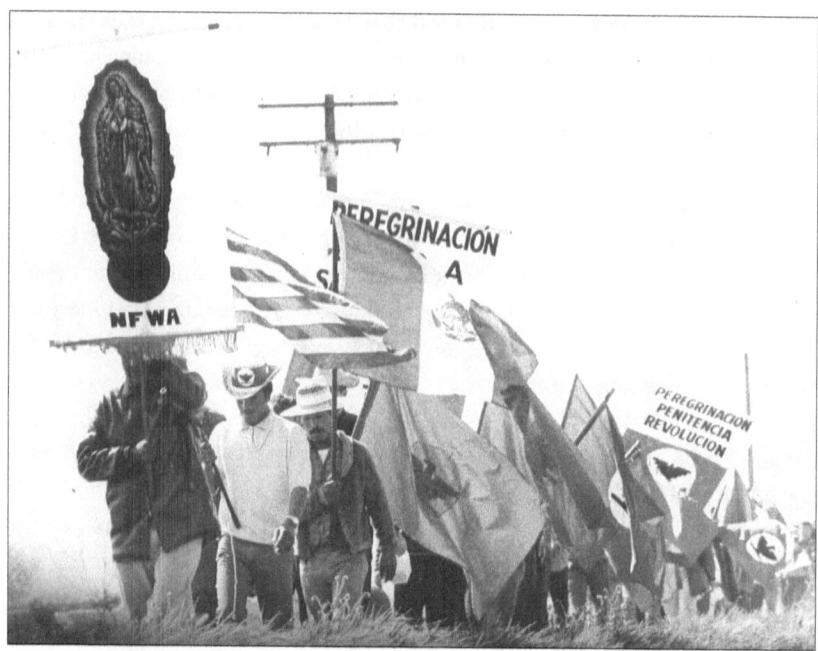

10.5.   United Farm Workers March from Delano to Sacramento. Photograph by Jon Lewis,
         ©1966. Courtesy of Jon Lewis and the Farmworker Movement Documentation
         Project, www.farmworkermovement.us.

national and political allegiances of the farmworkers and of the thousands of
students, teachers, activists, artists, actors, politicians, and urban profession-
als from across the Southwest who sympathized with the farmworkers' *causa*
and attended or participated in the procession. Similar Guadalupe banners
were carried by the millions of undocumented immigrants who marched on
Los Angeles in 2006 in an attempt to bring national attention to their desire
to remain in the United States, to have their lives legitimized through citizenship, and to be free to work for the American Dream. In 1993, the Virgin of
Guadalupe was used as an emblem in the student-led protest at the University
of California, Los Angeles that led to a two-week hunger strike and demands
for the institutionalization of a Chicano and Chicana Studies Department at
UCLA.[56] Indeed, every May 1, International Workers Day, the hundreds of
workers and laborers who gather in downtown Los Angeles march in the
Virgin's wake.

More than a symbol of Mexican cultural identity, La Virgen signified for Sedeño and other Chicano cultural nationalists the mythological Aztlán,[57] the original homeland of the Aztecs said to be located in the conquered Mexican north (now the American Southwest). To reconquer or reclaim Aztlán, in cultural if not territorial ways, was considered one of the goals of the Chicano movement, and the Virgin of Guadalupe, like the Mexican flag, was a signifier for that struggle. Indeed, by wrapping his human offerings in the Mexican flag—the term *human* offering itself is reminiscent of Aztec sacrifices—Sedeño's performance was alluding to the legendary *niños héroes*, or child heroes, of Mexico who, according to the myth, wrapped themselves in the Mexican flag and threw themselves from the ramparts of the castle at Chapultepec to protest the Anglo takeover of Mexico in 1848. In Sedeño's worldview, Alma López was ignorant of that history, and ignorant as well of the "true" significance of the Virgin of Guadalupe for Mexicans and Chicanos; therefore, she could be neither Mexican nor Chicana. And furthermore, as a feminist and a lesbian who dared to strip the traditional image of its vested purity and maternity, thereby robbing Chicanos of their cultural mother, she had betrayed her brothers in Aztlán and aligned herself with the Anglo conquerors who continued to colonize New Mexico.

THE EMBODIED AESTHETICS OF ALMA LÓPEZ

In "There's No Place Like Aztlán: Embodied Aesthetics in Chicana Art," I argue that the concept of Aztlán, with its twin tropes of loss and recuperation, functions as a place-based aesthetic in the work of Chicano and Chicana artists. "Place-based aesthetics" is the name I give to an artistic practice that expresses the artist's connection to place, and place is represented in the theme and content of the artwork not as landscape but, rather, as homeland, culture, region, community, neighborhood, family, and even memory. Over and over in the course of the controversy, Alma López stated that as a Mexican-born Chicana who grew up with the Virgin of Guadalupe in her East Los Angeles home, the Virgin "belonged" to her as much as and even more so than to men like José Villegas and Archbishop Sheehan. "Catholic or not, Chicana / Latina / Hispana visual, literary, or performance artists grew up with the image of La Virgen de Guadalupe, therefore entitling us to express our relationship to her in any which way relevant to our own experiences."[58] Her connection to the Virgin is based on a notion of place that is more than a homeland or site of origin (Mexico), more than culture (Chicano), more than religion (Catholic), and more than class (community)—although all of them intersect in *Our Lady*. For Alma López, the place at which she connects most intimately with the Virgin of Guadalupe is her own sex, that is to say, her body:

> [R]ather than expressing their attachment to place as either dispossessed of or exiled from their native land, Chicana artists have a more intimate and embodied connection to place . . . Chicanas are actively deconstructing and reconstructing . . . a politics of the body and of self-creation. Transmuted into art, this politics of the body produces an *embodied aesthetic*, one that frees the Chicana artist from the shackles of a relational identity as someone's wife, mother, daughter, or mistress. Instead of dispossession, ownership, or reclamation of a place outside the self, embodied aesthetics uses the body as the signifier for place. As such, the body functions as site of origin, bridge between worlds, and locus of liberation.[59]

Our Lady disrupted the conservative Hispano community's expectations of a cultural icon; the Mother of God was not just humanized but depicted as a second-rate human, that is, as a woman flaunting her sexuality rather than submitting to the biological imperative of her gender. Interestingly, depicting the Son of God as a baby boy suckling at his mother's exposed breast with his genitals exposed does not insult Catholics, because the naked breast is performing its biological function, and the holy being attached to his mother's lactating nipple has been incarnated in the male form; that is, he was made into first-class flesh, male flesh, a masculine and therefore universal subject. Nor does his nearly naked body on the cross offend anyone, as what we are taught to see in the image of the crucified Christ is not a sexual being, not a dead body with an erection under his loincloth, but a battered, tortured redeemer of our sins. Indeed, the suckling baby Jesus and the erect penis of Christ are semiotic signs of his humanity, of the "Word made flesh," as Tey Diana Rebolledo, paraphrasing Leo Steinberg's thesis in *The Sexuality of Christ in Renaissance Art and in Modern Oblivion*, points out: "[T]his iconography is not meant to be salacious, but rather to reflect the fact that God has become a male human,"[60] and has bodily needs like eating and ejaculating, like any other son of God.

In "Sons of La Malinche," Octavio Paz exemplifies what Chicana historian Emma Pérez calls "the colonial imaginary"—a way of imagining history that reifies the male colonizer—by describing the quintessential difference between two female icons of Mexicano and Chicano culture, both from the colonial period, and both of which serve the interests of patriarchy in the social construction of the feminine gender: the Virgin of Guadalupe and La Malinche, the interpreter and slave of Hernán Cortés who, it is rumored, willingly offered herself to her conquerors and for that is eternally blamed for the downfall of the Aztec empire. In short, the Virgin represents the good mother, the obedient daughter, the passive wife—all of the qualities that Mexican and Chicana girls are taught to desire and become. La Malinche, or "La Chingada," as Paz calls her, on the other hand, is the bad mother, the violated whore, the betrayer of her culture—the bearer of the most negative qualities of womanhood, which have the power to destroy not only the family but also the community:

> The Virgin is the consolation of the poor, the shield of the weak, the help of the oppressed . . . The Virgin is pure passivity . . . she consoles, quiets, dries tears, calms passions . . . [La Chingada] is even more abject . . . she does not resist violence, but is an inert heap of bones, blood, and dust. Her taint is constitutional and it resides . . . in her sex . . . She loses her name; she is no one; she disappears into nothingness; she *is* Nothingness. And yet she is the cruel incarnation of the feminine condition.[61]

When the protestor-pilgrims performed their "staged activism" against Alma López's *Our Lady*, they were protesting what they saw as La Chingada in the halo of La Virgen de Guadalupe. Who can respect, much less worship, a nameless, violated "Nothingness" who wears nothing but a bikini of roses and is held aloft by a naked-breasted butterfly angel rather than a cherub with a dangling participle between his wings? Even worse, the woman in the image is anything but an "inert heap of bones, blood, and dust." She is not immobilized by her long embroidered tunic or weighed down by the Coyolxauhqui stone that she wears tossed over her bare shoulders like the lightest of capes. Her defiant gaze, her confrontational stance, her bare feet and legs practically walk off the canvas. We can almost see her kicking her head back to challenge the viewer.

"I am woman, hear me roar," said Helen Reddy. "Ain't I a woman, too?" asked Sojourner Truth. "Soy woman, y qué?" says *Our Lady*. Who can feel consoled and nurtured by this rebellious woman, this shameless woman whose unabashed exposure of her female flesh invites one and all to partake of it?

One of the religious activists in the *Bikini Virgen on Trial* video speaks to this issue clearly. Holding up an image of the traditional Guadalupe, the man says: "We want to keep her dressed . . . Why does she need to be undressed? . . . Would you call it good judgment if two people undressed right here in front of us and started copulating each other?"[62] To this viewer *Our Lady* represented his unspoken arousal; the undressed female body signified for him the sexual act of copulation. Shamed by his desire for the representation of La Virgen, he blames the artist for what his dirty mind sees in *Our Lady*. Moreover, desire is something that should never be ascribed to the Virgin of Guadalupe, for she is beyond sex, beyond the body, and certainly beyond pleasure. The only sexual act the body of the Virgin is allowed to perform or, rather, the only act she is allowed to perform with her sexual organs, is giving birth to her half-human, half-divine hybrid son. Pregnancy, as a result of copulation, is not the issue, although the fact that Raquel Salinas is not portrayed as a pregnant Madonna is problematic for these male defenders of the faith. It is the all-too-real digital photo collage of Raquel Salinas and her muscular abs and thighs posing as La Virgen that animates *Our Lady* and makes it both so threatening and so desirable. This is no miraculous imprint of a meek brown pregnant woman on a *tilma*.

The protestor-pilgrims were selective, however. They did not object to any and all artistic renderings of the Virgin of Guadalupe or, apparently, to the myriad applications of their sacred symbol on consumer products from mouse pads and light-switch covers to bobble heads and tattoos. Indeed, even Archbishop Sheehan was selective about what he considered a promiscuous image. Three years earlier, the cover of the winter 1998 issue of *La Herencia del Norte* (a newsletter from northern New Mexico) featured a photograph by Miguel Gandert of a Guadalupe tattoo on a young woman's bare back. The photo accompanied a story called "The Lady Has Many Faces," by Jacqueline Orsini, author of *Viva Guadalupe!* In the article Orsini explains that "Nuestra Señora de Guadalupe is a lady with many faces, and each one finds favor with followers according to their personal needs. Guadalupe reaches out to friars, pilgrims, artists, lowriders, scholars, housewives, prisoners and

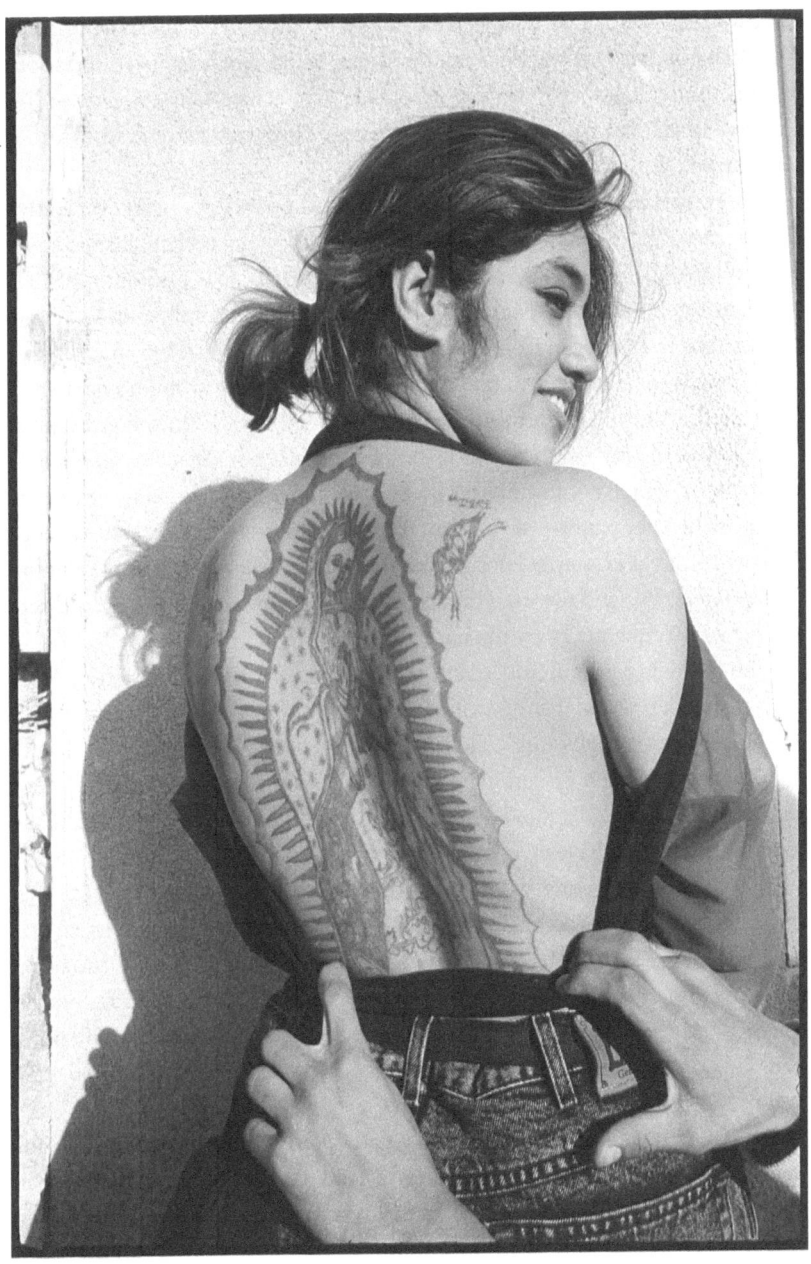

10.6. *Teresa Gutiérrez of Juárez, Mexico.* Photograph by Miguel Gandert, © 1992. Courtesy of Miguel Gandert.

street women. Guadalupe is especially sought by those who fall short of ideal Christian conduct, for she does not condemn sinners; she offers compassion, pardon, understanding. Nuestra Señora de Guadalupe's first words at Tepeyác were an offer of care for all folk of every kind without reserve, without retribution."[63]

The model in the photo looks like either a Mexican American or a Native American young woman in baggy jeans who has removed her shirt to show off the tattoo. In fact, she is identified in the title of the photograph: "Teresa Gutiérrez of Juárez, Mexico." Neither Chicana nor indigenous to New Mexico, she is a Mexican from the border. Also pictured in the frame is a pair of men's hands that seem to be pulling down the young woman's halter top to show the Virgin tattoo more clearly. The man's hands on the girl's waist suggest a familiarity with the girl's body, a nuanced sense of ownership or entitlement, which communicates that he has the right to pull down her shirt and, possibly, her pants as well. Also, there is a friendly coquettishness about the girl's smile and sexy sidelong gaze that suggests a heterosexual relationship between her and the man (not to mention the male viewer), who is represented synecdochically by the hands.

The following year, in the spring 1999 issue of the same newsletter, Archbishop Sheehan wrote the following short letter to the editor: "I was intrigued by the picture of the young girl on the cover of the Winter 1998 issue with the Guadalupe tattoo on her back. It seems like Our Lady of Guadalupe is a very friendly and understanding spiritual image that many people can relate to, even those who have terrible problems."[64]

What does the young woman in Miguel Gandert's photo represent that the archbishop seems to be able to relate to? Perhaps, as Orsini alludes to in her article, she is one of those "who fall short of ideal Christian conduct," not a pilgrim or a housewife, but a "street woman," openly offering herself to men and their cameras. Or perhaps she is someone with "terrible problems," as the archbishop's letter euphemistically states, who has found spiritual friendship with or forgiveness from Guadalupe.

If, as Orsini claims, the Virgin of Guadalupe "find[s] favor with her followers according to their personal needs" and also "offers compassion, pardon, understanding" to "all folk of every kind without reserve, without retribution," then why is it that the archbishop could not seem to follow in the Virgin's footsteps when it came to the incorrigible Alma López? If he can absolve pedophile priests;[65] if he could bring his archdiocese to the brink of bankruptcy, as he did in 1993, to pay the $50 million settlement that would help in some measure to atone for the rape, sodomy, and illicit sexual relationships that New Mexico's priests were perpetrating on girls and boys in their congregations, beginning with the former archbishop, Robert Sánchez;[66] if he could find visual gratification in the image of a Guadalupe tattoo on a young Mexican woman's naked back—why did the archbishop react so violently to *Our Lady*? What changed for Archbishop Sheehan between 1999—when he was so "intrigued" by Miguel Gandert's photograph that he felt compelled to send a letter of praise to the editor of *La Herencia del Norte*—and 2001, when he summarily condemned Alma López for turning Our Lady into a "tart and a street walker"? What difference did the archbishop perceive between Teresa Gutiérrez in Gandert's photo and Raquel Salinas in *Our Lady*?

The answer, I think, is obvious. *Our Lady* is not flirting with anyone. The hands on her waist are her own, not some anonymous male hands about to pull down her floral garment. Nor is she winking in coquettish response to the male gaze. And despite her naked breasts, the butterfly angel that sustains Our Lady offers no lactating solace to believers. The two Raqueles of *Our Lady* make up an interpretation of the Virgin of Guadalupe that refuses to be objectified or appropriated. By calling her a "tart" and a "street walker," Archbishop Sheehan not only gave permission to male viewers to bring their own illicit desire for the not-so-naked Virgin to the surface but he also gave her an identity that the men could control. Just as the protestor-pilgrims created an irreverent apparition, the archbishop created an inversion of the woman with "terrible problems" who "intrigued" him in 1999. He simultaneously sexualized Our Lady and punished her for not being [hetero]sexual enough.

Not only did López's digital depiction of Our Lady as a real live Everywoman "cheapen" the Virgin of Guadalupe in the eyes of López's detractors, that is, reduce the Virgin's value in the pantheon of sacred Catholic icons, but worse (and here is the key to the vituperative community response that was instigated by men), she was the tempting Devil in the rose bikini, the evil twin of the Lady of the Apocalypse. The bare belly, the bare legs and feet, the hidden cleavage vividly present in its absence—all aroused the unspoken heterosexual desire of her penitent male progeny. But it was the unseen parts, Our Lady's breasts and vulva covered demurely with roses, coupled with that defiant stance and the butterfly angel's pierced nipple that terrified and yet gave rise to other perversely pleasurable Catholic sentiments such as guilt and shame. As Luz Calvo tells us in "Art Comes for the Archbishop," Alma

López's "images seduce the spectator into new desiring positions by exposing Chicano/a libidinal investments—conscious and unconscious—in the Virgin of Guadalupe. Her images mobilize and disturb these investments, channeling Chicano/a desire in queer directions."[67] It is this seductive quality that is at the heart of López's "embodied aesthetic" or, rather, her use of the place-based Aztlán aesthetic to deconstruct and transform longings for an imaginary conquered homeland, which La Virgen de Guadalupe represents, into a reclamation and celebration of a brown female body that will not submit to any conqueror, which is *Our Lady*.

In trying to understand how the cultural icon of the Virgin of Guadalupe could signify her own life, Alma López sought the help of her friends, performance artist Raquel Salinas and writer/performer Raquel Gutiérrez. Together, they fleshed out Alma's vision of an embodied Virgin, not encumbered by the heavy robes that hide her limbs and keep her tethered to a one-dimensional existence. *Our Lady* shows a powerful, actual woman liberated from the yoke of a relational identity. Neither the "Mother of God" nor the "deliverer of the faithful," the Virgin in this artwork is rooted as much to the land (the earth, the continent, and the nation from which she sprang) as to the mysteries signified by the dark moon; she is anchored in the history of her Aztec past, which is encoded into her racial memory, just as the Viceroy butterfly's migrant journey between Mexico and United States is encoded into its genetic DNA.

By engaging in semiotics, deconstruction, and meta-ideologizing—the first three technologies in Chela Sandoval's "methodology of the oppressed"[68]— Alma López transformed the meaning of the Virgin of Guadalupe to more accurately signify her own experience as a sexed, gendered, raced, and classed body in patriarchy. Hers is what Margaret Montoya calls "a spirituality animated by transgression [that] makes us come to terms with different forms of repression."[69] Her unshakeable faith in the dignity of her creation, and her abiding love and respect for the revolutionary image that the Virgin of Guadalupe represents, gave Alma López the spiritual and political wherewithal to refuse to apologize, refuse to be stigmatized, and refuse to do penance: "When I see *Our Lady* as well as the works portraying La Virgen by many Chicana artists, I see an alternative voice expressing the multiplicities of our lived realities. I see myself living a tradition of Chicanas who, because of cultural and gender oppression, have asserted our voice. I see Chicanas creating a deep and meaningful connection to this revolutionary cultural female image. I see Chicanas who understand faith."[70]

THE SHADOW OF *OUR LADY* IN THE CITY OF FAITH

So large was the shadow cast by Alma López's one-and-a-half-foot *Our Lady* that it could only be eclipsed seven years later by a 12-foot, 4,000-pound bronze statue of the Virgin of Guadalupe. Standing at the corner of Guadalupe and De Vargas streets (an appropriate crossroads, indeed), perhaps over the very spot on which *Our Lady* received her mock burial in the ancient Catholic tradition of building Christian temples over pagan ruins, the statue is surrounded by offerings of roses on a platform of memorial bricks stenciled with the names of the parishioners who donated to her shrine and who now compose the Guadalupe Family: "She came to Santa Fe covered with bubble wrap and a blue tarp, lying on a flatbed trailer pulled by a red Dodge Ram truck. The Sirens signaled her arrival at the cathedral basilica of St. Francis of Assisi . . . When the procession came to a stop, Deacon Anthony Trujillo of Our Lady of Guadalupe Church and José Villegas, the police chaplain, began unwrapping the 12-foot, 4,000-pound bronze statue of Our Lady of Guadalupe. The parish, which is the oldest Marian shrine in the United States, raised the money and commissioned the work from a Mexican artist."[71]

It is no surprise that two of the most vocal protestor-pilgrims, indeed, the instigators of the protest—José Villegas and Deacon Trujillo—were involved in welcoming the statue to Santa Fe, undressing her, as it were, from her bubble-wrap veil, and raising her from her flatbed repose to her place of honor in front of the Guadalupe Santuario, as the church is called. As a consequence of the *Our Lady* debacle, no doubt, the parish's nonprofit Guadalupe Historic Foundation launched a campaign to build a permanent shrine to the "true" Virgin of Guadalupe in Santa Fe. Although the Santuario is considered the oldest church dedicated to Our Lady of Guadalupe in the United States,[72] and is itself a historic landmark as well as a shrine, parishioners felt it necessary to reassert the power of the traditional Guadalupe image in a sizeable and public way. Fund-raising for the shrine project began in 2001, the same year as the *Our Lady* controversy, and Deacon Trujillo was on the board of advisors for the nonprofit.[73]

Anne Constable, a journalist for the *Santa Fe New Mexican*, tracked the twelve-day pilgrimage of the statue and its *peregrino*/pilgrim escorts from Mexico City to Santa Fe in July 2008, where the statue was greeted with all the fanfare of a triumphal entrance reminiscent of another New Mexico Virgin, La Conquistadora, who was carried into New Mexico by the armored conquistador Diego de Vargas in 1692, when he reconquered New Mexico in the name of the Spanish crown and the Catholic faith.[74]

There is a reason that the protests against *Our Lady* took place in New Mexico and not, say, Mexico or Texas or California, where *Our Lady* has also been shown. Of all of the states of the Southwest, New Mexico is probably the most tricultural or mestizo—blending Spanish, Anglo-American, and Native American cultures—and yet, also, the most attached to its Spanish ancestry and the most celebratory of its Catholic colonization. Every year just after Labor Day, for example, Santa Fe observes its annual Fiestas de Santa Fe. Instituted in 1712, this popular celebration and tourist attraction, second only to Spanish Market and Indian Market, offers a reenactment of the Catholic colonial takeover of New Mexico from its indigenous inhabitants, who in the Pueblo Revolt of 1680 had burned down the Catholic mission and driven out the Spaniards and their Conquest Virgin. In 1692, Diego de Vargas and his army of conquistadors reentered Santa Fe carrying the Virgin of the Conquest and effected a peaceful and bloodless "reconquest" of New Mexico. Since 1712, New Mexicans have been commemorating the Spanish subjugation of the Indians and occupation of their homeland in an annual festival complete with royal processions of La Conquistadora through the downtown streets followed by a Conquistador King, a Virgin Queen,[75] a noble court of ladies and gentlemen, special masses in the cathedral basilica, native dances, an effigy burning, and a "historical/hysterical" parade in which the floats fall into the category of history or humor.[76]

A city that commemorates its history of conquest, a landscape of faith-healing earth, ancient adobe churches, and bloodstained brotherhood *moradas* (literally, chapels; symbolically, Stations of the Cross), a miraculous staircase,[77] a medieval cathedral elevated to basilica status by a pope, saint-carving *curanderos*, Easter pilgrimages and *penitente* re-creations of the Via Crucis and the Passion of Christ in the isolated communities of the Sangre de Cristo Mountains, an archbishop, a deacon, and a chaplain who rouse the Catholic community into a punishing rabble over an irreverent apparition of their own making, and a twelve-foot Virgin of Guadalupe city mascot—need we wonder at the City of Faith's historical/hysterical response to *Our Lady*?

As fate would have it, what the protestor-pilgrims most wanted to remove from the walls of the Museum of International Folk Art has now etched itself permanently into the cultural memory of the Land of Enchantment. Because of the protest's processions and pilgrimages, because of the media blitz, because of the way the controversy drew communities together in defense of their faith or in support of an artist's constitutional right to make personally relevant art, Alma López is now a household name in New Mexico. Her fame to some may be along the lines of the atom bomb or the UFO,[78] but to others she is "the bomb," that is, the example of an artist living true to her faith in the transformational power of her work. Along with La Conquistadora and the Virgin of Guadalupe, *Our Lady* forms a trinity of Virgins that preside over Santa Fe. Everyone finds solace now: the conquered, the penitent, and the queer.

NOTES

I thank Allison Wyper for her invaluable research assistance in the writing of this chapter.

1. "Even if Salman Rushdie repents and becomes the most pious man of all time, it is incumbent on every Muslim to employ everything he has got, his life and wealth, to send him to Hell." See the Ayatollah Khomeini entry in Wikipedia, www.wikipedia.org.

2. The "eye" part of this construction functions as a synecdoche to represent the body of the viewer and the material conditions that inform the experience of the body—race, class, gender, age, sexuality, ethnicity, language, etc.—and that consequently shape the subjectivity of the "I" that filters what the eye sees. For more about how the eye/I constructs positionality, see my *Chicano Art: Inside/Outside the Master's House: Cultural Politics and the CARA Exhibition* (Austin: University of Texas Press, 1998), 23–28.

3. John R. Linton, "'Our Lady' Artwork Is an Offense," *Albuquerque Tribune* (April 5, 2001).

4. Henry Casso, letter to Archbishop Michael Sheehan, June 20, 2001, *Cyber Arte* Collection, Museum of International Folk Art Archives.

5. See the *Our Lady* link on www.almalopez.com.

6. See www.sancta.org.mx; www.virgendeguadalupe.org.mx.

7. Rory McVeigh and David Sikkink, "God, Politics, and Religion: Religious Beliefs and the Legitimation of Contentious Tactics," *Social Forces* 79.4 (2001): 1426.

8. Hollis Walker, "Whose Lady? Laying Claim to the Virgin Mary," in *The New Gatekeepers: Emerging Challenges to Free Expression in the Arts* (New York: Columbia University/National Arts Journalism Program, 2003), 43.

9. Chela Sandoval, *Methodology of the Oppressed* (Minneapolis: University of Minnesota Press, 2000), 131.

10. Ibid. Meta-ideologizing is the third of five technologies of the methodology of the oppressed. The first two are semiotics and deconstruction, and the last two

are democratics (or the hermeneutics of love) and differential consciousness. In actuality, *Our Lady* is a representation of the five technologies working together. For more about Chela Sandoval's theories in relation to *Our Lady*, see Chap. 6 here.

11. Ibid., 83.

12. Stuart Hall, "Encoding/Decoding," in *The Cultural Studies Reader*, edited by Simon During (New York: Routledge, 1993), 100. Although this essay is about the reading of televised images, the same three readings or reference codes can apply to all cultural texts.

13. Richard Benke, "Bikini-Clad Virgin Mary 'a Tart': Archbishop," *Ottawa Citizen* (April 5, 2001), *Cyber Arte* Collection, Museum of International Folk Art Archives.

14. Quoted in Walker, "Whose Lady?" 43.

15. Ibid.

16. Ibid., 42.

17. *Cyber Arte* Collection, Museum of International Folk Art Archives.

18. Margaret Montoya, "Un/braiding Stories about Law, Sexuality, and Morality," *Chicano-Latino Law Review* 24 (2003).

19. Alicia Gaspar de Alba, *Chicano Art*, 162.

20. Alma López, artist's statement published online on April 2, 2001 as "The Artist of 'Our Lady.'" Downloaded from www.lasculturas.com.

21. "I'm embarrassed to think that we are still living in the age of the Inquisition" (*Cyber Arte* Collection, Museum of International Folk Art Archives).

22. To read the full text of all of these e-mails, see www.almalopez.com.

23. Sandoval, *Methodology of the Oppressed*, 183.

24. The show opened at Emanations Studio Gallery in Santa Fe. The six artists in the show were Delilah Montoya, Pola López, Goldie García, Vivian Marthell, Ana Rivera, and Alma López.

25. Tom Sharpe, "Artist Calls for Backing of 'Our Lady,'" *Santa Fe New Mexican* (June 2, 2001), *Cyber Arte* Collection, Museum of International Folk Art Archives.

26. Sandoval, *Methodology of the Oppressed*, 182.

27. Gaspar de Alba, *Chicano Art*, 162.

28. Museum of New Mexico press release, April 6, 2001, *Cyber Arte* Collection, Museum of International Folk Art Archives.

29. "Museum Director Denies Appeal: *Our Lady* Stays," museum press release, July 13, 2001, *Cyber Arte* Collection, Museum of International Folk Art Archives, box 1, folder 3.

30. Alma López, "The Artist of 'Our Lady.'"

31. Alberto López Pulido, *The Sacred World of the Penitentes* (Washington, DC: Smithsonian Institution Press, 2000), xiii–xiv. While the *penitente* rituals of New Mexico are considered not only sacred but also secret pageants exclusive to the northern

mountain hamlets and village communities in which they are staged, in Iztapalapa, Mexico, a town just outside of Mexico City, the Passion play—complete with an actual whipping and a real crucifixion of the chosen redeemer—"has become one of the largest and most fervent in the world, attracting more than two million annually." See Larry Rohter, "A Mexican Tradition Runs on Pageantry and Faith," *New York Times International* (April 12, 2009): 12.

32. See the "Chimayo, New Mexico" entry at www.wikipedia.org.

33. Ronald L. Grimes, *Symbol and Conquest: Public Ritual and Drama in Santa Fe* (Albuquerque: University of New Mexico Press, 1976), 62.

34. Ibid.

35. Ibid.

36. Ibid., 67.

37. Jennifer McKee, "Shouts, Shoves, Prayers Filled Foyer Outside," *Albuquerque Journal North* (April 5, 2001), *Cyber Arte* Collection, Museum of International Folk Art Archives.

38. Steven Robert Allen, "Our Lady of Eternal Conflict," editorial, *Weekly Alibi* (April 19–25, 2001): 14. *Cyber Arte* Collection, Museum of International Folk Art Archives.

39. Antonio López, "Our Lady Fleshing Out the 'Our,'" *Cyber Arte* Collection, Museum of International Folk Art Archives.

40. Peter Caster, "Staging Prisons: Performance, Activism, and Social Bodies," *The Drama Review*, 48.3 (Fall 2004): 114; original emphasis.

41. Catherine Coggan, "Our Lady: From Light Switch Covers to Bikinis," *Crosswinds Quarterly* (April 5–12, 2001). *Cyber Arte* Collection, Museum of International Folk Art Archives.

42. Peggy Phelan, "White Men and Pregnancy: Discovering the Body to Be Rescued," in *Unmarked: The Politics of Performance* (New York: Routledge, 1993), 130.

43. Ibid., 131.

44. Ibid., 132.

45. Ibid., 145; original emphasis.

46. Caster, "Staging Prisons," 107.

47. Report to the MNM [Museum of New Mexico] Committee on Sensitive Materials, *Cyber Arte* Collection, Museum of International Folk Art Archives.

48. Grimes, *Symbol and Conquest*, 67.

49. The American Society for the Defense of Tradition, Family and Property group started an aggressive letter-writing campaign with worldwide outreach to have the offensive art piece removed from the exhibition. The campaign included an image of the traditional Guadalupe, some inflammatory text about the blasphemous "Bikini" Virgin, and a preaddressed postcard that just needed to be signed, stamped, and mailed to the museum in New Mexico. The *Cyber Arte* archives

logged over 24,000 cards, some of them coming from as far as Belize and Brazil. The TFP/ANF group's website, however, states that their campaign brought 65,000 cards to the museum.

50. Sarah Horton, "Ritual and Return: Diasporic Hispanos and the Santa Fe Fiesta," in *Expressing New Mexico: Nuevomexicano Creativity, Ritual, and Memory*, edited by Phillip B. Gonzales (Tucson: University of Arizona Press, 2007), 199.

51. Jeremy Pawloski, "Church Gives 'Our Lady' Mock Burial," *Albuquerque Journal North* (October 29, 2001), *Cyber Arte* Collection, Museum of International Folk Art Archives.

52. J. C., "Idolaters Doth Protest Our Lady," unsigned letter to the editor, *Weekly Alibi* (April 26–May 2, 2001): 6, *Cyber Arte* Collection, Museum of International Folk Art Archives.

53. The performance was "censored by the museum," said Sedeño in a press release (*Cyber Arte* Collection, Museum of International Folk Art Archives).

54. Sharpe, "Artist Calls for Backing of 'Our Lady.'"

55. In 2009, Yale University's Beinecke Rare Book and Manuscript Library completed arrangements to acquire the entire Jon Lewis portfolio relating to César Chávez and the UFW.

56. I was one of the first six faculty hired in 1994 with full-time appointments in the newly instituted César E. Chávez Center for Interdisciplinary Instruction in Chicana and Chicano Studies, which was the compromise reached after the hunger strike agreement. In 2005, the Chávez Center became a department, of which I served as chair between 2007 and 2010.

57. Cultural nationalism is a form of identity politics that expresses allegiance to a culture instead of a nation. Regardless of where they located their birthplace, in the United States or in Mexico, Chicano cultural nationalists claimed Mexican culture, which included the Catholic faith and the Spanish language as their nation. Now seen as an outdated form of Chicano identity politics, cultural nationalism continues to be seen as a tenet of the Chicano movement and a seminal aspect of the ideology of Chicanismo.

58. Alma López, "The Artist of 'Our Lady.'"

59. Alicia Gaspar de Alba, "There's No Place Like Aztlán: Embodied Aesthetics in Chicana Art," *New Centennial Review* 42.2 (2004): 127; original emphasis.

60. Tey Diana Rebolledo, "The Archbishop Sees the Body of the Virgin: Art, Religion, Ideology, and Popular Culture," in *The Chronicles of Panchita Villa and Other Guerrilleras* (Austin: University of Texas Press, 2005), 179.

61. Octavio Paz, "Sons of La Malinche," in *The Labyrinth of Solitude: Life and Thought in Mexico* (New York: Grove Press, 1985), 85, 86.

62. See *Bikini Virgen on Trial*, directed by Cynthia Buzzard, Alma López private collection.

63. Jacqueline Orsini, "The Lady Has Many Faces," *La Herencia del Norte, Cyber Arte* Collection, Museum of International Folk Art Archives; emphasis added.

64. *La Herencia del Norte* (Spring 1999): 6, *Cyber Arte* Collection, Museum of International Folk Art Archives.

65. For more about the pedophilia scandals in the Catholic Church, with emphasis on the Santa Fe Archdiocese, see "Archbishop Asks for Forgiveness," *Associated Press State & Local Wire* (March 11, 2000); "Archbishop Says It Wasn't Easy to Put Priest on Leave," *Associated Press State & Local Wire* (January 19, 2000); Richard Benke, "Archbishop: New Mexico Dealt with Its Own Sex Scandals," *Associated Press State & Local Wire* (March 22, 2002); Anne Constable, "Sheehan: I Never Reinstated Molesters," *Santa Fe New Mexican* (June 18, 2002); Joseph B. Frazier, "Catholic Church, Accusers Reach Deal," *Associated Press Online* (October 10, 2000); Paul Logan, "Sheehan Wants Stricter Rules," *Albuquerque Journal* (June 10, 2002); Paul Logan, "Bishop's Denial Brings Back Pain," *Albuquerque Journal* (April 21, 2002); John J. Lumpkin, "Embattled Priest Says Goodbye," *Albuquerque Journal* (January 17, 2000); Fran Presley, "Lone Star Living: Sheehan Has Faith-filled Desire to Bring Christ to the People," *Associated Press State & Local Wire* (February 23, 2000); Isabel Sánchez, "Archdiocese of Santa Fe on Mend after Lawsuits," *Albuquerque Journal* (January 13, 2002); Meredith Wade, "Sheehan Can Fix It, Local Clergy Say," *Albuquerque Tribune* (June 18, 2003).

66. The archbishop called the settlement "Chernobyl on the Rio Grande"; quoted in Uwe Siemon-Netto "Analysis: Bishop's Trial in France," *United Press International* (June 15, 2001).

67. See Chap. 5 here.

68. Semiotics is the science of signs or, rather, the reading of cultural signs to unveil the dominant political ideologies inherent in them. Deconstruction refers to the practice of challenging the mythological constructs (as we see in the writing of cultural myths that have both historical and teleological functions) of these political ideologies. And, again, meta-ideologizing is the revolutionary appropriation of cultural signs for the purpose of transforming their mythologized meanings and resignifying those meanings for the empowerment of the oppressed. For more about how Alma López engages the methodology of the oppressed, see Chap. 6 here.

69. Montoya, "Un/braiding Stories," 9.

70. Alma López, "The Artist of 'Our Lady.'"

71. See the Santuario's website to read more about how to become a member of the Guadalupe Family, www.ologsf.50webs.com. Quotation from Anne Constable, "Parishioners Welcome Marian Statue after Safe Arrival from Mexico," *Santa Fe New Mexican* (July 23, 2008).

72. The oldest shrine to the Virgin of Guadalupe in the New World is actually not the Santuario in Santa Fe. The first and oldest Guadalupe Church is located in Ciudad Juárez, across the border from El Paso, Texas, having been built over a hundred years earlier than the Santuario in Santa Fe. In fact, it was to this site that De Vargas and his missionaries, colonists, and fellow conquistadors repaired in 1680 when the Pueblo Indians revolted and drove the Spaniards out of New Mexico. With the territorial redistribution of 1848, when the Mexican North became the American West and Southwest, but only after 1912, when New Mexico became admitted as a state, the honor of being the first and oldest church to Our Lady of Guadalupe *in the United States* fell to the Guadalupe Church in Santa Fe.

73. Anne Constable, "Journey of Devotion," *Santa Fe New Mexican* (July 26, 2008), www.santafenewmexican.com.

74. For more about La Conquistadora and the Fiestas of Santa Fe, see Chaps. 3 and 4 here.

75. There are strict nativity and marital requirements for the man and woman who are selected as the King and Queen of the Fiestas. They must both be born in New Mexico, but while the man is expected to be a family man, i.e., married with children, the young woman must be unmarried, i.e., a virgin, and remain that way through the end of the Fiestas.

76. For more information about the Santa Fe Fiestas, see www.santafefiesta.org.

77. Another big tourist attraction, the miraculous spiral staircase is located in the Loretto Chapel, a few blocks away from the cathedral basilica. According to local legend, it was Saint Joseph himself, in the guise of a nameless, humble carpenter looking for work, who paid a visit to the Sisters of Loretto, the first nuns of Santa Fe, and built the staircase that would connect the chapel's nave to the choir. What is "miraculous" is that the wood curves dramatically in 360-degree turns and is held together without nails.

78. New Mexico is the home of the penitent, the conquered, and the miraculous, but also of the explosive, the covert, and the alien. The atom bomb was invented in Los Alamos, New Mexico, and Roswell has long been associated with the sighting of Unidentified Flying Objects and the secret government laboratory known as Area 51, where supposed extraterrestrial aliens are studied.

11

It's Not about the Santa in My *Fe*, but the Santa Fe in My *Santa*

Alma López

> I want the freedom to carve
> and chisel my own face.
>
> GLORIA ANZALDÚA

MIGRANT VIRGEN

I WAS BORN IN LOS MOCHIS, Sinaloa, Mexico.[1] My family migrated to the United States when I was four years old. I grew up on both sides of the U.S.-Mexico border with the image of La Virgen de Guadalupe in my home. We traveled to Mexico at least once every other year, usually during Christmas vacation. On the mornings of those trips all seven of us would pile into the red Thunderbird and, after invoking the protection of La Virgen, begin our long drive south at dawn. La Virgen de Guadalupe was always present in each family home we visited in Mexico, including my godmother's house, where I was born. La Virgen was present in the churches we visited. She was present in the public vans, or *peseros*, and buses we traveled in, either dangling from a rearview mirror or glued to a dashboard. In Los Angeles, she was always present on a mural on the walls of the local bakery, taco stand, or corner store. I would see her all year long on holiday calendars given to us by our neighborhood bakery, El Águila. I would see her on tattoos. I would see intricately detailed pencil or ballpoint pen pinto art drawings of her in *Lowrider Magazine*. Occasionally, we would visit her in our neighborhood Catholic church, All Saint's Church on Portola

Avenue in El Sereno. Growing up, I wore Guadalupe earrings or a small gold medal hanging from a thin gold chain. Today, my Virgen de Guadalupe medal is accompanied by a larger medal of Coyolxauhqui.

In our home she was a migrant Virgen. We had a large, heavy, framed full-color poster print of La Virgen de Guadalupe hanging in our living room. When my mother needed to pray, she would take it down and move it from the living room to a bedroom, where she would place a candle before the print. If the bedrooms were occupied, which was highly likely with six children, she would take La Virgen to the bathroom. If the bathroom was occupied (again, highly likely), she would take her to a closet. It was usually in the closet where my mother and La Virgen would end their pilgrimage.[2]

I have lived all over Los Angeles, including Compton, Pico Union/Convention Center, El Sereno/Northeast L.A., Vernon/Huntington Park, West Adams, Santa Monica, Eagle Rock, Highland Park, and Westchester. In 1997, I moved from West Adams to South Los Angeles, the geographic area south of downtown Los Angeles formerly known as South Central Los Angeles. At this time, South L.A. was experiencing demographic changes. African Americans were moving north to places like Lancaster and Rialto, where they could afford larger, newer homes with swimming pools. The vacated homes were either rented or purchased by Mexicans and Central Americans, including Guatemalans, Salvadorans, Nicaraguans, and Hondurans.[3] In the 2000 census, South L.A. had a population of 520,461, and 55 percent of the residents were Latino, 41 percent were African American.

On November 18, 1999, the L.A. Weekly published a story on defaced Virgen de Guadalupe murals in South Central Los Angeles.[4] For months, someone had been destroying these murals on San Pedro and Central avenues from 27th Street to 60th Street. La Virgen's face was obscured with blotches of blue; on some "666" was plastered across her belly; or her entire body was painted white. Veronica Hernández at L.A. Meat Market suspected that the vandals most likely attended one of the Pentecostal or Evangelical churches competing with the Catholic church for Latino members.

I clearly remember this religious shift from Catholicism to Christianity in the Latino community. Within my own family, my mother and two brothers converted. One of my brothers successfully completed Victory Outreach's drug rehabilitation program and later, with his wife, directed the women's and men's rehabilitation homes.[5] According to the article in L.A. Weekly, pamphlets had circulated in the neighborhood declaring "God has no mother" and denouncing the "cult" of Mary.

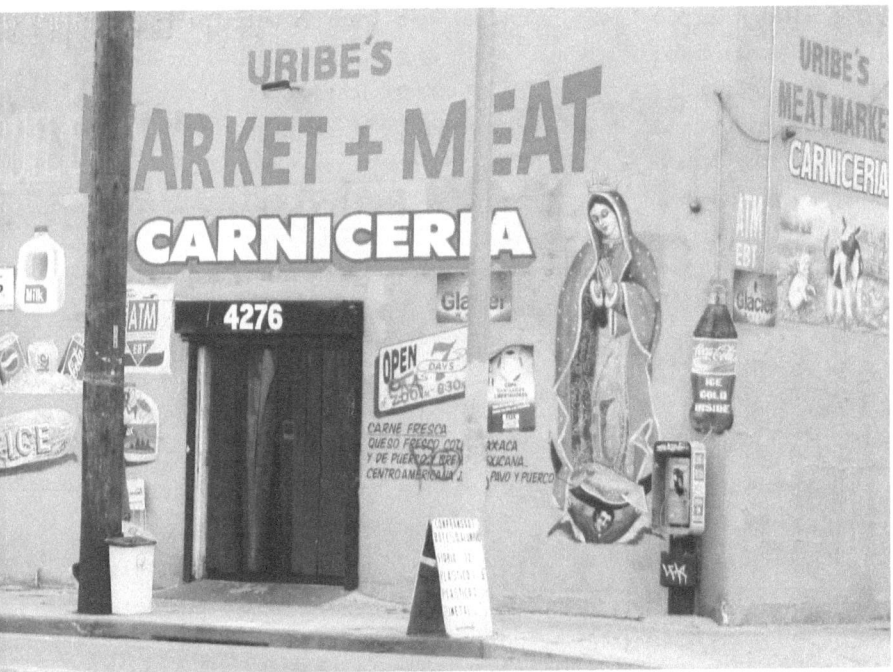

11.1.   Virgen de Guadalupe mural in South Los Angeles. Photograph by Alma López, © 2009. Courtesy of Alma López.

We were all really surprised by this defacement. Traditionally, the only walls safe from graffiti and vandalism in Los Angeles were the ones painted with La Virgen de Guadalupe. These events were so alarming that Senator Barbara Boxer asked Attorney General Janet Reno to investigate the vandalism of the Virgen murals as a hate crime. It is ironic to me, then, that only two years later, hate crimes against my own creation, *Our Lady*, would come to dominate my life as well as the popular culture of New Mexico.

On February 25, 2001, the *Our Lady* controversy began in Santa Fe, New Mexico. Since then I have lectured and exhibited internationally on this image and my work. In the intervening years, I have had time to reflect on my relationship to La Virgen de Guadalupe and what she means to me as an artist and as a Mexican-born Chicana who has lived most of her life in Los Angeles. I have also had time to reflect on the process of creating the image titled *Our Lady*, and I write this chapter as a way of sharing the evolution of the image and to document the process of my own activist art. Writing this chapter has given me the time to flesh out the ideas and beliefs I have had about La

Virgen's apparition since 1997, when I started placing photographs of Virgen de Guadalupe murals into my work as part of my 1848 series. In these images, I place Guadalupe directly on the fence that separates Mexico and the United States to signify the Treaty of Guadalupe-Hidalgo, which created the border and the border citizens who call ourselves Chicano and Chicana. Since then, La Virgen has taken many forms in my work. The first question I asked myself when I started to think about this chapter was, Who really was La Virgen de Guadalupe? A miracle, a fabrication, or, like my own work, an image with a purpose?

LA VIRGEN DE GUADALUPE APPARITION STORY

According to popular accounts, La Virgen de Guadalupe appeared four times to a fifty-seven-year-old indigenous widower, and now saint, Juan Diego Cuauhtlatloatzin (1474–May 30, 1548) on Tepeyac hill from December 9 through 12 in 1531.[6] She instructed him to notify bishop-elect Fray Juan de Zumárraga (1468–June 3, 1548) of her wish to have a temple built on Tepeyac. Disbelieving the native, the bishop asked for proof, and La Virgen of Guadalupe instructed Juan Diego to pick roses which she caused to appear from the side of the hill. She carefully rearranged the flowers on his *tilma* made of a coarse fabric derived from the threads of the maguey cactus. When Juan Diego dropped the roses at the feet of the bishop, La Virgen's image was miraculously imprinted on his *tilma*. Supposedly, this is the same image currently located in the Basílica de Guadalupe in Mexico City. Every December 12, people from all over Mexico, Latin America, and the United States participate in a pilgrimage to the basilica either to ask for miracles or to give thanks for miracles received. This pilgrimage is enacted in many Mexican Catholic neighborhoods throughout the Southwest on La Virgen's feast day.

This apparition story is retold in a multimedia presentation on the official Virgen de Guadalupe website and in a graphic novel titled *Nuestra Señora de Guadalupe*, which I purchased in Mexico City in 1998.[7] The graphic novel was written and illustrated with the approval of the Los Angeles Roman Catholic archbishop, Timothy Cardinal Manning (1909–1989), published by Franciscan Communications, and printed and distributed in Mexico by Ediciones Don Bosco. The introduction briefly illustrates the violent conquest of the Aztec empire and the destruction of sacred temples. Missionaries beg the king of Spain to send them to Mexico to help the native peoples. According to this

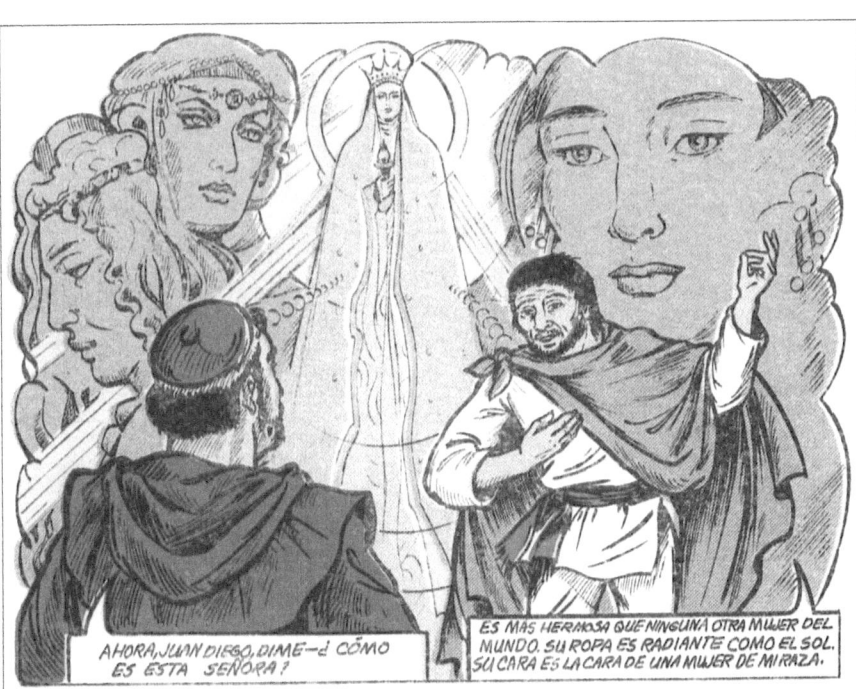

AHORA, JUAN DIEGO, DIME—¿CÓMO ES ESTA SEÑORA?

ES MAS HERMOSA QUE NINGUNA OTRA MUJER DEL MUNDO. SU ROPA ES RADIANTE COMO EL SOL. SU CARA ES LA CARA DE UNA MUJER DE MI RAZA.

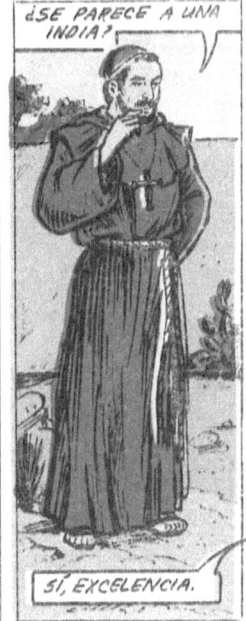

¿SE PARECE A UNA INDIA?

SÍ, EXCELENCIA.

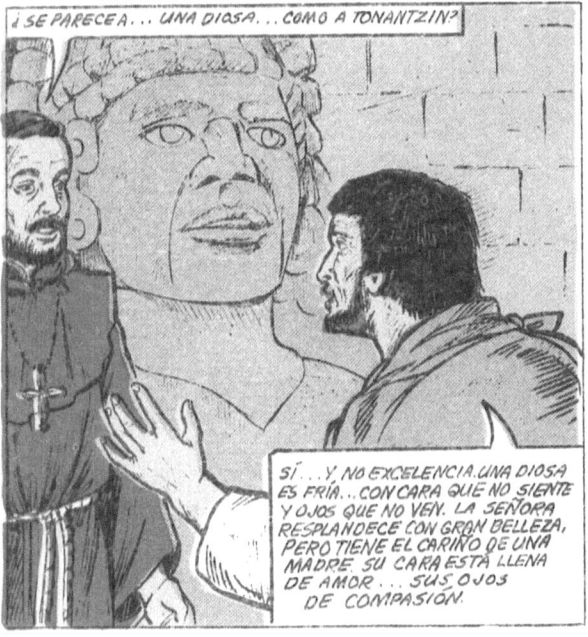

¿SE PARECE A... UNA DIOSA... COMO A TONANTZIN?

SÍ..., Y, NO EXCELENCIA. UNA DIOSA ES FRÍA... CON CARA QUE NO SIENTE Y OJOS QUE NO VEN. LA SEÑORA RESPLANDECE CON GRAN BELLEZA, PERO TIENE EL CARIÑO DE UNA MADRE. SU CARA ESTÁ LLENA DE AMOR... SUS OJOS DE COMPASIÓN.

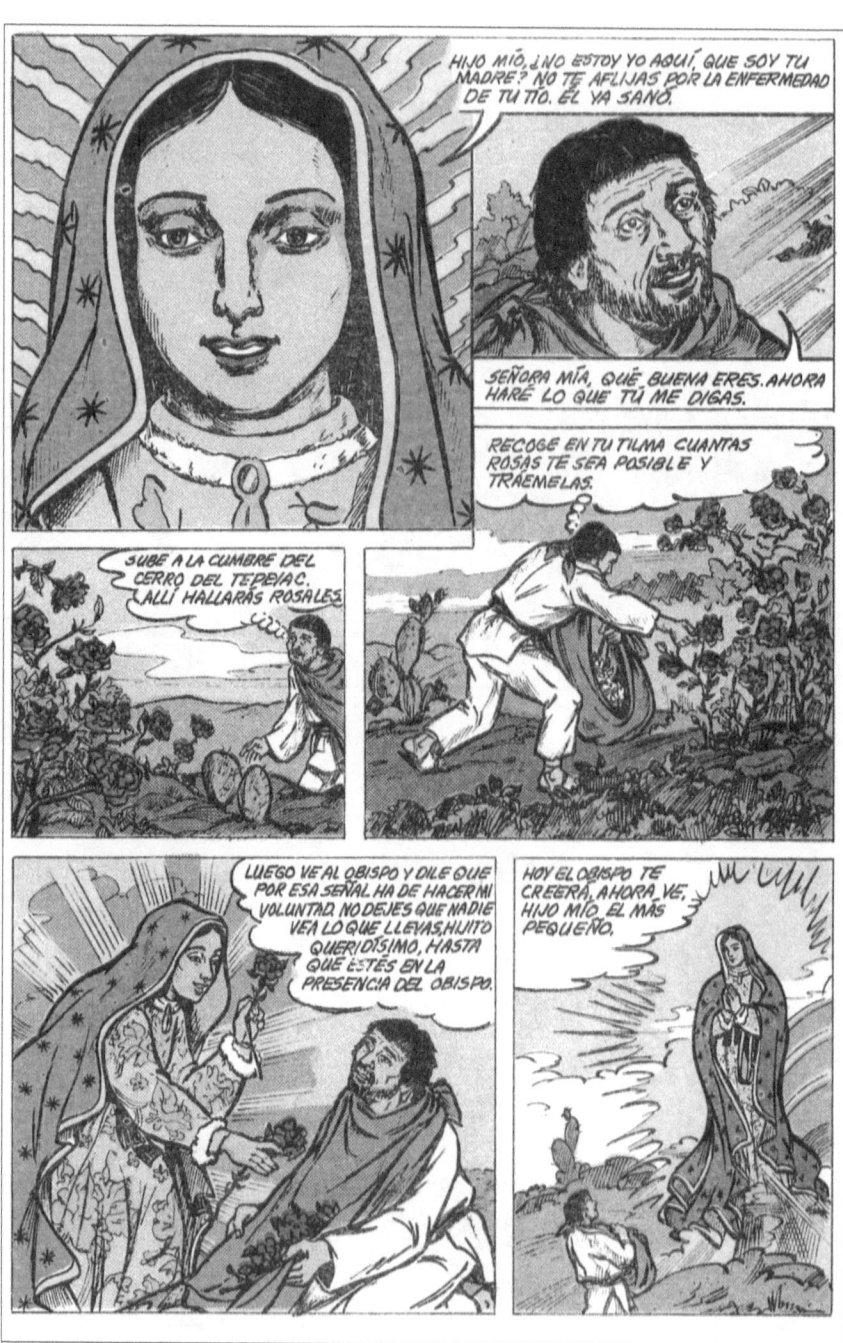

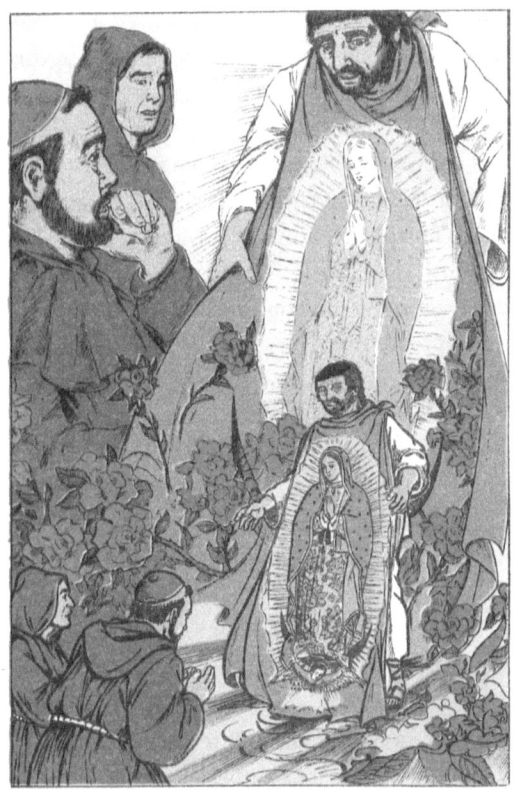

11.2.
Three pages from the graphic novel *Nuestra Señora de Guadalupe*, a publication of Franciscan Communications, Los Angeles, California.

graphic novel, La Virgen de Guadalupe appears to Juan Diego around the same time that Bishop Zumárraga prays for a miracle to help him intervene on behalf of the native people who have been enslaved, raped, and tortured by the conquering Spaniards.

Bishop Zumárraga questions Juan Diego to clarify whether the goddess apparition was in fact Tonantzin. Juan Diego responds: "Yes and no your Excellency. A goddess is cold, with a face that does not feel and eyes that cannot see. On the other hand, the beautiful, radiant lady has the tenderness of a mother, a face of love, and compassionate eyes."[8] After Juan Diego informs the bishop that the goddess demands that a temple be built on Tepeyac, the bishop asks Juan Diego to ask the goddess to prove that she is the mother of Jesus Christ. At the fourth and final apparition to Juan Diego, the goddess offers the roses as proof. We all know that when Juan Diego shows the bishop the roses, the image of La Virgen de Guadalupe is imprinted on his *tilma*.

The story of her apparition, spread via oral tradition, started a massive wave of indigenous conversion to Catholicism. Some scholars and historians believe that the Spaniards introduced the Virgen de Guadalupe image to represent syncretically both the Virgin Mary and the pre-Columbian goddess Tonantzin as an aid in this mass conversion. Some of us doubt this Catholic manipulation of the story. Some of us see La Virgen as a literal *fabrication*. I do not give credit to the Spaniards for the invention of this image. I have my own theory, which I will share below.

The Spanish priests recorded everything. Bishop Fray Juan de Zumárraga lived for seventeen years after the apparition, writing many letters, notes, and catechism. Most notably, he introduced the printing press to Mexico, where he acted as editor or publisher. Yet never in any of his lectures, homilies, or publications does he mention the apparition of La Virgen de Guadalupe. According to the apparition story, Fray Zumárraga was a primary witness. Why would he never write or print anything about this apparition, especially when he could have given himself credit for participating in such a miraculous event? Was he there? Did he know Juan Diego? Did he know about La Virgen's apparition? Or was the apparition of La Virgen on Juan Diego's *tilma* not a miracle at all, at least not in the church's eyes, but a survival story created by the natives? Whatever it was, the event was not significant enough in the bishop's life, or in the lives of his fellow New Spain bishops, to merit recording.[9]

The story of La Virgen's apparition was not published in Spanish for 117 years. *Imagen de la Virgen María, Madre de Dios de Guadalupe*, written and published in 1648 by Miguel Sánchez (1594–1674), a diocesan priest in Mexico City, is the first-known account of the apparition in Spanish. The *Nican Mopohua*, which translates as "Here it is recounted," documents the apparition in Nahuatl.[10] It is believed that Antonio Valeriano (c. 1531–1605) a Nahua scholar, politician, and assistant to Fray Bernardino de Sahagún (1499–October 23, 1590) wrote the *Nican Mopohua* in 1556 while compiling the Florentine Codex. A very old, damaged copy dating to circa 1556 along with two later copies are located in the New York Public Library. The *Nican Mopohua* was published with other Nahuatl texts on the apparition by the *criollo* priest and lawyer (and chaplain of Guadalupe from 1646 to 1656),[11] Luis Lasso de la Vega in 1649. That text had a really long title: *Huei tlamahuiçoltica omonexiti in ilhuicac tlatocaçihuapilli Santa Maria totlaçonantzin Guadalupe in nican huei alte-penahuac Mexico itocayocan Tepeyacac*, which translates from Nahuatl as "By a great miracle appeared the heavenly queen, Saint Mary, our precious mother of Guadalupe, here near the great altépetl of Mexico, at a place called Tepeya-cac." It is generally referred to by a shortened title: *Huei tlamahuicoltica*, or the great miracle.[12]

Why would the church neglect to record such a miraculous event for over one hundred years, especially since friars like Sahagún were involved in documentation and Zumárraga had access to a printing press? Why would scholars such as Sahagún worry that La Virgen of Guadalupe was referred to as Tonantzin, and why would Zumárraga's biographer, the nineteenth-century historian Joaquín García Icazbalceta, question the existence of Juan Diego?[13] Why would natives who endured invasion, rape, pillage, and torture by their Spanish conquerors, as well as biological and cultural genocide, for more than ten years suddenly convert?

LA VIRGEN AS A REVOLUTIONARY

When I look at the image of La Virgen de Guadalupe, I see a complex activist revolutionary cultural icon. To me, she is the poster image for the first successful act of mass nonviolent civil resistance/disobedience on this continent. Like the Aztec moon goddess Coyolxauhqui, La Virgen de Guadalupe needs to be deciphered and *re-membered*. Hundreds of years of conquest and Catholic misinformation shifted her meaning. She documents the spirit of indigenous resistance. We witness this spirit of resistance resurface throughout our Mexican, Mexican American, and Chicana/o history.

In 1810, Miguel Hidalgo y Costilla initiated the move for Mexican independence from Spain with his Grito de Dolores, exclaiming: "Death to the Spaniards and long live La Virgen de Guadalupe!" In 1914, Emiliano Zapata's and Francisco Villa's peasant armies marched against the dictatorial government of Porfirio Díaz. Their campaign slogan was "Tierra y libertad" (land and liberty) and their banner was La Virgen de Guadalupe. In 1966, during the United Farm Workers' pilgrimage from Delano to Sacramento to focus national attention on the plight of farmworkers, the marchers carried four flags: the Mexican, the U.S., the United Farm Workers' black eagle on white and red background, and La Virgen de Guadalupe (see Figure 10.5).[14] In 1994, the Zapatista Army of National Liberation (Ejército Zapatista de Liberación Nacional, EZLN) named its "mobile city" Guadalupe Tepeyac.[15]

In 1531, when La Virgen de Guadalupe appeared, the indigenous populations in Mexico were at risk of extinction. In 1519, Spaniards landed in what we now know as Mexico. They waged a bloody war and conquered Tenochtitlan and Mexico in 1521. The indigenous populations were raped, enslaved, tortured, murdered, and exposed to disease that led to near extinction. If brutally taking their bodies, their families, and all their material property were not enough, they were forced to replace their cosmology with European Christian beliefs.

As an activist artist, I imagine the indigenous community leaders meeting to develop strategies for survival. Like any grassroots social movement, this one is rooted in love for self and community. I imagine a room full of activists consisting of parents, teachers, students, artists, writers, scholars, priests, and even perhaps a few Catholic friars horrified at the atrocities committed against the indigenous peoples by their own kind. I imagine months or perhaps years of heated debate among these community leaders about how best to express their resistance and yet preserve their survival. The result of all this activism, I think, was what Jeanette Rodríguez calls a *"disfrasismo,"* "a way of communicating the most profound thought or feeling using a complementary union of two words or symbols, which expresses one meaning."[16] I can see the artists in the group suggesting that by uniting the symbol of the Christian Mother of God with their own creation goddess, Tonantzin, they could effectively disguise their resistance as obedience, and so curtail their suffering and end the bloodshed in their communities. Among this group of activists, perhaps, was the one selected to represent the "good native and Christian" double-agent messenger,[17] He Who Talks Like an Eagle or, as we know him, Saint Juan Diego.

It does not seem at all far-fetched to me that these community activists decided to create or commission a coded image that would be understood by the indigenous populations. They were, after all, experts in semiotics, as is obvious from studying their sculptures, pyramids, murals, and codices. This coded image was required to be European and Christian-looking enough to satisfy the conquerors and missionaries. This image would portray an indigenous Nahuatl-speaking goddess resembling the Virgin Mary as described in the Book of Revelations 12:1: "And a great sign appeared in heaven: A woman clothed with the sun, and the moon under her feet, and on her head a crown of twelve stars."[18]

From researching the Guadalupe image and the documents of her cultural myth, I believe that this revolutionary process had to have been longer and more extensive than the four days during which the apparition story takes place. The development of the oral tradition and the painting of the image most likely took several years. The first known handwritten account of the story of the apparition to Juan Diego was in Nahuatl in 1556 by Antonio Valeriano. Valeriano was born in 1531, the same year that Our Lady was said to have appeared to Juan Diego; he would have been twenty-five years old in 1556.

For hundreds of years, the image and the story have been debated. In 1556, in a sermon for the Viceroy and members of the Royal Audience, the head of the colony's Franciscans, Francisco de Bustamante, stated that "[t]he devotion that has been growing in a chapel dedicated to Our Lady, called of Guadalupe, in this city is greatly harmful for the natives, because it makes them believe that the image painted by Marcos the Indian is in any way miraculous."[19] He is referring to Marcos Cipac de Aquino, an Aztec artist, and to the "cult" of Our Lady of Guadalupe at Tepeyac that had developed in New Spain since 1531, to the alarm of the church fathers. In Bustamante's view, this Guadalupe cult, which was being sanctioned by the archbishop, Alonso de Montúfar, successor to Zumárraga as the archbishop of Mexico in the sixteenth century, would "threaten to uproot the fragile Christianity of the indigenous population."[20]

In 1754, Pope Benedict XIV declared Our Lady of Guadalupe the "patron" of New Spain. Two years earlier, at the request of Archbishop José Manuel Rubio y Salinas (1703–1765), Zapotec painter Miguel Mateo Maldonado y Cabrera (1695–1768),[21] made an early study of the Virgen of Guadalupe image. This painter is known for his *"casta"* paintings (representing the racial caste system of colonial Mexico) and his portrait of Sor Juana Inés de la Cruz, but he is also credited with creating the first portrait of Juan Diego and for making three replicas of La Virgen of Guadalupe. In 1752, Cabrera was allowed to access the original *tilma* to paint the three replicas and to affirm the 1666 declarations that the image was miraculous by using his expert knowledge and status as the recognized greatest painter in all of eighteenth-century New Spain. He concluded that there were four different types of paint media and techniques used throughout the image: La Virgen's face and hands were painted in oil; the tunic, mandorla, and angel were painted in egg tempera; the mantle was painted in gouache; and the rays seemed to be of gold dust woven into the palm fibers of the fabric.[22] Ultimately, Cabrera concluded that the image was miraculous because those techniques were not practiced in New Spain in 1531.

Three questions occur to me about this conclusion. First, how would Cabrera know if the materials and painting techniques that he found in the *tilma* image were not available in 1531 in New Spain, more than two hundred years before his lifetime? Second, was Cabrera unaware that gouache had been used in Europe since the fourteenth century followed by egg tempera and oil in the 1500s,[23] techniques that were probably transported to the New World by the Franciscans? Third, as the official painter of the archbishop of Mexico and favorite artist of the Jesuit order, was he pressured to testify in agreement with the church to avoid risking profitable commissions? These questions lead me to believe that maybe Cabrera's conclusions were unreliable. Worse, this faulty logic has been used and repeated by the Catholic Church as "evidence" that the imprint on the *tilma* could not have been painted by human hands; ergo, it had to be a "holy image," that is, a divine work of art. A slightly more famous "divine work of art" is Leonardo da Vinci's *Mona Lisa*,[24] painted approximately twenty-five years earlier than the Guadalupana. Why do we question the painting skills of the artists who might have rendered La Virgen de Guadalupe and not those of the painter of the *Mona Lisa*? Is it perhaps a Eurocentric conclusion that indigenous artists were not civilized, human, or advanced enough to know and practice painting techniques used by the great Leonardo da Vinci?

In 1938, German scientist Richard Kuhn found that the pigments in the image of La Virgen had no traces of mineral, vegetable, or animal dye, and synthetic colors did not exist in the sixteenth century. This, along with other new "scientific" studies of the *tilma*, further supported the miracle narrative that by now had become ingrained into the Mexican psyche. Consequently, in 1945, Guadalupe was pronounced the Queen of Mexico and Empress of the Americas by Pope Pius XII.

If I had been Cabrera and found that there were four different media and techniques utilized in the image of La Virgen de Guadalupe, my conclusion would have been that, perhaps the painting was a collaborative effort among a few artists with expertise in various media and that, obviously, the painting had been changed by artists over the intervening two hundred years. The original image did not have a crown, for example, and then somewhere along the way a crown appeared, and then for some reason, it disappeared. The hands were different sizes and colors, one larger and lighter, the other smaller and more mestiza. The wings of the angel did not originally correspond to the three colors of the Mexican flag, which came after independence, when the Mexican nation and its tricolored emblem came into being. It seems to me that La Virgen de Guadalupe is an evolving and collaborative image conscientiously created by human hands for a political purpose. I would wonder, then, who made the original as well as the changes, and for what purpose?

The debate about La Virgen de Guadalupe's apparition has never been settled, and, in fact, it grew even more heated when the Roman Catholic Church canonized Juan Diego as its first indigenous American saint in 2002. The controversy there was not whether La Virgen would appear to a lowly native—that had been Zumárraga's doubt way back in 1531—but whether Juan Diego existed at all, and whether La Virgen ever really appeared to begin with. Nonetheless, Pope John Paul II, devout follower of La Virgen de Guadalupe who celebrated several masses in the Mexico City basilica, beatified Juan Diego in 1990 and canonized him twelve years later. As recorded on the Vatican's website, in his canonization Mass in Mexico City, Wednesday, July 31, 2002, Pope John Paul II said the following:

> [W]ith deep joy, I have come on pilgrimage to this Basilica of Our Lady of Guadalupe, the Marian heart of Mexico and of America, to proclaim the holiness of Juan Diego Cuauhtlatoatzin, the simple humble Indian who contemplated the sweet and serene face of Our Lady of Tepeyac so dear to the people of Mexico . . . Beloved Juan Diego, "the Talking Eagle!" Show us the way that leads to the "Dark Virgin" of Tepeyac, that She may receive us in the depths of her heart, for She is the loving, compassionate Mother who guides us to the true God. Amen.[25]

My question in all of this, particularly for the neoindigenists of Aztlán, is why do we continue to believe the colonized interpretation of La Virgen's story? Even the pope called her the "Dark Virgin" and referred to her messenger by his Nahuatl name, Talking Eagle. Is it not more revolutionary to imagine that a culture celebrated throughout history for its advanced knowledge in mathematics, architecture, horticulture, astronomy, and medicine would know how to create an indelible painting?

LA VIRGEN DE GUADALUPE AS CODEX

The original image of La Virgen de Guadalupe reads like a postconquest codex. As Gloria Anzaldúa (1942–2004) explains in *Borderlands/La Frontera: The New Mestiza,* this is a mestiza image, blending iconography and concepts that are European, Christian, Aztec, and Nahuatl. The symbolism is complex and layered. It deserves close deciphering and researched interpretation. I will focus on only a few symbolic elements which have been researched and documented on the official Basílica de Guadalupe website,[26] and which I have thought about in my own attempts to understand this image. What follows is my own translation of and dialogue with some of the information presented on that website.

The image is imprinted on what some believe to be a coarse fabric made from the maguey plant that Juan Diego wore as a *tilma*. This image measures approximately four feet, eight inches in height (143 cm). It portrays a young woman with long hair holding her palms together as if in prayer and looking down toward her lower right. She stands in front of the sun on a black crescent moon, and an angel with green, white, and red wings holds her blue green robe with his right hand and her rose-colored floral dress with his left.

La Virgen's hair is loose, which, according to scholars of codex images, means that she was a young unmarried woman, perhaps a virgin. Her hands are held together in prayer and, some believe, form the shape of a small house or temple / church. Her right hand appears to be longer and lighter than her darker and rounder left hand, which some believe to symbolize the combination of two races, the Spanish and indigenous, and therefore the making of the mestizo race. She stands on a black moon. In Nahuatl, the root words for Mexico are "*Me*-tztli" (moon), "*xi*-ctli" (bellybutton or center), and "*co*" (in). The translation of all these Nahuatl terms would mean that Mexico is "in the bellybutton or center of the moon."

Her rose-colored dress represents Earth. On the dress, there are nine floral arrangements, which some believe to represent the nine original tribes that migrated south from Aztlán to Tenochtitlan. The roots of these nine floral arrangements are located where the dress and the cape meet. The stem or root of these floral arrangements is seen as rivers or water from which the leaves and flowers grow. To me, this could represent the concept of the god of rain, Tlaloc, or the water goddess, Chalchihuatlicue, and their importance in earth-life sustenance.

The large part of these flower arrangements is described as a "tepetl," or hill. It looks like an inverted heart or a hill engraved with many Aztec speech scrolls. Tepetl may directly refer to Tepeyac, or paired with the speech scroll it may perhaps refer to Teotlatoltepec, which means "hill of the divine word," or Teocuicatepec, which means "hill of the divine song." I argue that the speech scrolls within the tepetl could be the key element in the reading of this image as a codex, meaning that it states to those who can read it that this is an important story/message which needs to heard and retold throughout the land and among all the nine original tribes. In fact, these scrolls could be the graphic representation of *Nican Mopohua*.

La Virgen's dress has four kinds of flowers. There are small flowers at the stem base of the nine floral arrangements, or tepetl. There are flower buds. There are eight flowers of eight petals each. It is believed that these eight flowers document the Sun and Venus conjunction. There is only one flower of four petals. This single four-petal flower is located in the center of the image and the belly of La Virgen. This flower is believed to be the Nahui Ollin. This is the same symbol in the center of the Aztec calendar that records the past four suns, or ages, and the current fifth sun, the Sun of Movement. The glyph for movement is called "Ollin." On the tip of the tongue of the face in the center of the calendar is a small flower. This flower is said to predict the Sixth Sun, the Sun of Flowers.

La Virgen's robe is blue green or turquoise. The robe represents the sky. It is covered with forty-six eight-point stars, which some researchers believe are placed in such a way that they illustrate the alignment of the stars on the dark morning of her apparition to Juan Diego.

The angel holds this robe/sky with his right hand and the dress/earth with his left hand. He is believed to be an eagle angel representing Juan Diego Cuauhtlatloatzin. Cuauhtlatloatzin means "eagle who speaks" or "he who speaks like an eagle." Therefore, this eagle angel, the intermediary between the earth and the sky, or the human and the divine, is the one bringing the story of La Virgen's apparition. This eagle angel also reminds us of the eagle devouring a snake on a cactus that appears on the Mexican flag, which was the sign foretold in the Mexica prophecy that would signify the Aztecs' new homeland, Tenochtitlan. The three colors on his wings are the colors of the Mexican flag: red, white, and green.

The site of La Virgen's apparition is also coded. Tepeyac was the worship site of Tonantzin, who is known to be an earth/mother goddess. She has other names: Chicomexochitl, Seven Flowers; and Chalchihuatlicue, Woman of Precious Stone.[27]

Tonantzin is known by many other names and is associated with other goddesses like Coatlicue and Cihuacoatl. According to the story, when La Virgen appeared to Juan Diego's sick uncle, Juan Bernardino, she stated that her name was Coatlaxopeuh, or She Who Crushes the Serpent. Speaking in Nahuatl, La

Virgen shared with Juan Diego the concept of *in lak'ech*, which means "I am you, you are I." In essence, she was saying that he and the indigenous people could trust her because they were one and the same. By naming herself Coatlaxopeuh, by exchanging the idea of *in lak'ech* with Juan Diego, La Virgen was, I believe, being fabricated as a postconquest indigenous goddess such as Tonantzin or Coatlicue disguised as the Christian Mother of God.

The date of La Virgen's apparition is the most coded of all. The year 1531 witnessed interesting astronomical events similar to the galactic alignment we are expecting on December 21, 2012. In 1531, four important astronomical events occurred which are connected to the apparition. First, the day La Virgen appeared was winter solstice,[28] which signified the birth of a new sun. Second, the planet Venus crossed in front of the sun. In the Aztec cosmology, Venus represents Quetzalcoatl, the ancient god of love and creation, also known as the Feathered Serpent.[29] Third, the conjunction of the sun and Venus represented Nahui Ollin, or the birth of the fifth sun. Fourth, and most significant to me for supporting my theory about the revolutionary creation of La Virgen's image, a celestial body now known as Halley's Comet blazed across the Anáhuac sky in late August of that year. The layering of all these astronomical events resulted in La Virgen de Guadalupe's apparition. The Feathered Serpent (Venus) in front of a new sun (winter solstice) created the conjunction (Nahui Ollin) that announced the birth or coming of the new age appeared in the sky (Halley's Comet). How perfect was it that in trying to envision a new goddess who could deliver them from destruction, the activist artists who conceptualized the image of La Virgen de Guadalupe had these four astronomical signs to draw from and represent?

In the tradition of those activist artists of the sixteenth century who saw a need for creating a new goddess to deliver them from the evils of colonization, I have been creating, re-creating, and re-membering cultural icons since the 1990s. I have been engaged in *disfrasismos* of my own, trying to connect the different and sometimes hostile worlds of my history, my identity, and my community.

DIGITAL BEGINNINGS

From 1991 to 1997, I worked for the Social and Public Art Resource Center (SPARC), first as a painting assistant for muralist Judith F. Baca, SPARC cofounder and artistic director, and later as public art administrator, where

I coordinated the production of murals throughout L.A.'s diverse neighborhoods. Eventually I was promoted to the position of Digital Mural Lab production associate. While setting up the lab, I taught myself photo-based digital technology in order to teach Professor Baca's César Chávez Department of Chicana/o Studies mural students at UCLA.

In 1997, as a SPARC employee and UCLA research assistant, I coordinated the production of six 8' × 9' digital murals on vinyl at the Estrada Courts Community Center. As a California Arts Council artist in residence at SPARC, I was the principal artist of two of the six murals. Those two murals focused on women in Estrada Courts and were created with UCLA students. *María de los Ángeles* focused on the mothers and multigenerational matriarchy. *Las Four* focused on the daughters of Estrada Courts. Behind the four young women of Estrada Courts are four activists: Dolores Huerta, Sor Juana Inés de la Cruz, Adelita *la soldadera*, and Rigoberta Menchú. Rising behind these activists is the Aztec moon goddess, Coyolxauhqui.

A few weeks after this mural was installed, it was vandalized or, as I saw it then, "Coyolxauhquied";[30] that is, the vinyl mural was slashed and destroyed by the young men of that community. At the time, I was most shocked by the violent reactions of the young men toward the young women. Referring to the young women as "hoodrats," the young men felt entitled to destroy the one image in the Estrada Courts that featured their sisters. The excuse for the vandalism was that some of the young women had dated some of the young men in the neighborhood, and because the neighborhood was so small, their dating possibilities were limited, so now one of the young women was dating someone outside of the neighborhood. Jealousy and revenge, then, fueled the young men's rage. The young women felt that the young men treated them as if they were neighborhood property. I suppose I should have seen it coming when one of the young women originally photographed on the front steps of her home asked me to replace her in the picture. She did not want to be part of the mural because she had a black eye her boyfriend had given her.

Toward the end of 1997, I was exhausted. The previous year, I had earned a Master of Fine Arts degree from the University of California at Irvine while working at SPARC and trying to produce my own work. I felt that I was at a crossroads. I remember asking a good friend, artist Yreina D. Cervántez, for advice. She advised me to consult with a *santero* who later earned his PhD at UCLA and had his practice off of Soto Street near the 10 Freeway in East Los Angeles. He read my shells, performed a *limpia* (a spiritual cleansing), and advised me to ask my ancestors for guidance. My mother was orphaned at ten years old when her mother was stabbed to death while sleeping between my mother and my aunt Julia.[31] I have never met my father, who still lives in Los Mochis.

For Día de Muertos, I decided to take my mother to visit my maternal grandmother's gravesite in Los Mochis. My sister Leti and her daughter Melissa joined our pilgrimage. On November 2, we spent the day with relatives who travel far to meet every year at my grandmother's gravesite. Silently, I asked my grandmother for guidance. Her advice was clear and direct: "Life is short. Do what you enjoy most every moment." I stood up and walked around the cemetery, where I saw a little girl fluttering around in a white dress, gold bracelets, and colorful clown sandals. I asked the little girl and her mother permission to photograph her. I planned to create an image called Santa Niña de Mochis to thank and honor my grandmother. Like Juan Soldado, a secular "saint" created in the mid-1900s by border crossers to intervene for them with migration difficulties, green card issues, and citizenship matters, Santa Niña de Mochis is a young saint who speaks to the need of immigrants and dispossessed people to find their own calling in life. My logic for inventing a saint named Santa Niña de Mochis was that if people crossing the border could make up their own saint, then I could sanctify my own grandmother, who guided me to make the decision to prioritize my art.

My images of Juan Soldado and Santa Niña de Mochis are part of my 1848 series, which critiques the racist legacy of Manifest Destiny that under the governorship of Pete Wilson resulted in racist legislation that targeted undocumented immigrants in California. When I returned to Los Angeles, taking the santero's advice and my grandmother's message very much to heart, I quit my job at SPARC and since then have dedicated myself to my art.

ROSES, OF COURSE!

In 1998, I was a member of three art activist groups: Homegirl Productions, a black and brown public art collaborative; L.A. Coyotas, a Chicana/Latina visual and performance collaborative; and Tongues, a queer woman of color collaborative. Raquel Salinas was a member of L.A. Coyotas. Since 1993, she has written and performed work that "gives voice to the rage and creative form to that which is taboo within the cultural parameter of tradition, thus empowering all women universally."[32] One of her original performances is titled *Heat Your Own*. This performance illustrates multigenerational Chicanas/Latinas struggling to express themselves within confining culturally gendered roles. In one section of this performance, Salinas, dressed as La Virgen de Guadalupe, becomes irritated with the prayers of two men. One man prays for a woman to marry who can cook and take good care of him and his home, as his mother did. The other man stumbles in drunk praying for an extraordinarily beautiful woman who can sexually satisfy his every whim. Salinas as Guadalupe frightens the men, who scurry away when she climbs off her pedestal, angry at them for wanting a virgin mother or sex bunny for a wife instead of seeking a real woman with a mind, a career, and her own needs as an equal life companion. This is where Raquel Salinas was in her own relationship with La Virgen de Guadalupe at the time I asked her to pose as La Virgen for *Our Lady*.

Raquel Gutiérrez is a cofounding member of Tongues and Butchtlalis de Panochtitlan.[33] She is a Mexican and Salvadoran writer and performance artist who grew up in Bell Gardens, in Southeast Los Angeles, with a 93 percent Latino population, and was enrolled in Catholic schools.

Both Raqueles and I would have long discussions about our sometimes ambivalent and complicated relationship with the image of La Virgen de Guadalupe. For all three of us, Guadalupe had been an important icon in our childhood and a role model in our girlhood for how we were expected to behave and what we were supposed to become when we grew up. We discussed Salinas's Guadalupe performance, Gutiérrez's experiences in Catholic school, my mother's "migrant Virgen," the Chicana feminist Guadalupe art by Ester Hernández and Yolanda M. López, and the essays in the anthology by Ana Castillo titled *Goddess of the Americas*.[34]

Goddess of the Americas includes essays written by Mexican and Chicana/o artists, writers, and scholars. The one essay that stood out for me was titled "Guadalupe the Sex Goddess," by Sandra Cisneros. I identified with this writer's anger at and frustration with growing up with family expectations of her being virginal and "good" in a "culture of denial" that encouraged ignorance of our bodies and sexual selves by what she called "the cover-up." She writes that she was angry for many years when she saw La Virgen because she was "damn dangerous, an ideal so lofty and unrealistic it was laughable."[35] I became especially enraged as I thought about my nieces and other little girls growing up in a time of STDs, HIV/AIDS, and sexual violence. The most important defense for girls and young women is knowledge of themselves and their bodies.

Cisneros's anger was soothed by knowledge. Through her own research, she found Guadalupe's pre-Columbian historical past as the mother goddess Tonantzin. Tonantzin is associated with a pantheon of other mother and earth goddesses such as "Tlazolteotl, the goddess of fertility and sex, also referred to as Totzin, Our Beginnings, or Tzinteotl, goddess of the rump,"[36] and, of course, Coatlicue, the mother of Huitzilopochtli, the War/Sun God, and Coyolxauhqui, the Moon Goddess. She concludes that her Virgen de Guadalupe is not just the Mother of God, "she is God,"[37] but she is also a woman.

When identifying with her as a brown woman with a real body like her own, Cisneros wondered what La Virgen would wear under her exceedingly long dress and robe. My immediate response to her question was: "Roses, of course!" Roses proved La Virgen's miraculous apparition. Roses are offered to her on altars everywhere, including on La Virgen de Guadalupe street murals in Los Angeles. So, in my imagination, Guadalupe was wearing roses under her clothes. The image I saw in my mind's eye would evolve into *Our Lady* and later into *Our Lady of Controversy*.

I shared my concept with Raquel Salinas and Raquel Gutiérrez, who both agreed to be photographed as models for the image I wanted to make. In order to explain myself to them and to work out my own ideas, I made a quick drawing in a small sketchbook of a standing woman with long hair and hands on her waist. She was wearing a bra and panties on which I planned to collage roses, and a starry robe rested on her shoulders. Her full-body halo included oranges, which I probably thought to include in reference to the Latino street vendors who sell oranges and other fruits and flowers on the streets and at freeway exits of L.A.

This woman stands on a crescent moon held by a bare-breasted woman with a halo over her head. Three angels fly around in the background. All this is framed with drapery similar to that I used in the image titled *Lupe and Sirena in Love* (1999), which shows La Virgen in a loving embrace with the Sirena character from the popular Mexican *lotería* game. When doing quick sketches like this one, I tend to write notes to myself. At the lower left, I wrote the possible title of this work, *Nuestra Lady*. On the right I wrote an entire list of thoughts or reminders for myself: "California oranges? Virgen underwear roses. Background—storefront city in blue? Red? Angels or hummingbirds or butterflies? Children/young people in song/prayer? Add stars in gown/cape."

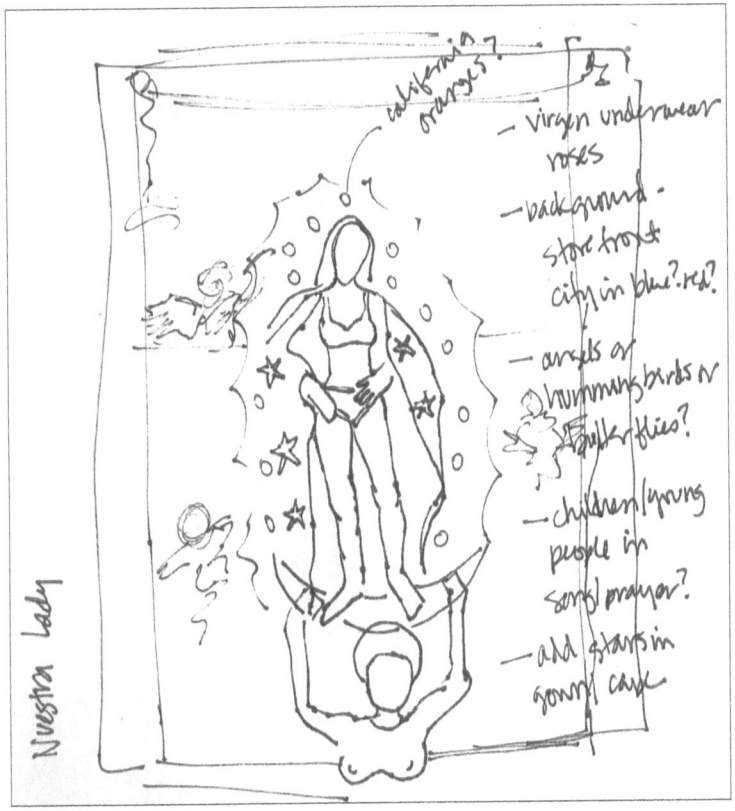

11.3. *Nuestra Lady.* Drawing by Alma López, ©1999. Courtesy of Alma López.

A REAL LADY

Raquel Salinas and I had our own reasons for collaborating on this project. As an artist, I wanted to illustrate a contemporary Virgen as a real, strong, and beautiful Chicana/Latina answering Sandra Cisneros's question: "When I see la Virgen de Guadalupe I want to lift her dress as I did my dolls' and look to see if she comes with chones, and does her panocha look like mine, and does she have dark nipples too?"[38]

The reason for this collaboration was more personal for Raquel Salinas. In an interview on April 20, 2001 with *Column of the Americas* writers Patrisia Gonzales and Roberto Rodríguez, she stated that she agreed to be photographed for this image in order to continue her lifelong healing process from "the shame and the guilt" of being raped at eighteen.[39]

Other women who saw the image and read about Raquel related to her story. Adriana from Santa Ana, California, e-mailed me on May 11, 2001.[40] In her personal and moving e-mail she writes about being acculturated and socialized to be silent. In *Borderlands*, Anzaldúa explains how "[c]ulture forms our beliefs."[41] Within culture, women have subservient roles, and "if a woman rebels she is a mujer mala. If a woman doesn't renounce herself in favor of the male, she is selfish."[42] In her e-mail, Adriana tells about being molested for years by a male cousin. She expresses that her pain, shame, and guilt have been suffered in silence.

Adriana turned to her mother for protection and guidance. Her mother was also a victim of culture and was unable to act and respond responsibly; she was shackled "in the name of protection."[43] So her mother encouraged Adriana to continue carrying her burden in silence for the sake of the appearance of normality, avoidance of community gossip, and the comfort of all other family members, including the molester. Meanwhile, her own daughter suffered and rotted from the inside. Adriana demanded: "¿Pero yo, qué? ¿Me pudro?"[44]

In regards to the image and the model, Adriana states: "You give the voiceless and unimportant like me a voice. I'm an artist myself and fascinated by the archetype of Guadalupe/Tonantzin, who in my eyes is all women with fire and pride in her eyes, just like Raquel."[45]

On the day of our first photo session, Raquel drove to my second-floor apartment in South Central Los Angeles. She brought the green gold-trimmed cape from *Heat Your Own* along with several possible matching Victoria's Secret panties and brassieres. She asked if I had a preference for an outfit. I told her my vision was to cover her in roses; therefore, she should wear whatever was most comfortable. After she selected her outfit and applied dark red lipstick, my only instructions were to stand and look tough and assertive. I shot several rolls of film.

When I developed the photos, I desperately tried to find one that worked, but I was disappointed with all the pictures. None seemed to convey the strength I was seeking. When I spoke with Raquel about the pictures, she admitted that she was not feeling good that day and therefore was not surprised that none of the photos conveyed strength. We arranged a second meeting.

Weeks later, we met for a second photo session. The day was cold and overcast. The light was almost fluorescent and seemed to bounce off everywhere so that there were no shadows. She removed her clothes, applied dark red lipstick, placed the green robe on her shoulders and her hands on her waist. As soon as I looked through my camera lens to take the first picture, I knew this was going to work. She looked confident and assertive. We took pictures inside and just outside the apartment in order to make the most of the natural light. This time, I took only one roll of film because I knew we had captured the photo I needed.

After developing this roll, I selected the one photograph that I felt was perfect. I scanned it. Using the graphic editing program Photoshop, I removed the background. Behind the model, I placed a halo surrounded by graphic roses scanned from a small Virgen de Guadalupe prayer card I had purchased in Mexico City. Below her I placed the Raquel Gutiérrez Viceroy butterfly angel holding up the black crescent moon. For the background, I created curtains with La Virgen's dismantled and rearranged dress. The stage was created with La Virgen's turquoise robe and golden halo rolled up and turned upside-down.[46]

By dismantling and rearranging La Virgen's dress, robe, and halo, I wanted to create a space where she was omnipresent but not suffocating the woman's body. I wanted the background to give the impression of La Virgen's dress and robe "blowing up" and clinging to the two-dimensional visual space of the digital print stage. I wanted to create a chiastic world, a world in reverse. This would be the world of my imagination where I take an icon like La Virgen and imagine it differently.[47] In this new world, La Virgen de Guadalupe is no longer buried under pounds of cloth or dragged down by a prematurely balding male angel. Instead, her body, the body of a proud and strong Chicana, stands in the center of *Our Lady* wearing roses.

Raquel's facial expression is the most important element of this new reality. She looks forward while slightly tilting her head to her left and lifting her chin. This look, accompanied by both hands on her hips, reminds me of my mother, my aunts, and the neighborhood *peleonera cholas* (feisty gang girls) ready for any confrontation. I believe the model's assertiveness is achieved not only from the facial expression and the hands on the hips but from the use of *contrapposto*.

Contrapposto is an Italian term meaning "counterpoise." This term is used to describe a human figure standing with most of its weight on one leg. In sculpture, it creates vertical support plus an illusion of a dynamic yet relaxed appearance. It is a pose in transition. The most immediate example of *contrapposto* is *David* by Italian Renaissance artist Michelangelo. In this sculpture, the artist portrays the biblical story of David and Goliath. According to some art historians, this sculpture portrays the moment when David has decided to kill Goliath. David stands tense, his veins bulge on his right hand, in which he appears to be holding a stone, while his sling drapes over his left shoulder. Other historians believe that this sculpture portrays the moment when he has slain Goliath and appears to be quietly contemplating his victory. Or perhaps he continues to stand somewhat tensely as he is making sure that Goliath will not rise while David is preparing to reload his sling with the stone he holds. In these interpretations there is an acknowledgment of a depiction of momentarily relaxed action. In *Our Lady*, the model Raquel Salinas in *contrapposto* portrays a relaxed assertiveness in which she appears prepared to act or react.

I changed the green cape Raquel was wearing when I photographed her to a cape embroidered with the image of Coyolxauhqui, the Aztec moon warrior goddess. According to the legend, she led her four hundred siblings, the Centzón Huitznahuas, to battle their brother Huitzilopochtli, the god of war. Their mother, Coatlicue, had conceived him miraculously with feathers she found as she swept the Templo Mayor. Huitzilopochtli, born in full military regalia, battled and defeated Coyolxauhqui and her siblings by dismembering his sister, casting her head into the sky and her limbs and torso down the steps of the temple pyramid. She became the moon, and her siblings became the stars. The fourteen-foot-diameter relief stone sculpture of Coyolxauhqui was found at the base of the Templo Mayor pyramid in 1978. This excavation site is situated off the Zócalo between the cathedral and the government palace.

This sculpture perhaps was intended to illustrate a change to a patriarchal government. For me and other feminist Chicanas, Coyolxauhqui illustrates not only an incredibly violent dismembering of a warrior woman but also the need to re-member and heal not only ourselves but also our histories and cultures from this violent and misogynistic past. I created this Coyolxauhqui cape because I wanted to illustrate that as feminist Chicanas, we have a long history of goddess warriors to guide and protect us. For those of us fortunate to have witnessed this bas-relief stone sculpture at the Templo Mayor museum, I wanted for us to remember its weight, and therefore consider how tall and strong Our Lady must be to be able to carry Coyolxauhqui on her shoulders like a floating cape.

BUTTERFLY ANGEL

I photographed Raquel Gutiérrez holding a metal pole so that she would be able to hold both hands equidistant from her body and at the same height. She was wearing jeans, a black-and-white beaded necklace, and a silver ring in her left nipple. Initially, I photographed her wearing a grey sports bra. The bra did not look right—too contemporary and unnatural. She offered to remove her bra. As I looked through the 35mm camera lens, I knew this was the correct choice. Her bare breasts were beautifully female and blended naturally with the Viceroy butterfly wings that I intended to substitute for the eagle feathers of the traditional male angel. Her bare breasts directly answered Sandra Cisneros's question about La Virgen's female body.

After developing the photographs, I selected the picture with all the required elements. Standing straight, her arms symmetrical, her hands slightly open as if to invite La Virgen's grace, Raquel Gutiérrez looked unabashedly at the viewer. There was nothing aggressive or confrontational in her eyes. Her face was angelic without being timid or coy. I scanned the picture and, using Photoshop, removed the background and the metal pole. I placed her on a Viceroy butterfly and had her hold the black crescent moon on which Raquel Salinas stood. She was perfect.

In my work, the Viceroy butterfly is a significant element of my own visual language. I found this butterfly while researching the Monarch butterfly. Monarchs are famous for their annual migration between the United States and Mexico. I was interested in the Monarch because, as I was developing a visual language in my work, I needed a symbol for migration. I was very interested in this little butterfly's migration pattern. I felt that this butterfly's migration could represent the migrations of Mexicans and other indigenous people of this North American continent. As Gloria Anzaldúa states: "We have a tradition of migration, a tradition of long walks."[48] Unlike humans, who get stuck on one side or the other of the border fence due to the United States racial and political practices since the U.S./Mexico War and the signing of the Treaty of Guadalupe Hidalgo in 1848, this butterfly completely disregards that dividing line. The border fence does not exist in the consciousness of the Monarch.

I was very interested in the Monarch's migration and its genetic memory. When the Monarch migrates "home," that is, back to its place of origin, which may be either north to the United States or south to Mexico, it is the child of the butterfly that originally migrated north or south. Instinctually, the child knows how and where to return. The journey home is encoded into its DNA.

Perhaps because I am a Chicana born in Mexico and raised in Los Angeles, I am attracted to this idea of genetic memory. All of us, but especially immigrants, no matter where we may come from, have a desire to know our ancestors, our history, and our culture and perhaps a preference for particular foods or sounds. We have this knowledge stored in our cells. Like the Monarch butterfly, we carry the genetic memory of our transformations and our "long walks."

At this time, I was meditating on the fact that as indigenous people we have always been here. We were here before the naming of this continent. We were Americans before this land was called America. Our cells have metamorphosed many times. We have shape-shifted from less than dirt to vegetable to animal to human in a constant cycle of materializing. We consume ourselves. In our cells is our memory, our genetic memory, which we struggle to remember. Of course, I was meditating on the writings of Gloria Anzaldúa and Walt Whitman.

I was in high school the first time I read Walt Whitman's epic "Song of Myself" in his controversial (mainly because of his questioned sexuality) and self-published poetry collection titled *Leaves of Grass* (1855). As a teenager, I remember imagining myself in this man's poem when he begins: "My tongue, every atom of my blood, form'd from this soil, this air, / Born here of parents born here from parents the same, and their parents the same" and ends with "I bequeath myself to the dirt to grow from the grass I love / If you want me again look for me under your boot-soles." This is when I first imagined myself as matter that has always been here. It was then that I realized that everything that is on this earth has always been on this earth. Except for some meteor debris, there is nothing materially new on this planet; everything is made from matter that has existed before. We are in a constant state of metamorphosis.

In my work, I use the Viceroy butterfly instead of the Monarch to allude to more than migration and genetic memory. Originally, the Viceroy butterfly was believed to be a Batesian mimic of the Monarch. It is now known that the Viceroy is actually a Müllerian mimic, meaning that this butterfly does not just look like the Monarch, it also shares the defensive properties necessary for survival. Monarchs and Viceroys feed on willows, poplars, and cottonwoods, making them taste chemically bitter and unpalatable and making them poisonous to their predators. Viceroys are shape-shifters. In areas where Monarchs are common, the Viceroys resemble them. Where Queen or Soldier butterflies are common, the Viceroys mimic them.

The only distinguishing visual difference between the Monarch and the Viceroy is the horizontal line on the Viceroy's secondary wings. In my visual vocabulary, the fact that the Viceroy mimics the Monarch but is different means that it is "queer." The Viceroy is part of the butterfly communities of Monarchs, Queens, and Soldiers, and yet she is different. The Viceroy is queer. I too am different. As a Chicana, as a lesbian, and as an artist, I am different, I am queer.

LUPE AND SIRENA IN LOVE

This queer Viceroy butterfly flutters into my work all the time these days. Before *Our Lady*, I had created an image titled *Lupe and Sirena in Love*. [49] The sacred Virgen de Guadalupe embraces the secular *lotería's* Sirena. Together they float on a Viceroy butterfly. This image appeared to me on my computer monitor late one night. This Lupe and Sirena apparition can have multiple meanings.

The most obvious interpretation is the physical. Lupe, as a "top," cradles Sirena's left breast with her left hand while lightly spanking her fishy bottom with her right hand. Sirena loses herself in Lupe's eyes as she strokes her hair with her left hand and reaches with her right hand to touch Lupe's hand. This is an intimate physical sexual embrace between two famous female Mexican icons.

Another possible interpretation was offered to me by the wife of the winner of the Primer Premio de Poesía Binacional Carlos Pellicer/Robert Frost at the Museo de Arte e Historia in Juárez, Chihuahua, Mexico, in 1999. I was in Juárez exhibiting *Our Lady*, *Lupe and Sirena in Love*, and other digital prints as that year's recipient of the Primer Premio Visual Binacional David Alfaro Siqueiros/Jackson Pollock. This woman said that to her, *Lupe and Sirena in Love* illustrates La Virgen embracing Mexico. Mexico's geographic land mass, she said, is in the shape of a fish or mermaid's tail surrounded by water.

My interpretation is so much sappier. For me, *Lupe and Sirena in Love* illustrates the concept of miraculous and unconditional love. It is a miraculous event when we meet someone to love who loves us back. Like La Virgen in the sky and La Sirena in the ocean, we live in different worlds or spaces. When and where would it be possible for La Virgen and La Sirena to meet and fall in love? When La Virgen appeared to Juan Diego, she loved him unconditionally. I believe this was the love message the indigenous community's activists were spreading with the speech scrolls on the *tepetl* of La Virgen's dress. For Cisneros, "to open the door and accept her," Guadalupe needs to be a woman like her. For me, Guadalupe needs to be queer.

REVOLUTIONARY VÍRGENES

In the spring of 1969, during the Chicano Youth Conference in Denver, Chicanas met in a workshop and reported to the full conference that "[i]t was the consensus of the group that the Chicana woman does not want to be liberated."[50] In 1976 and 1978, Ester Hernández and Yolanda M. López responded to that very disappointing statement with their feminist visual work. I believe that La Virgen de Guadalupe appeared to these two artists to guide us through our own Chicana feminist revolution in the arts.

In 1976, Ester Hernández was an undergraduate student at the University of California, Berkeley. She created a 16" × 14" aquatint/etching print on paper titled *La Virgen de Guadalupe Defendiendo los Derechos de los Xicanos*. This image portrays a young woman with long hair and dressed in a karate outfit and a starry robe and kicking with her left leg. Behind her is a halo as she balances on her right foot on the crescent moon held by an expressive and angry angel. Amalia Mesa Bains states: "This groundbreaking piece established the beginning of a Chicana/o artistic tradition of recuperating the Virgen de Guadalupe in a humorous and familiar fashion as well as a symbol of defiance."[51] (See Fig. 8.2)

In 1990, Ester Hernández printed a serigraph titled *La Ofrenda II*, based on her 1988 *La Ofrenda*, printed at Self Help Graphics in Los Angeles. This image is the cover of the first edition of the book titled *Chicana Lesbians: The Girls Our Mothers Warned Us About*, edited by Carla Trujillo in 1991. Hernández was unable to grant reprint permission for future editions of this book due to the homophobic attacks she endured from our community. *La Ofrenda II* portrays a topless young woman wearing red lipstick, a crystal earring, and a short punk Mohawk hairstyle. The young woman looks over her right shoulder. A full-color tattoo covers her entire back. The tattoo is a primarily green, red,

CHICANA LESBIANS

The Girls Our Mothers
Warned Us About

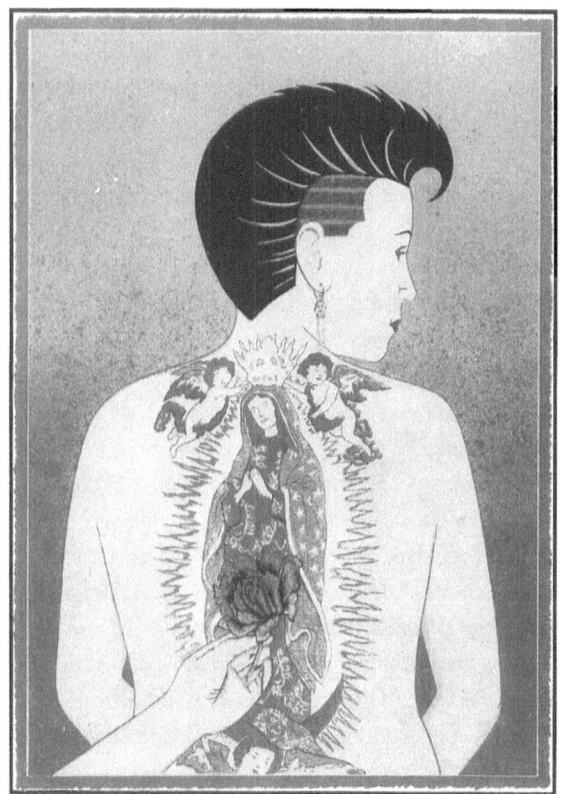

Edited by Carla Trujillo

11.4. *La Ofrenda II*, cover of *Chicana Lesbians*. Screen print by Ester Hernández, © 1990. Courtesy of Ester Hernández.

and gold illustration of La Virgen de Guadalupe held by an angel with a full head of dark hair. Two wavy-haired angels place a crown on La Virgen's head. From the lower left of the print frame rises a left hand holding a red rose. Is the hand a woman's hand? Is the rose an offering to La Virgen or to the young woman with the tattoo? What is so awful about this image's being the cover of a book that it elicited such hatred from our brothers and sisters of Aztlán?

In 1978, while earning her Master of Fine Arts degree at the University of California, San Diego, Yolanda M. López created her widely circulated Virgen de Guadalupe triptych. In this triptych she portrays ordinary women like a grandmother, a seamstress, and a self-portrait of a running young woman in the guise of La Virgen de Guadalupe. Each oil pastel on paper measures about 32" × 24". A self-proclaimed "artistic provocateur," Yolanda M. López states: "In 1978, there were no images of Latinos or Chicanos in the mass media. As for the movement media, the Virgin of Guadalupe was the most prevalent, continuous image of a woman."[52]

One of my favorite images in Yolanda M. López's Virgen de Guadalupe series is a small colored-pencil drawing titled *Walking Guadalupe* that Yolanda created in 1978. Yolanda portrays La Virgen peacefully walking, with her hands in prayer. Although she is on a break, she is still multitasking, walking as she prays. Her dress and robe are conservatively hemmed below her knees. She wears Candie's-style heels.

This image was the cover of the June–July 1984 issue of the feminist journal *Fem*, published in Mexico City. As a result of having this image on the cover, the journal offices received bomb threats. Why were the Mexicans so upset? Because she was showing her legs? Because the heels signified agency, the ability to move and go places and do her own thing? Did Yolanda M. López's *Walking Guadalupe*, like Raquel Salinas's Virgen in *Heat Your Own*, freak out Mexicans because she was off her sun halo–crescent moon–held–down–by–a–balding–male–angel pedestal instead of attending to their needs? Don't they understand that every working woman, including La Virgen de Guadalupe, deserves an occasional coffee break from labor and servitude?

These two artists are recognized for their revolutionary visual interpretations of La Virgen de Guadalupe, and today they continue to create images that illustrate our Chicana/o civil rights and feminist movements. Today, as in 1999, when I was creating *Our Lady*, I know that I am participating in a Chicana feminist tradition of reenvisioning La Virgen de Guadalupe. Like other Chicanas, I am reclaiming this goddess from the church and the patriarchy. I am proud to say that I am critically engaged in this activist visual labor.

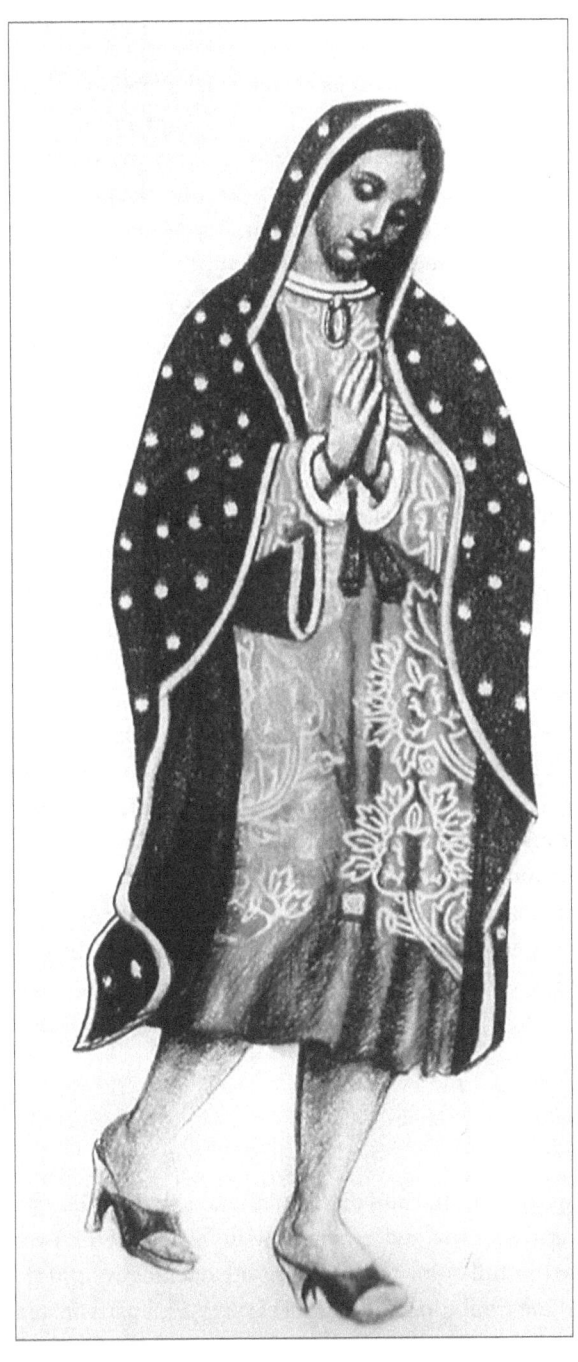

11.5.
Walking Guadalupe. Photo-
copy and colored pencil by
Yolanda M. López, © 1978.
Courtesy of Yolanda M.
López.

CYBER ARTE: TRADITION MEETS TECHNOLOGY

When I received the David Alfaro Siqueiros/Jackson Pollock Binational Prize in November 1999, I traveled to Juárez, across the border from El Paso, Texas, to the award presentation, which also featured an exhibition of my work. At this exhibition, I met Tey Diana Rebolledo, who was a juror for the binational poetry prize. She mentioned to me that her daughter, Tey Marianna Nunn, was a curator at the Museum of International Folk Art (MOIFA) in Santa Fe and was in the process of organizing an exhibition titled *Cyber Arte: Tradition Meets Technology* highlighting artists who used technology and cultural iconography in their work. She asked for slides, and fortunately, I had a sheet that I was able to give her to give to her daughter.

Months later, Tey Marianna Nunn e-mailed me regarding the exhibition she was organizing. This exhibit would feature four Chicana/Latina/Hispana artists who combined traditional cultural iconography with state-of-the-art technology. The artists included Elena Baca (photographer), Marion C. Martínez (sculptor), Teresa Archuleta-Sagel (weaver), and me. The curator, installation designer, and three of the exhibition artists were Nuevomexicanas. The curator and I selected the following images to include in *Cyber Arte: Our Lady, Heaven, Santa Niña de Mochis, La Línea, California Fashions Slaves, Juan Soldado, María de los Ángeles,* and *Selena in the Sky with Roses.* I signed a contract with MOIFA agreeing to lend it those images for the *Cyber Arte* exhibition from the opening of the exhibition on February 25, through the closing on October 28, 2001. After the work was installed, the museum decided to extend the exhibition for an additional four months, through February 2002.

I have always believed that this exhibition was pure insightful genius. It was a great concept to create a bridge whereby people familiar with the cultural iconography would be able to engage with new technologies, and perhaps younger people growing up tech-savvy would be introduced to cultural iconography.

CONTROVERSY BEGINS

In September of 2000, MOIFA printed and distributed 11,000 brochures; 750 were mailed, announcing *Cyber Arte* and other museum events (see Figure I.1). *Our Lady* was printed in full color to announce the opening reception, the panel discussion, and the exhibition dates. On February 25, I participated in an artists' panel moderated by Tey Marianna with the other artists, Elena, Marion, and Teresa. At the opening reception and panel discussion, I remember being informed of complaints about *Our Lady*.

On March 17, I received a long and threatening e-mail from self-proclaimed Chicano activist José L. Villegas Sr.[53] in which he attempted to educate me about La Virgen de Guadalupe as the apocalyptic Virgin Mary and northern New Mexico's history of land grant and political struggles after the signing of the Treaty of Guadalupe Hidalgo in 1848. He declared that I did not have a right to reenvision this sacred icon and threatened to publicly "admonish" any New Mexico supporters of *Our Lady* and *Cyber Arte*. He ended this nine hundred–word rant with "Que Viva La Raza! Que Viva La Causa! Que Viva Los Brown Berets! Que Viva Cesar Estrada Chavez!" At that moment, all I could think of was that this man remembered to include César Chávez's full name (perhaps he was afraid I would confuse the activist with the boxer) and yet he completely neglected to include the cofounder of the United Farm Workers as well as the other part of Chicana/o movement chants: "Que Viva Dolores Huerta! Que Viva La Mujer!"

In this e-mail, Villegas mentioned the first news article on *Our Lady* and the brewing controversy, reported that morning in the *Albuquerque Journal*. The story, written by Morgan Lee and titled "Skimpily Attired 'Our Lady' Protested," described *Our Lady* as a "scantily clad Virgin Mary" and a "Virgin of Guadalupe in a floral bikini." This was obviously the immaculate conception of the now-famous "Bikini Virgin." A few days later, on March 20, a news article appeared in Mexico City's *Reforma*.[54] It was titled "Consideran 'blásfema' obra Guadalupana" and was written by Antonio Bertrán, who mentioned the 1988 Rolando De la Rosa controversial Marilyn Monroe Guadalupe installation at the Museo de Arte Moderno.[55]

On March 18, I forwarded Villegas's e-mail to close friends, who immediately responded with words of encouragement. On March 23, Villegas, Deacon Anthony Trujillo, and other protestors met New Mexico Museum director Thomas Wilson, Cultural Affairs director Edson Way, and MOIFA director Joyce Ice. On the day of this meeting, a friend called me at work and told me to turn on my television set to Channel 52's *Primer Impacto*. There was a rally protesting *Our Lady*. The television cameras focused on older and grief-stricken Latina ladies. At this point, I knew this was not good. How would I be able to fight the image of suffering grandmothers with rosaries in their hands?

That weekend I visited my mother. She commented on the television program. In Spanish she said: "I believe I saw one of your images. Why were they protesting artwork in a museum instead of organizing a protest against the priest sexual molesters in their churches?"

The onslaught of e-mails and news articles was overwhelming. I remember spending entire days in front of my computer monitor responding to e-mails until my eyes glazed. Some of the e-mails were horribly disrespectful, sexist, and homophobic, but many more were incredibly supportive and insightful. I wanted to share them as an important and ongoing conversation of religious and cultural iconography in art and Chicana feminist thought. Susana Gallardo, *webjefa* of *www.chicana.com*, helped me think through the organization of the e-mails, and my sister, Leti, helped me save searches of web-based news articles. I placed these e-mails and news articles on the controversy on my Earthlink website and asked for support of my work and of the *Cyber Arte* exhibition. There was so much traffic that Earthlink closed my website account. I immediately authored a new site.

I survived this most-thorny controversy because there was so much support. My nieces would hear conversations between my mother, sister, and brothers, and they would say: "Drawing is fun. Why don't people want Tía Nina to draw?" Friends and Tongues members were always around to talk, especially at the most difficult moments, when I was being threatened and when I received an anonymous large yellow envelope with about fifteen handwritten letters by children who were instructed to write me hate mail.

Viceroy butterfly angel Raquel Gutiérrez drafted and distributed press releases. Tey Marianna Nunn and her family were actively involved in defending *Our Lady*, especially her mother, Tey Diana Rebolledo, who publicly denounced the principal controversy organizers and the archbishop, and Tey's father, who was instrumental in getting the original *Our Lady* print donated to MOIFA. Cyber *artistas* Elena, Marion, and Teresa stood in solidarity with me and Tey Marianna. The museum and others took the difficult high road, including New Mexico Museum director, Thomas Wilson, MOIFA director, Joyce Ice, and the exhibition docents and museum staff. There were countless people, artists, activists, and community organizations that spoke, wrote, and gathered in support of freedom of expression.

04-28-01

Tu queres que tu estas
Loca. tu piensa que s tas
may Sex. Nadie de nestra
familia te quiere. Te mires
Viendieja con ese bikini. y
tu eres una Descarada Vieja
Almona Lopoza. Por ezo nadien
te quiere. Cochina marana.
Sinseramente Elizabeth Salis

Leopoldo Moe
2/27/01

New Mexico Board of Regents Alma Lopes

I fell Sad becuse They but

a bikni on are lady and

If I will work at the Museum

I will but the bikni' owey.

11.6.   Hate mail written by children and mailed anonymously in a yellow folder, 2001.
Alma López private papers.

NO SPACE FOR DISCUSSION

Joyce Ice, Tey Marianna Nunn, and I prepared statements to present at a museum board meeting on April 4 at the Meem Auditorium in the Museum of Indian Arts and Culture (MIAC) across the museum plaza from MOIFA. As a Mexican-born Chicana artist, I wanted to explain my inspiration in creating *Our Lady*. The space was overcrowded and the meeting was cancelled. I read my statement at an impromptu press conference after Joyce Ice, Tey Marianna Nunn, and I were safely escorted back to MOIFA. An open forum to discuss *Our Lady* and the controversy was rescheduled for April 16 at the Sweeney Convention Center in downtown Santa Fe. I was unable to attend.

During the April 4 events, I refused to admit to myself that I was scared. I grew up in rough neighborhoods in Los Angeles. I painted murals and organized public art in communities like Skid Row. Like many women of color, I have an active *"facultad,"* that sixth sense described by Gloria Anzaldúa, as a "quick perception arrived at without conscious reasoning . . . an acute awareness . . . [that] those who do not feel psychologically or physically safe in the world . . . those who are pounced on the most—the females, the homosexuals of all races, the darkskinned, the outcast, the persecuted, the marginalized, the foreign— . . . [all develop.]"[56] In other words, I can sense danger. I knew that Joyce, Tey, and I were seconds away from being physically attacked by good Virgen de Guadalupe–loving Catholics.

The day after narrowly escaping a potentially physically violent event in Santa Fe, and before traveling to attend the National Association for Chicana and Chicano Studies (NACCS) conference in Tucson, Arizona, I took a detour for a day to San Antonio, Texas, to participate in a public-art panel discussion at the Guadalupe Center. After the event, the organizer took me to the Esperanza Peace and Justice Center to meet the director and the staff. They had heard of the controversy and questioned me: "Before doing your work, did you consult with community?" I remember being stunned. My *facultad* had not prepared me for this. I do not remember my exact response in that moment, but I was thinking: "Who is the voice of community? Are New Mexican men and a white male archbishop community? Does their voice count more than mine? I am a Mexican woman born in the same land as La Virgen of Guadalupe. Am I not community?"[57]

Over and over I had to keep telling myself that it was not the *santa* in my *fe* that divided me from the community; it was the conservative religious right, whether in Santa Fe or San Antonio, getting in the face of my *santa* that created the divide.

In June 2001, photographer Delilah Montoya and painter Pola López organized an exhibit called *Las Malcriadas: Coloring Outside the Lines* at Emanations Studio Gallery in Santa Fe as a response to the *Our Lady* controversy and as a public showcase of Chicana feminist solidarity. This exhibition featured the works of Goldie García, Ana Rivera, Vivian Marthell, Delilah Montoya, Pola López, and me—all fearless artists who were often labeled "bad girls" for their/our outspokenness. The show, which included my overtly lesbian *Lupe and Sirena in Love*, received very favorable press, and we were called "brave women."

CYBER ARTE EXHIBITION CLOSES

On October 28, Raquel Salinas and I attended the closing reception of *Cyber Arte*. The next morning, we borrowed Tey Marianna's silver Volkswagen bug and drove twenty-four miles northeast of Santa Fe to Chimayó. The drive—meditative and serene—was a huge contrast to the controversy. The leaves were transitioning to autumn colors of light green, yellow, and orange. We stopped at a *puesto* by the road to purchase snacks of nuts and seeds.

At the entrance of the Santuario de Nuestro Señor de Esquipulas, more commonly known as the Santuario de Chimayó, I noticed a tombstone dedicated to aborted fetuses. This entrance sign alerted my Chicana feminist instincts to the possibility that this might be a site of "cultural tyranny" rather than of spiritual healing for those who, like myself, believed in a woman's fundamental right to decide what to do with her own body.[58] Taking a deep breath, we entered.

The story of the Santuario in Chimayó is told on the Archdiocese of Santa Fe website.[59] The story goes that while Don Bernardo Abeyta, a *penitente* of the Hermandad de Nuestro Padre Jesús el Nazareno was performing penance on the night of Good Friday during Holy Week, he saw a light in the hills near the Santa Cruz River. He went to the site of the light and, scratching with his nails and bare hands, dug out a crucifix. He organized his neighbors to witness and worship the crucifix and to notify Fray Sebastián Álvarez at Santa Cruz Church. Fray Álvarez and the community participated in three consecutive "joyful" processions in which they carried the crucifix and placed it in a niche on the main church altar in Santa Cruz. Each morning after these processions, the crucifix was found back at the site of its original apparition. After the third time, it was obvious to everyone that the crucifix wanted to remain in Chimayó, and therefore the Santuario was built in 1816 for anyone who wanted to worship Nuestro Señor de Esquipulas. In 1929, it was given to the Archdiocese of Santa Fe, which has managed it since.

The Santuario of Chimayó is located on a mostly unpaved site. It hosts over 300,000 visitors a year who travel there because the soil miraculously springing from a hole in the back room is claimed to heal all manner of physical and spiritual illness. Like all other visitors, Raquel and I wanted to have some of this miraculous soil. With an empty black 35mm film canister, we scraped the sides and the bottom of the hole in order to retrieve the amount of a film canister for each of us. As I was carefully looking at and studying the blue-gowned image of the Dark Christ known as Esquipulas in this little back room, an Hispano man entered carrying a white five-gallon paint bucket. Raquel and I watched him as he unceremoniously dumped the soil he was hauling in the bucket into the hole of miraculous dirt.

THE *DISFRASISMOS* CONTINUE

In 2004, I painted *Coyolxauhqui Returns as Our Lady Disguised as La Virgen de Guadalupe to Defend the Rights of las Chicanas*. This image is the cover for Catrióna Rueda-Esquibel's book, *With Her Machete in Her Hand: Reading Chicana Lesbians*. I painted this image with Catrióna's book title, the controversy over *Our Lady* in Santa Fe, and Ester Hernández's 1976 aquatint etching *La Virgen de Guadalupe Defendiendo los Derechos de los Xicanos* in mind. In *Coyolxauhqui Returns*, a Chicana/Latina woman wearing an orange dress with the floral patterns of La Virgen's tunic stands in front of blue starry drapes. A strap of roses on her left shoulder betrays her true identity as Our Lady. In a pose reminiscent of Artemisia Gentileschi's paintings, she holds up her left hand, signaling to someone, perhaps the viewer, to wait a moment, hold that thought or that request, there's someone I need to protect right now. With her right hand she firmly holds a sword or machete. The sword's handle has a carving of the serpents wrapped on Coyolxauhqui's severed limbs. This image illustrates the rebirth of the spirit of the warrior Aztec moon goddess Coyolxauhqui reincarnated as a Chicana, who is Our Lady but who disguises

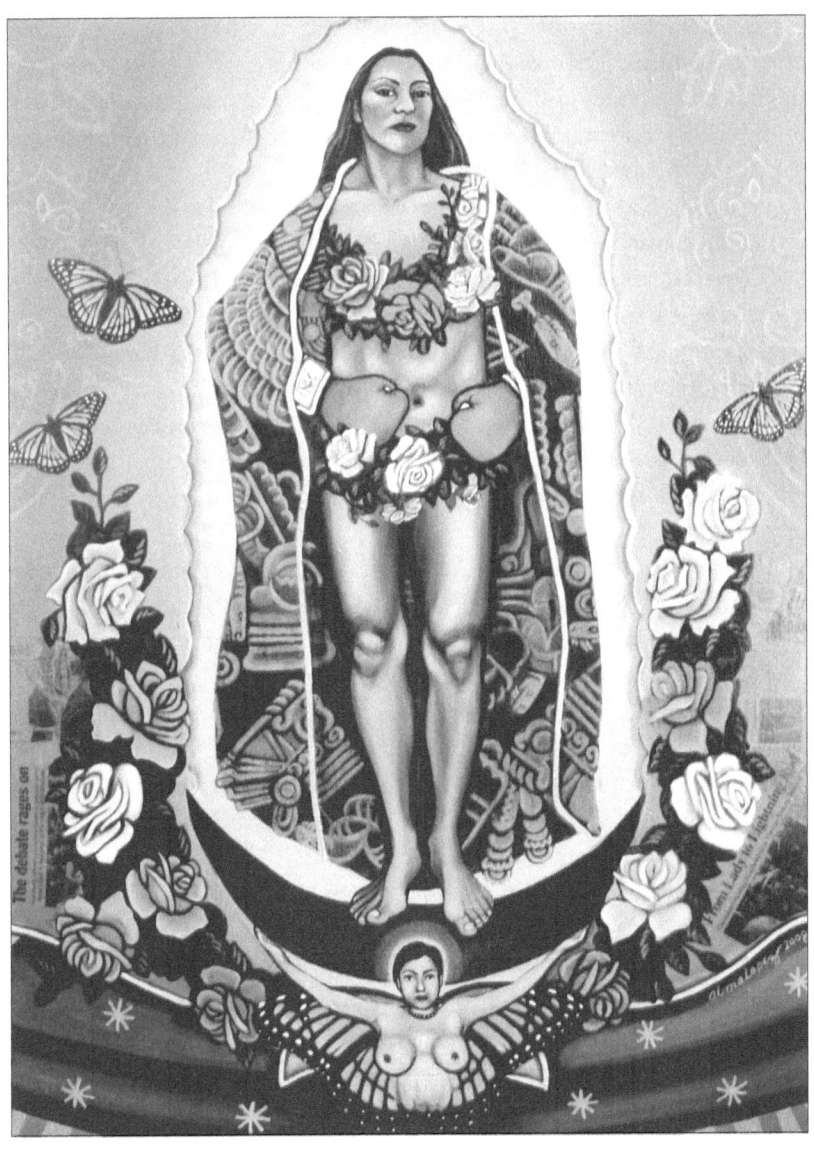

11.7.   *Our Lady of Controversy II*. Acrylic painting on canvas by Alma López, © 2008.
Courtesy of Alma López. From the collection of Alicia Gaspar de Alba.

herself (another *disfrasismo*) as the approved and respected Virgen de Guada-lupe. In this image, Coyolxauhqui is made whole once again; in her are united the human Our Lady and the divine Guadalupe, and together they make a revolutionary activist, the one inside each of us, to whom all Chicanas can turn for liberation and right-full intercession.

Reflecting on the *Our Lady* controversy, I decided to make a 30" × 40" acrylic on canvas painting titled *Our Lady of Controversy II*.[60] I painted Our Lady wearing red boxing gloves and prepared to defend herself, on a pink and orange background that signifies goddess colors with fading or perhaps reappearing *tepetls* from La Virgen de Guadalupe's dress. On the lower half of the background are photocopied news articles and political comics about the controversy. Viceroy butterflies flutter above the news articles and above the colorful rose arrangements growing from the butterfly angel. The Vice-roy butterflies spread the message that Our Lady has broken free of the controversy.

In her warrior incarnation, *Our Lady of Controversy II* returned to New Mexico in 2009. She was part of another exhibition organized by Delilah Montoya, this time in collaboration with Chicana scholar Laura E. Pérez, titled *Chicana Badgirls: Las Hociconas*, at 516 Arts in downtown Albuquerque. The show ran from January through March 2009, and I have heard no repri-sals or invectives or even rumors of scandal.

Delilah Montoya calls New Mexico home and feels strongly about orga-nizing activist exhibitions like *Las Malcriadas* and *Chicana Badgirls*,[61] which she sees as a continuation of the feminist conversations that began with the *Our Lady* controversy and the *Las Malcriadas* show in 2001. "What was at stake then and what is being addressed now is the right to create work that repre-sents our experience as Latina artists whose work is based on the lived reality of the struggles we encounter."[62] These two exhibitions, like *Our Lady* and *Our Lady of Controversy II*, subvert and reclaim terms like *malcriadas*, badgirls, and *hociconas* (loudmouths) to refer to women who refuse to remain silent, women who express their own realities and who are therefore rebels—wom-en who are not afraid to fight back, using our hands, our minds, and our art.

NOTES

1. Epigraph from Gloria E. Anzaldúa, *Borderlands/La Frontera: The New Mestiza* (San Francisco: Aunt Lute Books, 1987), 22.

2. I find it ironic that my mother would take La Virgen into the closet, and I would take her out of the closet in 1999 with the Lupe and Sirena series.

3. See the "South Los Angeles" entry, www.wikipedia.org.

4. Judith Lewis, "Virgin Territory: Who's Defacing Our Lady of South-Central," *L.A. Weekly* (November 18, 1999), www.laweekly.com.

5. www.victoryoutreach.org.

6. www.virgendeguadalupe.org.mx.

7. Juanita Vaughn and Joanne McPortland, *Nuestra Señora de Guadalupe*, a graphic novel (Mexico City: Ediciones Don Bosco, n.d.), published by Franciscan Communications with ecclesiastical approval by Timothy Cardinal Manning. I was in Mexico City presenting and exhibiting for the National Association of Chicana and Chicano Studies (NACCS) conference, where I briefly met Tey Marianna Nunn after a panel on Chicana art.

8. Vaughn and McPortland, *Nuestra Señora de Guadalupe*; all translations are mine.

9. The Rev. Stafford Poole, C.M., *Our Lady of Guadalupe: The Origins and Sources of a Mexican National Symbol, 1531–1797* (Tucson: University of Arizona Press, 1995), 34–38.

10. www.virgendeguadalupe.org.mx; www.vatican.va.

11. Jeanette Rodríguez, *Our Lady of Guadalupe: Faith and Empowerment among Mexican-American Women* (Austin: University of Texas Press, 1994), 17.

12. See "Huei tlamahuiçoltica" entry in www.wikipedia.org.

13. See "Virgen de Guadalupe" entry in www.wikipedia.org.

14. Documented in photographs by Jon Lewis, a retired Marine, photographer, and full-time union volunteer during 1966 and part of 1967, www.farmworkermovement.us.

15. See "Our Lady of Guadalupe" entry, www.wikipedia.org.

16. Rodríguez, *Our Lady of Guadalupe*, 37.

17. www.virgendeguadalupe.org.mx.

18. Art historian Jeanette Favrot Peterson also traces the development of the image from the apocalyptic Virgin in the Book of Revelations. See Jeanette Favrot Peterson, "Creating the Virgin of Guadalupe: The Cloth, The Artist, and Sources in Sixteenth-Century New Spain," *The Americas* 61.4 (April 2005). Peterson states that the image was most likely painted in the 1550s by Marcos Cipac de Aquino. She also states that in November 1982, José Sol Rosales, conservator and director of the Centro de Registro y Conservación in Mexico City, conducted a microscopic exam of the *tilma*. As a result of that study, Sol Rosales concluded that the "image was the result of human craft" (n2, p. 573).

19. See "Our Lady of Guadalupe" entry, www.wikipedia.org.

20. Ibid. See also "Alonso de Montúfar" entry.

21. See "Miguel Cabrera (painter)" entry, www.wikipedia.org.

22. See "Miguel Cabrera" entry in www.wikipedia.org.

23. See "gouache" and "egg tempera" entries in www.wikipedia.org.

24. See "Mona Lisa" entry in www.wikipedia.org.

25. www.vatican.va

26. www.virgendeguadalupe.org.mx.

27. See "Tonantzin" entry, www.wikipedia.org.

28. This date is according to the Julian calendar. The papal bull that established the Gregorian calendar as the official calendar was not decreed until 1582 by Pope Gregory XIII.

29. According to legend, Quetzalcoatl was prophesied to return to Tenochtitlan after a long sojourn in Yucatán, where the Maya also honored him. He is said to have abolished human sacrifice, which angered the followers of Huitzilopochtli, and had him driven to Mictlán, the land of the dead. The return of Quetzalcoatl, said to have been a light-skinned, bearded man, was a prophecy that even the great Moctezuma II believed in, which is what kept him from ordering the immediate massacre of the Spaniards when they arrived in Tenochtitlan. Cortés knew of the myth and used it to gain advantage over Moctezuma.

30. This neologism was coined by my friend Rigo Maldonado.

31. My grandmother, too, was Coyolxauhquied.

32. www.lawtf.com.

33. www.raquefella.com.

34. Ana Castillo, ed., *Goddess of the Americas / La Diosa de las Américas: Writings on the Virgin of Guadalupe* (New York: Riverhead Books, 1996).

35. Sandra Cisneros, "Guadalupe the Sex Goddess," in *Goddess of the Americas / La Diosa de las Américas: Writings on the Virgin of Guadalupe*, edited by Ana Castillo (New York: Riverhead Books, 1996), 48.

36. Ibid., 49.

37. Ibid., 50.

38. Ibid., 51.

39. See www.voznuestra.com and www.almalopez.com.

40. Alma López, "Silencing Our Lady: La Respuesta de Alma," in *I Am Aztlan: The Personal Essay in Chicano Studies*, edited by Chon A. Noriega and Wendy Belcher (Los Angeles: UCLA Chicano Studies Research Center Press, 2004), 191–193.

41. Anzaldúa, *Borderlands*, 17.

42. Ibid., 18.

43. Ibid., 20–21.

44. López, "Silencing 'Our Lady,'" 192.

45. Ibid.

46. Alicia Gaspar de Alba points out that without knowing it, I was giving *Our Lady* a chiastic twist by making the halo the stage on which she stands, and the folds of the starry cloak the steps leading up to the stage. In essence, it could be said that *Our Lady* is La Virgen's crown, a crown that disappeared and returned in the form of Raquel Salinas.

47. This is how I created the space in *Heaven* or how I imagined Popocatepetl leaving so that another Aztec princess could awaken Ixtaccihuatl.

48. Anzaldúa, *Borderlands*, 111.

49. The first time I exhibited the Lupe and Sirena series, which includes *Our Lady*, was in the City of Los Angeles (COLA) group exhibition from May 5 through June 20, 1999, at the Barnsdall Municipal Art Gallery in Hollywood.

50. Sonia López, "The Role of the Chicana within the Student Movement," in *Chicana Feminist Thought: The Basic Historical Writings*, edited by Alma M. García (New York: Routledge, 1997), 103.

51. www.esterhernández.com.

52. Karen Mary Dávalos, *Yolanda M. López* (Los Angeles: UCLA Chicano Studies Research Center Press, 2008), 80.

53. www.almalopez.com.

54. Ibid.

55. For more about the Rolando De la Rosa controversy, see Chap. 8 here.

56. Anzaldúa, *Borderlands*, 60.

57. The following year, my work was targeted again in San Antonio, when *Our Lady* was censored from the annual Virgen de Guadalupe exhibition at the Aztlán Cultural Center. I was in San Antonio participating in an artist residency exchange between the Guadalupe Center in San Antonio and Self Help Graphics in Los Angeles. Artist Vincent Valdez was guest curator of that year's Virgen de Guadalupe exhibition at the Aztlán Cultural Arts Center and invited me to submit work. I gave him several prints, which he matted. When I came to the exhibition's opening reception, he informed me that he was unable to include *Our Lady* because the directors were afraid of controversy, which could jeopardize their funding. Yet he included *December 12*, an image of me as a female version of Juan Diego with Lupe and Sirena imprinted on my dress.

58. Anzaldúa, *Borderlands*, 16.

59. www.archdiocesesantafe.org.

60. The first *Our Lady of Controversy* is a serigraph I produced at Self Help Graphics in 2002.

61. *Chicana Badgirls: Las Hociconas* featured the multimedia visual works of three generations of artists from California, New Mexico, and Texas, including Elia Arce, Nao Bustamante, Marie Romero Cash, Diane Gamboa, Maya González,

Tina Hernández, Elisa Jiménez, Pola López, Amalia Mesa-Bains, Delilah Montoya, Celia Álvarez Muñoz, Cecilia Portal, Anita Rodríguez, Isis Rodríguez, Maye Torres, Consuelo Jiménez Underwood, Rosa Zamora, and me.

62. Delilah Montoya, exhibition catalogue, "Introduction," *Chicana Badgirls: Las Hociconas*, curated by Delilah Montoya and Laura E. Pérez, 516 Arts Gallery, Albuquerque, New Mexico, January 17–March 21, 2009.

APPENDIX

Editor's note: The comments have been transcribed as written. No spelling or grammatical corrections have been made. Names have been substituted with initials.

I am very glad that people who would not normally visit museums are doing so due to the modestly provocatively dressed Virgen.
P.S. Please read "Holy Blood, Holy Grail"
—Unsigned, 3/24/01

Thank you for bringing this most creative + thought provoking show. If it hadn't been for the protest *AGAINST ART* I might have missed this wonderful exhibit!!!
—M.A., AlbuQuirky, NM, 3/24/01

Excellent! Yes—art has always been controversial leave it on the wall—it makes everyone think—I don't see anything offensive—go look at religious art in Europe—Italy—nudity is common.
—M.G., Wisconsin, 3/24/01

I believe it was a great exhibit. The exhibit by Alma L. was an interesting piece although I was a little disturbed by the nudity but in general the artist has a right to self expression. In all I enjoyed the show & look forward to more of her work.
—C.A.V., 3/24/07

Applaud the Artist for pushing the button. Some in the public need to look @ their emotional responses—it would be better for the protesters to become more rational.
—D., 3/24/01

* Taken from the *Cyber Arte* Collection, Museum of International Folk Art Archives. Used by permission.

Sorry, but one comment that may seem negative among the many positive exhibitions in the entire museum, is the Alma Lopez representation of Our Lady of Guadalupe in a bikini with an angel bare-breasted below her. Especially annoying and disrespectful in my opinion, is that it was placed in the local Hispanic section of the museum. That art is not our Hispanic local art. Sincerely,
—Brother S. A., F.S.C., 3/25/01

It is very important for all of our citizens that the museum system support artistic expression. I'm in full support of the museum's position.
—A.W., Santa Fe, 3/25/01

Great exhibit—represents the transition of a generation out of colonization into self expression and personal interpretation. "Our Lady" in particular represents to me a young woman's vision of her tradition within a rapidly changing context—no disrespect was meant here—it is a glorification of Faith and the world we live in today. Keep it up!
—Unsigned, 3/25/01

After seeing the photography exhibit in the New Mexico Museum of Art in which normal people are portrayed as mystical/religious people I can see that no insult was meant by the portrayal of the *Virgin* Our Lady of Guadalupe was intended. However, I still feel by my normal standard the portrayal is inappropriate.
—G.M., 3/25/01

Artists must be protected to do what they believe the Holy Spirit leads them to express. The modern portrayal of the Lady of Guadalupe is only a problem to those trying to control others, and to get attention to their own interests. Ultra-conservatives in any realm of life are more destructive than helpful, except to draw attention to what they complain about.
—R.K.H., 3/25/01

We visited the museum of International Folk Art to see Alma Lopez' *Our Lady* and found it truly beautiful and a sincere expression of her faith. Any idea that this is profane is ridiculous. The whole exhibit, *Cyber Arte* is wonderful! We thoroughly enjoyed it and commend the curator, Dr. Tey Nunn, for presenting such a meaningful show.
—A.O., president, Folk Art Society of America, Richmond, VA, 3/27/01

Please do not crucify the messenger (museum staff) for displaying this freedom of personal expression which could only offend those who are troubled by viewing the human body!
—W.O., founder, Folk Art Society of America, 3/27/01

Good for you—International Folk Art Museum
The Lady is still a Lady!
—J. & J.C., 3/28/01

I'm disappointed + deeply offended that a museum of this caliber decided to exhibit this sacrilgiouss image. Those involved showed very poor judgment in my opinion.
—L.L.P., 3/28/01

Juan Diego himself had to prove the veracity of the apparition of the Virgen of Guadalupe to the officials of the Catholic church, the Gnostics were martyred for believing that God was within each of us contained, and that God's word was revealed in our own conscience. Every human being contains parts of the soul that are reflective of the beauty which we represent as we are part of God. Every woman is part virgen and part Guadalupe. Whether her body is covered or shown in a bikini, a woman should be venerated and not subjugated and covered as shameful. Those who see the woman's body as indecent should look into the oppressive attitudes that they are perpetrating. Alma Lopez seems to reflect that even what may be considered the most common and marginalized woman by our society, carried the integrity of holiness within her.
—P.G.F., 3/28/01

The Our Lady of Guadalupe exhibit should *not* be censored. I personally find it thought-provoking and I am not offended by it in any way.
—S.S., W. Springfield, MA, 3/28/01

The Cyber Arte Exhibit should remain WHOLE & COMPETE. It is wonderful and Beautiful. I love the depiction of strength in women and the almagamation of art & computer. Thank you Alma.
—H.K, Albuquerque, NM 3/28/01

To the Foundation Board of Folk Art.
Please remember that this museum is a state institution & responsible to all
the voters, not one church. I thought the show of cyber-arte was very beautiful & comes from women of the catholic faith who do not disrespect their
religion but express it as part of their life.
—Unsigned, 3/28/01

Three of us from Houston visited today. We love your museum but very
much object to the Mary in the bikini exhibit—it is very offensive to us and
offends Catholics! Please don't do it again.
—Unsigned, 3/28/01

Loved! That controversial Virgin
Clever, meaningful & passionate
—Unsigned, 3/28/01

The work by the hands of Marian Martinez is rightly validated by this Folk
Art Museum, the machine work by the others seems to me out of place. The
question of whether it is religious art or feminist political art is something I
guess only Alma Lopez can say of "Our Lady." If feminist political art contextualized with religious imagery gleaned from "La Morenita" image, *Yolanda
Lopez* did that 25 years ago, in my opinion, in a much more eloquent way—
handpainted too!
—P.R., M.F.A., 3/28/01

I hope the next time I visit this Museum the deplorable image of Our Lady
of Guadalupe will be gone forever. Shame on you Ms. Lopez. Your distorted
view of art is non appreciated in our state.
—M.B., 3/29/01

To the museum and anyone else to whom this may concern—I support you
in exhibiting this piece of artwork concerning "Our Lady of Guadalupe" with
her floral swim suit. I am an artist and my best work deals with the nude—I
do it in a classical manner, i.e. tasteful—I have for years run into discrimination but I refuse to stop dealing with this subject matter—I also think the
church does not have the right to tell government, and or the people, who are
not catholic, what kinds of artwork they may or may not exhibit—I resent
these "ART POLICE" invading the arts—my hat is off to you—keep on . . .
—Unsigned, 3/29/01

All images may be used by artists and others for expressive purposes in a democracy. Only a theocratic government assumes "rights of censorship." Perhaps the archbishop would like to see images of his Priests molesting altar boys, as happened in New Mexico? Can you say "hypocrite"?
—Unsigned, 3/29/01

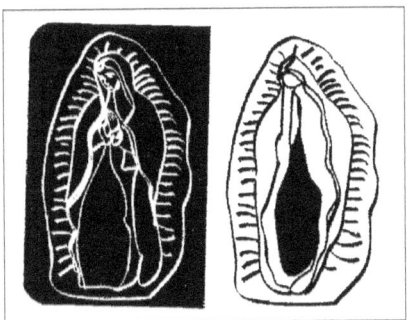

Please, let the artists do their work, let the curator's make their professional decision as to what to display, & let the public see the art! This is a public institution, not a place of worship.
—P. & J.G., 3/30/01

The representation of Our Lady of Guadalupe is not only sacriligious but has no place in Our "New Mexican" Museums, or for that matter in any other setting. She is "Our Mother." How dare the museum have her represented in any other manner. I Teach New Mexico History at the college level and to date have not had to deal with anything as repulsive, hateful, & hurtful to "Nuestra gente."
—Professor R.L., MA, PhD, TVI—Albuq. AE/S, History Instructor, 3/30/01

Our country was founded on the principle of freedom—religious and otherwise. We should honor that by allowing all people to express themselves as they wish. Let's not give in to people who feel they've been offended. No one is forcing anyone to come here and see the controversial image.
—Unsigned, 3/30/01

No more disturbing than all the bloodied figures of christ wrapped in nothing than a loin cloth. Don't like it? Don't look at it.
—Unsigned, 3/30/01

This is a wonderful museum. Please do not let the Catholic Church or any religious organization dictate what art can be here.
—D.C., Santa Fe, 3/30/01

I think this is an excellent exhibit & I strongly support Alma Lopez's art, she has every right to seek her understanding of "Our Lady" and to present it for the public to interpret. The museum's role should be to stimulate dialogue and thinking thru art. WE cannot all agree on anything so why art. Can a few dictate? As a Jew I find it hard to identify with the cross—so what.
—J.& D. S., 3/29/01

As at least a nominal Catholic I am in no way disturbed by the Alma Lopez painting. It seems to show the virgin as a figure of power . . . with enough of her female attributes emphasized to make it clear that it is *womanly* power. Good for Ms. Lopez.
—Unsigned, 3/29/01

This was an excellent exhibit of modern creativity. Please keep it *all in tact*. There was nothing offensive about it!
—R.W., Tuscaloosa, AL, 3/30/01

Great exhibit, I don't understand the controversy. Our Lady of Guadalupe never looked better.
—T.M., Indianapolis, IN, 3/30/01

Came all the way from Texas for this wonderful exhibit. As a Hispanic I see nothing insulting about this exhibit. Thank you. FEAR NO ART.
—L.M., Midland, TX, 3/31/04

The lady on the bottom *did* look like a cherub. Beatific, and holy, and pure.
—M.K., 3/31/01

The "virgin" could have had a less sullen expression.
—Unsigned, 4/1/01

I came to see Our Lady of Guadalupe dress in a "bikini"—I do not think it is in any way disrespectful to her image. *What* I find more disturbing is that a certain group can attempt to dictate what is shown here and what is not to

be shown here.
—Unsigned, 4/1/01

While the Lopez Virgin is done in a medium that does not particularly appeal to me, the sense of the piece that it is both religious in its honoring of the image of the Virgin, while claiming it as an inspiration for contemporary life is important and impactful. It is excellent that the museum continues to be committed to displaying it as a work of art.
—A.F., 4/1/01

What is outrageous are the people who outraged!
—N.S., 4/1/01

Came specifically to see the offending Guadalupe. It was great! Madonna w/ an attitude. Those who oppose it out to actually *see* it. Typical fundamental censorship. Keep it!
—Unsigned, 4/1/01

Understanding Traditions/traditional viewpoints is well understood—it seems harder in that its realistic/photography & mostly w/ the angel. It's just modern Chicanismo & not derogatory but raising in that a person's highest sense of self would be to raise oneself to the same status & therefore ideals of our heroes-saints. In the image of . . .
PS—Viva Tey Mariana
—R., 4/1/01

I support the museum's freedom to display art that the curators find worthy of artistic merits, regardless of its political or religious "correctness." Personally, I don't find the Alma Lopez piece offensive. It seems more demure to me than many contexts in which the Guadalupe is displayed in popular culture.
—R.K., Santa Fe, 4/4/01

In regards to Alma Lopez: I find her work amazing. Contrary to uninformed belief, she is not targeting the catholic religion or the virgin. She has so many issues and aspects of her piece, but more importantly I think she addresses the issue of oppression of women in the church set-up. She is not disgracing the virgin, she is merely displaying her beauty as a woman.
—A., 4/4/01

PLEASE DO NOT REMOVE ANY OF THE STAFF INVOLVED WITH
THIS SHOW!! *THANK YOU.*
—S.B., Big Sun Ranchos de Taos, 4/3/01

I think it is terribly disrespectful—but we should not have censorship—
—Unsigned, 4/4/01

Somehow I don't believe the Virgen Mary would be insulted. I suspect she
might even smile.
—Unsigned, 4/4/01

It's not a matter of Free Speech but *respect* for my rights and Belief.
—J.B., 4/4/01

It is a sacrilige against mankind & against Our Blessed Mother, the Mother
of God.
—M.R., 4/4/01

I am saddened at the degradation of the Christian Religion as shown in this
public institution.
—B.B.G., 4/4/01

I am glad my grandmother isn't here to see this. She could be devastated. All
respect in this world is gone.
—H.K.S., 4/4/01

Poor planning! Not aware of the cultural heritage of NM!!
—N.B., 4/4/01

It is a blasphemy bring it down!
—C.V., 4/4/01

What a sacrilege.
—M.E.R., 4/4/01

New Mexico must not be a fascist state! Censor censorship.
—T.M., 4/4/01

IT'S NOT A BIKINI!
—R.D., 4/4/01

For the Love of God and all that is good stop displaying art that is offensive to our Religion, culture and people.
—T.V., 4/4/01

Get rid of the trash.
—N.M., 4/4/01

We are not censoring! We are protesting sacrilegious rendering in the land of the penitente, the matachine & chimayo—would you even consider similar treatment to a Frida Khalo self-portrait—of course not!
—M.M.-A., 4/4/01

Why is Archbishop Sheehan missing such a great marketing opportunity? With more bare breasted angels in Catholic churches more men would attend mass!! Alma Lopez could single handedly revitalize the Catholic Church!
—Unsigned, 4/5/01

Although La Virgen is a sacred image I think this alternate depiction is worthy as art and has its place as well.
—C.S., El Paso, 4/5/01

I agree with C. from El Paso. I enjoyed seeing all of Ms. Lopez's pieces and hope she continues to develop her art.
—G.B., Albuquerque (Roman Catholic for 60+ years), 4/5/01

Ms. Lopez—I enjoyed your work. Please bring "Our Lady" to New York City. Our esteemed mayor will double your fame.
—R.L., New York City, 4/6/01

Overwhelming and type of work that *should be shown* in museums!
—Unsigned

As a visitor for the first time to New Mexico, I am amazed at the controversy over such a simple & beautiful piece of art—why don't you focus on the *poverty* that I have seen here—that is more shocking than your art.
—J., Washington, DC, 4/7/01

Our Lady—I came with a school group to do a project and I feel its disrespectful and foul for people to make images like that of such an important symbol
for Catholics like myself.
—C., 4/7/01

Our Lady
I feel that it is wrong the way our Lady of Guadalupe was portrayed. The Artist has no religious convictions. She should be ashamed of what she did and
by how she justified her actions. The so called art was very distasteful.
—C.B., R.G., 4/7/01

Please put this controversy aside. The total exhibit is an honor of these four
Latina Artists. No harm is done & it would be a great dishonor to our in-
dependent voice as artists to censor this exhibit. I love La Guadalupe, I'm a
Catholic and I feel she is smiling on us at this time. Mil gracias,
—I.O.L., Las Cruces, 4/10/01

The Cyber Arte exhibit is wonderful including the controversial piece! It
would be a shame to remove it. Everyone should see the exhibit before passing judgement. It is unfortunate that this whole issue is taken out of context
of the exhibit.
—Name undecipherable, Las Cruces, 4/10/01

Alma Lopez is an exceptional artist. The picture of "Our Lady" is beautiful.
However, the large breasted angel below may be objectionable to some older
folks. I am catholic not from this area and there is no confusion for me. It is
obvious that Alma Lopez has a lot of respect & reverence for "Our Lady of
Guadalupe". I enjoyed her work very much and wish her much success.
—M.K.G., Santa Fe, NM, 4/10/01

Welcome to Santa Fe Alma Lopez you are a great artist.
—P.V., 4/10/01

The piece of artwork is done in good taste & shows strength more than anything. I am a catholic & see no degrading element to the exhibit.
—L., 4/10/01

The image of Guadalupe is charming & lovely and—dare I say it?—a little lighthearted. I love it and it's clear to me that Alma did the work from her heart. Who are we to condemn the product of another's heartfelt devotion? Viva Guadalupe!
—Unsigned, 4/12/01

The representation of "Our Lady", at one level is a shameful example of the vulgarization of America, disrespectful even, for "well-meaning" non-Christians. At a different level, for Christians, who truly believe in the divinity of Jesus, the Christ, and of Our Lady, His Mother, it is deeply sacreligious.
—Unsigned, 4/13/01

Remember the 1st amendment!
—Unsigned, 4/14/01

One of the important roles of an artist is to challenge our traditional thinking. This collage does that very effectively. Leave it up!!!
—G.K., Santa Fe, 4/14/01

The function of the artist is to provoke thought, discussion and even controversy in order to enable us to better understand ourselves and the world we live in.
—T.B., Minnesota, 4/14/01

I came to Santa Fe at this time just to see Alma López infamous painting/photo/cyberart of "Our Lady." The newspapers & email chats I've read have completely misrepresented Ms. López' work. It is not in any way offensive; rather, it is in line with the artistic work of Yolanda M. López and Ester Hernandez, who have also depicted the Guadalupe in non-traditional ways. That is exactly the point—to represent the earthly woman who became a saint via motherhood—a very human occupation! There are many, many critical works on this topic—i.e., the re-representation of La Virgen. It is a representation that both celebrates the Virgen and empowers women to believe in their own strengths and possibilities. It would be a sin (and go against censorship ideals) to take down the artwork Ms. López has created. I hope the Regents and other powers-that-be recognize the limits of peer pressure and refuse to bow down to unfounded complaints about the artwork, naked angel and all!
—Professor K.L.R., University of Colorado at Boulder, 4/14/01

Very interesting! Our Lady by Alma really doesn't deserve the fuss—I like it & it should stay!
—Unsigned, 4/14/01

What's the fuss? Four good artists producing good art. Didn't raise *my* blood pressure.
—Unsigned, 4/14/01

I feel that Alma Lopez's art is appropriate for a public museum.
—J.F., Santa Fe, 4/17/01

I deeply question why this state-funded institution would choose to exhibit such a revolting piece of "art". It is not only inappropriate, it makes me question the integrity of Drs. Wilson & Nunn. It is solely their discretion to choose what to display and no one is questioning the constitutional rights to do so, however, is it necessary to continue to display an image that has caused such pain? I pray for the soul of Alma Lopez, Dr. Wilson and Dr. Nunn, may the Lord have mercy on you! I can only hope the regents of this museum rightly take it down and send it back to California!
—M.V., 4/18/01

I dreamt I went walking in my Maidenform.
—Unsigned, 4/18/01

Please do not succumb to the community pressure to remove Alma Lopez's artwork. It is important to all of us and our free America to keep open a dialogue about art and freedom of speech.
—Unsigned, 4/18/01

"Our Lady" should stay in the museum!! Hang in there & don't let the turkeys wear you down. She was BEAUTIFUL!!!
—Unsigned, 4/18/01

I find no irreverence in the piece entitled "Our Lady." To me the virgin as mother of god represents the essence of all that is beautiful in womenhood. I feel that this art work is quintessentially in that spirit.
—Unsigned, 4/22/01

¡La virgen en el bikini está bonita! Católicas—get a life!
—Unsigned, 4/22/01

Love the Virgin. When they stop making kokopelli bathmats, then we can talk about disrespect of religious/cultural icons. Please keep her!
—Unsigned, 4/22/01

Alma Lopez has given us a *powerful positive* female image of La Guadalupe. An interpretation which honors both yesterday *and* today. Let the work *shine*!
—Unsigned, 4/22/01

This is a very sad image of what you as a "artist" thinks of our most sacred things; saints, church, Our Lady. I am very sad for you and I will pray for you and your sick mind.
—Unsigned, 4/21/01

I cannot understand why 4"-high, glow in the dark plastic wobbling head virgins are acceptable, and Ms. Lopez's virgin is not? Don't the crass mass produced figures trivialize a religious symbol far more seriously than Ms. Lopez's beautiful image?
—Unsigned, 4/26/01

I love this show—we're family members and this type of show—contemporary interpretation of traditional subject matter—is *exactly* what I want to see at an *international* museum of this stature. Thank you for serving us, the local community, so well by bringing this show to us.
—R.C.C., Alameda, NM, 4/27/01

Seeing the whole Cyber Arte exhibit was great. I liked the work of Eileen Baca, Marion Martinez and *Alma Lopez*. All humans living today are living in the 21st century. We have varied ways of seeing God's power in our lives and God would be diminished if we did not recognize feminine power as well as masculine. Brava a las artistas!
—K.B., Albuquerque, 4/28/01

Finally! Someone figured out what the mother of Jesus (who was arrested and killed as a result of capital punishment because he dared to challenge accepted dogma) really looks like. Well done.

PS—My tax money goes to MOIFA, too, and I demand that they keep this picture on display.
—D.K. (Jewish carpenter & teacher)

Amen!
—Unsigned

Please remove artwork of Blessed Virgin Mother. It is very offensive to the millions who revere & respect all that she stands for. Thank you.
—J.M.

I think the exhibit is wonderful. Thank you for showing it. I especially liked to see several works from each artist. They were very expressive. However, New Mexico (Northern) is a special place, with special concerns. It's not an easy issue. I wish you well in deciding what to do. I do not think it should be removed.
—M.K.

May is traditionally the month dedicated to Our Lady. In the early 1500's she came with a message that many still cannot discern. . . . Continuing now ushering our New Dawn . . . our interpretation continues with new voic-es, new images. Bouquets of Roses to this museum for allowing those new expressions. Alma's other images are most worthy, especially in critiquing Guadalupe.
—M.C.H., 5/4/01

On Cyber Art:
I enjoyed the show. I am a tax payer & paid the admission. When the protest-ers talk about the public money, they forget that the public is comprised of a larger, diverse group of people. Not only religious fanatics pay the tax. The public include me. I support the show and the museum. Also when viewing the very work being attacked there is nothing anti or sac religious aspects about the work. Being female, the piece shares the notion of empowering female, celibrating the very sacrad figure as a liberated & responsible and beautiful female. Also where the "bikini"? It is beautifully dressed with flow-ers. The T.V. news takes whatever the scandals and makes nothing big deal. Go Elena, Go Girl.
—K.M., 5/5/01

"Our Lady" is completely inappropriate and disrespectful and should be removed.
—Unsigned, 5/5/01

This is a wonderful show and Tey Rebolledo Nunn is to be commended for her visionary approach to contemporary folk art. It would be a terrible mistake to remove the controversial virgin.
—S.R., 5/5/01

Please do not let hysterical pressure groups make you take anything off display. Guadalupe is powerful—one person's interpretation cannot do her harm!
—Unsigned, 5/6/01

The uproar over this rendition of "Our Lady" is pathetic. God please save us from such narrow minds.
—T., 5/6/01

Alma Lopez' "Our Lady" is wonderful. It is inspiring to see Our Lady manifested as, in this exhibit, both a voluptuous female and a child. She (Our Lady) is truly everything and can manifest in an infinite number of ways. Thanks for the courage and integrity to display and support Ms. Lopez' work.
—J.R., Dallas, TX, 5/6/01

I am not in support of censorship nor does the Catholic institution represent my views. I think Cyber Arte should remain up as it shows the depth of *ignorance* the dominant culture and its "model" subordinates have about what is cultural tradition, ignorance about the cultural significance of the Guadalupe/Tonantzin, ignorance of Mexican & New Mexican cultural tradition, i.e. Guadalupano devotion and also ofrendas. To use the Catholic forms of expression to present the extremist political propaganda of Alma Lopez is stupid. This is not relevant to Mejicano/Hispano culture Cyber Arte, where technology defaces tradition is intellectually bogus.
—P.R.S., MFA, 5/6/01

A vital religion generates new symbols and new meanings for old symbols. To do otherwise is to freeze a faith in time, make it brittle, and unwittingly

bury it as a force in life. Alma López is one of these individuals breathing new life into old symbols. Museum: keep up your fine work!
—R.W., G.V.-W., 5/10/01

The contents are nothing special. The same themes with slightly (or sometimes noticeably) different images are being made by latina artists all over the USA. The sexy Virgin Mary is nothing new, either. It's tasteless but hardly outright offensive to anyone who can just say, "Tasteless, juvenile attempt to shock," and then moves on.
—C.K., professor of fine arts, New York University

Spiritual Nazis dictate what you do. To take it down would further erode the separation of church & state.
—Unsigned, 5/20/01

I have just learned that the committee has recommended not removing "the painting". I congratulate them for their backbone. "Book burners" will always be with us, especially if the read/seen/heard themes challenge their narrow perception of the world. Remove one painting from the museum, one book from the library because of their pressure, and no image, no idea will ever be safe again. You make me proud I say I am a New Mexican, & more important, to say I am an American. The fragile First Amendment & artistic freedom are in good hands.
—L.G., 5/22/01

There is such fear in this world that women won't act nice, be good, etc. The whole focus of religion is to *control*. The artists piece, showing Guadalupe in a "bathing suit" is powerful—the woman representing Guadalupe was raped— she has suffered and survived. She is "in your face" with her power. "You go, girl."
—C., 5/22/01

The exhibit intrigued me with the computer [involved] images.
Likewise, except the one of "our Lady" did seem to be a gratuitous slap in the face to Hispanic Catholics.
—Unsigned, 5/23/01

Ok, so is the piece offensive? Clearly, to some it is. "Remove it," they say. I'm pretty offended by child poverty, and surely I'm not alone, but I've never seen demonstrations in the streets. Let's lighten up, Folks.

Besides, if you *are* offended, then simply *be* offended. Christ took up his cross with his mouth shut. Go forth and do likewise. Protest if you must, but to demand removal of the piece is to act as the state—and this ain't no theocracy.

Finally, if sexuality is a gift from God, then what's wrong with a sexy Mary? Was she the *one* sexless woman? Bah! I would argue that if God himself chose her to bear his son, then she must have been the *sexiest* of women. Is merely being attractive a sin? No.

Anyway, it's a great piece and part of a really neat idea of colliding the ancient with the modern.

Way to go Alma Lopez! (Sorry if I missed an accent—I'm from Canada) *response welcome*
—R.T., 5/25/01

I think Alma Lopez has no scruples. This is not art but a very disgusting picture. I see no talent whatsoever.
—M.V., Denver, 5/26/01

I am an Art Historian, a very liberal Catholic and not Hispanic—but I feel the Museum should not have exhibited the painting of Alma Lopez knowing the history of Santa Fe and knowing it would offend many people that live here.
—P.S., Albuquerque, 5/30/01

The logical conclusion to the argument to remove is to dismantle the collections of the Vatican, the Louvre, the Uffizi and Etc.
—N.K.W.

This exhibit brought me to the museum for the first time. I really enjoyed Alma Lopez work.
—Unsigned, 8/8/01

The exhibit is excellent—a testament to the strength of today's women who still acknowledge and respect their heritage.

I'm glad the Museum did not remove Alma Lopez' controversial work. I am a practicing Catholic woman and do not find anything offensive about any of the art in the exhibit.

Since a compromise was necessary, cutting the exhibit short was the best answer.

—L.K., 8/9/01

A wonderful exhibit, brought me to the museum & my good friend, a former Catholic nun. I would like to work with the curator to bring the exhibit to "Silicone" Valley, San Francisco, Oakland, & Berkeley.

I also think that you should publish a book containing both copies of the work, newspaper clippings, letters to the editor, and *all* of the letters via cyberspace & snail mail.

PS. *"blasphemy is in the eye of the beholder"* [emphasis added]

—D. del S., 8/9/01

It is scary to think that museums should face censorship. I'm sorry the exhibit offended some religious people but I consider myself quite devout and I enjoyed the exhibit. People should come & see some of the "Days of the Dead" altars in San Francisco if they consider Alma Lopez sacrilegious.

—Unsigned, 9/15/01

ABOUT THE CONTRIBUTORS

LUZ CALVO (luz.calvo@csueastbay.edu) is a professor in the Department of Ethnic Studies at California State University, East Bay. She received her PhD in history of consciousness at University of California, Santa Cruz. Her research focuses on Chicano/a visual culture, queer theory, and critical race psychoanalysis.

KATHLEEN FITZCALLAGHAN JONES is from Santa Fe, New Mexico. Growing up in this culturally rich city, she was always interested in the visual arts and the cultural and art history of New Mexico and Mexico. Kathleen was specifically drawn to the cultural and spiritual devotion to La Virgen de Guadalupe and the depictions of Guadalupe throughout the region, which she would later go on to study. Kathleen received a Bachelor of Arts in history and a Master of Arts in fine arts/art history at the University of Colorado in Boulder. Her major area of study was contemporary American art. She later earned an education license at Regis University in Denver and an endorsement in social, multicultural and bilingual foundations of education with an emphasis in linguistically diverse education as part of a Master's program at the University of Colorado's BUENO Center. Kathleen is currently an elementary school teacher and lives in Lafayette, Colorado, with her husband and daughter.

ALICIA GASPAR DE ALBA is a native of the El Paso/Juárez border and professor of Chicana/o studies, English, and women's studies at UCLA, where she also served as the chair of the César E. Chávez Department of Chicana and Chicano Studies from 2007 to 2010. She has published nine books, among them three novels: *Sor Juana's Second Dream* (1999), which was named Best Historical Fiction by the Latino Literary Hall of Fame in 2001; *Desert Blood: The Juárez Murders* (2005), which received both the Lambda Literary Foundation Award for Best Lesbian Mystery and the Latino Book Award for Best English-language Mystery in 2005; and *Calligraphy of the Witch* (2007). Besides

Our Lady of Controversy, she has also edited *Velvet Barrios: Popular Culture &*
Chicana/o Sexualities (2003) and *Making a Killing: Femicide, Free Trade, and La*
Frontera (2010). Her website is www.aliciagaspardealba.net.

DEENA GONZÁLEZ is a historian and author of *Refusing the Favor* (1999) and
was co-editor-in-chief of the *Oxford Encyclopedia of Latinas and Latinos in the
United States*, which was awarded honorable mention for the Dartmouth
Medal, among other prizes. She is completing two projects: a book on New
Mexico women's wills, and a collection of essays. She chaired the Department of Chicana/o Studies at Loyola Marymount University in Los Angeles
from 2001 to 2009.

ALMA LÓPEZ is a Mexican-born Chicana artist, activist, and visual storyteller.
She has a Bachelor's degree in fine arts from the University of California,
Santa Barbara (1988) and a Master's of Fine Arts from the University of California, Irvine (1996). Her work ranges from serigraphs, paintings, and photo-
based digital prints to public murals and video. She is dedicated to issues of
representation and social justice, taking as her subject the daily lives, mythologies, and dreams of people of color. Her arts activism lives at the critical intersections of race, class, gender, sexuality, love, and resistance. Through her
visual scholarship, she deconstructs and re-figures cultural icons, including La
Virgen de Guadalupe, Coyolxauhqui, the *lotería* Sirena, and La Llorona. Since
the 1992 Los Angeles uprisings, she has been engaged in collaborative public-
art making that helps bridge black and brown communities. Her artwork has
appeared on the covers of more than twenty publications. In fall 2009 she
was named Regents' Lecturer at UCLA in Art History and Chicana/Chicano
Studies. See her website at www.almalopez.net.

TEY MARIANNA NUNN is a native Nuevomexicana and the curator of the
National Hispanic Cultural Center (NHCC) in Albuquerque, New Mexico.
She is the director and chief curator of the Visual Arts Program at the NHCC
in Albuquerque and was formerly the curator of contemporary Hispano and
Latino collections at the Museum of International Folk Art in Santa Fe. She
received her PhD in Latin American studies (with a focus on art history and
history) from the University of New Mexico. She is the author of *Sin Nombre: Hispana and Hispano Artists of the New Deal Era* (2001). *Sin Nombre* was
awarded the Ralph Emerson Twitchell Award for "significant contribution to
history" by the Historical Society of New Mexico. She has curated numerous

exhibitions, and she lectures widely on various aspects of contemporary and traditional Hispano and Latino art and cultural identity. Nunn was voted Santa Fe Arts Person and Woman of the Year in 2001.

EMMA PÉREZ, originally from El Campo, Texas, is professor of ethnic studies at the University of Colorado, Boulder, and the author of *The Decolonial Imaginary: Writing Chicanas into History* (1999) and *Gulf Dreams* (1996). Her latest novel, *Forgetting the Alamo, or, Blood Memory*, from the University of Texas Press (2009), won the Christopher Isherwood Writing Grant, was a finalist in the Lambda Literary Awards for fiction, and received second place in historical fiction from the International Latino Book Awards. She lives in Denver, Colorado, with her young Leo daughter.

CLARA ROMÁN-ODIO is professor of Spanish and Hispanic American literature, with a specialty in late-twentieth century literature, visual arts, and society. Her research encompasses theoretical and practical models that galvanize feminist movements of women of color in the United States. Román-Odio has numerous publications on modern and postmodern aesthetics, including "Octavio Paz en los debates críticos y estéticos del siglo XX" (2006). Her book project, "Transnational Imaginaries: Chicana Mestizaje and the Virgin of Guadalupe in 1974-2008 Cultural Productions," reconceptualizes Chicana studies within a transnational context by examining connections between globalization, religious iconography, and contemporary Chicana literature and visual art.

CATRIÓNA RUEDA ESQUIBEL is a queer Chicana of northern New Mexican and Sonoran ancestry. Daughter of Leonora and Alfonso; granddaughter of Guadalupe and Libradita; great-granddaughter of Juanita, Altagracia, Catalina, and Celsa; great-great granddaughter of Deluvina, Altagracia, Serafina, and Bernadette. She is an associate professor in the Ethnic Studies Program in the College of Ethnic Studies at San Francisco State University and author of *With Her Machete in Her Hand: Reading Chicana Lesbians* (2006).

CRISTINA SERNA, a native of Boyle Heights in East Los Angeles, is a queer Xicana community activist and scholar. She is a doctoral candidate in the Department of Chicana/o Studies at the University of California, Santa Barbara. Her research focuses on queer and feminist Mexican and Chicana activists and visual artists.

INDEX

Page numbers in *italics* refer to images.
Images in plate section are designated by *ps*.